FAMILIES AND CHANGE

FAMILIES AND CHANGE

Social Needs and Public Policies

Rosalie G. Genovese
editor

Foreword by Jessie Bernard

PRAEGER SPECIAL STUDIES • PRAEGER SCIENTIFIC
BERGIN & GARVEY PUBLISHERS, INC.

Library of Congress Cataloging in Publication Data
Main entry under title:

Families and change.

Bibliography: p.
Includes index.
1. Family policy—United States. I. Genovese, Rosalie G.
HQ536.F333 1983 362.8'2'0973 83-22497
ISBN 0-03-070636-X

Bergin & Garvey Publishers, Inc.
670 Amherst Road
South Hadley, Massachusetts 01075

Published in 1984 by Praeger Publishers
CBS Educational and Professional Publishing
A Division of CBS, Inc.
521 Fifth Avenue, New York, New York 10175 U.S.A.

456789 056 987654321

Printed in the United States of America

To My Mother

Acknowledgements

My thanks are owed to many, especially the contributors who cheerfully met deadlines, Theresa Kusse and Cyndy Castell who efficiently typed sections of the manuscript, and Jean Taber who created the cover design. I also want to thank Jim Bergin and Jenna Schulman of Bergin and Garvey for guiding the book through various stages to publication.

Sylvia Fava has my gratitude for her encouragement in the early phases of the book's evolution and her continued interest as it progressed. I appreciated her thoughtful suggestions and comments.

Above all, I want to acknowledge my debt to my spouse, who backed up his enthusiasm and support for this book with the very concrete contribution of countless hours at a terminal, struggling with bits and bytes to generate the final camera-ready copy.

Rosalie G. Genovese

CONTENTS

IV. THE ECONOMIC STATUS OF FAMILIES: INCOME MAINTENANCE AND SOCIAL WELFARE OVER THE LIFE CYCLE

V. HOUSING AND COMMUNITY

VI. POLICY ISSUES FOR THE EIGHTIES

FOREWORD

On June 22, 1983, an annual Great American Family Awards Program was instituted by Mary Elizabeth Quint of the White House Office of Public Liaison, with the help of the seven-year-old American Family Society, in a White House ceremony with Nancy Reagan, honorary chairman of the American Family Society, serving as mistress-of-ceremony. The ceremony was the culmination of a ten-month project launched when President Reagan proclaimed National Family Week in November, 1982. The judges who selected the nine award-winning families were: NBC weatherman, Willard Scott; entertainers Marilyn McCoo, Billy Davis, Jr., and Marie Osmond; the 1982 Junior Miss, Susan Lea Hammett; and National Geographic Society vice-president, Robert E. Breeden. Corporate sponsors who paid the travel expenses of the winning families included: The Reader's Digest, Procter and Gamble, Atlantic Richfield, Kiplinger Foundation and Holiday Inns. The nine families were selected because they showed what the American family can be in today's complex world, supplying both roots and wings--security and inspiration--for their members. The event was a public relations triumph. "All the local television stations want to cover their local families," said Nancy Reagan's press secretary, Sheila Tate (Donnie Radcliffe, "Loving Those Families," *Washington Post*, June 23, 1983).

This book assembles and organizes a cache of materials on the manifold family-related issues currently confronting policy makers, including: the care and needs of the young (Part II); the employment, un- and non-employment of mothers (Part III); the impact of poverty on families (Part IV); the housing of families (Part V); and such newly emerging skeletons as domestic violence as well as more benign innovations springing up to supply new life styles where traditional families no longer serve. All this in an ambience of value dissensus that sometimes results in gridlock (Part I). Implicit in much of the discussion here is the attempt in process at the present time to inaugurate a policy called--mistakenly--the New Federalism, which is designed to return the support of families to local communities and to the private sector. It is actually, a return to an Old or--better perhaps--a Quasi, if not Non, even Anti, Federalism which was replaced in the 1930s by the New Federalism of Roosevelt's New Deal. For those unfamiliar with this trend, a brief historical sketch may be in order.[1]

Starting at the beginning, we note that the Elizabethan Poor Laws of 1602 had been brought to this country by the colonists. The theory underlying them may be stated approximately as follows:

> Human nature is essentially bad, so that unless you make relief as difficult and as humiliating as possible, people will just naturally take advantage of you. There must, therefore, be means tests of some sort or other, that is, people must prove their destitution and be willing to pay the price in humiliation, or even sacrifice of civil rights, if need be. Those receiving relief must be kept below the level of self-supporting families because economy in the administration of funds is a prime consideration and the taxpayer must be protected against a potential horde of chislers or...swindlers... There should be no "coddling" of clients... Public relief must be made as disagreeable, as punitive, and as unendurable as possible in order to reduce the numbers asking for it. Generosity would inevitably lead to abuse. Economy in the use of public funds,...demanded that the natural tendency for people to take advantage of generosity be curbed (353).

Along with this system, there arose in the nineteenth century another one, mainly in the hands of women and funded by private charity. These women became the models for the stereotype of the "lady bountiful," the woman who did good, who took baskets on Thanksgiving or Christmas to needy families in the community. In time, they became organized into voluntary groups and extended their concerns beyond the indigent to, among others, the aged, the prostitute, the poorly paid working girl (Bernard, 1981:303-04).

There were, therefore, two parallel systems of care for the needy, a sort of omnibus category that included the sick, the weak, the disabled, the elderly, the widowed, the orphaned, the homeless--the dispossessed in general. One was the publicly sponsored system based on the poor-law philosophy administered by local Overseers of the Poor, mainly men. The other was mainly the work of women and was funded by private charity.

The public system carried a larger part of the load. But the "Friendly Visiting" movement in the so-called charity organization societies came in time to achieve a high level of professionalism. It called for careful and detailed study of every case--for wealthy donors as well as tax payers had to be protected against frauds and imposters--and thus accumulated a body of research dealing with a variety of cases. A leader in the field, Margy Richmond, codified the investigatory procedures and laid the groundwork for "social diagnosis." Friendly visiting became social case work. In time it achieved academic recognition and status as a bona fide profession. Although case work was freed from the grosser aspects of the old poor-law philosophy, still in many ways it remained only a humane, kindly, well-intentioned form of the means test (356). It still spoke of worthy or deserving, unworthy or undeserving clients. When psychoanalytic concepts were added in the 1920s, treatment took the place of reform.

The elite, well-trained professional social workers had little but contempt for the public welfare system administered by local political hacks, not far from the ward healer. "The only public social work they accepted wholeheartedly was institutional care. They suspected and rejected outdoor [non-institutional] relief as administered by public agencies. Their opposition...was almost adamant" (361). Aware of the skills they had acquired, these women would have nothing to do with their male counterparts administering the public systems.

> It was natural, perhaps, that workers who had been taught to look upon their work as a profession with rigorous standards should maintain an attitude of snobbish condescension toward workers in public agencies who had no training for their work at all. So great, indeed, was the aversion of social workers in private agencies toward public welfare agencies that during the early years of the century, when there was a strong movement for state-supported Mother's Aid or Widow's Pension Laws, many outstanding leaders...opposed the movement on the basis that it would be administered by non-professionals, by political appointees who might do more harm than good. Private workers were still in the process of revolting against the whole tradition of the poor law and could see only the evils and dangers involved in the administration of public assistance (362-63).

Still, it became increasingly difficult for the elite social workers to buck the tide in the direction of public systems. As the title of this book reminds us, social needs direct public policies. Social needs were changing. The depression of the 1930s and the New Deal's response to it forced the profession to take a new look. "As private agencies staggered under their loads, they were forced to admit that they could not handle the job" (364). Local public agencies arrived at the same conclusion. It was obvious that the Old--Non, Anti, Quasi--Federalism had become anachronistic.

In 1931, for the first time in U.S. history, state funds had to be used for relief. They proved inadequate. So much for local responsibility. The next year the federal government, through the Reconstruction Finance Corporation, expressed willingness to lend money to states for relief purposes. But, in practice, since these loans had to be cancelled later, they amounted to federal grants to states for public relief. It was the moment of truth when the time-honored system had to give way to the then-New Federalism.

> The dissatisfaction of the public with these improvisations expressed itself in the campaign of 1932. The new administration frankly faced the fact that the problem was national in scope, stemming from national causes, and that it could be handled only by national programs. Thus public outdoor relief, which had always been local as the poor-law philosophy prescribed, became national in extent (364).

There was a long anti-intervention tradition in nineteenth-century thought. Herbert Spencer, the archtypical nineteenth-century proponent of laissez-faire and opponent of state intervention in the economy, had used a figure of speech to illustrate its futility. Here is a plate of metal with a bump on it. You can flatten it with a blow of a hammer. But straightway another bump bulges up elsewhere. For we live in a social system all parts of which are inter-related so that whatever happens to one part has reverberations elsewhere. For, as Robert Merton had noted (1956:61-2), there are often unintended consequences to even the seemingly best interventions. Thus, Moroney (Chapter 2) reminds us, even the best planned policies have "often created new 'problems' in other areas or operated at cross-purposes to other policies. More often than not, the secondary effects were neither intended nor anticipated." And sometimes, counterproductive. The bump that rose when we flattened the original bump was just as disturbing as the first one. It was not a trivial suggestion by then-Senator Walter Mondale that any contemplated policy be subject to scrutiny for its impact on families. How could unwanted new bumps be forestalled? How to trace such impact is by no means either theoretically or technically as yet feasible. We are thus left with widely differing beliefs about such impacts, conservatives seeing one kind, innovators, another (Hess, Chapter 1).

The absence of precedents for public programs on the scale called for in the 1930s made it possible to try fresh attacks on the many-faceted problems. Under the leadership of a trained social worker, Harry Hopkins, numerous bumps were hammered down in programs as diverse as: a work-relief program for young people (the Civilian Conservation Corps, 1933); a direct-relief program (Federal Emergency Relief Administration, 1933); a number of work programs (the Civil Works Administration, 1933 and the Works Project Administration, 1935); a rural rehabilitation program, 1934. In addition, there were surplus commodity distribution systems, garden programs, transient relief programs. But, as Spencer had predicted and as Moroney notes vis-à-vis later experience, other bumps kept popping up. Much re-thinking finally arrived at the approach embodied in the Social Security Act of 1935. It was to take some time before resulting new bumps showed up.

The expansion of federally aided programs would have been impossible if the trained social workers had continued to boycott public welfare work. Miss Gertrude Vaile is credited with being the first privately trained worker to make the case for public agencies in 1915. "Private workers began to recognize the importance of socializing and improving public agencies and the harm of ignoring them" (363). By 1922, the Family Welfare Association of America admitted a public agency for the first time. So that by the time of the New Deal, "many social workers, trained in private agencies had changed their minds about public service" (365). For whatever reason--including the decline in support for private agencies--the old aloofness of trained social workers disappeared. It was no longer considered demeaning to accept employment in a public agency.... Public welfare administration was in process of becoming professionalized. Newer philosophies and psychologies invaded the public field, bringing a revolution against the poor law philosophy and psychology with them" (366).

In 1942, one social work educator summarized the new philosophy:

> It is not good for people to be poor, not good for them or for others. We should not permit people to be poor.... The new philosophy is to go out and find cases rather than wait for them to come for help.... Aid or assistance should be given on the basis of need alone; no other consideration such as residence, age, citizenship, or even moral conventionality, is justified.... Community resources should be developed and created to remove the sources of poverty and dependency (353-54).

By the 1960s, some of the new public welfare workers sought to change the circumstances that created the bumps in the first place; they were radical and political. They created a certain mentality in recipients who were taught to see welfare services as rights, not as charitable hand-outs. They demonstrated.... In time traditional social case work became private family counseling or therapy, a privilege for those who could afford it. In time, many welfare workers became overworked bureaucrats.

The "right to relief" did not meet universal acceptance. In time, it was found that the public was indignant at many of the principles which social workers had slowly and painfully evolved over the past quarter of a century" (382). Public hostility sometimes lead to legislative efforts to "cleanse" relief rolls, to get rid of "welfare queens." Opposition was also expressed by neighbors of relief recipients who saw it as subsidization of immoral or lazy people. It was questionable how far any community would let welfare workers go with tax monies.

This book is, in its way, the story of some of the bumps this first New Federalism hammered down and the new bumps that resulted. The story of programs and policies of the last 35 to 40 years, especially those of the Great Society of the 1960s is traced in it. So also is the current attempt to "repeal" the first New Federalism of the New Deal and the Great Society and to revert back to the original Non or Anti or Quasi Federalism with its emphasis on local systems and reliance on the private sector. Some of the new bumps are already beginning to show (Joe, Chapter 17).

Along with the reversion of policy there has also been going on dramatic changes in the kinds of bumps it has had to deal with. A considerable part of the social security system and subsequent modifications dealt with women and presupposed the traditional family. Thus the provisions of Aid to Dependent Children, later Aid to Families of Dependent Children, had assumed widowed mothers and their children. But more and more they came to be separated or deserted or unmarried mothers and their children, a change revealing itself in enormous increases in numbers of female-headed families. Or they were divorced women for whom there was no provision when they became displaced homemakers untrained for employment. There was no provision for women subjected to domestic violence, not a new phenomenon but only recently coming out of the closet. There was no provision for housing for the poor. Although there was income provision for the elderly, later augmented to include health care, both poor and independent, increased longevity and the costs of care were changing the scene. In brief, along with the transition from a repressive, punitive poor-law mentality to a preventive or treatment or positive mentality, there had also been in process a change in the nature and structure of families themselves.

Although the focus of this book is on families rather than specifically on women, the message running through its pages is that public policies frequently do not improve women's economic status or their general well-being. Policies and programs sometimes even perpetuate inequities based on sex as well as on race.

Carl N. Degler, a historian, is, in fact, convinced that women's individuality and the family are difficult to reconcile (1980:472). "Where the women's movement has called for a recognition of individualism, the family has insisted upon subordination of individual interests to those of the group" (471). Degler is touching a tender spot here. But, as this book documents in detail, the policy issues vis-à-vis women transcend individuality; they may be life-and-death matters, as in the case of domestic violence. They may be issues of sheer survival as in the case of female-headed families or displaced housewives. Degler implies that policy is not involved.

> The family...is at bottom nothing more than a relation between a man and a woman and their offspring. What they work out for themselves as a mutually satisfying relation today depends in large part upon them. For some people that will mean a continuation of the established relation, with perhaps an opportunity for the woman to work outside the home, though for supporting rather than individualistic ends. For others it may mean abandoning family entirely in pursuit of complete individual fulfillment. The ideal goal...would be one in which the values of family and the realization of women's individuality could be reconciled" (472-73).

The concept of the family as "at bottom nothing more than a relation between a man and a woman and their offspring" flies in the face of reality. Families are shaped and profoundly influenced by policy at some point or other. Every one of Degler's solutions for their problems depends directly or indirectly on policy. No family is an island unto itself.

Jessie Bernard

Note

1. Unless otherwise noted, the quotations and citations are from Jessie Bernard, "Social Work," Pp. 345-81 in Philip L. Harriman, Joseph S. Roucek, and George B. deHuszar, eds. *Contemporary Social Science*, Harrisburg, Pa.: The Stackpole Company, 1953.

References

Bernard, Jessie.
1981 *The Female World.* New York: Free Press.

Degler, Carl.
1980 *At Odds.* New York: Oxford Press.

Merton, Robert K.
1957 *Social Theory and Social Structure.* New York: Free Press.

PREFACE

This book was originally conceived as a report on the status of public policies that affect families at the beginning of the 1980s. Its direction became modified, however, as actions taken by the Reagan administration suggested both a shift in the philosophy that has guided many social policies and programs since the 1930s and a lower priority for social and entitlement programs in the budget-allocation process. In its completed form, the book provides a look at past and current programs and policies, as well as some possible future directions.

Some chapters illustrate the lag between the reality of family life today and policies that recognize such changes as the growth in single-parent and blended or reconstituted families. Other chapters have specific life-cycle stages as their focus. Although public policies have been directed primarily toward the extremes of the life cycle, childhood and old age, family members in their middle years have unmet needs which current policies could address, as various authors suggest.

Sections of the book are devoted to the following policy areas: needs of children and youth; the interaction between work and family life; programs to help insure the economic security of families; and housing and community policies. Some policy issues for the 1980s are raised in the last section. In several chapters, the needs of individuals and nontraditional households are considered, since increasing numbers of people do not live with relatives for major portions of their lives.

When chapters analyzing Reagan administration policies are placed side by side with chapters on programs and policies adopted by previous administrations, the contrasting philosophies and goals concerning government's role in ensuring the well-being of families, and citizens in general, become apparent. Taken as a whole, the book provides some preliminary insights into which policy areas are undergoing the most change and which families are most affected by the cuts in social programs. Programs that have best withstood cuts so far are the universal ones for older citizens, but recently enacted changes in Social Security policy end this trend.

It comes as no surprise that the poor, the working poor, and the disadvantaged are most hurt by program and policy changes, with women and children especially affected (see Joe in Part IV). However, even in the 1970s, major legislation to benefit children did not gain approval, so the neglect of children's needs is not new, as the chapters by Moroney and others indicate. Cynics think the explanation lies in the inability of children to vote and in the absence of a well-organized lobby, comparable to the one representing senior citizens, to advocate for children's interests. "Singles," who have been ineligible for various social programs in the past, are unlikely to find their prospects for assistance improved in the near future.

From this overview of issues and policies affecting families, readers may be able to assess whether recent shifts in policies and programs represent long-term trends or temporary changes that will be reversed by future administrations. They may also try to determine the next areas to be given priority by policymakers, as well as what these choices signify for individuals and families underserved or neglected by current programs.

I

FAMILIES AND PUBLIC POLICY:

Differing Viewpoints?

The increased interest, concern and research on families over the past decade culminated in the 1980 White House Conference on Families. Many policy analysts, family advocates, individuals and groups thought that government should take action to improve family life. However, their analyses of problems, needs, and remedies often conflicted drastically. As Moroney indicates, such disagreements have always surrounded the issue of government's role vis-à-vis the family. (In Part II, Grotberg discusses this issue with regard to policies directed toward children.) The only point of agreement seemed to be that the family was changing. Policies that affected families were criticized as inadequate on grounds ranging from their failure to reverse the trend away from what some consider the "ideal" family (male breadwinner and family head, stay-at-home wife and mother, and two or three children) to their failure to provide supports to meet the needs of *all* families, whatever their composition or life-cycle stage.

Coalitions representing opposing viewpoints formed. The National Coalition on the White House Conference on Families included professionals in government social programs, social workers, and social welfare personnel. The National Pro-Family Coalition was formed by groups protesting policies that, in their view, weakened the traditional family. As Bernard noted (1981:57), this group opposed "contraception, sex education, homosexuality, cohabitation, shelters for battered women, child care, the ERA, and divorce."

But Bernard (1981:58) also thinks that the White House Conference on Families was a milestone signifying national recognition of the passing of the "old traditional family." This event was symbolized by the name change from "White House Conference on the Family" to "White House Conference on Families" to acknowledge the diversity in family composition and lifestyles. Numerous recommendations to make it easier for women to combine work and family responsibilities were approved, including parental leaves, expansion of child-care programs, sharing of social security credits by spouses, and elimination of the marriage penalty for dual-earner couples (White House Conference 1980). There was also agreement on policies and programs to aid the handicapped and aging and their families who care for them at home. Full employment, antidiscrimination efforts in employment, and housing aid for families were other measures supported. Controversial recommendations favored by one or the other coalition were not supported by all three regional conferences. These measures included stands on abortion (pro and con), the Equal Rights Amendment (ERA), and the Family Protection Act, which did not get support from all three regional conferences. Support for experimental forms of marriage was rejected, too.

This book takes into account both changes occurring in American families and recent shifts in the public policies that affect them. The White House Conference recommendations demonstrate the delegates' beliefs that families need various kinds of government programs and policies to support them. During the 1970s, many policy makers and professionals who work with families had pressed for new and expanded programs and policies to meet the needs of families and individual members. There is little optimism that the current administration will take steps in this direction. Indeed, even efforts to save existing programs that benefit families--especially the poorest--have been unsuccessful (see the chapter by Joe in Part IV). The Reagan administration's position is that government intervention should be limited and targeted only to those most in need--what Moroney terms "selective provision."

In its first year, the Reagan administration justified these cuts in social programs as contributing to its goal of achieving fiscal responsibility. Now, however, further cuts in domestic social programs have been more than offset by greatly increased funds for defense. The budget deficit is the highest ever and the goal of a balanced budget has been dropped. Therefore, these cuts can be seen as part of the administration's efforts to reorder spending priorities to reflect its conservative philosophy about the federal government's responsibility to its citizens. After the continuous expansion of government programs since the New Deal, the current administration seeks to stop and even reverse the trend. Some critics charge the administration with unprecedented callousness toward those in need, while it simultaneously enacts tax changes that benefit the well-to-do and big corporations.

Challenges to family programs are being made on moral as well as economic grounds. Objections to programs and policies that do not conform to their philosophy come from President Reagan's supporters on the right, members of "Moral Majority" and "pro family" groups who emphasize traditional family structures and roles. The Family Protection Act, analyzed by Hess, reflects their position. They want less interference in family life by societal institutions, yet they also want a government ban on abortion, a private matter, and are pressing for a Constitutional amendment to do this. President Reagan's support for the agenda of these groups has not been strong so far, and no major social legislation has been passed as this book goes to press. In fact, the Department of Health and Human Services' parental notification requirement for minor daughters who seek contraceptive devices from government-supported clinics has run into stiff opposition from a wide range of groups. These and other changes proposed by the administration affect low-income and poor women the most.

The White House Conference on the Aging, held in 1981, also generated a good deal of controversy, with some groups charging that the administration tried to pack the conference with delegates who represented its conservative viewpoint. Criticism is being leveled at the conference report as well for selectively reporting recommendations. In light of such activities and controversies, this seems a good time to review and to assess current policies that affect families.

Changes in Families

First, let's consider families today. Recent changes in family composition have meant greater diversity in households and lifestyles, accompanied by changes in the functions and roles of family members. The changing role of women, especially the high labor-force-participation rates of those with children, has been a major factor in these developments.

The statistics on increases in divorce and separation rates are well known. Divorce rates have more than doubled since 1965. The tendency of young adults to postpone marriage is another recent occurrence. In 1979, half of all women between the ages of 20 and 24 had never been married (Kitagawa 1981:5). At the same time, the number of unmarried couples more than doubled between 1970 and 1979 so that they represent 2 percent of all households. Another recent trend has been the increased proportion of out-of-wedlock births, with the rates among teenagers rising sharply. (see "Youth Problems" in Part II.) This development led the Census Bureau in 1970 to begin asking never-married women how many children they had borne (Kitagawa 1981).

One consequence of these changes has been the considerable increase in the proportion of children living with one parent. In 1979, one-fifth of all families with children present were one-parent families (Kitagawa 1981:4). Women head many of these families, a cause for concern since about half of the families below the poverty level have female heads. Consequently, an increased number of children will grow up in poverty.

The decline in birth rates is another important development. The fertility rate declined by 50 percent between 1960 and 1975, although it has leveled off since (Kitagwa 1981:1). In part, this reflects the tendency of many women to postpone childbearing until they reach their late twenties or thirties while they pursue educational and career goals. As childlessness becomes more generally acceptable, some will choose not to have children. Declining birth rates also reflect a trend toward smaller families.

Experts are watching these trends with interest, but are cautious in drawing conclusions about the long-term implications for the family. As Hess points out, over 90 percent of American men and women will marry at least once, so the institution has not gone out of style. Levitan and Belous (in Part III) are also optimistic about the future of marriage. Many divorced persons remarry and children often grow up in blended or reconstituted families. Moreover, women who postpone marriage or who bear children out of wedlock tend to marry at a later time. Declining birthrates may end as women who postponed motherhood have children at a later age (Kitagawa 1981:11, 13). Therefore, some argue that the family is merely developing or evolving, rather than dying.

However, such changes as increases in the labor-force participation of married women and in single-parent households have already had a considerable effect on the roles and relationships of family members. In some households, spouses share parenting and housework, although women still assume major responsibility for these tasks. In other families, children undertake household chores and care of siblings on a regular basis. Of course, one of the most significant recent changes in families has been the reliance on outside individuals or agencies to provide child care while parents work (see Part II).

The reactions of individuals and groups to these developments loosely place them in two major camps: (1) Some fear that the changing roles of men and women, particularly the tendency of more mothers to work outside the home, will weaken the family. They point to divorce statistics as confirmation of their position. They especially want to prevent further erosion of the core functions of the family. In their view, too much responsibility for children's socialization has already been taken over by other institutions like the schools. Family policy should not only reinforce the *status quo*, but even encourage a return to prior family structures and roles, or to their idealized view of those structures and roles.

In the first chapter, Hess analyzes the Family Protection Acts (FPAs), which reflect these conservative viewpoints. The proposed legislation seeks to reverse many previous policies. For example, it would place limits on government intervention in family life even when intervention is deemed necessary for the good of a child. It also goes against many experts' recommendations that policy should be neutral with regard to family structure and composition and that it should respect pluralism in family lifestyles and values. Instead, the FPA would make the traditional family with gender-specific roles the "right" one. Deviations in individual and family lifestyles would be measured against this standard. Adoption of FPA policies would be in sharp contrast to the more value-neutral approach taken by other industrialized countries. Moreover, elements of the proposed legislation work against the rights of women and would reverse some of their gains toward equality.

(2) The other major position is held by groups who support recent changes in roles and who support policies that recognize and encourage greater flexibility and choice in individual and family lifestyles. They would like new government programs and policies to ease the burdens of families headed by single parents or by two wage earners. Feminist groups believe that greater equality for women will permit those who head families to improve their economic status and they stress the importance of job training and advancement programs for women. Their policy recommendations also include improved maternity benefits and low-cost, high-quality child-care facilities (Kamerman & Kahn 1978:13). However, legislation favored by such groups has failed to pass the Congress or has been vetoed by past presidents, as Moroney and Grotberg indicate. Numerous chapters in this book document that public policy has not kept pace with the changes in women's lives.

Moreover, it is clear that policies framed with the traditional family in mind do not meet the needs of the majority of today's households. For example, few policies and programs exist to help either children or adults adjust to such changes in status as becoming a single parent, displaced homemaker, or member of a blended family, yet these transitions are faced by more and more family members.

Today there is not agreement even about what constitutes a "family." In fact, delegates from thirteen countries who attended the International Working Party on Family Policy Conference in 1977 spent considerable time on this question. Some suggested that policy makers should refer to "all types of families" to avoid the implication that there is only one "normal" type. In this vein, Morris (1979:155) commented, "Children with only one parent, adults living together without children, communal living groups of unrelated individuals, permanent liaisons between individuals of the same sex are all considered families in much modern thinking." The definition of family adopted in some countries is "at least one adult and one minor child" (Kamerman & Kahn 1978:9).

Other analysts suggest that the policy should focus on households rather than families. However, household members may lack emotional commitment to one another, an essential attribute of families (Kamerman & Kahn 1978:9). The United States Bureau of the Census defines a family as "two or more persons who live together" but the term also applies at times to persons living together as an economic or social unit (ibid:443-44). Contributors to this book define "family" in different ways and often consider the needs of nontraditional households, for example, those composed of individuals who live together but are unrelated by blood or marriage.

The Current Status of American Family Policy

"Public policy" rather than "family policy" appears in the title of this book since the United States does not have a comprehensive family policy. Rice (1977:79) suggests that a major reason why government has failed to develop a family policy is that "the implicit contract of the Constitution was to be between government and the individual citizen, without reference to the family." The rationale for this approach was to avoid social stratification based on inherited status. However, since government regulation was necessary in such areas as marriage, divorce, and inheritance, individual states developed their own family law. Social welfare services also came under the jurisdiction of the states, resulting in fragmentation and inconsistencies in family services (ibid.). If enacted, the new federalism is likely to increase those disparities among states which federal control was designed to minimize. (In Part IV, Joe points out the differences in public assistance payments by state.)

The value placed on individualism is consistent with this country's history. The assumption seems to be that too much emphasis on the family might interfere with individual rights (Rice 1977:79). The related value of privacy leads to the belief that government should intervene in family life only under special circumstances.

In Chapter 2, Moroney reviews the philosophy underlying social welfare policies since the 1930s. He emphasizes that, despite a broad consensus that the federal government should assume some responsibility for meeting citizens' needs in the areas of income, employment, housing, and medical care, little agreement has been reached on how to accomplish this goal. For the most part, programs and policies have been directed toward the needy, so that they are selective rather than universal in coverage and problem-oriented.

Still, some citizens resent the use of their taxes to support those unable to "stand on their own two feet," because it runs against beliefs in independence and individual initiative. So, although government support for the needy is no longer labeled charity, the philosophy of entitlement is not overwhelmingly accepted in this country. In contrast, many policies and programs in other countries are universal and do not require proof of need.

To limit government intervention and discourage unnecessary dependency, policies often require that families and government share the responsibility for their members' care, as indicated by the title of Moroney's book, *Families, Social Services and Social Policy: The Issue of Shared Responsibility.* The fear is that if government does too much, family members will abdicate their responsibility, a special concern with regard to care of the elderly.

Programs also tend to be problem-oriented. The consensus is that families with special kinds of problems need outside help; for example, when members have mental or physical handicaps or when elderly members can no longer care for themselves. However, critics argue that this approach stigmatizes recipients, and is both shortsighted and costly in the long run. The single-problem focus of many programs means that families with multiple needs have to search out support from several agencies or go without. An emphasis on programs was especially strong during the 1960s, when many new programs were established. As the overlap and conflict among programs became apparent, some policy analysts pressed for the development of comprehensive policies rather than this narrower "categorical approach" (Rice 1977:1). A comprehensive family policy was proposed for the same reasons.

Public policy also is supposed to reflect pluralism and respect for the diverse national, ethnic, and cultural backgrounds of Americans (see the material from the Report to the President on the International Year of the Child in Part II). Some would argue that this value receives only lip service. In practice this emphasis on pluralism, combined with individualism, often results in a preference for private or market-place decision making. Health-care policy provides a good illustration of government's tendency to make cash payments to citizens who then are expected to meet their needs in the marketplace (Morris 1979:19). With the Reagan administration, the reliance on the private sector has become even stronger (Palmer & Sawhill 1982:16-17). Those who cannot compete in the marketplace have limited options.

Kamerman and Kahn (1978:4) divide policies that affect families into three types: (1) those with specific family objectives, (2) those that affect families but were not primarily designed to do so, and (3) those whose impact on families is the opposite of what was intended. The first category is referred to as "explicit" policy," the second as "implicit policy" (ibid.:3). Policies of the second type include guidelines and decisions about the location of industry or highways.

Many examples of policies with a negative effect on families can be drawn from the field of social welfare. There is a continuing controversy about how Aid to Families with Dependent Children (AFDC) affects the stability of families. Some argue persuasively that families break up because women and children become eligible for aid only if there is no male in the household (see Moroney in this Part and Pearce & McAdoo in Part IV). Other researchers, however, question this conclusion (MacDonald & Sawhill 1978). Social security regulations provide other examples: older people are penalized for marrying and are rewarded for living alone rather than with their family if its income is above the poverty level (Kamerman & Kahn 1978:470).

The Family Impact Seminar at George Washington's Institute for Educational Leadership counted more than 250 federal programs that affect families. Because there are so many, some researchers recommend that new programs be required to include family-impact statements similar to environmental-impact statements. Given the diversity of lifestyles today, Rainwater (1978) suggests that a policy's impact on various family types be considered. He further recommends that policy be assessed from a life cycle rather than family perspective, with separate consideration given to a policy's effect on men and women (ibid.:9). Such an approach makes sense when many current programs are directed toward the individual rather than the family unit.

Family Policy in Other Countries: Some Major Differences

Although comprehensive family policies were not established until the twentieth century, many European countries have such policies today. (For a review of family policy in fourteen countries, see Kamerman & Kahn 1978). Several differences are immediately apparent when family policies in other industrialized countries are compared with those in the United States. Since their philosophies are often universalistic, benefits are available to all, not just the needy. However, the escalating costs of such programs are leading some countries to consider introducing a degree of selectivity.

A brief consideration of family policy in two Scandinavian countries, Sweden and Norway, illustrates their goals and values. Three major themes are reflected in Sweden's family policy. First, programs and policies are designed to assist the unprotected, for example, children and unmarried mothers. Second, some programs and policies are designed to support population policy and income equalization goals. A third set of programs and policies encourages equality and role sharing by men and women (Liljeström 1978:19).

Norway's family policy can be divided into the following categories: "Measures of substitution," in which experts and public agencies provide substitutes for traditional family services and care; "measures of support," such as child allowances and housing subsidies; and "measures of direct maintenance." Programs in the last category, which became important in the 1970s, include leaves for fathers and support for public family-guidance agencies. These represent a shift in focus from individuals to the family as a unit because of fears that past policies might have inadvertently shifted responsibility for family members from relatives to public agencies and government, thereby weakening the family as an institution (Henriksen & Holter 1978:65-66).

This brief summary points out only a few differences and similarities in public policies affecting families, but additional differences between the United States and other countries will be brought out at various points in this book.

References

Bernard, Jessie.
1981 "Facing the Future." *Society* (Jan./Feb.):53-59.

Henriksen Hildur Ve, and Harriet Holter.
1978 "Norway." Pp. 49-67 in Kamerman & Kahn (1978).

Kamerman, Sheila B., and Alfred J. Kahn (eds).
1978 *Family Policy: Government and Families in Fourteen Countries.* New York: Columbia University Press.

Kitagawa, Evelyn M.
1981 "New Life-Styles: Marriage Patterns, Living Arrangements and Fertility Outside of Marriage." *Annals,* 453 (Jan.):1-27.

Liljeström, Rita.
1978 "Sweden." Pp. 19-48 in Kamerman & Kahn (1978).

MacDonald, Maurice, and Isabel V. Sawhill.
1978 "Welfare Policy and the Family." *Public Policy* 26 (Winter):89-119.

Morris, Robert.
1979 *Social Policy of the American Welfare State: An Introduction to Policy Analysis.* New York: Harper & Row.

Palmer, John L., and Isabel V. Sawhill.
1982 "Perspectives on the Reagan Experiment." Pp. 1-28 in John L. Palmer and Isabel V. Sawhill (eds.), *The Reagan Experiment.* Washington, D.C.: Urban Institute.

Rainwater, Lee.
1978 "Notes on U.S. Family Policy." *Social Policy* (Mar./Apr.):28-30.

Rice, Robert M.
1977 *American Family Policy: Content and Context.* New York: Family Service Association of America.

White House Conference on Families.
1980 *Listening to American's Families: Action for the 80's.* Washington, D.C., October.

Suggested Additional Readings

Aldous, Joan, and Wilfried Dumon (eds).
1980 *The Politics and Programs of Family Policy: U.S. and European Perspectives.* Notre Dame, Ind., and Leuven, Belgium: Notre Dame University and Leuven University Press.

Donzelot, Jacques.
1979 *The Policing of Families.* New York: Pantheon.

McAdoo, Harriette P. (ed.).
1981 *Black Families.* Beverly Hills, Cal.: Sage.

Ross, Heather, and Isabel V. Sawhill.
1975 *Time of Transition: The Growth of Families Headed by Women.* Washington, D.C.: Urban Institute.

1. PROTECTING THE AMERICAN FAMILY: Public Policy, Family and the New Right

Beth B. Hess

INTRODUCTION

I firmly believe that the Federal Government should not interfere or intrude into personal family life relationships. Families that have not been able to solve their personal problems have traditionally looked to their community's spiritual and religious leaders for direction.

Our role as elected officials should be one of protecting the freedoms of families as well as individual citizens. The time has come when protection that reflects the will of the people must be provided for and defined through legislation. With the accelerated erosion of basic family values due to Government intrusion and growing secular humanism--the time for family protection legislation has arrived.

The results of the November 1980 election clearly reflected the desire of the American people to see a change in the direction of our country's economic, educational, moral, and social policies [*Congressional Record*, 17 June 1981, p. S 6327].

With these words, Senator Roger Jepsen (R-Iowa) introduced Senate Bill S. 1378, the Family Protection Act (FPA) of 1981. This version is a reincarnation of legislation proposed two years earlier by Senator Paul Laxalt (R-Nevada). Laxalt's bill languished quietly in committee, while the senator became an increasingly powerful figure in the presidential campaign of Ronald Reagan. With the Reagan election and the replacement of a half dozen leading liberals by extreme conservatives in a Republican-controlled Senate, it seemed likely that the new FPA would receive a thorough hearing. A similarly titled, though not identical, measure (H.R. 311) had already been presented to the House of Representatives in the opening session of 1981 by George Hansen (R-Idaho), with the following declaration of purpose:

The Congress find that-

(1) a stable and healthy American family is at the foundation of a strong American society;

(2) the Government has frequently fostered policies which undermine the viability of the American family, through its policies of taxation and spending; and

(3) a reversal of Government policies which undermine the American family is essential if the United States is to enter the twenty-first century as a strong and viable Nation". [H.R. 311, p. 1-2].

Since sponsors of this legislation are widely regarded as spokesmen for the "New Right" in contemporary American politics, and since they have heretofore enjoyed the firm support of the President, we can take the provisions of the Family Protection Acts of 1981 as representing a blueprint for family policy of the current administration. Whether or not any parts of these bills are eventually enacted--and at this writing none of the important provisions has--the documents stand as clear statements of conservative ideology.

I. THE CONTEMPORARY FAMILY AND THE NEW RIGHT

In the New Right's view, the contemporary family is in the process of disintegration from some previous ideal state, but can be rescued by appropriate action from those who campaigned with the promise of "getting the government off the back of the American people." In the remainder of this chapter, we shall examine the major thrust of these proposals and analyze their potential effects on families, particularly female members.

First, however, it is necessary to review some basic sociological data on family structure in the early 1980s. If there is an "ideal type" of married couple, with dependent children and one wage-earner (male), then fewer than one in five families qualify today. It should be kept in mind that many families, not technically of the ideal type at any given moment, have been or are soon to be so constituted. That is, child-free families can be older couples in the postparental stage or newly marrieds before childbearing. Many single-parent families will be reconstituted through remarriage. Conversely, a single-earner family may, at various times, expand to include dual-earners, or contract to a no-earner type through unemployment or retirement. In 1982, over half of all married women, husband present, were in the labor force, the great majority as full-time workers, including over one-third of mothers of children under the age of three.

Of all couples marrying in 1980, only one-half will still be married to the same person in 2005. Although remarriage rates are also very high--varying inversely with the age of the woman (the higher her age, the lower the probability of remarriage)--large proportions of men and women and children will spend some part of their lives in single-parent households. Yet it is important to remember that in the not-too-distant past, a large proportion of families were disrupted by death, so that the increase of single-parent households is considerably less dramatic than often portrayed in the media or in the Congress of the United States. Moreover, the great majority of children and adults will still spend most of their lives in intact families.

Also, on the more positive side, increased life expectancy in this century has wrought profound changes in the family life course. For those men and women who do remain married past the child-rearing stage, a full two decades of joint survival is highly probable. And despite all that has been written about "the death of grandparenthood," a child today will actually know more of her/his grandparents for longer periods of time than ever before! Further, if we consider the possibility that remarriage adds another set of grandparents to the child's complement of kin--and that the noncustodial grandparents are likely to retain their links to their offspring's children--a young person could interact with at least three sets of older relatives throughout childhood and adolescence. Further, if the factor of fewer offspring per family could be translated into a grandchild/grandparent ratio, we would find today's young people better endowed with links to the past than has ever been the case in human history.

We must also make note of the extremely high marriage rates of the past two decades--well over 90 percent of men and women in the United States will marry at least once, and over 90 percent of these will have at least one child. Both of these percentages are higher than in the past and can be interpreted as evidence that marriage and childrearing are not going out of style but simply occurring under changing social conditions. What is "dying" appears to be the pattern of relationships internal to family functioning--from the traditional model of authoritarianism, male dominance, and separate spheres for males and females, to the more companionate model of relative egalitarianism across generations and between spouses. It is this change that has evoked the fears of supporters of family protection legislation.

The various titles of the FPAs directly reflect the concerns expressed by the political right in the 1980 election. Looking at the full agenda associated with this segment of the political-religious spectrum--against the ratification of the Equal Rights Amendment and for a Constitutional amendment conferring personhood on fertilized ova; the abolition of the Federal Department of Education and increased responsibility at the state level for social welfare programs; for school prayers and against "secular humanism"--the provisions of the FPA can be seen as embodying the deeply conservative impulse to return to that classical family of Western nostalgia in which parents controlled their children and wives obeyed their husbands. In this sense the FPA *is* the basic agenda of the New Right--stretching beyond the purely familial to embrace religious and educational goals.

Yet, as historians and sociologists of the family have long acknowledged, the family of the past has been romanticized and idealized beyond reality. It is doubtful, for example, that more than a minority of families--and then for only a short time--lived in multigenerational households, typically for financial rather than emotional advantages. It is also a dubious proposition to assume that individuals were more fulfilled in their affective relationships than is the case today. Indeed, since there are no laws against shared households, the fact that very few adult offspring live with their parents should alert us to the possibility that they do not wish to do so. If most young people and wives were perfectly content to remain dependent upon the finer impulses of the family's father-husband, one assumes that there would be no women's movement or statements of children's rights. Yet, as we now turn to the specific provisions of the Family Protection Acts, we shall see how very compelling the idealized image remains.

II. THE FAMILY PROTECTION ACT OF 1981

Although the bill presented to the House of Representatives by Representative Hansen represents the New Right philosophy more clearly than the 1981 Senate version (which had been modified to meet objections of civil libertarians within the conservative movement itself), the Senate proposals are more likely to receive a serious hearing.

In general, H.R. 311 is more punitive and inclusive than S. 1378. For example, where the Senate bill states that no federal initiative could be "construed" as prohibiting certain actions by state and local authorities, and gives aggrieved parties access to the district courts, the House version absolutely forbade or mandated specific outcomes. Sometimes the differences are simply a matter of style, as when the Senate bill speaks of barring federal funds to "school districts which require teachers as a condition of employment to pay dues or fees," while the House version described "forced payment of dues or fees." Similarly, the Senate's rather sedate mention of "homosexual advocacy" replaced "so-called gay rights" in the House version.

While none of the major provisions of either version has actually been adopted by Congress in the first two years of the Reagan Administration, and it appears unlikely that family matters will take precedence over economic issues in the near future, the FPAs remain important documents for what they tell us about an underlying vein of discontent in the country. One need not be a New Right activist to worry about the future of the family or be concerned about one's children. McGrath (1982) notes that the FPA should be taken seriously because of a generalized perception that government and social welfare entrepreneurs have breached the privacy of family life, most particularly in the area of parent-child relations and spousal violence.

For all these reasons, it is worth examining the basic provisions of the FPA (Senate version) for what we can learn about the New Right's family agenda and the family policy of the current administration, regardless of the likelihood of enactment. Attention must be paid to the discontent of political and religious conservatives as well as to that of the dispossessed.

Family Preservation

The title on family preservation is designed "to preserve the integrity" and "to foster and protect the viability of the American Family" in the following areas.

Rights of parents are defined as the "legal presumption in favor of an expansive interpretation of the parental role in supervising and determining the religious or moral formation of the child." In practical terms, an "expansive interpretation" would limit the intervention of authorities in family life--presumably educational authorities, social workers, or other bureaucrats.

Specifically, religious and sex education are at stake here, so that an expansive interpretation would give parents control over their children's participation in school-sponsored programs.

Parental notification requires that no program may receive federal funds unless parents or guardians are given notice of the provision of contraceptive, abortion counseling, or abortion services to an unmarried minor. This section is self-explanatory in its assumption that minor children have no rights to privacy in the area of sexual behavior. As explained by Senator Jepsen:

> For over a decade now there has been a concerted effort to detach sexual activities in young people from the imperatives of morality and responsibility. What began as an effort by the Federal Government to provide health care services for low-income women has expanded into other untouchable areas of family planning. The Federal Government now is funding abortion referrals and counseling and is distributing contraceptives to minors without parental consent [*Congressional Record*, 17 June 1981, S. 6327].

Such organizations as Planned Parenthood and others that promise to respect the privacy of clients will not be able to do so in the future, thus eroding the rationale for family planning services for teenagers. The sponsors apparently hope that fear of parental knowledge will inhibit sexual activity among minors.

Juvenile delinquency. This section stipulates that no federal program, directive, guideline, or grant shall override existing state law regarding juvenile delinquency, and that states preserve their integrity with respect to any program for the return of runaway youth. In essence, this section removes the federal government from intervention at the state level, which might seem unexceptionable until one realizes that many states have especially punitive legislation in this area. In general, federal intervention has heretofore been in the direction of protecting juveniles from arbitrary and unusual treatment.

Child abuse. Similarly, the child-abuse section reaffirms state primacy, with the further specification of the definition of child abuse to *exclude* "discipline or corporal punishment applied by a parent or individual explicitly authorized by a parent to perform such function." This latter undoubtedly refers to school authorities. The fear being addressed here is that the government will unduly interfere in family matters, even to the point of snatching children from their homes.

Spousal abuse. Again in the section on spousal abuse, the primacy of state law is reaffirmed against all federal presence in the area not only of spousal abuse but of domestic relations *in toto*. Since there are many parts of the United States in which the husband's dominance over his wife is a cultural norm, this section obviously affects the legal standing of the abused spouse as well as federal assistance in remedial services. Phyllis Schlafly, founder of Eagle Forum and a Stop-ERA leader, frequently refers to battered-women's shelters as "rest and relaxation" havens for irresponsible homemakers.

Legal assistance. The Legal Services Corporation (LSC), a federally funded entity providing legal aid to indigent citizens has long been a target of the New Right, in large part because over its two decades of activity the LSC has successfully represented poor clients against local and state authorities and other vested interest groups in class-action suits based on denial of equal treatment. The FPA specifically bars the LSC and any of its grantees from providing legal representation in any proceeding seeking to procure an abortion, or arising out of a divorce, or adjudicating an issue of homosexual rights. These restrictions may be unnecessary if the Reagan administration succeeds in ending funding for the LSC, a step thus far resisted by Congress. Failing total elimination, the administration has succeeded in crippling Legal Services through appointments to its board of directors of persons notoriously hostile to many of the LSC's goals.

Homosexual advocacy. Based on "the proposition that the government should not support either directly or indirectly homosexual advocacy...particularly...in regard to the use of taxpayers' dollars," the section on homosexual advocacy bars "federal funds from going to any public or private individual or entity which presents that male or female homosexuality is an acceptable lifestyle." Homosexuals may, however, continue to receive Social Security, welfare, veteran's benefits, student assistance, and other legal entitlements.

This section appears to be aimed at educators, textbooks, civil-liberties organizations, and any other broad-based advocacy group that embraces homosexual rights (e.g., many segments of the women's movement).

Taxation

Although Reagan, when a candidate, and other conservatives as well have decried the use of the tax system to accomplish social ends, some goals, it seems, are more worthy than others, namely that of fostering and protecting the American family. To this end, the tax system can become an instrument of social engineering through the following sections.

Educational savings accounts provide for tax-deductible contributions of $2500 per year per child in a savings account to be used for tuition at any qualified school. Since elementary and secondary public schooling requires no tuition, this section is obviously designed to enhance the attractiveness of nonpublic education. However, the number of families able to set aside $5000 per year for two offspring is quite limited.

Tax-exempt schools. This section specifies the attributes of a "qualified school." Although discrimination on the basis of race and ethnicity is prohibited, the attorney general must establish a pattern for four consecutive years before filing suit to remove the tax exemption. A school thus need only admit minority students or hire minority teachers once every four years to remain in good standing. Further, a school policy requiring adherence to certain doctrines or beliefs may *not* be considered a policy of deliberate discrimination.

Multigenerational households. In what might seem a particularly welcome provision, the FPA permits a limited tax credit or deduction for every year that a taxpayer maintains a household for a dependent aged 65 or over. Here is the rationale provided by Senator Jepsen:

> All too frequently, low and moderate income families are forced to put their elderly parents into subsidized nursing homes because they cannot afford to keep them at home...[The provisions of the Act] are certainly more cost-effective and more humane than putting an elderly relative out of sight in a federally regulated, subsidized, and controlled institution [*Congressional Record*, 17 June 1981, S 6328].

These remarks completely distort the factual condition of old people. Very few low- and moderate-income families place elderly relatives in nursing homes, nor do they do so for want of tax deductions. Institutionalized elderly are typically extremely old (the average age is over 80), ill, and frail women with few, if any, surviving offspring. Those old people who are found in state-supported institutions would not be spared their indignities by a tax credit to their families. Since 80 percent of the home care provided to old people is given by relatives, some families could well benefit from these revisions of the tax code, but many if not most caretakers would prefer government assistance in the form of community-based services--respite care, health and nursing assistance, transportation, and the like.

Yet we are speaking here of only a small portion of old people; the overwhelming majority (80 percent) prefer to maintain independent residences and have been able to do so precisely because of the income effects of Social Security and Medicare. Typically, neither the older person nor her family wants to share a household; they do so only as a last resort, by which time their service needs are overwhelming.

But most important are the latent consequence of an emphasis on family responsibility for the aged. First, given the philosophical thrust of the New Right, such a legislative stance could be the opening wedge in removing altogether public sponsorship of elderly care. Why should all taxpayers support government intrusion into what ought to be left to the natural support system? Public programs thus become perceived as destructive of family ties.

A second latent effect is to assign this responsibility to the elderly relative's female offspring. What better way to involve the energies of middle-aged women no longer occupied with child-rearing and perhaps about to be "misled" by antifamily forces into believing that self-fulfillment lies in returning to school or entering the labor force?

Corporate day care. If, however, a younger woman should need to leave home for work, the section on corporate day care provides a business-expense deduction for costs of an on-site day care center for employees. To the extent that corporate day-care centers are encouraged, this section should be of great benefit to working mothers. The net effect will be to replace one type of publicly subsidized day care (government-sponsored) with another (corporate), which is clearly in line with conservative goals of transferring powers from public to private entities.

Exemptions for childbirth and adoptions. The FPA takes a blatant natalist stance by allowing taxpayers an additional $1,000 deduction in the year of a child's birth or adoption, and $3,000 for the adoption of a handicapped or racially mixed child under age six. This exemption is to married couples who file a joint return. Expenses incurred in the adoption process are also deductible.

In effect, such "baby bonuses" are designed to encourage fertility and to make it easier for others to adopt the issue of unwed mothers (as an alternative to terminating an unwanted pregnancy through abortion).

Education

It is a basic assumption of the New Right that parental authority has been undermined by the schools--both through a secular curriculum that denies absolute values and through unionization of teachers effectively excluding parents from participation in their children's education. To remedy this situation, the FPA proposes the following:

Community participation in religious instruction and education. Under the section on community participation in religious training, no educational entity receiving federal funds may (1) fail to provide ways for parents to participate in establishing courses relating to religion; (2) limit rights of parents to visit schools or classrooms and to inspect children's records; (3) fail to "provide for parent review of textbooks prior to their use in public school classrooms"; or (4) "purchase or prepare any educational materials which tend to denigrate, diminish, or deny the role differences between the sexes as...has been historically understood in the United States."

Under these rules, aggrieved parents may bring civil action in district court. This point will become crucial when discussing differences between the Senate and House versions, since this requirement in the Senate bill places the burden of proof upon the individuals who feel that its provisions are being disregarded.

Rights of state and local educational agencies are reaffirmed, so that no federal funds will be withheld or any federal law construed to prohibit the rights of state and local educational authorities to set teacher qualifications, attendance requirements, or to prohibit and limit "the intermingling of the sexes in any sport or other school-related activity."

This section is obviously designed to circumvent many provisions of the Education Act of 1965, particularly Title IX of that act, in the matter of sex discrimination. In case there was any misunderstanding of the sponsor's intent, this section absolutely repeals Titles I, II, III, IV, VII, and IX of the Education Act in favor of state discretion in spending block grant monies.

Parenthood education as provided by religious institutions is favored: no federal law can be construed as prohibiting release time for parenthood education to be conducted by churches in fulfillment of school requirements.

In this section, the thin line between church and state that has long been a central concern of religious conservatives in America is paradoxically breached by representatives of these very denominations. The effect of this provision is, of course, to ensure that sex education and family-life instruction are presented under religious rather than secular auspices.

Voluntary Prayer and Religious Meditation

The confluence of religion, education, and family is epitomized in the Voluntary Prayer and Religious Meditation title. As Senator Jepsen describes it, "this section is designed to reverse the last nineteen years of Supreme Court decisions and subsequent case law" in which the free-exercise clause of the First Amendment has been subordinated to the establishment clause. In other words, that part of the First Amendment which prohibits the establishment of religious influence on secular affairs has been emphasized at the expense of that part of the amendment guaranteeing freedom of religious expression--and it is this latter right that the FPA sponsors seek to raise to equal standing. Thus, voluntary prayer is a constitutionally protected exercise of religious freedom, and cannot be inhibited by federal actions.

Rights of Religious Institutions and Educational Affiliates

The title on rights of religious institutions and educational affiliates is designed "to preserve and protect the integrity of religious institutions and their related activities from government intrusions, regulations, and other acts of ...intervention."

Although to some analysts the logical connection between this title and the family may appear attenuated, in the minds of the FPA's sponsors the two institutions are naturally and inextricably interwoven.

Rights of religious institutions bars the federal government from any intervention--other than safety regulation--in the internal affairs of any organization directly or indirectly operated by a church or religious body. These include child-care centers, foster homes, emergency shelters for abused family members, and delinquency or drug-abuse centers, as well as schools. All such programs are to be exempt from federal guidelines regarding affirmative action or racial balance.

III. THE NEW FAMILY AGENDA

If these proposals can be taken as embodying the Reagan administration's family policy--and there is nothing in the public record to date to suggest otherwise--several conclusions can be drawn.

One of the most obvious of these is that the "new American family" is perceived as a religious entity. Parents and spiritual leaders will guide the moral development of the child. Such development will be of a traditional type, particularly with respect to gender roles within the family and in the world outside. Parental authority stops only at the nebulous line between abuse and "responsible discipline." The position of the male head of household is reinforced ideologically and materially through his control of various funds and trusts established for dependents.

The legislation is also markedly pronatalist, from withholding of federal funds for family planning to the tax incentives for large families. Two proposals in this vein--retirement accounts for full-time homemakers and tax credits for care of elderly relatives--might on their face appear to be in line with feminist goals of upgrading work in the home, financial protection of home workers, and more humane treatment of frail elderly (almost all of whom are women). Yet the FPA is a profoundly antifeminist document and intentionally so. As Senator Jepsen put it: "[W]ith the eroding away of the values of the man-wife, mother-father, sister-brother relationship, the family as a basic unit, there is also the eroding away of the value and the beauty of a woman being a mother and a homemaker" (S. 6328).

Almost every aspect of the FPA is designed to "preserve and protect the American Family" by enlarging its role through increased responsibilities for the wife/mother, and through increased economic dependence on the husband/father. This, of course, has the effect of reducing the attraction, or possibility, of work outside the home. Yet the truly clever aspect of FPA is to place feminists in opposition to "the family" as thus defined--a position that can only hamper feminist efforts to reach out to other constituencies. Who else but an unnatural woman would object to encouraging childbearing, adoption of the handicapped, home care of the elderly, pensions for homemakers, prayer in the schools, wholesome textbooks, and the removal of homosexual influence in the culture?

A third facet of the FPA and New Right ideology in general is the attempt to reduce the influence of the public schools. Not only does the proposed legislation enlarge the role of parents vis-à-vis school authorities, but it also contains anti-union provisions. Further, several sections make it easier both for parents to afford nonpublic schooling and for private and parochial schools to operate without surveillance or tax liabilities. The ultimate aim is nothing short of creating a dual system of education in the United States. The claim that public schools teach a "religion" called "secular humanism" serves to diminish the image of public education as impartial, objective, and scientific. By referring to secular humanism as a religion, the New Right seeks to raise parochial education to an equal level with the public schools--if they both embody a religious ethos, then ought they not both to be publicly supported?

In sum, the family of the future envisioned by the New Right will have a drastically different relationship with the other institutions of society than in the recent past. Whereas public policy had been increasingly supportive of the rights and privacy of minors, it will now support an expansive interpretation of parental control. Where policy had funded family-planning services, the new guidelines will effectively remove public financing in this area. Yet government influence will not be lacking or even neutral; rather, tax policies will encourage childbearing, as well as social service activities performed in the home by the wife/mother.

The FPA seeks to restore a family pattern that most members of the society have rejected--in practice if not ideologically: the dominant father, the dependent wife/mother, and the obedient children; a family reinforced by religious sanctions and, in turn, supportive of sacred institutions. To the extent that the fact that such a family has not spontaneously developed and survived in the mid-twentieth century reflects the imperatives of late industrialism, a return to a nineteenth-century ideal may be problematic if not impossible. Will women gladly forsake the burdens of choice? Judging from the strength of the antifeminist backlash, this may be the case.

At this writing, the future is up for grabs. Many Americans--perhaps a majority--are deeply disturbed over what they perceive as a disintegration of social order. All of us probably long for a serene and stable family experience. A profound nostalgia grips us; the vision of a simpler time enthralls; eternal verities are almost irresistible in an age where all seems relative. It should therefore be no surprise if the vision of the family embodied in the FPA is sufficiently compelling to win widespread public support. Whether or not most Americans will actually endorse the specific proposals enumerated in the FPA remains to be seen. Although it is doubtful that family closeness and trust will be enhanced by this legislation, there may be many willing to give it a try, encouraged by a persuasive president and others seeking to divert public attention from other problems. In this case, the broad outlines of the FPA may shape the American family in the 1980s.

References

The Family Protection Act--S. 1387--appears in the *Congressional Record* of 17 June 1981, pages S 6324-6344. Senator Jepsen's explications of the various titles and sections are included, as is a brief statement of endorsement by Senator Laxalt.

A copy of H. R. 311 can be obtained from Representative Hansen's office. The primary source used in this essay is entitled: "97th Congress, lst Session, H. R. 311: To strengthen the American family and promote the virtues of family life through education, tax assistance, and related measures...January 5, 1981."

McGrath, Dennis.

1982 "Taking the Family Protection Act Seriously." Paper presented at the American Sociological Association Annual Meeting, San Francisco, September.

2. FAMILIES, SOCIAL SERVICES AND SOCIAL POLICIES

Robert M. Moroney

Families and Social Policy: The Context for Discussion

In the best tradition of the modern Welfare State, this country has repeatedly expressed a commitment to meet the basic needs of its people.[1] In this same tradition, this evolution has produced a series of policies, programs, and services that are often contradictory and counterproductive when assessed holistically. This does not mean that specific policies when taken individually were not of value. Rather, the specific intervention often created new "problems" in other areas or operated at cross-purposes to other policies. More often than not, the secondary effects were neither intended nor anticipated. Some examples are well known, e.g., the disruption of family life through the Aid to Families with Dependent Children Program (AFDC). The program, as structured, penalized two-parent families and encouraged fathers to desert. Recently, the Senate Finance Committee and the House Ways and Means Committee discussed procedures to enforce child support payments, to establish paternity for dependent children, and to require mothers to cooperate in locating fathers. As one observer noted, "This requirement is not only an invasion of privacy; it acts to split poor families apart by pitting women against men within the family unit" (Stack & Semmel 1974). Less known examples are certain housing policies and current emphasis on deinstitutionalization in the field of mental health. In the former, housing policies have had unintentional negative effects on local neighborhoods to the point of destroying informal support networks and of physically separating children from their aged parents. The policies were, in fact, quite successful in providing adequate housing to those who previously had been living in a substandard physical environment (Young & Willmott 1975; Hearings before the Subcommittee on Executive Reorganization 1966: Pt. 9, p. 2030, Pt. 11, p. 2837). The recent emphasis on efforts to reduce hospital care for the mentally ill and mentally retarded, defensible on both therapeutic and financial grounds, has brought with it increased pressure on families. The reduction of institutional

---

Excerpted from Robert Moroney, *Families, Social Services, and Social Policies: The Issue of Shared Responsibility*. U.S. Dept. of Health and Human Services, Public Health Service, ADAMHA. Washington: 1980, pp. 6-13.

places and increased discharges to the community have not been balanced with a comparable expansion of residential care places and community support services. Many families now find themselves under considerable stress with few external resources available to assist them (Moroney 1976)....

Since the 1930s, the State has assumed that it has the responsibility to meet, either directly or indirectly, the income, employment, housing, and medical care needs of its citizens. In a sense, it guarantees their physical and social well-being. While this principle has been upheld by successive administrations, there has been little consensus as to which specific types of policies best promote welfare or to which interventions are most appropriate.

There have been continuous and often bitter debates around these issues. The disagreement can be reduced to a number of fundamental questions. Should services be provided as a right or only made available to individuals and families when they demonstrate their inability, usually financial, to meet their basic needs? Should benefits be provided to the total population or restricted to specific target groups, usually defined as "at risk"? Should the State develop mechanisms to continuously improve and promote the quality of life, or should it restrict its activity to guaranteeing some agreed-upon minimum level of welfare, a floor below which no one is allowed to fall? Should it actively seek to prevent or minimize stressful situations, both environmental and personal, or should it react to problems and crises as they arise?

On one level these questions are shaped by financial considerations, on another by disagreements on basic values. Arguments are offered supporting the thesis that the country can afford only so much social welfare. Resources are limited and need to be given to those with the greatest need. Selective provision rather than universal coverage is viewed as more effective and less costly. In fact, selective provision is more likely to result in more services and higher levels of benefits for those truly in need...not "wasted" on those individuals and families who can manage on their own. Finally, by introducing means testing or other criteria for eligibility determination, potentially excessive demand or use is minimized, and the State indirectly encourages individual initiative and responsibility. This position is countered with the argument that a residual approach, one that basically reacts to crises or problems after they have occurred, is shortsighted and that present economies might result in tremendous future demands. Furthermore, policies and services developed from this stance tend to stigmatize recipients, segregate them from the mainstream of life, and strengthen an already fragmented service delivery system.

These questions and concerns are value laden. They are presented in normative terms to emphasize the idea that policy formulation cannot be equated with technical decision making and that the process is open to disagreement. On two levels the issues transcend the technician or analyst and are firmly grounded in politics. Questions of what the State should do or must do presuppose some degree of consensus as to the desired nature of a specific society including the relationships among individuals and between individuals and formal institutions.

On another level, and after the first two questions are resolved, analysts have a role to play. They can translate goals into resources and can also generate particular courses of action to achieve those goals. Unfortunately, the criteria for choosing among alternatives are often economic, and the implications of policies are not traced through sufficiently.

Despite this ambivalence and disagreement, there tends to emerge a general consensus that when policies are proposed, the family should be considered in all deliberations. Most, if not all, argue that families should be protected and strengthened as a basic social institution. For some, this position is philosophical and moral; for others it is a political necessity. Reasons aside, the family continues to be very much a part of the social welfare debate. Even a cursory review of the past forty years shows that social legislation has been promoted on the premise that it would benefit family life and, in doing so, benefit the country. In turn, opponents counter with the argument that such action, if taken, would weaken the family. Because little rigorous analysis accompanies these claims and countercharges, for the sake of argument it does not matter which group is "right" on a specific issue. Nor is it possible to determine what the motives are of the various groups involved, since motives are at best imputed from an individualized perception of what is "good." Regardless, the notion that the family will benefit or be harmed becomes a key part of the debate.

[In a report to then-Governor Jimmy Carter, Califano stated]...that "Families are America's most precious resource and most important institution. Families have the most fundamental, powerful and lasting influence on our lives. The strength of our families is the key determinant of the health and well-being of our nation, of our communities and of our lives as individuals" (Califano 1976). Following...[Carter's] election, welfare reform emerged as a top priority for legislative action. The rationale presented was to the point, and it argued that existing welfare policies were detrimental to family life. Proposed reforms were necessary to restore families to positions of strength. This concern for restructuring the system, however, has not been unique to one political party, nor is it a new subject for political debate. Another administration, eight years earlier, introduced slightly different proposals with the argument that the welfare system had been "successful in breaking up homes, robbing millions of the joys of childhood, contributing to social unrest, and undermining family life in general" (*Congressional Record* 1969). Still another administration fifteen years ago suggested amendments that would refocus efforts on the family and family life (House Committee on Ways and Means 1962).

Each of these criticisms generated a series of reforms that were to overcome the deficiencies of the public assistance programs that evolved from the Social Security Act of 1935. The legislation in turn had been promoted as a major break from the Poor Law tradition, an innovation to strengthen the quality of family life by providing a protective floor against the risks of income loss through unemployment, death of the wage-earner, disability, or unemployment. The designers of the earlier reform saw a guaranteed income as enabling families to remain intact. The merits or limitations of these policies will be addressed later. They have been introduced here to emphasize that each measure was introduced with the explicit assumption that it would benefit families.

Take another example. In 1971, the Office of Child Development proposed that universal day care, available for all families and not just the poor, was both a right and a service with the potential of "improving the well-being of the total family" (Office of Human Development 1971). The Administration disagreed, and in his veto of the proposed Comprehensive Child Development Act, the president argued that universal day care would "diminish parental authority and involvement with children." Furthermore, he suggested that such public provision would be harmful to the family and would not "cement the family in its rightful position as the keystone of our civilization" (Presidential Veto Message of the Comprehensive Child Development Act 1971). Four years later, when the Child and Family Service Act of 1975 was introduced, this country experienced a unique campaign to discredit it. It was charged that, if enacted, children would be raised in a "Soviet-style system of communal child care" and that "it would take the responsibility of parents to raise their children and give it to the government" (House of Representatives 1976). And what principles did this legislation propose? In the preamble it states that "The Congress finds that the family is the primary and most fundamental influence on children; child and family service programs must build upon and strengthen the role of the family and must be provided on a voluntary basis only to children whose parents or legal guardians request such services with a view toward offering families the options they believe to be most appropriate for their particular needs" (H.R. 2966, Section 2, 94th Congress, 1st Session).

This listing could go on with examples drawn from the areas of housing, mental health and mental retardation, family planning, employment and manpower, and even various proposals for tax reform. Legislation is defended on the principle of strengthening family life and attacked by opponents on the assumption that it has harmed or will harm families.

Families, Social Welfare, and the Current Debate

Assuming that these positions are more than political rhetoric, it is necessary to search for their rationale and to unravel their implications. The family is viewed by many as a social institution under attack, one that has been weakened over the preceding decades, one that is in danger of annihilation. How real is this concern for families? As importantly, why the concern and what families are being discussed? Regardless of ideological or political preference, many agree that the breakdown is occurring and that it is in the best interest of society that the family be restored to its earlier position. The underlying assumption is, of course, that previously the family was stronger. There tends to be less agreement, however, on the causes of the perceived breakdown or on ways to reverse the trend.

Historically, this concern is not new. For example, the issue of family responsibility for the care of dependent persons, e.g., children, the handicapped, the elderly, has been the subject of continuous debate over the past 350 years. Most social welfare programs have been developed on the premise that the family constituted the first line of responsibility when individuals had their self-maintaining capacities impaired or threatened. It was further expected that families would support these persons until the situation became overwhelming and only then would society, through either the public or private sector, intervene.

This approach has been based on the principle that family life is and should be a private matter, an area that the State should not encroach upon. The family was and is viewed as the last sanctuary that individuals could retreat to and as a fragile institution [that] needed to be protected (Bane 1976). The appropriate role of the State, then, was to develop policies that would protect and strengthen families, more often than not resulting in intervention only when absolutely necessary. "Necessary" involvement was, however, unclear and subject to various interpretations.

There seems to have been agreement that society, through the State, had the right and responsibility to step in when individuals could no longer meet their own needs and did not have resources to fall back on. As early as the seventeenth century, the Poor Law made provision for widows with children through its outdoor relief policy. Children could be and were removed from their families and apprenticed if the State felt the family environment was not suitable. Today, this principle has been interpreted to cover the State's right to intervene in a family situation in which a child has been or is in danger of being abused or neglected. The child is accepted by society as an individual with certain rights, one...[being] protection from physical harm. Furthermore, few today feel the State interferes with individual privacy when it removes an isolated elderly person to a nursing home when he or she is unable to meet basic survival needs. To the contrary, people are shocked and angry when they hear of an elderly person starving or freezing to death unattended. The emphasis in these situations is on the need to protect the individual who might harm himself or others or be harmed. In clear-cut cases, the State becomes a substitute family in that it provides for some basic survival needs.

The State has also assumed a degree of responsibility in less extreme situations where it is thought that families or individuals are unable to cope adequately. In practice, each generation appears to define what form of intervention is appropriate and under what conditions, but each generation does not discard past policies and develop its own. The process is incremental, characterized more by marginal adjustments than by radical change. Examples are the numerous income maintenance, food stamps, manpower, and educational programs. Intervention usually takes place after a crisis or breakdown, whether individual or structural. While in the earlier period of the Poor Law, services were made available only as a last resort, forcing families to admit to pathology or "family bankruptcy," the current role of the State is still seen as marginal though not as repressive or personally demeaning. Legislation, by and large, still views social welfare as a system that should be concerned with a relatively small proportion of the population, a residual group unable or unwilling to meet its own needs (Titmuss 1963). In general, then, the State has been reluctant to intervene if that intervention in any way is perceived to interfere with the family's rights and responsibilities for self-determination.

This residual approach, consistent with earlier social philosophies of laissez-faire and social Darwinism, is gradually becoming balanced with the belief that society, especially as represented by government, should assume more direct responsibility for assuring that basic social and economic needs...[are] met. However, this evolution, incorporating many of the earlier Poor Law policies, has produced a number of uncertainties, and the borderline between society assuming increased responsibilities through its social welfare institutions and the family retaining appropriate functions has become less clear.

For example, over forty years ago, the federal government established a program of social insurance and public assistance that provided retired persons a guaranteed income. Implicitly, the principle was established that adult children were not to be held responsible for the economic needs of their parents, a position that ran counter to previous policies. In practice, however, the principle was not totally accepted. A number of states still have various statutes regulating filial responsibility (granted, they are not enforced in most situations), and early drafts of current welfare reform proposals state that adult children have a duty to care for their infirm parents.[2] The State has also assumed major responsibility for the education of children and youth. It has justified this intervention, a policy strengthened by legal requirements, from a human investment rationale, i.e., children are the adults of the future and will be responsible for the social and economic well-being of the next generation. And yet, it has been reluctant to expand this intervention to preschool programs, despite the fact that the same rationale could be used for developmentally oriented day care.

Notes

1. The phrase "Welfare State" is used more in an ideological sense than as a description of a specific set of policies and programs that could be used to differentiate a Welfare State from a non-Welfare State or to locate individual societies on a Welfare State continuum. It refers to the gradual evolution of most societies from periods characterized by laissez-faire and little or minimal governmental intervention to periods when the State accepts increased responsibility for meeting basic human needs. The term "social welfare," as used in this context, refers to the particular set of instrumentalities that a particular society develops to fulfill the goals.
2. Earlier drafts, later amended, required that the income of all relatives in a household be counted when determining eligibility for welfare benefits of anyone in the household. This requirement would have penalized many families because aged members would not have been eligible to Medicaid or Social Security.

References

Bane, M. J.
1976 *Here to Stay: American Families in the Twentieth Century.* New York: Basic Books.

Califano, J., Jr.
1976 "American Families: Trends, Pressures and Recommendations." A Preliminary Report to Governor Jimmy Carter.

Congressional Record.
1968 "Message from the President of the United States Relative to Welfare Reform, 1969." August 11, p. 59582.

Hearings before the Subcommittee on Executive Reorganization.
1966 *Federal Role in Urban Affairs.* Senate Committee on Government Operations, 89th Congress, Second Session.

House Committee on Ways and Means.
1962 Hearings. Office Memorandum. "Administrative Actions Necessary to Improve Our Welfare Programs." 87th Congress, 2nd Session, p. 161.

House of Representatives.
1976 *Background Materials concerning Child and Family Services Act, 1975, HR 2966.* Washington, D.C.: U.S. Government Printing Office.

Moroney, R.
1976 *The Family and the State: Considerations for Social Policy.* New York: Longmans.

Office of Human Development.
1971 *Day Care: A Statement of Principles.* DHEW Publication no. (OHD) 72-10. Washington, D.C.: U.S. Government Printing Office.

Presidential Veto Message of the Comprehensive Child Development Act.
1971 Dec. 10.

Stack, C., and H. Semmel.
1974 "Social Insecurity: Breaking Up Poor Families." In B. R. Mondell (ed.), *Welfare in America: Controlling the Dangerous Classes.* Englewood Cliffs, N.J.: Prentice Hall.

Titmuss, R.
1963 *Social Policy.* London: Allen & Unwin.

Young, M., and P. Willmott.
1975 *Family and Kinship in East London.* London: Routledge & Kegan Paul.

II

NEEDS AND RIGHTS OF CHILDREN AND YOUTH

Policies directed toward children need to be reexamined today as changes in family composition and lifestyles mean that many are growing up in circumstances different from those of their parents or grandparents. The first chapter, excerpted from a Health and Human Services report, *The Status of Children, Youth and Families*, provides some basic demographic data on children in our society. It also describes the changing family settings in which children are growing up, especially the increasing numbers who live in single-parent households or blended families.

Issues in Programs and Policies for Children

Nowhere are the inconsistencies and fragmentation in public policies more evident than in programs and policies directed toward children. These contradictions reflect ambivalence concerning government's role in ensuring the healthy development of children. On the one hand, there is a strong principle in our society that government should not interfere in individual lives, especially in those areas long considered private, as Grotberg notes. The New Right takes this position. On the other hand, although child rearing is considered outside the government's jurisdiction by many, in some instances it is not only appropriate but necessary for it to intervene to protect the rights of children who are abused or neglected or who require special care or treatment that families cannot provide (see Moroney in Part I). Since children are unable to look after their own interests, the state is expected to assume responsibility when questions arise about their welfare.

In addition, some government programs for children have been designed to compensate for the conditions of poverty and deprivation under which many children grow up. The Headstart program, discussed by Grotberg, provides such an example. To supporters, these programs and policies are essential in redressing inequalities in our society. To critics, they are an unacceptable overstepping of government authority and an unwarranted expenditure of public funds. Similar differences in viewpoints occur with regard to introducing programs to meet the needs of children in single-parent families.

In reviewing changes in the federal government's involvement in child care and child-rearing over time, Grotberg elaborates on differing views about the federal role. Headstart and foster-care policies illustrate how national concern about the needs of children has grown. Yet several attempts to pass child-care legislation during the 1970s were not successful, suggesting that there is still ambivalence about how much government should intervene in family life. This discussion echoes that of Moroney in Part I. In her final section Grotberg reviews the status of federal involvement at the present time.

Government's reluctance to intervene in child-rearing stems from what the Carnegie Council calls the myth that the family should be self-sufficient. Yet families already have relinquished much of their control over child-rearing to others, including the schools and day-care centers. A second, equally powerful and influential myth is that all problems tend to originate in the family (Keniston 1977). Critics point out that such myths have resulted in services that too often treat symptoms, not causes of problems. In their view, the conditions leading to social problems--poverty, inequality, unemployment and inflation--should be attacked. "Minority Children" describes how inequality in our society limits opportunities for minority children and suggests policies to help redress these inequities. The authors also emphasize that governmental programs and policies must recognize and respect cultural diversity in our society.

Keniston (1977:26) estimates that from one-fourth to one-third of all children grow up in families that experience basic deprivations. Such poverty has a widespread impact on the health, education, and life chances of these children. Many War-on-Poverty programs tried to decrease the inequities so prevalent in our society. Nevertheless, this country is still far from ensuring the rights in the 1959 United Nations General Assembly Declaration of the Rights of the Child, which include "the rights to a name, nationality, nutrition, shelter, medical care, love, family and legal protection" (*New York Times*, July 21, 1981:B4). At the present time, poverty is increasing in this country as a result of bad economic conditions and the cutting back or elimination of entitlement and other social programs.

A frequent criticism of programs and services directed toward children is that they are fragmented, uncoordinated, and developed to alleviate crises or conditions defined as "problems." At various times, the focus has been on specific problems like abuse, delinquency, drugs, and handicaps. But the programs developed as a response to these issues often have not been integrated into existing programs and services and basic services may be neglected. A *Report on Federal Government Programs That Relate to Children* (U.S. DHEW 1979:i-ii), prepared for the International Year of the Child, lists programs in twenty-nine agencies from the Agency for International Development to the Veterans Administration. As might be expected, Health, Education and Welfare administered the most legislated programs for children. Some focus entirely on children and youth, for example, Child Abuse and Neglect or Head Start programs. Others, like the Indian Health Service, meet the needs of specific ethnic groups and their children. Still others, like Social Security and Immunization, have a major impact on children although not focused primarily on them.

This proliferation of unrelated programs has led organizations like the Carnegie Council on Children and many family-policy analysts to recommend development of a national family policy to deal with these interrelated problems in a systematic and comprehensive way. In Canada, the Vanier Institute (1979:1-1) has taken a similar position, stating that the problems of children cannot be separated from those of society as a whole. Otherwise, individual families are held responsible for their situation, with little attention paid to societal conditions.

The National Research Council of the National Academy of Sciences and the Carnegie Council on Children both recommend that a broad network of support services be made available to all families. Keniston (1977) recommends expanding the concept of entitlement to avoid stigmatizing poor families, and the National Research Council has a similar viewpoint. The Council recommends that services be free to poor people, with others paying according to their means (National Academy of Sciences 1976:95). Keniston and the Council also agree that services should be clustered, perhaps in multiservice centers, and that the first priority should be to provide the economic and social support families need to stay together. Such an approach often costs less in the long run than placing children in foster-care settings or institutions. Since so many problems relate to economic status, the Carnegie Council also emphasizes the need for jobs and a decent living standard for all families (Keniston 1977:216). This approach is particularly important in light of recent changes in family makeup and the growth of single-parent families.

Child Care

Child care is a policy area of great concern to government and families. In the 1960s, many War-on-Poverty and Great-Society programs included child-care provisions (McCathren 1981:103). In the 1970s, some federal programs authorized and supported child-care and other services for the disadvantaged through Head Start, Title XX, and the Elementary and Secondary Education Act, Title I. Child care under Title XX grants to the states for social services, a provision of the Social Security Act, is the "largest single federal channel of support for child care" (McCathren 1981:136). During fiscal 1977, approximately 800,000 children in low-income families received such services under Title XX. Child care for the nonpoor was provided mainly by relatives or by services purchased on the open market, since proposed legislation authorizing broad child-care and child-development services was not enacted during the 1970s, as Grotberg and Moroney discuss.

Some policy analysts like Steiner (1976) interpret this failure to mean that there are two philosophies concerning the government's role in child care: intervention is all right on behalf of the poor, especially when associated with job-training programs for parents, but is considered threatening by the nonpoor. Opposition to universal child-care and child-development services comes from groups who fear that intrusion by government and experts will weaken families and modify traditional family relationships and values. The proposed Family Protection Acts reflect this viewpoint. Wallach (1981:163) characterizes the 1970s opposition to child-care legislation as directed against the following concepts: "government as parent," "control of the standards of child-rearing by experts," and "children's rights against parents." Organized campaigns, circulating misinformation about the provisions and impact of the Comprehensive Child Development Act of 1971 (vetoed by President Nixon), the Child and Family Services Act, and the Child Care Act, played an important role in the failure of all three proposals to become law.

Yet the need for child care occurs at all economic levels. Increasing numbers of families seek day-care services as more mothers with young children enter the labor force and as more households contain only one adult (see "The Status of Children" in this section). For female-headed households, many of them below the poverty level, the problem is especially acute, as the chapter by the Civil Rights Commission in Part III shows. A mother may be unable to obtain job training or to enter the labor force to improve the family's standard of living if she cannot afford to pay for child care. Those able to purchase day care in the marketplace find it costly. Those who cannot, must compete for a small number of places in subsidized or cooperative centers, which require parent participation in day-to-day activities. Some employers provide day care for their employees' children or contribute to the cost of day care purchased by employees (U.S. Department of Labor 1980, 1981). Finally, many families rely on baby sitters or other informal arrangements (Bane 1979). Parents in dual-worker families may arrange their work hours so that one parent is at home most of the time, with baby sitters or relatives filling the gaps. Nevertheless, there are many "latchkey children," on their own when they finish school each day.

The child-care controversy also revolves around who should provide care. There seem to be at least three positions on a national day-care policy: (1) government should stay out of the area completely; (2) there should be a federally supported and comprehensive program tied to the public school system; (3) there should be a comprehensive federally funded program, but not under the jurisdiction of the schools (Berger & Neuhaus 1977:24).

Those who oppose day care under school auspices tend to favor a family-oriented approach, with parents playing a central role in determining the nature and extent of the services provided (Rice 1977:63). The American Enterprise Institute, a conservative group, favors a program similar to Head Start because sponsors could be "private or public, voluntary associations, neighborhood groups or simply parents getting together to run a day care center..." They also urge that centers be not-for-profit and as "inexpensive and unintrusive as possible" (Berger & Neuhaus 1977:24). The state's role would be limited to such areas as financial accountability and health and safety.

The American approach to policy on children differs from that taken by most Western industrialized countries, whose family allowance programs add to the income of parents regardless of need. Kamerman surveys child care and family benefits in five European countries and compares them to the United States, where fewer policies and programs exist. The discussion of the role played by government and schools in child care gives readers an idea of how other countries assign responsibility. It seems unlikely that the United States will move in the direction of parental leaves at this time. Kamerman also raises issues about coordinating work and family responsibilities, the subject of the next section in this book.

In the United States, most programs are directed toward children in poor or low-income families, with a few policies like child-labor laws applicable to all. Services to children in this country also differ from those in some European countries because private organizations here often are reimbursed by government for the services they provide (Morris 1979:153). The Carnegie Council favors continuing this policy to give families choice in the marketplace. It also recommends greater participation by parents in organizations whose accountability to clients should be increased (Keniston 1977:150).

Needs and Problems of Youth

Problems of youth also need to be considered. According to Conger (1981:75), "adolescents are currently one of the most poorly served population subgroups in the United States." This verdict encompasses a whole range of areas--education, physical and mental health, vocational preparation, social services, foster care, out-of-home placement, and criminal justice. Moreover, budget cutting will eliminate or greatly truncate programs for youth, including child-care homes and special education teachers.

"Youth Problems" deals with three important issues: abuse (taken up again in the chapter on domestic violence in Part VI), teenage pregnancy, and runaway youth. According to the National Center on Child Abuse and Neglect, there were 711,142 reported cases of child abuse in 1979 (Collins 1981:B4). The actual incidence of abuse must be much higher.

Opinions differ on how to deal with the problem of teen pregnancy. The so-called Moral Majority favors educational programs to promote chastity. Liberals, women's groups, and family-planning groups favor making contraceptives available to teenagers and leaving abortion decisions a private matter between the woman and her physician. Changes in Department of Health and Human Services regulations, introduced since this report was completed, will require family-planning clinics that receive federal funds to notify parents of teenagers who request contraceptives. Critics predict that more teenage pregnancies will result, since young people would not want their parents notified and would not go to the clinics. Charges of discrimination arise, since boys can obtain over-the-counter contraceptives but girls would be faced with parental notification. Legal challenges to the requirement are expected, so the issue may be decided in the courts. Government cuts in nutritional programs for poor pregnant women and their infants will add health problems to the economic difficulties faced by teenage mothers.

Runaway youth, a problem that seems to be growing, is another issue attracting the attention of policy makers and social agencies. In 1979, according to the FBI, the police took 164,000 runaway children into custody (Collins 1981:B4). Many of these youths are homeless, sometimes because they have run away or have been pushed out after abuse or neglect by their families (Subcommittee on the Constitution 1980).

Children's Rights

Policies for children are designed to ensure that their basic needs for food, housing, medical care, and an adequate living standard are met, as well as their need for education, care, and support until they reach the age when society decrees them able to care for themselves. Until that time, the assumption has been that children's best interests are represented by their parents. However, this belief is sometimes inaccurate. The extent of child abuse in this country especially underscores this fallacy, as the chapter on "Youth Problems" demonstrates. In some instances, for example, teenage pregnancy, youths and their parents may disagree about the best course of action. While some groups recommend that the parents' decision in such matters be final, others argue that children should be given whatever assistance they need to reach their own decisions.

The breakup of families also raises concern that children's needs and interests be adequately considered in such situations. Many children in poor or low-income single-parent families would live under better conditions if court-ordered child support payments were paid regularly. The proportion of divorced, separated, never married, or remarried women with children who receive child-support payments is astonishingly low at all income levels, only about one-third according to recent estimates (Levitan & Belous 1981:73).

Some experts recommend that parents be given joint custody so that they continue to have a fairly equal say in child rearing (Roman & Haddad 1979). Moreover, divorce has a new connotation since the state of Connecticut made it possible for children or their parents to divorce each other. It is questionable whether this option always works to a child's advantage, since parents may use this means to rid themselves of responsibility for children with whom they cannot cope. With such situations increasing, a move has grown to ensure that children's interests are represented in legal proceedings. Children under the jurisdiction of the state, especially those in institutions, similarly need advocates to see that their rights are protected, as do children or youth without permanent homes.

Children in foster care (more than half a million) represent another group whose needs are not always adequately considered. Many are shunted from family to family; others are kept in limbo although foster parents may wish to adopt them (National Commission on Children in Need of Parents 1978). At the same time, policy makers and children's advocates know that some children would not need to be removed from their homes if various kinds of support for parents were available. Grotberg discusses the changing role and policies of the Department of Health and Human Services in the area of foster care.

The issue of how to divide responsibility for a minor's welfare among parents (who may be divorced or separated), government, the child or adolescent, and foster parents is an extremely difficult one with compelling arguments to support differing viewpoints. However, as a result of both legislative enactments and court decisions, the states' role has been widening. Increasingly, states are intervening when parents' ability to care for their children is not certain, for example, in cases of child abuse and status offenders (National Research Council 1981:83). Therefore, the National Research Council is calling for research into this shift in responsibility from parents to the state and how this change (or perceptions of it) affects parent-child relationships (ibid.).

It is possible that the balance now may begin to swing back toward parents. A recent Supreme Court decision declared unconstitutional a New York State law permitting the state to take children permanently from the custody of parents who abuse or neglect them on the grounds that the statute, which requires only "a fair preponderance of the evidence" to support the judicial finding of permanent neglect, did not give parents due process of law (*New York Times* 1982:A28). Thirty-three states have gone farther than New York in requiring "clear and convincing evidence" to terminate parental rights. On the other hand, the dissenting opinion in the Supreme Court decision stated that the majority had overlooked the essential purpose of parental termination laws, that is, to protect abused and neglected children. When parental rights are terminated, a child may be adopted instead of remaining in foster care.

Therefore, consideration of public policy that affects children must include the relatively new concept of children's rights. Under this heading come such widely debated issues as when children should be granted the same rights as adults. The 1967 Supreme Court ruling in *In re Gault* represented a landmark in children's rights because it "held that children have rights to due process in court proceedings, including the right to a lawyer, to privilege against self-incrimination, and the right to be tried before witnesses who could be cross examined" (Collins 1981:B4). Before this decision, children did not have "rights." Their parents or guardians were expected to represent their interests. In the event that parents did not fulfill this responsibility, the state was expected to step in (Keniston 1977:184). In this country, various advocacy organizations have been formed to ensure that children's rights are protected. In other countries, including Norway, Sweden and the Netherlands, official ombudsmen for children have been appointed to monitor their rights. [For a discussion of recent policy and programs in Sweden, see Adamo (1980) and Howard (1981).] Some groups oppose the lessening of parents' rights implicit in such policies; and proposed measures to redress the balance include the Family Protection Acts discussed by Hess in Part I.

Future Policy Directions

Many Reagan administration policy initiatives are aimed at eliminating or curbing many programs and policies expanded by governments since the 1930s. Drastic cuts have been made in major federal programs that affect children (Collins 1981:B4). Poor and low-income children are affected by decreased funds for health, education and welfare programs ranging from maternal and child-health programs to educational services and school lunches to cuts in educational grants and loans, summer jobs, and vocational training. Children will be even more adversely affected in the future if proposed changes in Department of Health and Human Services regulations are put into practice. These modifications would allow states to curtail or do away with many benefits now available under a Medicaid preventive health program for which more than 11 million children are eligible (Pear 1982:A20). States could decrease their burgeoning Medicaid costs by eliminating existing services, including perhaps immunizations.

Just as crucial for children's services is the administration's proposal to lump some five hundred programs which are now funded by categorical grants, under block grants to be distributed by the states according to their own priorities. Past experience with block grants suggests that funds would be shifted from programs for the disadvantaged to programs that directly benefit localities and that keep local taxes down. Programs would vary even more widely from state to state. Such an approach is in keeping with Reagan's promise to "get [the federal] government off people's backs." Unfortunately, children will lack needed services as a consequence.

In addition to those policy issues dealt with in this section, issues that affect children are found in readings throughout the book: teenage unemployment in Part III, economic needs in various chapters in Part IV, and policies and practices that affect housing for families with children in Part V.

References

Adamo, Amelia.

1980 "Year of the Child Provides New Rights for Sweden's Kids and Parents." *Social Change in Sweden*, no. 19. Sept. Swedish Information Service.

Bane, Mary Jo, et al.

1979 "Child-care Arrangements of Working Parents." *Monthly Labor Review* (Oct.):50-56.

Berger, Peter, and Richard J. Neuhaus.

1977 *To Empower People: The Role of Mediating Structures in Public Policy.* Studies in Political and Social Processes. Washington, D.C.: American Enterprise Institute.

Collins, Glenn.

1981 "Debate over Rights of Children Is Intensifying." *New York Times* (July 21): A1, B4.

Conger, John Janeway.

1981 "Hostages to Fortune: Adolescents and Social Policy." Pp. 75-100 in Wallach (1980).

Howard, Frances H.

1981 "The Children's Ombudsman in Sweden: Spokesperson for All Children." *Social Change in Sweden*, no. 22. Feb. Swedish Information Service.

Keniston, Kenneth, and the Carnegie Council on Children.

1977 *All Our Children.* New York: Harcourt Brace Jovanovich.

Levitan, Sar, and Richard Belous.

1981 *What's Happening to the American Family?* Baltimore: Johns Hopkins Press.

McCathren, Randall R.

1981 "The Demise of Federal Categorical Child Care Legislation: Lessons for the '80s from the Failures of the '70s." Pp. 101-44 in Wallach (1981).

Morris Robert.

1979 *Social Policy of the American Welfare State: An Introduction to Policy Analysis.* New York: Harper & Row.

National Academy of Sciences, Advisory Committee on Children and Families.

1976 *Toward a National Policy for Children and Families.* Washington, D.C.: National Academy of Sciences.

National Commission on Children in Need of Parents.

1978 *Who Knows? Who Cares? Forgotten Children in Foster Care.* New York: Child Welfare League of America.

National Research Council, Committee on Child Development Research and Public Policy, Assembly of Behavioral and Social Sciences.

1981 *Services for Children: An Agenda for Research.* Washington, D.C.: National Academy Press.

New York Times.

1981 "General Assembly Adopted Declaration of Children's Rights." (July 21):B4.

1982 "Court Overturns Child Abuse Law." (March 25):A28.

Pear, Robert.

1982 "U.S. Would Relax Rule on Child Health Exams." *New York Times* (June 8):A20.

Rice, Robert M.

1977 *Family Policy: Content and Context.* New York: Family Service Association.

Roman, Mel, and William Haddad.

1979 *The Disposable Parent: The Case for Joint Custody.* New York: Penguin.

Steiner, Gilbert Y.

1976 *The Children's Cause.* Washington, D.C.: Brookings Institution.

Subcommittee on the Constitution of the Committee on the Judiciary, U.S. Senate, 96th Congress, 2nd Session.

1980 *Homeless Youth: The Saga of "Pushouts" and "Throwaways" in America.* Washington, D.C.: U.S. Government Printing Office. Dec.

U.S. Department of Health, Education and Welfare, Office of Human Development Services, Administration for Children, Youth and Families.

1979 *Report on Federal Government Programs that Relate to Children.* Prepared by the Representatives of the Federal Interagency Committee for the International Year of the Child and compiled by the HEW Secretariat for the IYC--January. DHEW Pub. no. (OHDS) 79-30180.

U.S. Department of Health and Human Services, Social Security Administration, Office of Policy.

1980 *Social Security Programs throughout the World.* Research Report no. 54. Washington, D.C.: U.S. Government Printing Office.

U.S. Department of Labor, Office of the Secretary, Women's Bureau.

1980 "Child Care Centers Sponsored by Employers and Labor Unions in the United States. Washington, D.C.: Department of Labor.

1981 "Employers and Child Care: Establishing Services Through the Workplace." Pamphlet 23. Washington. D.C.: U.S. Government Printing Office.

Vanier Institute.

1979 "Children and the Familial Society. A Work in Progress." June.

Wallach, Harold C. (ed.)

1981 *Approaches to Child and Family Policy.* AAAS Selected Symposium 56. Boulder, Colo.: Westview Press, for the American Association for the Advancement of Science.

Suggested Additional Readings

Everett, Joyce.
1981 "The Merits of Child Support Payments as an Income Source for Female Headed Households." *Working Paper no. 75.* Wellesley College, Center for Research on Women, Wellesley, Mass.

Hubbell, Ruth.
1981 *Foster Care and Families: Conflicting Values and Policies.* Philadelphia: Temple University Press.

Keniston, Kenneth, and the Carnegie Council on Children.
1977 *All Our Children.* New York: Harcourt Brace Jovanovich.

3. STATUS OF CHILDREN

U.S. Dept. of Health and Human Services

NUMBERS AND DISTRIBUTION

General

On July 1, 1978, the number of American children under age 14 totaled 46.7 million. The number of children in the United States has declined by 13 percent since 1970.... This continues a trend begun in 1960 of children becoming a steadily decreasing proportion of the total population. The fewer number of children is the result of a decline in the total fertility rate (the average number of lifetime births expected by young women). The fertility rate peaked at 3.8 in 1957, and by the early 1970s, it had dropped to 2.5. By 1978, the rate had dropped to about 1.7. This represents both a growing preference for the two-child family as well as an increasing proportion of women expecting to remain childless or to have only one child. Young women are postponing childbearing to pursue their own education and career goals and tend to have fewer children. In addition, the cost of rearing a child is growing, and incomes are not keeping pace with inflation.

Although the fertility rate may continue to fall, the absolute number of children is likely to increase over the next 10 years.... This is caused by the large number of postwar babies (members of the baby boom) who are reaching childbearing age.

While all societal institutions and programs have been influenced by changes in the childhood population, the changes have not occurred evenly. More than other areas, central cities and rural areas have been affected by large decreases in childhood populations. These two areas are likely to have empty classrooms and little prospect for filling them. Maternity wards are decreasing in size or closing down in some hospitals.

Mobility. Like their parents, American children are "on the move." In 1978, 53.4 percent of children, ages 3 and 4, and 41.4 percent, ages 5 to 9, had moved

---

Excerpted from U.S. Dept. of Health and Human Services, Office of Human Development Services, Administration for Children, Youth and Families, *The Status of Children, Youth, and Families, 1979*. Washington: US Government Printing Office, 1980, pp. 51-56.

during the previous three-year period. One-third of those under age 5 and one-quarter of those between 5 and 9 years who moved remained in the same county. The high degree of mobility often removes the child and his/her family from the support system that grandparents, uncles, aunts, cousins, and long-term neighbors can provide.

Ethnic and regional distribution. The Census Bureau reports that 83 percent of all children under 14 were white, 15 percent were black, 6 percent were of Spanish origin, and 2 percent were of other races. Over two-thirds of white children (64.9 percent) lived in metropolitan areas, with the largest number living in the suburbs. Black children and Hispanic children also lived primarily in metropolitan areas, but the largest number was located in the central city.... Recent years have seen a slight increase in the percent of children living outside metropolitan areas, which follows a general trend toward moderate gains in population of cities of medium size.

Family Setting

Although 99 percent of both white and black children live in families, the form of the family is changing. The percentage of children living with both parents has declined dramatically since 1960. In 1978, 78 percent of all children under 14 lived with two parents, a decrease of almost 10 percent from 1960. In absolute terms, this means that over 8 million children under 14 are living with one parent, and another 1.7 million are living with neither parent. Most white children (84.8 percent) lived with both parents, while less than half of black children (42.6 percent) lived with both parents. Black children were also more likely to live with a nonparental relative....

The decline in the number of children in two-parent families is mainly the result of a soaring divorce rate. One in three marriages now ends in divorce. Current estimates show that between 20 percent and 30 percent of children growing up in the 1970s eventually will have divorced parents. Another 5 percent to 10 percent will be living with a single parent because of annulment, separation, or death.

However, yearly statistics on children living with one parent are slightly misleading. The majority of these children eventually will have a two-parent family with one biological parent. Four out of five divorced persons remarry within a five- to six-year period.

Effects of divorce. The five- to six-year period before remarriage may represent a psychologically and socially significant part of a child's life span. Stress in parental relationships causes stress on the child and may warrant temporary outside support to prevent permanent problems. The specific kind of support depends on the age of the child, but all children need help in understanding difficult periods. The parent may be unable to provide the necessary support when it is needed.

Traditionally, children of divorce have been considered more likely than others to be delinquent, psychologically disturbed, and low achievers. However, recent research using adequate controls for economic status suggests that differences in long-term behavior between children from one- and two-parent homes of comparable economic status are small or even nonexistent. The fact remains, however, that divorce is more prevalent among poor families and that children are more likely to remain with their mothers. Only 47 percent of divorced women receive alimony or child support; the median amount received is about $1,350 a year. Many children of divorce are burdened, at least temporarily, with the economic hardship that is characteristic of female-headed households.

Step-families. America's high divorce rate and high remarriage rate have created in growing numbers the phenomenon of the step-family. Between 10 percent and 15 percent of all households, with eight to ten million children, are step-families. Understandably, children with step-parents face difficult adjustments. Current research on the long-term effects of these adjustments is inconclusive. Issues common to all families, but exacerbated in the step-family, include the problems of consistent discipline, money policies, and establishing supportive relations with members of the extended step family.

4. MINORITY CHILDREN

National Commission on the International Year of the Child

Although our major concern...[during the International Year of the Child] has been the fundamental qualities that unite all children and families in the United States, we have also reflected on the racial and cultural diversity of this society and on the special contributions and special problems of minority group families and children.

The minority population is, of course, many populations. These populations consist of 24.8 million Blacks; 12 million Hispanics, not counting the residents of the territory of Puerto Rico; 3 million Asian-Americans and Pacific Islanders; 827,000 American Indians and Alaskan Natives; and numerous other, smaller minority populations. Even within each group, there is striking diversity. For example, of the 12 million Hispanics (who are also called Latinos), 7 million are of Mexican origin, 1.7 million are Puerto Ricans living in the continental United States, 774,000 are Cubans, and the remaining 2.5 million come from a variety of other Spanish origins (Bureau of the Census 1979). The Asian-Americans and Pacific Islanders include Chinese, Japanese, Koreans, Filipinos, Vietnamese, Hawaiians, Guamanians, Samoans, Laotians, Thais, Cambodians, and others who differ in religion and language as well as in place of origin. The American Indians and Alaskan Natives represent well over 150 tribes, organizations, and communities (Bureau of Indian Affairs 1979).

Although we have cited figures, the numbers in the country's minority populations are difficult to estimate because, for various reasons, the census undercounts these groups. For instance, the United States Census Bureau acknowledges that as much as 7.7 percent of the Black population went uncounted in 1970. Beyond baseline population counts, data on the facts of life of minority children and families are, to a very great extent, either uncollected, unanalyzed, or unpublished. Currently, data on the population and conditions of Hispanics, American Indians and Alaskan Natives, Asian-Americans, and Pacific Islanders are poor to nonexistent.

Reprinted from National Commission on the International Year of the Child, *Report to the President*. Washington, D.C.: U.S. Government Printing Office, 1980, pp. 69-74

Over the course of this year, we heard a great deal about what it means to be a minority child in the United States. Again and again, we saw how minority children and families have benefited from the unique strength and human resources of their cultural and ethnic communities and traditions. But we also saw evidence of the discrimination that has set the context in which minority children grow up.

Perhaps the greatest obstacle that many minority children in the U.S. face is the poverty of their families. The proportion of black families with incomes less than $5,000 is almost three times the proportion of white families; for Hispanics, the proportion is almost twice that for the rest of the white population (U.S. DHEW 1979). Minority adults suffer a higher unemployment rate than do whites, earn less than non-minority workers, and are more likely than whites to be employed in hazardous or unsafe occupations (ibid.). A young black college graduate has the same chance of being unemployed as does a white high school dropout; a black high school graduate has the same chance of being unemployed as a white grade school dropout (Bureau of the Census 1979). All of this, translated into family income, means that minorities are often less able than others to purchase health care or medicine, adequate food, decent housing, and services such as counseling or babysitting for their families and children. These aspects of living in a family with low income have a cumulative effect on most minority children's present lives and future hopes.

The historical denial of equal opportunity to minority children persists in the present. A few facts highlight this reality:

- Among children aged one to four, minority children die at a rate 70 percent higher than white children; minority children aged five to nine die at a rate 40 percent higher than white children (Children's Defense Fund 1978).
- American Indian children are twice as likely to die from heart disease, influenza, and pneumonia as other children (National Council on Children's Television 1979).
- For every two black high-school graduates, one black child drops out of school. The same rate holds for Hispanic children. For every ten American Indian children who graduate, eight drop out. Black children are more than twice as likely to be suspended from school and to receive corporal punishment in school as are white children (Edelman 1979).
- Black and Hispanic children are more likely than white children to grow up in a female-headed family (ibid.).

The personal experiences of individuals often tell an even more powerful story. Last year, we heard about a Sioux Indian teenager who was pregnant. When she went into labor her friends took her to a city hospital's delivery room. Upon arrival, she was told that her Indian health card was not acceptable at the hospital and that she should find an Indian Health Care Hospital or go back to the hospital on the reservation. Enroute back to the reservation hospital, she started to hemorrhage. By the time she had arrived, she was critically ill and the baby had died (Public Forum 1979).

A pervasive lack of recognition and respect for cultural and language diversity destroys children's sense of identity and acceptance. Nowhere around them in the mainstream culture are minority children, no matter from what background, likely to find material from which to build a positive self-image. The printed and electronic media do little to depict people from their backgrounds as they really are. Television may be the most obvious offender, but printed materials, books and textbooks are no better.

Minority children often encounter attitudes and practices hostile to retaining their own culture and language. Few services, for example, are offered in a language other than English. An illustration of the challenge to a child who does not speak English comfortably was related to us by a young Chinese immigrant:

> Imagine for a moment that you have lost your power of speech and that it will take a good deal of effort on your part to regain it. At the same time, in order to survive and carry on your daily activities, you have to communicate. Sign language, body language, and pantomime will work to a degree, but how can you tell someone in sign language that George Washington was the first President of the United States? If you can imagine this perhaps you can feel for the immigrant child who has to deal [not only] with the total adjustment of being uprooted and transplanted in a new country, but also with the sudden loss of almost all of his ability to communicate [Sung 1979].

Government policies do not respond to the diversity of minority populations, nor to their individual characteristics. Although it is undeniable that minority populations differ greatly, government programs do not sufficiently reflect or respond to their differences. The strengths of each community are neither recognized nor utilized. Health care services for American Indians do not draw on traditional healing methods. In immigrant populations, programs for translating and interpreting differences between native cultures and practices and the American approach in a variety of areas are needed but rarely exist. For example, the situation of the 250,000 refugees from Southeast Asian, an estimated 40 percent of whom are children, is unique; apart from leaving their home countries far behind, these refugees have undergone traumatic experiences of war, of risking their lives in the process of escape, and of losing family members. Services designed for this population must be responsive to these experiences.

Present assistance programs tend to undermine populations for which they were originally intended. For example, policies that deny services to undocumented children force families to choose between getting the help they know they need and risking involvement with immigration officials. American Indian families often must send their children away from home for schooling because no school has been provided nearby. Some foster-care regulations deny reimbursement costs to agencies that place children with relatives or extended family members, so children are often sent to live with strangers when the extended family wanted to keep them.

To learn more about the situation of minority children...we convened a special conference on minority children and families. This was an exciting undertaking in which representatives of different minority groups met together with a common focus on children. One hundred and twenty participants attended, met in general sessions, separated in various caucuses and attended workshops on intergroup cooperation, on strategies for making public agencies responsive to minority children's concerns, and on current legislation.

What emerged from these intensive two days of deliberation and debate was a fresh picture of the special and diverse needs of minority children and a recognition that by working together minority groups can address those needs for all minority children more effectively. Those who attended insisted that the continuing racial and cultural discrimination that victimize minority children and families within our education, health care, juvenile justice, child welfare, social services, welfare, and employment systems must be eliminated.

Toward that goal, participants put forward several specific principles for action:

☐ *Accurate, up-to-date and reliable data on minority groups must be collected, while, at the same time, the privacy rights of individuals are protected.*

Good data are essential for obtaining appropriate services. Poor data can underplay the need altogether. Therefore, federal agencies must gather, analyze, and publish information on the needs of diverse minority group children and on whether and how well those needs are being met. In particular, increased data on conditions of Hispanics, American Indian and Asian-American children are required. Moreover, major federal reporting systems should break down each minority group into component populations. Unless differences between and within minority groups are known and documented, tailoring services to specific needs will be impossible. For example, the Census Bureau recently reported the percent of children who were under eighteen and living with a single parent; the report was broken down by Hispanic sub-population groups. There were significant differences among these groups, with 15 percent of Mexican-American children, as contrasted with over 45 percent of Puerto Rican children, living in single-parent families... Clearly, the needs of these groups differ.

☐ *The design and implementation of programs must recognize, respect, and build upon the contributions and strengths of minority families and communities.* Programs to help minority children and families must have strong minority participation and direction and be sensitive to the varying needs, languages, cultures, traditions, values, and informal support systems of the minority populations being served.

☐ *Greater minority-group unity in advocating for improved policies for minority children is needed,* focusing in particular on the budgetary and resource allocation processes and calling for increased funding for programs that will meet the needs of minority children.

☐ Internal and cross-cutting communications, coordination, and action *networks must be established within and among diverse minority groups* in order to use the political process effectively to achieve specific goals for minority children. Minority communities must rely on themselves, their votes, their organizations, and their strengths in ensuring that their children's needs are visible and responded to by policy makers and political leaders.

References

Bureau of the Census.

1979 *Population Characteristics.* Washington, D.C., April.

1979 *The Social and Economic Status of the Black Population in the United States: An Historical View, 1790-1978.* Current Population Reports, Special Studies Series P-23, no. 80. Washington, D.C.

Bureau of Indian Affairs, Public Information Office.

1979 Telephone Interview with Thomas Oxendine Jr., Dec.

Children's Defense Fund.

1978 "Doctors and Dollars Are Not Enough." Washington, D.C.: Children's Defense Fund.

Edelman, Marion.

1979 "The Status of Black Children in the United States." *Children: Mankind's Greatest Resource.* Congressional Black Caucus, Ninth Annual Legislative Weekend, Sept. 21-22.

National Council on Children's Television.

1979 "Towards Policies for Children and an Agenda for the Media," *Forum,* 2, no. 1 (Winter).

Public Forum for National Commission on the International Year of the Child.

1979 "National Indian Child Care Conference." In cooperation with Save the Children's Federation, Phoenix, Arizona, Nov. 27-28. (Information in the Commission's unpublished conference file, National Archives.)

Sung, Betty.

1979 *Transplanted Chinese Children.* Department of HEW, Administration for Children, Youth and Families, under Grant no. 90-C-920.

U.S. Department of Health, Education and Welfare, Public Health Service, Office of Health Research, Statistics and Technology.

1979 *Health United States, 1979.* Washington, D.C.

5. FEDERAL INVOLVEMENT IN CHILD-REARING AND CHILD CARE

Edith H. Grotberg

There is probably nothing that underscores the conflict between the federal government and private citizens more than the issue of child-rearing as this involves child-care. The issue is further narrowed to child care for preschool children. The reasons for the conflict around the child-care issue include (1) attitudes toward government involvement with families; (2) the changing role of the federal government concerning child care; (3) changing policies of the different branches of government in response to emerging needs of families. This chapter will address each of the reasons for the conflict around child care and will summarize the status of the issue as of early 1982.

Attitudes toward Federal Involvement with Families

The attitudes toward federal involvement with families, particularly where young children are concerned, may be organized around political ideologies, state perspectives, business interests, consumer and advocacy views, and parent perspectives (Grotberg 1980). Two clearly defined political ideologies are expressed by those resenting federal involvement with families and by those supporting such involvement. The former groups hold strong feelings about any government role in the personal lives of the citizens, especially where families with young children are involved. They strongly oppose what they perceive as government intrusion into the lives of young children, fearing the danger of state-reared and state-controlled children. The other political ideology holds that the government has an important role in contributing to the well-being of young children by providing funds, programs, standards, and monitoring functions to meet their needs. They point out that families cannot meet the needs of their young children without government support.

State perspectives of federal involvement with families, particularly where child care is concerned, are expressed by officials in various branches of state government and in human services agencies. Their general view is that the federal government should not be involved in a direct way with child-care services. Rather, the federal roles should be limited to redistributing federal funds and to helping states accomplish what they want by providing support for training and for technical assistance.

The prevailing business view is that government involvement in child care interferes with those in the child-care business. Government regulations and standards, they claim, are too costly to carry out and prevent child-care entrepreneurs from making sufficient profit to stay in business. They do not, however, oppose government subsidies--only government regulations and standards.

Consumer and advocacy views are expressed by groups such as women's groups, professional associations, and child-care organizations. These groups feel that child care is a right of parents and children and that it should be supported by public funds. Their concern is primarily for the needs of working mothers, especially as mothers with young children increasingly enter the labor force.

Parent perspectives are reflected in consumer studies (U.S. DHEW 1976; *Family Day Care* 1981) determining parental attitudes toward government involvement in child care. With regard to child-care facilities, parents generally accepted regulations on fire and building safety, cleanliness and sanitation of facilities, health conditions of staff and children, program content and activities, space, and counseling and referral agencies. However, for family day care specifically, parents agreed that "the internal social dynamics of the family day care home should not be regulated" (ibid. 1981:24).

In essence, overall American attitudes about federal involvement in families are summarized in two studies. One study by the Education Commission of the States (1975:1-2) expressed these attitudes as follows:

> American praise for the institution of the family has long been accompanied by a hands-off policy. Attempts to support and guide the directions of family efforts in child-rearing can quickly raise fears for the sanctity of the family. Some persons and groups feel such efforts to be an intrusion into private life...Others fear the undermining of their cultural traditions and mores...Any program of aid to families must therefore clearly demonstrate its aim as support to parents in achieving more effectively their own goals for their children.

The other study, conducted under contract with the Administration for Children, Youth and Families, concluded:

> While supporting a federal role in standard-setting and in environmental and health protection, there is widespread distrust of any direct federal participation in individual services outside of financial support, and fear of the possible consequences of a federal family policy (Lazar 1980:555).

The conclusion was that respect for differences among families and respect for family integrity had to dominate government actions. The 1980 White House Conference on Families (1981) echoed these attitudes and beliefs throughout the nation.

The Changing Role of the Federal Government Concerning Child Care

While attitudes about government involvement with families have remained more or less constant over time, the role of government has changed. Historically, the federal government was involved with parenting in one form or another from the formation of the nation. Rural families received and continue to receive information and services concerning parenting through the agricultural extension programs. These programs, which combine federal, state and county support and involvement, include home visiting, parent education, crisis services, and opportunities for future homemakers and parents. The preventive services sponsored by the federal government have included prevention of child abuse and neglect, prevention of parents' exploiting their children for labor, and prevention of family breakup by removing children when it is at all possible to keep the family intact. Maternal- and child-health services have been available for more than fifty years, as have family support services.

In reviewing the child welfare policies of the nation over a two-hundred-year period in honor of the bicentennial, Lois-ellin Datta (1977), a staff member of the National Institute of Education (NIE), summarized the changes succinctly as follows:

> Child welfare policies have changed, obviously, in the past two hundred years. They have expanded, contracted, and re-defined the population served along five dimensions:
>
> *focus*: public concern began with food, shelter, clothing and education of orphaned, destitute, indigent children (economic problems). It has *expanded* to include the psychological welfare of poor children as well as the emotional health and safety of children whose parents have enough money to provide for their physical needs;
>
> *responsibility*: paying for child welfare has *expanded* from mostly parish, private citizen, charity organizations or municipal monies to a larger proportion of funds from state and federal governments;
>
> *strategy*: approaches have *expanded* from direct action on or with the individual child such as indenture or placement in orphanages to indirect and preventive action such as income maintenance and parent education programs;
>
> *tactics*: the approaches have *shifted* (not expanded) from punishment of mothers bearing illegitimate children and removal of poor children from their families to income maintenance. A cushion of public funds helps many poor but otherwise competent families care for their children. Public policy includes an emphasis on strengthening the family's ability to care for children in their own homes and integrating children with special needs into the community;
>
> *oversight*: accountability has *changed* from primarily oversight by parish, private citizen, charity organization, and municipal committees to establishment of national and state standards for child welfare services, and development of professional organizations concerned with expansion and quality of child welfare. *Unchanged*, however, is the role of individuals whose eloquence and evidence catalyze public reform on behalf of children [Datta, 1977:222-23].

With the shift in family life concerns from philanthropy to specialized services came the "professionalization" of responses to family needs and problems, and the strong single-service advocacy that supports and directs governmental responses. Thus, a sick person needs a licensed physician, an uninformed one needs a teacher, child care should be in a licensed day care center, families with no or low income need a social worker, etc. In general, professionals questioned the capacity of the family to perform effectively and did not very often consider the value of informal, familiar ways of meeting family needs. The importance of problem prevention was obscured for many years by the emphasis on treatment, for which professionals were trained.

As the government became more sensitive during the 1970s to the importance of the family as the basic social unit of the nation, it supported studies on the family and especially on the impact of government policies on families. Many federal government policies do not necessarily address the family directly, but impact on families and their parenting role; e.g., tax benefits for child-care costs, ability to use public funds to pay relatives for child care, inclusion of men as qualifying for Aid to Families with Dependent Children (AFDC), location of services and resources, provision of educational services to handicapped children and their parents, etc. Policies on foster care and adoption, services to teenaged pregnant girls and teenaged parents, even interest rates for building loans, affect families and parenting. Two examples illustrate the new concern for families. One resulted from a request of the secretary of the Department of Health, Education and Welfare--later changed to the Department of Health and Human Services. This 1978 request was responded to by the Administration for Children, Youth and Families in an analytical paper written by Dr. Ann O'Keefe, an ACYF staff member. The highlights of her executive summary provide the salient information on the role of a Federal program that reflects the new concern for families:

> "Head Start Is Building Families." Although this was the theme of a recent national Head Start Association conference, it might surprise many a "man on the street" who still views Head Start at best solely as a preschool educational program for poor children. However, the fact is that the Head Start program was conceived and implemented from its earliest moments as a broad comprehensive program which, while providing educational, health and social services to low income children, would do so in the context of the child's family and would emphasize parent involvement and participation in all aspects of the program. Parents have always had a key role in Head Start, and Head Start has served and worked with parents and families of enrolled children from the very beginning....
>
> There is considerable evidence showing how Head Start is actively involving parents, families and communities, as mandated by the program requirements (although much more needs to be learned about the "invisible" kinds of involvement that may be meaningful to individual parents and families). Parents are an integral part of the decision-making process and comprise a majority of each local Head Start policy council. They are part of the staff hiring (and firing) process, the program self-assessment teams, and the program-planning process--to name only a few of the general areas of parent participation in the decisions which affect the operation of their local Head Start program.
>
> Parents are also offered innumerable opportunities within Head Start to strengthen and further develop their understanding and skills as parents. These opportunities include conferences with Head Start staff, parent meetings and discussion groups, suggestions on how to capitalize on the home as a learning environment and how to follow up at home on the activities which are begun at the center. [O'Keefe, 1979:v-vi].

The second example of the government's new concern for families is foster care. There were few attempts until the 1970s to examine the problems of foster care from the perspective of the families involved. Historically the concerns were limited to such issues as: the child has no case; plans, the child moves too much, or there are no appropriate placements. During the 1970s, however, studies examined the impact of foster care policies on families and consistently found the following patterns:

1. Children are cut off from their own families. Parents are often discouraged from visiting their children. Families seldom receive the social services needed to help the family stay together or to be reunited. The funding patterns provided more money to pay foster parents than to support parents in caring for their own children. Foster care can continue for years.
2. If children cannot be reunited with their own families, they are also likely to be denied permanent adoptive families. Termination of parental rights is difficult to obtain. Bureaucratic fragmentation frequently impeded the transfer of a child from the foster care unit to the adoption unit. The economics of foster care acted as a disincentive to permanent adoption; money can be obtained for foster-care but there was no subsidy for adoption.

The research clearly identified the value of parental visits to their children, family services to help the family function, and clear efforts to prevent family breakup in the first place. The results of examining the literature and assessing foster-care policies from a family perspective led to government legislation, P. L. 96-272, 17 June 1980 (Adoption Assistance and Child Welfare Act of 1980). This bill addresses the problem of foster care from the family perspective and requires the following policies and regulations for carrying out the family-focused legislation:

1. emphasis is shifted from foster care to services to help families;
2. emphasis is on returning children to their families or on funding adoptive homes;
3. states are limited in the amount of federal funds they can use for room and board for foster children; greater emphasis on family services;
4. 6-month case reviews on each child in foster care are required to determine why the child is not reunited with the family or considered for adoption; a court dispositional hearing is required after 18 months;
5. case plans written for each child are designed to achieve placement in the most family-like setting close to the parents' home;
6. guarantee of parent visits and involvement in decisions affecting their children;
7. states will develop a service program designed to strengthen families under stress and to prevent foster placement of their children;
8. adopting families can be subsidized for children with special needs: handicapped, older, or minority children and sibling groups;
9. long term goal of prevention of foster-care actions.

In summary, the federal government has always affected families and parenting through legislation, policy and regulation. Its role has changed over time, but what is new is a greater awareness of the interrelatedness and interdependency of laws and policies with families and parenting. Also new in this country is the increased sensitivity to the needs of families as distinct from the needs of individual family members or the past tendency to remove children from their families.

Changing Policies of the Different Branches of Government in Response to Emerging Family Needs

The branches of the federal government have changed many policies over the years concerning child care in response to emerging family needs. One sequence of policies is directly responsive to the growing numbers of middle-income families where mothers with young children are joining the labor force. Another is concerned with the costs, program characteristics, and quality standards of child-care services. And a third involves the extent to which the federal government supports child care.

Child-care tax credit or deduction. The history of the child-care tax credit or deduction reflects the changing policies of the executive and legislative branches of government over the years (Hayes 1980). Taxpayers began in 1939 to challenge the Internal Revenue Service's disallowance of child-care costs as an income deduction. The issue was dormant until 1953 when the following arguments were made to revise the tax laws: (1) child care expenses are necessary to the employment of the parent (usually the mother) and are therefore business expenses; (2) since most working mothers work out of necessity, the tax relief is needed; (3) mothers on public welfare would be attracted to obtaining employment and would remove themselves from welfare.

By the early 1950s married women with children were entering the labor force in unprecedented numbers, with 2.25 million women with minor children working. That figure would continue to rise dramatically over the years. The issue, however, had become critical by 1953.

The supporters of the tax law revision in 1953 included several unions who hired women, some employer organizations who also hired women, and some professional organizations concerned with tax equity in business deductions. Opposition came from many members of Congress who were against labor-force participation of women with young children and from the Treasury Department, fearful of the potential impact upon the tax structure of expanded employee business deductions. The proposal lost in the House. The Senate set income limits for families claiming a child-care-cost deduction and also a deduction maximum, thereby addressing the concerns of the opposition and meeting some needs of supporters. The child-care deduction became law in 1954.

The impact of the law was negligible, with only a small proportion of households with working mothers benefiting from the deduction. This situation prevailed until 1963 when President Kennedy in his message to Congress on tax revisions recommended liberalizing the child-care deductions. The major argument was that child-care costs and median income had risen since passage of the law in 1954. It was also argued that women were needed in professions then predominantly female: nursing and teaching. The issue now had proponents in the executive branch as well as in Congress.

During the late 1950s and early 1960s there was a dramatic shift in attitudes concerning working women. The shift occurred not only in attitudes toward their working but also in attitudes about equal pay. The Equal Pay Act of 1963 indicated that sexual equality was becoming a rationale for policy initiatives. The act, however, was not very helpful in relation to child-care credit or deduction changes. The House of Representatives was still reluctant to provide incentives for mothers to work, but did agree to increase the deductible amount. The Senate also increased the deductible amount, but increased the income ceiling as well.

Over the years the members of households claiming the deductions increased but the tax benefit continued to drop. Yet the participation of women in the work force continued to rise dramatically. By March 1979, for example, 30.1 million children had mothers in the labor force, almost 20 percent more than in 1970. Slightly over half of all children under 18 living in two-parent families had mothers in the labor force, as did over 60 percent of those in single-parent families. Comparable proportions at the beginning of the decade were 38 and 53 percent (*News* 1979:4).

The more recent changes in the role of women probably finally ended Congressional opposition to liberalizing the child-care credit or deduction. Working women, the media and lobbying groups shifted the attack to claiming "sexism" in the tax code, which was intended to prevent women from choosing to work at home or in the marketplace.

The fruits of the efforts over the previous years began to emerge in the 1970s. A "family assistance program" with a large publicly financed child care component and the "comprehensive child care program" with a similar publicly supported child-care component were both defeated in the early 1970s. The debates then returned to liberalizing the tax benefits for child care and the notion of a tax credit for child care gradually emerged. Thus, while a 1975 bill attempting to make all child-care costs deductible lost in Congress, the tax credit notion was alive and by 1976 the Child-Care Tax Credit became law.

The advantages of the tax credit were that all income brackets qualified. Thus, in 1975 only 134,000 households earning over $20,000 per year claimed the tax credit while in 1976, 959,000 claimed it. The tax-credit allowance was again increased in 1981, and the number of users continues to increase. The benefits to middle-income families are clear. Low-income families tend to rely more on publicly supported child care and to use the tax credit minimally.

Costs, programs, and standards for child care. The cost of child care to the consumer depends on the kind of care used, the age of the child, the nature of the caregiver (relative vs. nonrelative, for example), the geographic location, and other factors (Bruce 1978). A significant amount of care is provided free or for in-kind compensation or other nonmonetary reimbursement. Nevertheless, it is estimated that consumers pay between $6 and $7 billion a year for child care, including intermittent baby sitting as well as more formal arrangements. About 33 percent of this amount is spent for in-home care, 40 percent for family day care, and 27 percent for center-based care.

Most day care in this country is paid for by the parents of the children receiving the care or with other private funds. However, the federal government has become increasingly involved in day care and has affected the extensive growth of the day-care market. In fiscal 1977, for example, the government obligated about $2.5 billion for federal child-care programs. Of that figure, approximately $800 million was planned spending under the Title XX program for the direct purchase of day care, more than twice the amount provided in 1977 under Title XX's predecessor, Title IV-A.

Child care purchased in part or in whole with federal funds (FFP) differed from nonfederally funded day care (non-FFP) in a number of significant ways: who used it, who paid for it, and what it cost.

Nonfederally funded care is purchased directly by the parent, whose choice is limited primarily by income. Of course, even families at the same income level choose to spend widely varying amounts of money for child care. Federally funded care, in contrast, is purchased by a government entity and provided to qualified recipients. The government-as-purchaser is bound both by law and by bureaucratic considerations. Not only is the government required to purchase care that meets legal requirements, but the agency making the purchase generally determines the modes of care. Sharp differences are found among states in their choices of care purchased. For example, under its Title XX and Work Incentive (WIN) programs for children in day care full time, Michigan used in-home care 54 percent of the time. California chose center-based care 75 percent of the time. Wisconsin used center care 45 percent of the time and family day care 35 percent (Bruce 1978).

As a result of its role as a purchaser of day care, the federal government has been concerned both with the costs of care and the effects of different arrangements on children and parents. In 1968, the Department of Health, Education and Welfare, the Department of Labor, and the Office of Economic Opportunity adopted a uniform set of standards intended to control the type and quality of care purchased with federal dollars. These standards, the Federal Interagency Day Care Requirements (FIDCR), apply to all day-care centers and family day-care homes receiving federal subsidies and are designed to protect children from harm and to promote their development.

The 1968 FIDCR were made part of the Code of Federal Regulations in early 1969. Late in 1974 Congress enacted an amendment to the Social Security Act, Title XX. Grants to States for Services, in which a slightly modified version of the 1968 FIDCR became law, effective October 1, 1975, with potentially severe financial penalties for noncompliance. The modification added staff-child ratio requirements for children under three and made optional the inclusion of an identifiable educational component. However, because of controversy at the state and local levels, Congress delayed full implementation of the FIDCR staff-child ratio requirements.

During the period from 1975 to 1978, Congress mandated a study on the appropriateness of the FIDCR (1978) and required the Administration for Children, Youth and Families to complete the study. New day-care requirements were signed by the Secretary of the Department of Health and Human Services in 1980, but then Congress postponed their implementation until July 1982. The issue of who controls child care had become more important than the quality issue, as the following discussion indicates.

Federally-supported child care. The 1972 Family Assistance Program supported by President Nixon, which included child care, was defeated in Congress. The 1974 Comprehensive Child Care Program supported by Congress was vetoed by the president. The issues increasingly were government intrusion into family life and the role of the federal government in child care. Again in 1979, a Child Care Act (S4) was introduced to respond to the needs of working parents and to draw on all past knowledge and experience accrued in the nation to assure state, local, and parent involvement in the act. Since the president was not interested in the Act, the bill was withdrawn from Senate consideration. The federal government could provide tax benefits for parents; it was increasingly unwilling to provide federally-supported child care.

Beginning in 1981 with the new federalism, this reluctance to be involved in child care reached another level of policy. In effect, the policy decentralized the responsibility for child-care standards, costs, and services to the state and local levels. The federal government was turning over the responsibility for child care to the states and, through the pooling of money into block grants, was directing funds back to the states, but at reduced levels. The states were expected to increase their share of funding over the years. Both the legislative and the executive branches seem to support this trend. The sharp difference between middle-income families who use tax benefits and select their own child-care services and low-income families who rely on publicly supported child-care services is easily obscured. The federal government has focused almost exclusively on child-care services for low-income families. Even the standards were restricted to those child-care services where federal moneys are provided. However, it should be noted that as soon as the federal government began considering laws for comprehensive child-care programs for all income groups, concern about government intrusion into family life surfaced.

Summary and Status in 1982

By integrating the attitudes toward government involvement with families, the changing role of the government concerning child care, changing family structures and emerging needs, and changing political policies, a composite of the present status of the child-care issue is discernible. The public will accept some standards for quality child care, but wants the freedom to choose informal child-care arrangements with no regulation over any other form. The federal government became increasingly involved in child-care issues over the years at the same time that the concern about maintaining the integrity of the family was gaining in importance. The changing family, particularly resulting from a dramatic increase in the number of working women with young children, focused new attention on child-care needs. The changing government policies included providing different help to different economic-level families, introducing and then withdrawing standards, and providing leadership and funding and then decentralizing the efforts.

This administration apparently considers federal government involvement in child rearing and child care an issue for states and families to decide. Tax benefits will persist but the federal government, if all goes as planned, will not only turn back the responsibility of child care to the states and families, but will reduce its involvement financially. The Head Start program is the single exception to the decentralization effort, but it is seen more as a child development program for children from families with low incomes than as a child care program. It will be important to examine how the states and families respond to this situation.

References

Bruce, P.
1978 *Early Childhood Day Care in the United States.* Washington, D.C.: U.S. Department of Health, Education and Welfare, Administration for Children, Youth and Families.

Datta, Lois-ellin.
1977 "Watchman, How Is It with the Child? Some Aspects of Child Welfare Policy from 1776-1976." Pp. 221-279 in Edith H. Grotberg (ed.), *200 Years of Children.* Washington, D.C.: U.S. DHEW.

Education Commission of the States.
1975 *The Role of the Family in Child Development: Implications for State Policies and Programs.* Denver: ECS, December.

Family Day Care in the United States:
1981 *Executive Summary.* Final Report of the National Day Care Home Study. DHHS Publication No. (OHDS) 80-30287. Sept.

Grotberg, Edith H.
1980 "Regulation and Maintenance of Quality Child Care." Pp. 19-45 in Sally Kilmer (ed.), *Advances in Early Education and Day Care.* Greenwich, Connecticut: JAI.

Hayes, Cheryl (ed.).
1980 *Final Report: Panel for Study of the Policy Formation Process.* Grant 90-C-1414. Washington, D.C.: Administration for Children, Youth and Families.

Lazar, Irving.
1980 *Final Report: Formulating National Policies on Child and Family Development.* Contract no. HEW-105-77-1053.

O'Keefe, Ann.
1979 *What Head Start Means to Families--Executive Summary.* Washington, D.C.: Administration for Children, Youth and Families, Department of Health, Education and Welfare.

U.S. Department of Health, Education and Welfare.
1976 *Statistical Highlights from the National Child Care Consumer Study.* Pub. no. (OHDS) 76-31096. Washington, D.C.: Department of Health, Education and Welfare.

U.S. Department of Health, Education and Welfare, Office of the Assistant Secretary of Planning and Evaluation.
1978 *Appropriateness of the Federal Interagency Day Care Requirements (FIDCR): Report of Findings and Recommendations.* no. 260-923/5035 (78). Washington, D.C.: U.S. Government Printing Office.

U.S. Department of Labor, Office of Information.
1979 *News.* Washington, D.C., Oct.

White House Conference on Families.
1981 *Report to the President.* Washington, D.C.: U.S. Government Printing Office.

6. CHILD CARE AND FAMILY BENEFITS: Policies of Six Industrialized Countries

Sheila B. Kamerman

The pattern of segregated roles of men and women in work and family life has changed dramatically over the past two decades throughout the industrialized world as many more women, especially married mothers, have entered the labor market.[1] At present, more than half the children under 18 years of age in the United States have mothers in the labor force. Our country's most prevalent family type is now the two-parent, two-wage-earner family. If we add to this group the many single-parent families in which the sole parent (overwhelmingly likely to be a woman) works, then the "typical" American family in the 1980s is one with working parents.

"Working families" have previously established themselves as the norm in many European countries and are becoming prevalent in others.... Governments and employers are now beginning to react to this change by initiating activities in response. This article discusses the nature of the resultant lifestyle and analyzes the different types of benefits that the United States and several European countries have provided to help working parents cope.

Clearly, work and family life can no longer be viewed as separate domains. This is especially true because of the high U.S. labor-force-participation rates of young women of childbearing age, 25 to 34 years. In 1978, the highest rate ever for this age group were in the labor force--62 percent--which was nearly the highest rate for women of any age. Included among these were close to 40 percent of those mothers with children under age 3 (41 percent in 1979).... Therefore, women are now working during the peak of their childbearing years, whereas in the past, it was common to stay at home once one married and had children.

Reprinted from *Monthly Labor Review* (Nov. 1980):23-28.

Society Places Demands on the Individual

As these changes occur, two issues emerge of central importance:

- □ How are adults, regardless of gender, likely to manage increasingly demanding daily routines involving home as well as job responsibilities?
- □ How will society respond to individual family lifestyles in which most adults are likely to be in the labor force during the same years that they are at the peak of their childbearing and childrearing responsibilities?

Given an earlier history of growth in female labor-force-participation rates, we studied several European countries to explore alternative public-policy responses to the growing proportion of working families. We chose five countries with similar levels of industrialization and the following characteristics: (1) about half of the adult women or more are in the labor force, (2) where women with school-age children are expected to be in the work force and a similar pattern is emerging for those with preschool-age children, and (3) where recent government attention has focused on the problems of working parents with children under age 3--when the demands of child-care responsibilities are the heaviest and the tension between work and family life is most severe, and most visible.[2] The countries were selected initially because each suggested a distinctive policy stance:

- □ Supporting mothers at home (Hungary)
- □ Supporting mothers in the labor force (German Democratic Republic)
- □ Supporting parental choice in selecting how to allocate work and family roles (France)
- □ Supporting the opportunity for all adults to manage work and family roles simultaneously (Sweden)
- □ Assuming that adults make personal and private arrangements in adapting to this lifestyle (Federal Republic of Germany)

Countries Have Similar Problems

As we explore what is occurring in other countries, there is the emergence of a common list of problems needing attention. Although not all these needs arise simultaneously in every country, gradually the lists become very similar.

The concerns tend to be in one of four areas:

- □ The need for some financial assistance to help with the costs of childrearing.
- □ The need to care for children while parents are away from home at work.
- □ The need to make possible a more equitable sharing between men and women of home and family tasks and responsibilities.
- □ The need to facilitate a better balance between work and home so that adults may fulfill their roles as parents without either gender suffering penalties in the labor market.

Emergence of Family Benefits

The European countries have a long history of acknowledging that children are a major societal resource and that the whole society should share in the costs of rearing them. The cash benefits provided families with children are increasingly being referred to as a "family benefit system," part of a country's Social Security system but distinguishable from traditional social insurance and assistance.

This principle was reflected first in family or child allowances, in the form of cash benefits provided monthly (or weekly) for every child (or second or subsequent children), usually regardless of family income and the labor-force attachment of parents. Family allowances began first in France in the 1930s; in Sweden, Finland, and several other countries by the 1940s. By now, sixty-seven countries, including all the developed countries except the United States, provide such a supplement to the income of adults who are rearing children. The benefits, which are usually tax free, range in the Western European countries from $300 to $600 or more per year. In both Eastern and Western Europe, these benefits represent a significant percentage of median wages, usually between 5 and 10 percent (where there is one child) and substantially higher for single mothers (whose wages are likely to be low), and families with several children.

Regardless of the specifics, these benefits provide a significant supplementary contribution to family income, particularly for low and median wage-earners, for whom the cost of rearing even two children can be a financial burden. They reflect a recognition of the lack of correspondence between wages and family responsibilities--and of the societies' stakes in child-rearing.

An alternative approach to providing income supplementation to families with children is the provision of a similar child benefit through the tax system. In contrast to the $1,000 tax exemption for dependents in the United States (many countries have such exemptions), of value only to those who pay taxes and of more value to those with higher incomes, the child benefit tax credit is provided at a fixed amount and paid to families at all income levels. Furthermore, it is refundable to those whose incomes are so low as to preclude any tax obligations.

France provides an additional, income-tested special supplement to low- and middle-income families with children under age 3 or with three children or more. The assumption here is that very young or many children make it increasingly unlikely that a woman can be in the labor force and, therefore, such families may suffer an extra financial hardship in trying to manage, even briefly, on the wages of one adult.

If income supplementation for families with children is a longstanding policy in many European countries, defining childbirth as a social risk which may result in temporary unemployment, and providing a cash benefit as an earnings replacement under such circumstances, is a much more recent policy. Accordingly, there are two parallel policies in most European countries to protect family income at the time of childbirth in those families where mothers are employed.

First, there is a guarantee of a right, around the time of childbirth, to leave work for a minimum of three months (Denmark and several other countries), a maximum of three years (Hungary), and an average of six months to one year, with the assurance of full job protection, seniority, and pension entitlement. In Sweden, this right can be shared equally by both parents. Some countries have supplementary rights to extended leaves, but with more limited protection.

Social Security Covers Maternity Leave

The second, parallel policy is the provision (in connection with leave right before childbirth and after it) of a cash benefit through the Social Security system, replacing the full wage covered under social security (or a significant portion of it). These benefits are available to almost all employed women of childbearing age and under certain circumstances--or in certain countries, such as Sweden--to their husbands, too. The benefits may be tax free or considered as taxable income.

In effect, these two parallel policies comprise what is usually described as the statutory provision of maternity or parental benefits and leaves. The key portion of the policy is the leave from work which is covered by a cash benefit replacing earnings foregone at the time of childbirth. In France, this covers 16 weeks, including 6 weeks before childbirth, and is equal to full wage replacement. In West Germany, 7-1/2 months are covered, the first 14 weeks with a statutory flat rate benefit equal to the wage of about 70 percent of the working women, but supplemented to full wage by the employer for those women earning more, and the remainder of the time at the statutory benefit level only. The German Democratic Republic provides full wage replacement for 26 weeks (and for an additional 26 weeks at the birth of second and subsequent children). Sweden is unique in providing a benefit covering 9 months, available to either parent, and capable of being prorated so that parents can use the benefits to cover full-time work, half-time work, or three-quarter time while the children are young. This enables parents to share all child-care responsibilities between them for the child's first year to year and a half of life.

The Hungarians provide an unusual benefit from the end of maternity leave until the child is 3 years old. Here, the mother is entitled to a cash allowance equal to about 40 percent of an average female wage, as long as she remains at home to care for her child. During this time, she continues to be defined as a member of the labor force and therefore maintains her seniority and pension entitlements, while assured of job protection.

These benefits are all contingent on prior labor-force attachment and represent some attempt by the larger society to replace all or a significant portion of earnings at the time of childbirth and for some limited period of child-caring time thereafter. Although not yet widely implemented, one growing trend in Europe seems to be to extend these rights to both parents and to parents of adopted children.

The benefits thus far discussed *supplement* incomes of parents rearing children or *replace* income in connection with the period right after childbirth. Very few countries provide a *substitute* for earned income beyond the time a child is age 3, and the scale and scope of Aid to Families with Dependent Children in the United States is rare, even though Britain, West Germany, Canada, Israel, and Sweden do give some cash benefits to single mothers with low incomes. Canada and Britain have the closest equivalent of the U.S. system.

Meeting Child-Care Needs

The paid leaves from work following childbirth range from three months to three years. In most countries, six months is typical, with growing discussions about extending the leave to nine months or a maximum of one year. All European countries permit additional unpaid but job-protected leaves of somewhere between six months and two years, although few women avail themselves of this benefit. This means that most working families in Europe need some form of out-of-home child-care service beginning when a child is about 6 months old, except where one adult works part time. Compulsory school usually begins at age 6, as it does in the United States; but in Britain 5 years is the age of entry, and in Sweden, Poland, and several other countries it is age 7, although all 6-year-olds in these countries already attend a preschool.

For the typical working family in Europe, all day, out-of-home child-care services are needed for children who are about 6 months to 6 years old. What is provided for these children now?

Most children age 3 to 6 years are already attending a free public preschool program, based in the educational system, covering the normal school day and attend it on a voluntary basis regardless of whether or not they have "working mothers."

France has the most extensive such provision in any European country--serving 95 percent of the 3- to 6-year-old age group. Moreover, 32 percent of the 2-year-olds (largely those age 2-1/2) are now attending and the programs are expected to serve close to half this age group within the next two years. (Hungary and West Germany also recently have opened kindergarten to the two year-olds as space has become available.)

Belgium has a similar program serving about 95 percent of its 3- to 6- year-olds. West Germany serves about 75 percent of this age group in such a program, although it is still largely for half a day (8:00-1:00), as in all primary schools in Germany. (But a "long school day" is becoming more prevalent, especially in schools located in working class neighborhoods.) Italy has place for about 70 percent of the age group, but most of the Eastern European countries serve between 75 and 90 percent of this group in full-day preschool programs, with the highest coverage in East Germany. Sweden has only a little more than half this age group in their child-care programs which, in contrast to the others, are part of an independent free-standing program, not part of the public education system.

Preschools Viewed as Healthy

Most of Europe assumes that children from age 3 (and increasingly from age 2-1/2 or 2) will attend a preschool program, because these programs are viewed as being good for children, whether or not mothers work. Incidentally, as does primary school, preschools fulfill important child-care need of working parents. Thus, for most working families in Europe, child care is available from the age of 2, 2-1/2, or 3 on, at least to cover the normal school day.

Only the United States, Britain, Canada, and Israel continue to maintain an artificial distinction between child care under social welfare auspices and that under education auspices; and only these countries continue to support two parallel systems for all children under compulsory school age. In Israel about 90 percent of the 3- to 5-year-olds already attend a preschool in any case, although these are largely under private auspices as they are in the United States, where more than half of this age group now attend such schools.

Except for Sweden and Finland, which have a separate but integrated special child-care program for children up to age 7, day care is viewed largely as the care of children under age 3 in Europe, and in most countries is administered under health ministry or department auspices. Infant and toddler care for children of working families is not nearly as extensive as care for children from about the age of 2 or 3 and older.

East Germany has by far the most extensive group provision for infants and toddlers--with 60 percent between the ages of 6 months and 3 years in care (48 percent of children from birth to age 3), and plans to expand provision to include space for 70 percent. France leads among western countries, with about one-third of the under-threes in some kind of out-of-home care. The public preschool program serves a significant number of 2-year-olds and another small percentage are served in publicly subsidized day-care centers, subject to income-related fees. The largest group is cared for by licensed family day-care mothers; France has the most extensive provision of this type of care. Hungary has only a limited amount of group care, because its primary policy focus for the under-3s is to subsidize the mothers' own care. In contrast, Sweden has an official policy of expanding such coverage to meet most existing needs. However only about 14 percent of the children under age 3 can be served in publicly subsidized care today, while an equivalent amount are still cared for in private, informal, family day-care arrangements....

Family Day Care Versus Group Care

Thus, most countries still have a long way to go before there are enough out-of-home places to care for children aged 6 months to 3 years, while their mothers are at work, but the policy is clear for the 2-year-olds already and emerging, too, for younger children. While family day care dominates currently, especially given the unlicensed, unregulated provision, many experts now assume group care will ultimately predominate as more and more women are working and the potential labor force for family day care disappears and the costs increase (as standards are raised). If and when this occurs, family day care may be available, but is likely to be viewed as a high-priced therapeutic program intended for children with special needs.

Before- and after-school care, for the pre- and primary-school-age children of working parents when school hours and days do not coincide with work schedules, is recognized as a universal need. No country provides adequate coverage or even has systematic data indicating where children of this age are cared for now. Several of the Eastern European countries do provide extensive after-school programs or a long school day. French schools, especially those in large metropolitan areas and in working-class districts, often provide children with supervised care before and after school hours and on holidays. The Swedes are encouraging the establishment of separate after-school programs called leisure-time centers, often located adjacent to the preschool programs where children of different ages have an opportunity for interchange in "sibling groups." Similar provision is expected to grow in Germany. Such programs are important and their scarcity represents a significant weakness of child-care services.

None of the research reported here covered intrafamilial adaptations or workplace response to the new realities of work and family life.[3] We would note, however, that for some years policies in many countries have supported, or been predicated on, traditional role assignments within the family. Modifications will be necessary if intrafamilial equity is to increase.

Most adaptation in the home will reflect the values and behavioral changes of the adults living there, but there is evidence (particularly among the younger cohorts) that as women have entered the labor market, men do participate more actively in home and family responsibilities. We assume that such changes also would affect children: they may begin to get more attention from their fathers than they have previously.

Employers Provide Important Rights

The workplace itself remains an essential arena for change; here we refer both to marketplace and statutory benefits and to the organization of work. Special attention is currently being directed in a number of countries to the social security status of women (for example, in the work force, homemakers, and widows). We already have described Swedish parent insurance as a major innovation. Among countries making provisions for supplementary but unpaid post-childbirth leaves, France offers a two-year leave for either parent under certain circumstances. Norway provides a parental leave of up to one year. Sweden permits an unpaid leave after the conclusion of the parent insurance benefit until a child is 18 months old, and guarantees parents the right to work part time (a six-hour day) until their child is age 8. Assuring workers a right to take a specified number of days off from work to care for an ill child at home, or to visit a child in school, while receiving the same wages they would receive if they were ill themselves, is receiving attention in Europe, too.

There are also efforts by industry to modify employment practices or to provide selected benefits through labor contracts or as part of private fringe benefit systems. Similarly, there is growing experience with flexitime and other alternative work schedules such as part-time and shared work.

If adults are to manage work and family life simultaneously, attention will have to be paid to all four arenas we have discussed.

Government policies have been the major focus of what we have studied in Europe; and one major finding, apart from the specifics mentioned above, is the trend towards the development of family or child policy "packages" that go far beyond any single policy strategy. The European experience clearly suggests the need for a policy strategy that includes income transfers, child-care services, and employment policies as central elements even if the specifics may vary as they are modified to fit the ideology, demography, and needs of each country....

This discussion is predicated on the recognition that employment and labor market policies are a cornerstone of social policy in industrialized countries. Work remains the primary role for all adults and a central ethic. It seems likely that unless it becomes possible for adults to manage work and family life without undue strain for themselves and their children society will suffer a significant productivity loss in the labor market and economy, and perhaps an even more important loss in the quantity and quality of future generations. The developments now occurring in other countries can provide the basis for discussion in the United States.

Notes

1. For U.S. data, see Janet L. Norwood and Elizabeth Waldman, *Women in the Labor Force: Some New Data Series*, Report 575 (Washington, D.C.: Bureau of Labor Statistics, 1979); Elizabeth Waldman and others, "Working mothers in the 1970's: A Look at the Statistics," *Monthly Labor Review*, Oct. 1979, pp. 39-49; and Beverly L. Johnson, "Marital and Family Characteristics of the Labor Force, March 1979, *Monthly Labor Review*, April 1980, pp. 48-52. For comparative data, see *Equal Opportunities for Women* (Paris: Organization for Economic Cooperation and Development, 1979).
2. A full report of this study...[is in] Sheila B. Kamerman and Alfred J. Kahn, *Child Care, Family Benefits and Working Parents* (New York: Columbia University Press, 1981). We acknowledge the support of this research by the U.S. German Marshall Fund. Additional data are included here as relevant from an eight country study... "Income Maintenance Policies from a Family Policy Perspective," and a report by Sheila B. Kamerman, *Maternity and Parental Benefits and Leaves: An International Review* (New York: Columbia University Center for the Social Sciences, 1980).
3. The report of a U.S. study of how a sample of suburban working families manage this family lifestyle is: Sheila B. Kamerman, *Parenting in an Unresponsive Society: Managing Work and Family Life* (New York: Free Press, 1980).

7. YOUTH PROBLEMS

U.S. Department of Health and Human Services

Adolescent Abuse and Neglect

Any attempt to document the incidence of adolescent abuse and neglect on a nation-wide basis must suffer from the problems that have plagued researchers in attempting to analyze the incidence of child abuse and neglect. Official statistics are incomplete. Uniform definitions of abuse and neglect are not used in all areas. Reported cases make up only a fraction of all true cases of abuse and neglect. In regard to adolescent reporting, even more problems exist. Society tends to accept overly strict disciplining of adolescents more readily than they do that of children. There exists a popular belief that adolescents can fight back, can run, or can report on their parents. While there is some truth in this belief, it still belies the subtle issues of guilt, submissiveness, and family protectiveness that adolescents face in confronting their own abuse. With all these caveats, recent studies show, nevertheless, that incidence of abuse and neglect is remarkably even at all ages from birth through age 17.... There is a higher than average incidence at ages 1 and 2, a slight dropoff at age 10, and a rapid drop at age 17. Overall, there is a slight decline from age 2 through age 16, but the data clearly contradict the commonly held assumption that adolescents are much less frequent victims of abuse and neglect than are younger children.

In regard to sex, the numbers of male and female victims vary dramatically as the age group of the victim increases. The greatest percentage of male victims occurs at age 3 (54 percent), but at age 16, females constitute 63 percent of the total number of incidents reported.

Sexual abuse in 1977 comprised only 4 percent across all age groups; and 7 percent of victims ages 12 through 17. Of all substantiated reports of sexual abuse, 71 percent involved persons ages 9 through 17. Thus, one of the most surprising findings was that abuse of children, ages 0 through 8, comprised 29 percent of all substantiated sexual abuse cases.

Excerpted from U.S. Dept. of Health and Human Services, Office of Human Development Services, Administration for Children, Youth and Families, *The Status of Children, Youth, and Families, 1979.* Washington: US Government Printing Office, 1980, pp. 109-113.

Of all validated reports of maltreated adolescents in 1977, the great majority, almost 70 percent, involved reports of neglect as opposed to physical or sexual abuse.

Adolescents live in a broader world than small children, and as such, they are in contact with a greater number and variety of adults. In consequence, there exists a wide range of agencies, organizations and people who can work with maltreated adolescents and their families. Thus, it is common for staff from schools, police, social services, churches, courts, mental health agencies, medical agencies, and many others to contribute to alleviating problems of abuse and neglect.

A view widely held in service-delivery systems (although not so widely practiced) is that services will be more effective if the victim is treated within the context of relevant social systems, such as the family, the peer group, the classroom, and so forth. In practice, treatment programs such as this are difficult to carry out, in part because they require a great deal of shared knowledge among the service providers. To this end, much federal effort in this area has been in the development and dissemination of information and training materials for different professionals--police, teachers, doctors and nurses, and others--who are in a position to aid maltreated adolescents.

Two agencies within the Administration for Children, Youth, and Families--the National Center on Child Abuse and Neglect and the Youth Development Bureau--are coordination and administrative centers for federal government activities in this area.

Teenage Pregnancy

Childbearing during adolescence is a high-risk experience for mother and child alike, especially if the mother is a very young adolescent, or if she does not receive proper prenatal care and nutrition. Yet one-fourth of American teenage girls have had at least one pregnancy by age 19. Every year about 1 million adolescents under age 19 become pregnant, including perhaps 300,000 under age 15--which represents an annual rate of 10 percent for all teenage girls. Two-thirds of them are unmarried. At least three in ten elect to terminate their pregnancies. Birth rates for teenagers, ages 16 to 19, are declining but they are increasing for girls under age 16.

Those mothers, who are very young adolescents or who do not receive proper prenatal care and nutrition, have greater risk of bearing low birthweight infants, with consequent developmental problems and risk of infant death associated with low birthweight. Often they also face significant social problems: disruption of schooling, high rates of repeat pregnancy, and public dependency. A substantial proportion of school districts, by not providing for continuing education, still encourage expectant mothers to drop out of school; more than 25 percent of the young mothers become pregnant again within just a year after their first delivery.

A major underlying problem that urgently needs addressing for this age group is the inadequate knowledge of, and access to, information on sexual behavior and family planning services. In 1976, an estimated 40 percent of unmarried teenage girls, ages 15 to 19 (two-thirds by age 19), had engaged in sexual intercourse, and 25 percent of them had never used any form of contraception.

Birth control methods currently prevent an estimated 750,000 unwanted pregnancies annually. If all sexually active young people, who do not want to become pregnant, were to use some form of contraception regularly, it is estimated that premarital pregnancies would drop by more than 300,000 a year.

There is growing evidence that comprehensive programs for the pregnant teenager and her baby, especially those that emphasize continued schooling, are associated with fewer repeat pregnancies. An example is a program at the Johns Hopkins Medical Institutions in Baltimore. There, staff members provide young mothers with comprehensive medical and psychological services, conduct classes from the first prenatal visit through labor, delivery, and for three years after delivery, and, perhaps most important, form close supportive relationships with the young women. Recent results indicate that 85 percent of mothers enrolled at the center have returned to school and only 5 percent became pregnant again within a year after delivery. Of all Baltimore teen mothers, only 10 percent return to school and 47 percent become pregnant again within a year. Teen mothers in the program also have had fewer obstetrical complications and fewer premature deliveries, and have given birth to larger and healthier babies than Baltimore's teen mothers in general.

Federal concern in these matters was shown in 1978 by the establishment within the Department of Health, Education, and Welfare of the Office of Adolescent Pregnancy Programs. The mission of the agency is to assist in setting up networks of community-based services for adolescents at risk of unintended pregnancies, for pregnant adolescents, and for adolescent parents. In 1979, the Office completed its first cycle of grant awards and also began a series of technical workshops in different regions of the country.

Runaway Youth

A survey conducted in 1975 found that approximately 733,000 youth, ages 10 to 17, left home annually without parental consent for at least overnight. A major contributing factor was family conflict. The survey also presented evidence that large number of homeless and neglected youth were not being served by traditional social service agencies.

In response to concerns raised by this situation, the Runaway Youth Act was authorized and signed into law in 1977 for the purpose or providing assistance to those youth, who, while away from home and living on the streets, were vulnerable and exposed to exploitation and other dangerous encounters.

By 1978, the National Runaway Youth Program, within the Youth Development Bureau, had undertaken funding of 166 individual runaway youth programs that were providing services to over 32,000 runaway youth and their families located in forty-eight states, Puerto Rico, the District of Columbia, and Guam. The program also was funding the National Toll-Free Communications System to serve runaways, other homeless youth, and their families. Since its inception, three years earlier, the Program had served over 75,000 youth in its individual programs, and over 250,000 youth had used the National Toll-Free Communications System....

Intake data gathered at the various programs throughout the country yield the following profile of youth served:

- Sex--female (59.4%)
- Age--16 years (25%)
- Race/ethnic origin--white (74%)
- Living situation past three years--home with parents or legal guardians 82.4%)
- Juvenile Justice System involvement--no involvement (59.4%)
- Reasons for seeking services--poor communication with parent figures (51.8%)
- Parent participation--one or both parents (51.9%)
- Length of stay--less than fourteen days (84.1%)
- Disposition--home with parents or legal guardians (30.4%)

Most of the individual programs throughout the country have developed or are developing multiple service components addressing various needs by young people in the local communities. At the same time, the programs are becoming viewed as legitimate members of the community social service network and are being used by other social service agencies and by the law enforcement/juvenile justice system as resources for youth and families.

III

WORK AND FAMILY:

An Area for Policy Initiatives?

Goals and Values Underlying Work-Family Policies

The idea that there should be government policies to help family members manage the often conflicting demands of work and family is relatively new in this country. It has arisen largely because of changes in family composition and in views about men's and women's roles. For women in the labor force with young children, the pressures of integrating work and family responsibilities are great. Although the women's movement has given voice and legitimacy to efforts to modify the sexual division of labor within the family, researchers have found that women still tend to do the lion's share of household and child-care work (see Chapters 9 and 11).

Until recently workers have been expected not to let their private lives interfere with their jobs. Now there is growing support for policies to ease the strains on parents. However, unlike Sweden for example, the federal government has not adopted policies to encourage men and women to share household and child-rearing responsibilities, as described in Chapter 10 in this section and Chapter 6 in Part II. On the contrary, the new right and other groups who share their viewpoint want government policies that favor the traditional nuclear family, as indicated by Hess (Chapter 1).

This is not to say that government policies do not have direct and indirect effects on the interrelationships between work and family. Ideology and values concerning preferred family composition and relationships have influenced laws and regulations governing work--and still do today, as Lehrer (Chapter 8) suggests. Lehrer looks at the rationale behind protective labor legislation for women, analyzing how beliefs about women's family roles have influenced views about them as paid workers. She also illustrates how this legislation, considered such an advance when introduced, has served to reinforce societal beliefs about women as providers of "secondary" income and to justify their inequitable treatment with regard to pay, advancement, and other aspects of work. Women in some industries today are still treated differently from men because of their reproductive role. The Civil Rights Act and subsequent legislation sought to undo the effects of past policies that permitted differential treatment of men and women in education, work and other areas of life.

Yet the belief that woman's place is in the home has been swept aside during periods when economic policy goals required women's labor-force participation. During World War II, as Levitan and Belous point out in Chapter 11, patriotic appeals were made to women, whether married or single, to support the war effort by working. Not only were traditional male and female roles disregarded, but occupational segregation broke down as women held jobs in male-dominated occupations. "Rosie the Riveter" was a symbol of this campaign. After the war, beliefs about the traditional nuclear family's importance were restated as men reclaimed the jobs they had left. Women were expected once more to stay at home and care for their children. Postwar suburbanization trends, which separated the locations of work and residence, helped delineate separate spheres for men and women and reinforced the belief that woman's place was in the home.

The situation in many European countries was different because women were needed in the workforce to compensate for the men killed in the war. Benefit packages and programs and other incentives were developed to lure women into the labor force. Today, governments in many countries encourage women to work by providing child care, maternity allowances, and other programs to facilitate combining motherhood with full-time work. Kamerman describes many of these programs in Part II.

Some policies affecting families were devised primarily to serve population policy objectives--for example, to increase the birth rate. Governments have often used family allowances and other benefits to encourage women to stay home to raise children. On the other hand, Chinese policy encourages small families, and governments in developing countries often have extensive birth-control programs. A country may adopt conflicting policies at different periods, depending on whether labor-force or population policies have priority. Sometimes policies in different spheres are incompatible.

For example, when the Norwegian government wanted to increase the labor-force participation of women in the latter half of the 1960s, its policy was to reduce the "family support" part of men's salaries to make them lag behind the cost of living. The purpose was to encourage women to work during a period of tight labor markets when a recession seemed possible (Henriksen & Holter 1978:56). However, that policy conflicted with official views that mothers should be at home with their children. This ambivalence has been somewhat resolved. In the 1970s, day care became an important component of government policy, resulting in the development of various types of child-care facilities, including playgrounds and youth centers (ibid.:57, 61). Part of the rationale for this changed direction was that children might be exposed to "a richer cultural milieu" in the centers than is found in some homes and could interact with their peers.

Newland, in Chapter 10, explores the coexistence of traditional and egalitarian definitions of women's labor-force position and makes apparent how these inconsistencies in values are reflected in government policies which, on the one hand, seem to endorse equality for women but which, on the other hand, demonstrate how powerful the image of the traditional nuclear family remains. Newland shows how ambivalent the governments of many countries are about "women's proper place," despite their support for legislation to provide equality in paid employment. Given this inconsistency among policy makers, it is not surprising that employers frequently hold onto myths about women working for pocket money or only "until" they get married or have children. Newland also discusses the ways in which the traditional division of labor within the home works against equality between men and women in the labor force.

Some countries have made progress in encouraging equality between men and women. Newland describes initiatives taken by the Swedish government to bring about greater equality between men and women in employment and other areas of life. Various programs and policies help resolve work-family conflicts and make it easier for women who are single parents to provide for their families. Moreover, Sweden's system of individual taxation gives advantages to families with two earners.

Recent policies in many countries have been designed especially to assist or strengthen families, although views differ on whether government should encourage any specific family types or arrangements. In Denmark, the aim of family policy is much discussed. Questions arise about whether government policy should encourage the traditional family, help liberate both parents, or be neutral on this issue. Disagreements exist too about the parents' role when children are young, perhaps because conflicts arise among family needs, industry needs, and women's rights (Vedel-Petersen 1978:320).

American views differ about whether mothers should be at home with their children or in the labor force. Furthermore, if they are expected to stay at home, should they be compensated for their work and, if so, how? The Family Protection Acts, discussed in Chapter 1, attempt to make staying at home more attractive. This traditional view of woman's place is at odds with the belief that each individual has the right to develop his or her potential and with policies to achieve sexual equality. In single-parent and low-income families where the woman's income is essential, the debate becomes irrelevant. For these women, child care is a major need, affecting their ability to improve their own and their children's lives.

"Equal Opportunity and the Need for Child Care" assesses the extent to which the need for child care stands in the way of equal opportunity for women. Lack of care, or inadequate care, prevents women from taking jobs or advancing at work. Some women have to forgo job-training possibilities because they cannot afford child care, thus passing up the chance to improve their economic status. Research cited from a variety of sources provides evidence of the problem's dimensions. The report recommends increases in various types of child care, including at-home care, group day care, family day care, and evening child care.

American policy makers only recently have begun to examine the interactions between family and work to determine whether strains and conflicts felt by both men and women might be reduced (see Kanter 1977; Bohen & Viveros-Long 1981; Fava and Genovese 1983). Some of their recommendations are aimed at dual-worker families, while others seek to help single parents manage work and family with less strain. For example, dual-career couples may profit from new corporate programs that offer employees a cafeteria of benefits so that spouses do not duplicate unneeded medical or other benefits, but may substitute partial payment of child care or increased vacation time instead (Catalyst 1981). Some corporations are expanding relocation services for spouses so that men or women who give up jobs to follow their transferred spouses do not face unemployment or interrupted careers (ibid). However, more families are resisting transfers, not only because the move may disrupt a spouse's career, but also because of the emotional costs of uprooting children and the economic costs of relocation.

Not all observers think that corporations will make significant changes in work to accommodate family-related needs of workers. On the contrary, Hunt and Hunt (1981) suggest that there will be a polarization between work and family, with employees having to choose whether to put career or family first. Those in the former group, who will often be child-free, will advance fastest and farthest in the corporate hierarchy in the Hunts' view.

Some parents try to resolve work-family conflicts by experimenting with shared positions or with permanent part-time work. These alternatives may be a mixed blessing, since they tend to offer less chance for advancement and fewer benefits. Technological change now makes it possible for some workers to avoid the separation between work and family life by carrying out their duties in the home. Although there has always been "cottage industry," some men and women now do sophisticated jobs like data processing at home terminals, sometimes as employees of large corporations. Parents with young children find obvious advantages to combining child care and employment. Work hours are flexible and may be concentrated at times when family responsibilities are less. However, efforts to relax regulations concerning work at home have run into opposition from groups like the garment workers' unions who fear that those who do piecework at home will be exploited as they were in the past.

As this discussion suggests, explicit government policies and programs play a small role in affecting the relationship between work and family. In this respect, the United States has much to learn from other industrialized countries which provide extensive leaves and other work-related benefits for parents.

Wives and Mothers in the Labor Force

Westcott and Bednarzik (Chapter 12) provide data on changing labor-force patterns, especially the increase in multi-earner families. Since 1978, there were more families with both spouses employed than with only the husband employed. Another interesting finding is that few women leave the labor force because of family or home responsibilities. Consequently, their earnings represent an integral part of the family income.

During the current recession, the labor-force participation of women has continued to rise (see Chapter 12). Between 1980 and 1981, 1.2 million additional women entered the labor force, so that 52.1 percent of all women 16 years or older were working or looking for work (BLS #663, n.d.: 1). The earnings of many women are essential to their household income, as various statistics indicate. In fact, despite the increased labor-force participation of women, the number and proportion of families with dual-workers did not change between 1980 and 1981. (There were about 25.6 million dual-earner, married-couple families in 1981, an increase of 25 percent over 1971.) One explanation lies in higher unemployment, especially in male-dominated fields like manufacturing. In some one-earner families, the wife is the worker. There also has been an increase in families with no workers. Many are couples over 65, but others are families with both husband and wife unemployed.

High divorce rates provide another answer. Sixty percent of the women who maintain families were in the labor force, up from 53 percent in 1971. However, the median income of such families in 1980 was only one-half that of married-couple families with one earner--$10,120 compared to $20,470--and an even higher $27,750 for families with husband and wife in the labor force (Bureau of Labor Statistics, n.d.:1). Women continue to earn substantially less than their male counterparts. The median income of full-time working women is just over 60 percent of men's income, a percentage that has remained virtually unchanged for decades. Although government affirmative-action policies have had an impact on the occupational distribution of women, whose numbers are increasing in some male-dominated fields, for the most part women's median salaries remain substantially below those of men in the same occupations (Bureau of Labor Statistics 1982a).

Past administrations have introduced a wide range of programs to improve the status of women and minority workers. However, the Reagan administration has eliminated or eased guidelines in hiring and promotion and has backed away from back pay awards for discrimination in employment. Many job-training programs, which gave poor or low-income minorities and women needed skills and helped them to improve their economic status, have been ended. Such actions are consistent with the administration's conservative economic policies and lack of support for social programs. Moreover, the president has held "ladies" largely responsible for the rise in unemployment rates, seeming to imply that women are secondary workers whose income is not essential to themselves and their households. Convincing evidence to the contrary is provided by Westcott and Bednarzik (Chapter 12) and Pearce and McAdoo (Chapter 16, in Part IV).

Analysts expect that women will continue to enter the labor force in large numbers for the rest of the decade if present trends continue (Smith 1979b). These projections may lead to the introduction of new programs and policies in the work-family area, especially if recognition grows that their earnings represent all or an essential part of household income. Job-training, child care, affirmative action and flexible work schedules that do not confine women workers to the secondary labor market would help women upgrade their own and their family's economic status (see Smith 1979a).

Does increased labor-force participation of women, along with high divorce rates, imply that the institution of marriage is on its way out? Levitan and Belous (see Chapter 11) disagree with those who predict the end of marriage in the future. As they note, "going it alone" tends to be temporary for many adults. Without denying the strains that beset families today, they are optimistic about the continued resilience of families. They recommend modifications in federal income tax and social security policies to reflect changes in families, but they do not think that a comprehensive family policy is feasible. Instead they suggest incremental changes that respect the diversity of family types.

Families and Unemployment

Unemployment can be traumatic for all families. For example, the median income of families with an unemployed member was 21 percent lower than that of families without unemployment (Bureau of Labor Statistics 1982b). But its impact is most devastating in households with only one worker. Families maintained by women are hit the hardest, since they are least likely to have more than one earner. For example, in the second quarter of 1982, 1.6 million families maintained by women had one unemployed member. More than one-half of these families had no other worker (Bureau of Labor Statistics 1982c). The effect of unemployment also varies according to an individual's life-cycle and family stage.

Teenagers are most likely to be unemployed, with rates for black teenagers as high as 50 percent. Their plight is of special concern today, since the Reagan administration has discontinued or slashed funding for job-training programs. The inability of young adults to enter the work force may have serious long-term implications. Their families may need multiple earners just to stay above the poverty level. Some youths may have to delay their own family formation. The longer they remain without work, the greater the likelihood that they will become permanently unemployed.

This problem of youth unemployment is discussed by Jaynes and Loury (see Chapter 14) in an excerpt from *Urban Policy Issues*, a report prepared for Community Development Block Grant recipients. One of its proposals, that a subminimum wage for teenagers be introduced, is controversial, but the authors explain the rationale for the recommendation. The Reagan administration is reportedly considering such a subminimum wage for teenagers. Especially interesting is the suggestion that the minimum wage raises white and middle-income family earnings more than it helps black and lower-income families. The importance of job training for low-income urban youth is stressed in the report, too. Current federal policies have drastically reduced such programs. However, as high unemployment rates persist, programs for retraining and relocating unemployed workers are receiving more serious consideration by Congress and the president.

In addition, public-service-employment jobs have been eliminated. A Congressional Budget Office report (1982) analyzed the effect of this action on government expenditures as well as on individuals and families. It found that the savings from these programs would be offset somewhat by lost tax revenues and increased costs for government benefits like unemployment insurance, public assistance, and food stamps. While some individuals who lose government-supported jobs will find other jobs, others will have to turn to these social programs to provide the necessities for themselves and their families. About 10 percent of former public-service-employment workers would get neither jobs nor benefits.

"Unemployment among Family Men" (Chapter 13) examines men in their middle years who were unemployed between 1967 and 1976. Unemployment rates for these men reflected changes in the economy, and did not decrease with age as expected. The researchers also found that blacks, the poor, blue- collar workers, the less educated, and those under 45 years were much more likely to have been unemployed at some time during the ten-year period. When unemployment hits workers at midlife, families face an array of problems, including paying for housing, children's schooling, and other fixed expenses. Moreover, middle-aged workers find employers increasingly reluctant to hire them. With one or more family members employed, the family unit has more economic security to plan for major expenditures. Such considerations motivate many wives to enter or to remain in the labor force. Yet there is no commitment to a full employment policy in this country despite the extent of unemployment. In fact, new policies discourage labor-force participation by members of low-income families.

Government policies in the area of employment are closely intertwined with those in other areas like income maintenance and social welfare. Policies enacted in one sphere may have unintended or unwanted effects on another. The effects that employment and social welfare policies and programs have on each other will become even more apparent in Part IV.

References

Bohen, Halcyonne, and Anamaria Viveros-Long.
1981 *Balancing Jobs and Family Life: Do Flexible Work Schedules Help?* Philadelphia: Temple University Press.

Bureau of Labor Statistics, U.S. Department of Labor.
1982a "1981 Weekly Earnings of Men and Women Compared in 100 Occupations." *News* (March 7): 1.
1982b "Unemployment and Its Effect on Family Income in 1980." Bulletin 2148. Washington, D.C.: U.S. Government Printing Office.
1982c "Employment in Perspective: Working Women." Second Quarter, 1982. Report 669.
n.d. "Employment in Perspective: Working Women." 1981 Annual Summary. Report 663.

Catalyst.
1981 "Corporations and Two-Career Families: Directions for the Future." New York: Catalyst.

Congressional Budget Office.
1981 *Effects of Eliminating Public Service Employment.* Washington, D.C.: U.S. Government Printing Office.

Fava, Sylvia F., and Rosalie G. Genovese.
1983 "Family, Work and Individual Development in Dual-Career Marriages: Issues for Research." In Joseph H. Pleck and Helena Z. Lopata (eds.), *Research in the Interweave of Social Roles.* Vol. III. Greenwich, Conn.: JAI

Henriksen, Hildur Ve, and Harriet Holter.
1978 "Norway." Pp. 49-67 in Kamerman and Kahn (1978).

Hunt, Janet G., and Larry L. Hunt.
1981 "Dualities of Careers and Families: New Integrations or New Polarizations?" *Social Problems* 29 (June):499-510.
Kamerman, Sheila, and Alfred J. Kahn.
1978 *Family Policy: Government and Families in Fourteen Countries.* New York: Columbia University Press.
Kanter, Rosabeth Moss.
1977 *Work and Family in the United States: A Critical Review and Agenda for Research and Policy.* New York: Russell Sage Foundation.
Smith, Ralph E. (ed.)
1979a *The Subtle Revolution: Women at Work.* Washington, D.C.: Urban Institute.
1979b *Women in the Labor Force in 1990.* Washington, D.C.: Urban Institute.
Vedel-Petersen, Jacob.
1978 "Denmark." Pp. 302-323 in Kamerman and Kahn (1978).

Suggested Additional Readings

Adams, Carol T., and Kathryn T. Winston.
1980 *Mothers at Work: Public Policies in the United States, Sweden and China.* New York: Longman.
International Labour Organization.
1980 *Work and Family Life: The Role of the Social Infrastructure in Eastern European Countries.* Geneva: ILO.
Kamerman, Sheila B., and Alfred J. Kahn.
1981 *Family Benefits and Working Parents: A Study in Comparative Policy.* New York: Columbia University.
National Commission for Employment Policy.
1981 *Seventh Annual Report: The Federal Interest in Employment and Training.* Washington, D.C.: National Commission for Employment Policy.

8. WOMEN VS. PROTECTIVE LABOR LEGISLATION

Susan Lehrer

One of the key targets of the recent women's movement has been laws that restrict or regulate working conditions of women. These laws, that apply to women workers only, typically contain provisions which limit the number of hours per day and per week that women may work, prohibit women entirely from certain jobs, regulate the hours of the day or night when they may work, set standards for working conditions (e.g., lighting, seating), etc. These laws vary considerably from state to state. For example, bartending was closed to women in ten states, night work has been regulated or prohibited in forty-seven states, and minimum wages have been set for women and not men in seven states. Women's rights groups now condemn these laws because they violate the principle of equal treatment under law, and also because they maintain and perpetuate a false doctrine about the specific capabilities of women. Rather than protecting working women, legislation of this kind is viewed as reinforcing their inferior position in the labor market by keeping them out of skilled, well-paying jobs, and by implying that woman's primary place is "in the home."

By contrast, when this legislation was first enacted at the beginning of this century, it had the support of almost all liberal social reformers, labor unions and women's organizations. They considered it desirable and necessary to pass protective legislation to improve the conditions for women workers, who were unable to do so for themselves. Men, women, and children alike frequently worked twelve hours or more a day at dirty, dangerous, monotonous work and, especially in the case of women and children, for very low pay. In this context, labor legislation for women was considered a positive reform in the spirit of the Progressive Era, and it was more often found acceptable by the courts than legislation that included men workers. Today, seventy years later, these laws are not only considered obsolete but are directly counter to Title VII of the Civil Rights Act of 1964.

Title VII, passed in the wake of the black civil-rights protests in the South, outlaws employment discrimination based on race, religion, sex, or national origin. The inclusion of "sex" was suggested by a Southern congressman in an attempt to defeat the entire bill; instead the measure passed, and sex discrimination in employment, like racial discrimination, has become illegal. According to the guidelines for implementing Title VII, employers cannot use stereotyped characterizations of a group as the basis for refusing to hire an individual--for example, that men are less capable of assembling intricate equipment or that women are less capable of aggressive salesmanship. The guidelines state: "The principle of non-discrimination requires that individuals be considered on the basis of individual capacities and not on the basis of any characteristics generally attributed to the group" (Kanowitz 1974:309). An exception in the form of "bona fide occupational qualification" does exist, but the Commission has stated that this must be interpreted narrowly and does not include the refusal to hire a woman because of assumptions about the general characteristics of women in general. It is counter to these guidelines, then, for employers to question prospective women employees about their children, child-care arrangements, and so on. Concerning sex-specific state employment laws of the kind to be discussed here, the Equal Employment Opportunities Commission stated, "The Commission has found that such laws and regulations do not take into account the capacities, preferences, and abilities of individual females and, therefore, discriminate on the basis of sex" (Kanowitz 1974:310). An employer who provided protection or benefits for women only, like special rest periods required by state law, would be required to extend the same benefits to male employees, rather than to deny them to both men and women.

How, then, did these laws, which were considered liberal, progressive reforms when first passed, come to be accepted as legitimate in the first place? A historical look at the social conditions and the legal reasons used to justify these laws reveals how this kind of legislation served to delimit the position of working women in industrial capitalism. The development of protective labor laws for women, which took place in the United States roughly between 1900 and 1925 (the Progressive Era), raises the issue of how women's position within the family, that is, their responsibility for domestic work and reproduction of the labor force, relates to their situation as wage workers with a separate, lower wage structure than men.

Women's Work and Industrialization in the United States

Before 1800 there was very little manufacturing or industry in this country. The mainstay of the economy was agriculture and commerce. During this early period, the home was a center of production, with women engaged primarily in domestic work, including spinning, weaving, and dying cloth, rather than in farm work. If more was produced than needed for home use, the surplus could be sold to the local store. Women also were employed from colonial times as shopkeepers, innkeepers, printers, and teachers (for girls' schools); a very few owned sawmills or other industrial establishments (Abbott 1910:16). The beginnings of the factory system meant little more than that women first began to work on commission in the home for small cloth-making establishments and then, when the looms were installed by some businessmen under one roof, in the "factory." Work of this sort for women, and children too, was valued not only for its productive aspect, but as a puritan virtue and a defense against the sins of idleness and sloth.

With the introduction of labor-saving machinery, women in the factories continued the work they had previously done at home--spinning and carding to make yarn and then weaving as well. Male labor was scarce and expensive in this early period since agriculture was still the main source of employment for men. The textile mills thus provided "the means of employment to thousands of poor women and children [with] no [other] opportunities for earning a livelihood."[1]

It can be seen from the foregoing that women participated in the industrial work force right from the beginning. However, women's factory work was viewed as secondary to their functions as wives and mothers. There was rapid turnover among these mostly young "mill girls," who saw their jobs as temporary (Abbott 1910:129). Thus, from the beginning of their participation in the labor force, women have never been considered primary wage-earners, despite the fact that many were.

The period 1860-1880 saw the beginnings of a national labor movement in the United States. During this period, rapid industrial development in this country had consequences for both the nature of work in the factory and the consequent role of the family in supporting a labor force. The introduction of machinery meant the decline of traditional craft processes and the replacement of formerly skilled craftsmen, trained through years of apprenticeship, by relatively unskilled wage laborers. With increased immigration to this country there was no longer a scarcity of workers, and immigrants and women, as well as blacks, became sources of the needed unskilled, low-paid labor. The family, no longer a focal point of production, became a refuge from the increasingly alienating conditions of industrial labor (Aronowitz 1973:201). The ideology of "woman's place" in the home and family then increasingly came into conflict with the reality of women as workers in an industrial labor force. Protective labor legislation can be viewed as an attempt to mediate this conflict in defining women's role by accepting them into the industrial work force, but at the same time restricting their participation in it. In the next section we shall examine how this was accomplished.

From the beginning, labor organizations have reflected a kind of ambivalence toward women as workers. Unionists voiced both economic and ideological reasons for their opposition to women workers: Women were competition for jobs (and a source of low-paid labor as well). They also felt that women's prime function was maternal and that factory work was physically and morally bad for a woman. In this early period of unionization, union leaders were opposed to using legislation as a means of achieving better conditions for men workers. They argued that this end was better achieved by the unionizing efforts of men workers themselves than by passage of protective laws on behalf of men. Women, however, were a different story. Since they were considered impossible to unionize (and hence unable to fight effectively for their own interests), legislation would help them to get what they were unable to provide through their own efforts.

Origins of Protective Labor Legislation: 1905-1925

In discussing protective labor legislation, it is necessary to distinguish the development of legal arguments applied to all workers from those applied to some special characteristic of women which justified legislation for women only. Arguments opposing labor legislation usually appealed to the principle of formal equality under the law, despite substantive social inequality.

Initial opposition to protective labor legislation (and the right to unionize as well) was justified by referring to eighteenth century notions of the liberty of the individual and sacredness of private property; these became incorporated into judicial decisions by using the Fourteenth Amendment to the Constitution to strike down labor laws, on the grounds that they interfered in the "wage bargain." This was interpreted as the unabridgeable right of the worker freely to make an agreement with his employer regarding wages, hours and conditions of work, without interference from the law. Proponents argued that the substantively unequal bargaining position of worker and employer justified the need for formally unequal treatment. They also contended that the state had a legitimate interest in "strong, robust, healthy citizens, capable of self support...Laws to effect this purpose, by protecting the citizen from overwork and requiring a general day of rest to restore his strength and preserve his health, have an obvious connection with the public welfare."[2] These opposing legal considerations of formal rights under the Constitution and of substantively unequal power relations were explicitly articulated in the course of the struggle for better working conditions at the turn of the century.

Statutes limiting work to six days a week were, as indicated, upheld as necessary protections of the "physical welfare of the citizen," which interest justifies the interference of the state and therefore "does not go beyond the limits of legislative power by depriving any one of liberty or property within the means of the Constitution."[3] Some cases were decided upon grounds that plainly indicated recognition of the substantive (i.e., real, economic) inequality that existed between workers and employers, and the need for judicial protection of workers' interests.

Simultaneously, judicial opinion was tending in the direction of extending protection to workers based not only on physical health and safety, but also on the rationale of extending social rights: the need for a better standard of living.

Thus the first cautious steps in the direction of substantive protections for workers was beginning to result in acceptable judicial doctrine, despite the apparent and recognized conflict with the principle of the civil right of formal equality under the law.

At the same time that these basic questions were being considered regarding the overall judicial legitimacy of protective labor legislation and its relationship to basic civil rights under the Constitution, another set of issues was arising around legislation that applied only to women. The general context for the debate was set by the same considerations that had affected men. The question was whether women were also considered able freely to contract the conditions of their employment, or whether they were under some disability because of their sex, which would warrant special legislation.

In England, the early Factory Acts had limited protection to women and children. In this country, the rationale for special legislation concerning women workers constituted an area of judicial debate throughout the time period being considered here. It was necessary to justify restrictive legislation either in the same way as for men, or on the basis that women were in special need of protection. Arguments vacillated between the two positions. The first was based on their general equality with men but stressed the need for protection of workers of both sexes standing in a position of substantive inequality in relation to the employer. The second was the opening wedge for a large body of legislation which frequently did result in improved working conditions for women, but contained explicit assumptions of their inferiority in relation to men in general and men workers in particular. These included woman's physical frailty compared to men and their special disabilities resulting from actual or potential motherhood. This had the corollary of further justifying state intervention by virtue of its legitimate interest in insuring healthy mothers for the future of the nation.

These laws, then, set up a kind of protected status for women which appeared to be responding to their special needs as working women, but which did so by leaving the major premises about women's position intact. That is, these laws do not challenge but rather reinforce the traditional assumption that woman's place is properly, or at least primarily, in the home.

The earliest state law regulating conditions of labor for women (and children) appears to have been an unenforceable Massachusetts law of 1876 limiting working hours to ten per day, sixty per week. By 1896, thirteen states had such legislation on the books, none of which had any real effect. When subjected to legal challenges, these laws were usually struck down on the grounds that they were interfering with a woman's right to contract (e.g., an 1895 eight-hour factory law in Illinois). This reasoning was echoed in a later case involving a prohibition on night work for women in which the judge's opinion commented that the act in question "attempts to take away the right of a woman to labor before 6 o'clock in the morning, or after 9 o'clock in the evening without any reference to other considerations (e.g., of health)...This was the first attempt on the part of the state to restrict their liberty of person, or their freedom of contract, in the pursuit of a vocation." Specifically condemning the abridgement of Constitutional rights that this act would entail for women, the opinion states: "It is certainly discriminative against female citizens, in denying to them equal rights with men in the same pursuit." It further distinguished women from children: "The right of the state...to restrict, or to regulate the labor and employment of children is unquestionable; but an adult female is not to be regarded as a ward of the state, or in any other light than the man is regarded."[4] In this instance, the equality of women with men was used to strike down the law; in other cases, it was used to demonstrate the need for protective legislation to cover women and men alike.

The principle of legislation for women only was clearly established in *Muller v. Oregon* (1908), regarding the constitutionality of a state law limiting the hours of work of females in factories or laundries to ten hours per day. This landmark decision, in which the brief was prepared by Louis Brandeis and Josephine Goldmark (and called "the Brandeis brief"), stressed the innate disadvantages of women, arising from "woman's physical structure and the performance of maternal functions," the injurious effect of standing up for long periods of time, and "the fact that woman has always been dependent on man." Justifying its decision, the court stated, "[T]he physical well-being of woman becomes an object of public interest and care in order to preserve the strength and vigor of the race." This decision invoked both the physical disabilities and the overall dependency of women on men that would exist "even though all restrictions on political, personal and contractual rights were taken away" (Baker 1925:65-66). The extensive brief in this case, as well as the decision handed down by the court, made use of substantive, purposive-legal arguments to justify the legislation and did not rely on formal reasoning. It helped set a precedent for future protective legislation for women as substantive, socially desirable policy. It also defined the primary function of women as maternal, and found the situation of women as workers to be in conflict with this.

It is important to remember that during this period the right to vote and improvements in working conditions for women (along with settlement-house concerns like assimilation into American culture and so on) were the main focus of women's rights organizations. Protective labor legislation for women was developed during a period when it was taken for granted that woman's role in the home and her duties as mother were her most important job. In fact, any modification of that role that might result from her working outside the home was seen as detrimental and a threat to the foundations of family life. Opponents of women working claimed that it resulted in broken homes, juvenile delinquency, and the like; proponents simply claimed that a woman could work outside the home (and had to), without sacrificing her family responsibilities if only she were granted certain protections on the job. Legislation then became the means by which women could take care of their traditional responsibilities in the home while working full time outside the home. (By contrast, the women's movement today is also concerned with the "politics of housework," questioning the assumption that such tasks as child care, cooking, and cleaning are the proper responsibility of the woman in the family and contending that men should share these tasks.)

The immediate effects of these various pieces of legislation differed according to the concrete situation. In those occupations where women predominated, the general effect was to extend the benefits of the protective legislation (especially hours) to men also. Where women were a less essential part of the productive process, the restrictions on the conditions of their labor tended to eliminate them entirely, frequently from skilled or better-paying classifications. Where an occupation was forbidden entirely to women, even proponents admitted that the motive for the legislation was to eliminate them as competition for men. Thus, Rose Schneiderman, an officer of the National Women's Trade Union League, was opposed to women working at "men's jobs," since those "who want to work at the same hours of the day or night and receive the same pay, might be putting their own brothers, or sweethearts, or future husbands out of a job" (Baker 1925:202) Opposition to women in skilled trades frequently came from (male) trade unions, sometimes with the claim that their occupations were physically or morally unfit places for women to work, or that women were employed simply because their labor was cheaper, or that their place was properly in the home.

Although protective legislation for women generally was supported by all major groups except business interests, opposition did develop from a few women's groups. The Women's League for Equal Opportunity was formed to oppose protective legislation for women on the grounds that "Welfare legislation...will protect women to the vanishing point....It will drain women out of all highly-paid and highly organized trades" (Baker 1925: 190). This group drew much of its support from women printers, after the prohibition against night work for women had eliminated the latter entirely from their occupation. The National Women's Party also had to choose between their beliefs in women's equality with men (and hence opposition to special legislation for women), and the economic inequality of women (and therefore the need for it). They resolved the conflict by opposing all "welfare bills" for women only, in favor of extending their protection to men as well.

Recent judicial reasoning seems to be that conditions deserving regulation for women are equally deserved by men and, conversely, that "women must be permitted to take their chances along with men" in rough occupations. This attitude, stated in a ruling by a California court, also challenged the state's interest in interfering with woman's right to choose her occupation: "The state has not only failed to establish a compelling interest served by...[the restrictive statute], but it has failed to establish any interest at all."[5] California thus in this ruling accepted sex as a "suspect classification," and challenged the earlier ground of the state's interest in protective laws, which define women as inherently frail and as mothers of the nation.

However, although labor legislation is now generally accepted as a legitimate means of protecting all workers, in recent years the argument that women workers are in special need of protection has resurfaced. Although Title VII clearly states that workers are to be considered on the basis of individual capacities, it has been argued that pregnant women or women of childbearing age ought to be excluded from jobs that present hazards to women's reproductive organs or the developing fetus. Women have been fired from industrial jobs on the grounds that chemical and other dangerous substances present a danger to their reproductive capacities.

A large number of women do continue to work throughout pregnancy, and concern for the effects on future generations of industrial chemicals, for example, is certainly valid. However, the only jobs where this has become an issue were a few well-paid skilled job categories where women had succeeded only recently in gaining a foothold; the large number of traditionally female jobs with equivalent hazards have not received similar attention. In addition, those hazards to reproduction and to the fetus continue to present hazards after the child is born and grows up, as Chavkin (1979) points out. Damage to *male* reproductive systems is also likely to result from exposure to radiation, chemicals, and so on.

Concern for the health and safety of all workers, male and female, is critical to the conception, development and growth of future generations. Focusing this concern solely on women workers serves to perpetuate the definition of women in terms of their reproductive capacities and their roles as wives and mothers; it also serves to deflect attention away from the employer's responsibility to ensure a safe working environment for *all* workers.

Historically, women workers have worked both as wage laborers outside the home and within the home. These laws can be seen as one means by which women were defined primarily in terms of their importance within the family, but also permitted limited access to wage labor outside the home. The state, then, has contributed to maintaining the subordinate position of women in the workforce through its support for a certain kind of family structure--one based on the wage labor of the husband and (unpaid) domestic labor of the wife. These laws were intended to allow limited participation of women in the paid labor force, while also defining their primary function in terms of the family and the reproduction of the "race." Social reformers demanded a "living wage" for men at the same time that they were working for restrictive legislation for women workers. Women were never seen as self-supporting, let alone as the sole support of a family.

In the present period, increasing numbers of women are not only full-time, permanent members of the workforce, but they are often the sole wage-earner in many families. Both the unequal wage structure for women and the legal impediments that remain continue to place women at a disadvantage in the labor force. The Equal Rights Amendment, which would have overturned the legal presumptions of "special handling" for women, has been defeated in state legislatures. Nevertheless, the basic issue remains. Laws that distinguish on the basis of sex, that define women primarily in terms of their role within the home as mothers, and that limit women's participation in the workforce in ways that do not apply to men (for example, laws against night work), do women no service. Some observers feared that in the present period of economic crisis and erosion of benefits for all workers, the ERA, had it been passed, would have been used as a pretext to deny benefits to workers, rather than to extend existing ones to the entire workforce. Whether or not these fears were justified depended upon the legal means available to defend workers' rights and upon the social and political forces available to back them up. Not the least of these would be the insistence of the present women's movement that the place of both women and men is properly on the job as well as in the home.

Notes

1. Manufacturer quoted in Abbott, 1910:16.
2. Baker (1925:30-31), quoting from the opinion of Judge Vann in New York regarding barbers' right to one day's rest in seven, *People v. Havnor*, New York, 1896.
3. Baker (1925: 31), *People v. Havnor.*
4. Baker (1925:72-73), opinion in *People v. Williams*, New York, 1907.
5. Johnson and Knapp (1971:675), quoting decision in *Sail'er Inn v. Kirby.*

References

Abbott, Edith.
1910 *Women in Industry*. Appleton and Co.

Aronowitz, Stanley.
1973 *False Promises.* New York: McGraw-Hill.

Baker, Elizabeth Faulkner.
1925 *Protective Labor Legislation, with Special Reference to Women in the State of New York.* New York: Columbia University Press.

Chavkin, Wendy.
1979 "Occupational Hazards to Reproduction: A Review Essay and Annotated Bibliography." *Feminist Studies* 5, 2 (Summer):310-25.

Hutchinson, Emilie.
1919 *Women's Wages: A Study of the Wages of Industrial Women and Measures Suggested to Increase Them.* AMS reprint.

Johnston, John D., Jr., and Charles L. Knapp.
1971 "Sex Discrimination by Law: A Study in Judicial Perspective" *New York University Law Review*, 46:675.

Kanowitz, Leo.
1974 *Sex Roles in Law and Society.* University of New Mexico.

Van Kleeck, Mary.
1913 *Women in the Bookbinding Trade.* New York: Russell Sage Foundation.

9. EQUAL OPPORTUNITY AND THE NEED FOR CHILD CARE

U.S. Commission on Civil Rights

□ Mary Smith, one of the 80 percent of all employed women who work in clerical, service, sales, or factory jobs, is a secretary in a small insurance firm in the Midwest. She is committed to her work, ambitious, and highly capable, and her supervisors recognize her talents. To help Mary advance to a policy writer position, they will even pay so that she can join two of the company's salesmen at a course in a real estate insurance law at the local college--three evenings a week for the next thirty-six weeks. Mary's husband, a fireman on a rotating shift, is often not home in the evening. Because she cannot find reliable evening care for a 2-year-old, a 5-year-old, and an 8-year-old, Mary's opportunity to advance like the men in her company is closed.[1]

□ Cheryl Petska is not employed at a "typical" woman's job. In 1978 she became the first woman state trooper in Virginia. During the coalworkers' strikes in late 1978, Petska was ordered on forty-eight hours' notice to report for a two-week tour of duty in the coalfields, four-hundred miles from her home. Although she had a daily child-care arrangement for her children and had made special arrangements for the intensive twenty-three-week training program necessary to become a trooper, she was unable to find anyone to babysit her children overnight for two weeks on such short notice. When she refused the assignment, she was fired for "insubordination." (Cheryl's husband, Mark, also a State trooper and undercover narcotics agent, is frequently called on out-of-State assignments on a moment's notice (*Washington Post* 1978:37).

□ Hannah Robinson, a single mother, was completely supported by welfare until she found a job as a nurse's aide at the Veterans Administration hospital. Because her wages were so low, Robinson was still "income eligible" for government support of the child-care she needed in order to work. After six months, a cost-of-living wage increase put her over the threshold for child-care support; however, it did not provide enough to cover the child-care expenses for her 4-year-old son, Robert. Robinson was only permitted to refuse the salary increase--and thereby keep her child care--by accepting a demotion (Working Family 1974).

Excerpted from the U.S. Commission on Civil Rights, *Child Care and Equal Opportunity for Women.* Clearinghouse Publication No. 67. June 1981, pp. 7-15.

□ Sue de la Cruz, a low-income mother in San Mateo County, California, cannot find better employment without more education, but cannot attend the local community college unless some sort of child-care facilities are available in her area. When the San Mateo Community College District "refus[ed] to allow District funds to be used for these purposes,"[2] Sue de la Cruz and six other low-income mothers filed suit in federal court. To earn a living while the suit is pending, Sue had to take a low-paying job in a glass factory and still does not have regular care for her three children.[3]

These are familiar stories for women throughout American, for women of all races, ethnic groups, and levels of income. Because of the need for child care, women routinely drop out of school or the labor force or pass up opportunities for advancement; poor women are kept poor; women are disenfranchised from job opportunities and benefits.

A few of these stories, like Cheryl Petska's or Sue de la Cruz's, make headlines; their individual child-care problems become matters of public concern for a week, a month, as long as the local paper carries the story, or as long as the story has an unusual twist to it. But most of the stories do not make headlines. They are simply the stuff of women's lives, shared by women at all levels of educational background, and rarely shared by men. A "successful" Radcliffe graduate tells of having to bypass "top executive positions" for which she was qualified because "most employers provide [no] facilities for child care, much less infant care or breaks to nurse your child or even part-time, flex-time or shared-jobs" (Sreedhar 1979:20). A welfare recipient in Chicago tells the U.S. Commission on Civil Rights that she has been unable to take any job, even though there are many advertised equally for men and for women in the local paper. "The main problem" is that "you got children to take care of. And a man does not have that hanging around his neck. You have to be superwoman in order to get the same job that the man would very easily fall into because he doesn't have to worry about the children going to the doctor; he doesn't have to worry about the children getting sick."[4]

Only rarely, as in the 1980 movie *Kramer v. Kramer*, is child care displayed as a man's problem, and then it is clearly one that takes its toll on employment opportunity. When arranging child care and doctor's appointments appear to make him less "committed" to the advertising agency he works for, Ted Kramer is fired.

As a matter of public policy, the extent to which the need for child care constitutes a barrier to equal opportunity for women has received relatively little attention, even though many people have urged increased Federal support of child care. Major women's groups, such as the National Organization for Women, have repeatedly made child care part of their platform.[5] Over and over again, national surveys have identified child care as one of the most crucial unresolved needs facing both unemployed and employed women (National Commission on Working Women 1979:1; Whitbread 1979:88). Prestigious panels concerned with the well-being of children, such as the National Academy of

Sciences Committee on Child Development (1976:4-5) and the Carnegie Council on Children (Keniston 1978:79 and passim), have called for federal support of alternative forms of child care, so that parents who work out of necessity or preference are not forced to put their young ones at risk.

Still, the need for child care has rarely been explicitly and systematically related to women's equal opportunity. National debate and research about child care has been far more concerned with the effect on children of their mothers working outside the home than it has been with the effect of the lack of child care, or of inadequate child care, on women and their families. Because the number of mothers in paid employment keeps increasing, it is often assumed that child care is not much of a problem, much less a barrier to equal opportunity. During the last twenty-five years, the rise in the number of mothers working outside the home, especially mothers of young children, has been dramatic. As the Congessional Budget Office (1978:44) reports:

> In 1950, just over one-fifth of the mothers with children under 18 years of age were in the labor force; by 1978, over half were...The largest proportional increases in labor force participation have occurred among mothers with children under 6 years old. Between 1950 and 1978, the participation rate of mothers with children only between 6 and 17 years old increased 82 percent, while the rate among mothers with children under 6 more than tripled (from 14 percent in 1950 to 44 percent in 1978).

The fact that mothers are working does not mean that families have made satisfactory child-care arrangements. Most mothers, like most women and most men, work outside the home because of economic necessity. According to the U.S. Department of Labor, "Nearly two-thirds of all women in the labor force in 1978 were single, widowed, divorced, or separated, or had husbands whose earnings were less than $10,000" (Women's Bureau 1978:1). In more and more two-parent families, two incomes are necessary for economic viability. "It is frequently the wife's earnings that raise a family out of poverty. In husband-wife families in 1978, 6.1 percent were poor when the wife did not work; 2.7 when she was in the labor force" (ibid.:3).

Several recent analyses indicate that large numbers of employed mothers do not report having adequate--or, in many cases, any--child-care arrangements (National Commission on Working Women 1979:1, 6; Whitbread 1979:88, 92, 102-3). Sandra L. Hofferth (1979:99, table 15) of the Urban Institute has estimated that in 1975, 32,000 preschoolers were caring for themselves. According to Senator Alan Cranston, chairman of the Senate Subcommittee on Child and Human Development, "Census data tell us that at least 2 million school age children between the ages of 7 and 13 are simply left alone without any supervision."[6]

Results of a 1978 national survey of working women conducted by the National Commission on Working Women (1979:6, chart) indicate that 29 percent of those mothers in clerical, service, sales, factory, or plant jobs--i. e., in the types of jobs held by some 80 percent of all women in the United States--cite child care as a "major problem"; among professional, managerial, and technical women the figure was even higher, 36 percent. When *Family Circle* magazine did a similar survey, also in 1978, it too found widespread problems, including inadequate care for infants, toddlers, young schoolage children, and children who are sick (Whitbread 1979:88, 92, 102-3).

Among single mothers--who are more likely to be in the labor force than married--the problem of arranging satisfactory care is especially great (Waldman et al., 1979:46). According to Dorothy Burlage (1978:295-96), a clinical and research psychologist who has studied them extensively:

> Separated and divorced mothers are under pressure to take the first job they can get and worry about child-care arrangements later. Because separated and divorced mothers are unlikely to have a financial cushion...they cannot afford to risk losing their jobs. This economic insecurity becomes an additional source of stress and anxiety as they are trying to patch together child-care arrangements, take care of children when they are ill, attend their children's performances at school, and meet their mothering obligations. They are likely to work full time and to work whatever schedule is necessary to provide enough income for the family. This means that they have little flexibility in adjusting their employment situation to meet the needs of their children.

In sum, whatever their marital status, substantial numbers of women are employed in spite of, not because of, their child-care arrangements.

To what extent then, do child-care problems act as a constraint on equal opportunity for women? Existing data from a variety of sources...indicate that lack of child care, or inadequate child care, prevents women from participating in federally supported education and training programs, reduces the amount of time they can devote to employment or education, makes them unable to take advantage of job promotions or training necessary for advancement, and conflicts with their ability to perform their work.

Lack of child care or inadequate child care prevents women from taking paid jobs. Some argue that the "availability of employment is overwhelmingly more important" in determining labor-force participation than the availability of child care (Woolsey 1977:138). However, the pattern of women's participation in the labor force and the results of a number of studies during the last decade suggest that a substantial number of women, especially minority women, are prevented from taking paid work because of unavailable or inadequate child care (Congressional Budget Office 1978:47; Presser & Baldwin).

Even though overall participation in the labor force is increasing steadily, there are still striking differences among subgroups of women. Women without children are most likely to be in the labor force (Smith 1979:8). Mothers with children age 6 or over, for whom the nation's public schools provide a regular type of care for approximately six hours per day, are almost twice as likely to be in the labor force as mothers with preschoolers, for whom there is no such regularly available arrangement (ibid.:11, figure 2). Indeed, mothers with young children are the group of women least likely to be in the labor force (ibid.:11).

As the Congressional Budget Office (1978:45) notes, relatively few studies have sought to determine the extent to which the lack of day care inhibits women's labor force participation. Most have been based on hypothetical situations, asking mothers how they would behave if a certain type of child care were provided; and, according to Joseph Pleck,[7] director of the Family and Work Program at the Wellesley College Center for Research on Women, estimates have sometimes varied considerably, depending upon methodology. Moreover, most studies have ignored the double bind situations that face many women; they cannot afford child care unless they have a job, but they cannot get a job unless they have child care (Abbot 1974:20).

Nevertheless, a number of studies suggest that approximately one of every five or six unemployed women is unemployed because she is unable to make satisfactory child-care arrangements. A national survey of sources of variation in labor market behavior in 1971 asked women who were not in the labor force if they would be willing to seek employment if they could place their children in free day-care centers (Shortlidge 1977). Seventeen percent of the white mothers and 50 percent of the black mothers with children under 6 responded positively (ibid.). Harriet B. Presser of the University of Maryland and Wendy Baldwin of the Center for Population Research at the National Institute for Child Health and Development, in a literature review, cite a panel study by the Institute for Social Research at the University of Michigan, which found that 16 percent of unemployed mothers with children under 12 believed that child-care arrangements were not available at all if they wanted to take jobs (1980). Moreover, a 1971 Westinghouse Learning Corporation (1971) study of unemployed women with family income under $8,000 and at least one child under 9 found that 18 percent were not employed because they could not make or afford satisfactory child-care arrangements. Presser and Baldwin's (1980:1205-06) own analysis, based on census data from June 1977, yields similar results:

> Many more mothers with children less than 5 years of age would be working or working more hours if suitable child care were available...close to one out of five mothers with preschool-age children who are not in the labor force say they would be looking for work (or employed) if suitable child care were available...it is generally women who are most in need of employment who are most likely to report that the unavailability of satisfactory child care at reasonable cost affects their labor-force participation: the young mother (18-24), the unmarried mother, the black mother, the nonhigh-school graduate, and those with family incomes of less than $5,000.

Lack of child care or inadequate child care keeps women in part-time jobs, most often with low pay and little career mobility. Twenty-three percent of the adult women in the U.S. labor force either worked part time or were looking for part-time work in 1977, compared with 7 percent of adult men (U.S. Office of the President 1978:17). Various studies show that a major reason why women are overrepresented in part-time work is that they are combining child-care responsibilities with jobs in the paid labor market. For some women this is undoubtedly a choice; for others it is a constraint.

National statistics, collected and tabulated for the Bureau of Labor Statistics by the Bureau of the Census, show that a larger percentage of mothers with young children are employed part time than are adult women in general. Of the mothers with children under 18 in two-parent families who were employed during

1977, 38 percent held part-time jobs (one to thirty-four hours per week). Another 27 percent of those mothers were employed less than fifty weeks per year, leaving only 35 percent employed on a year-round, full-time basis. In two-parent families with children under 6, only 25 percent of the mothers in paid employment held year-round, full-time jobs (Waldman et al. 1979:44).

Both small- and large-scale studies indicate that women are constrained from increasing their hours of employment by the unavailability of adequate child care. For example, an intensive study of limited-income families with preschool children, directed by Laura Lein of the Wellesley College Center for Research on Women, found that in most cases child care was a major factor in determining women's job options (Working Family Project 1974:136). For many women, this meant working only during the hours their husband was not at his job, so that he could stay with the children (Lein 1979:12). According to Presser and Baldwin (1980:1205), "many more mothers with children less than 5 years of age would be...working if suitable child care was available...about one out of four part-time employed mothers indicate they would work more hours."

The economic cost of part-time work to these women and their families is great. Part-time jobs tend to be concentrated in low-skill, low-wage occupations without benefits. More than one-third of part-time working women are in food service, retail, and private household jobs (Smith 1978:44). The wage rate of women on part-time schedules is 25 percent less than that of women who work full-time. Smith reports that in May 1976 part-time women workers earned an average of $2.71 per hour compared to an average of $3.59 per hour for full time women workers. Some of the gap is attributable to lower wage rates for part-time work in the same occupation and some to different occupational distributions for the two groups of workers. Many part-time workers do not receive fringe benefits such as sick days, holidays, vacations, health insurance, training programs, and pensions. These negative features of part-time employment combine to create an isolated class of workers, predominantly women, who are cut off from high wages, prestigious occupations, benefits, and career mobility (Daski 1979:60-62).

Lack of child care or inadequate child care keeps women in jobs for which they are overqualified and prevents them from seeking or taking job promotions or the training necessary for advancement. Although no national data exist about this situation, several studies in different parts of the country bring evidence to bear on it.

In a New York City area study of one hundred black and one hundred white full-time employed mothers with at least one child aged 5 or younger, Sheila Kamerman[8] frequently found women taking jobs for which they were overqualified because they couldn't make satisfactory child-care arrangements. Lein's (Working Family Project 1974:136) Boston area study found women taking unsatisfying jobs due to child care and other family pressures.

According to Dorothy Burlage (1978:262-63), single mothers--most of whom do not receive child support--are in a double bind when it comes to advancement. To keep jobs producing even minimal income, they need child care; to upgrade their jobs, they need additional child care. Burlage found single mothers refusing promotions and better paying jobs and being unable to attend school because they could not find adequate child care. One woman, for example, "worked as a bottle-washer in a hospital for about a year and a half until she was finally able to arrange for her mother to take care of her children for two weeks while she took a refresher course from a secretarial school. After the period of retraining, she got a job as a secretary" (ibid.: 257-58). For others who could not solve the child-care problem and who needed the income from working, education was the first thing to go. Some single mothers reported "being late to school, missing classes, [and] having difficulty completing homework to the point that their grades suffered"; others reported cutting their school load to minimum or dropping out (ibid.:260).

A 1978 survey of undergraduate and graduate students at Portland State University in Oregon found a similar pattern among women with children. Three-fourths of all parents who had dropped out of school for a term or more indicated that they missed an average of 1.7 terms each due to child-care problems; among parents who stayed in school, over 58 percent reported dissatisfaction with child-care arrangements, and one-third of that number would be able to "increase their courseload an average of 3.6 credits per term if child-care problems were resolved" (Box 1979:13, 15-16).

Lack of child care or inadequate child care can conflict with women's ability to perform their work. Employed mothers are well aware of the difference that satisfactory child-care arrangements can make in the way they do their jobs. In *Family Circle*'s 1978 survey, some 70 percent said that "adequate child care helps their job performance" (Whitbread 1979:102).

However, recent analyses of national survey data by Pleck (1978: table 7) have shown that 23 percent of employed wives with children and 23 percent of employed female single parents who use a formal child-care arrangement find that their child care causes them to be late to work or to miss work. By contrast, almost no fathers in families using formal child care reported the same problems.

Among women who work on assembly-line jobs with heavy machinery, inadequate child care may have a relationship to higher accident rates. According to Wendy Cuthbertson,[9] international representative with the United Auto Workers in Toronto, "stress was presented as a significant factor in industrial accidents, and worry about inadequate child care was presented as the single greatest cause of stress" by forty female assembly-line workers at a 1978 conference on Occupational Health and Working Women."

Lack of child care or inadequate child care restricts women's participation in federal employment and training programs. During the 1960s and 1970s, women were underrepresented in federal employment programs. In 1977, for example, women made up approximately 56 percent of the population eligible for Comprehensive Employment and Training Act (CETA) programs, but only about 44 percent of the enrollees.[10] In 1978 women were only 74 percent of the registrants for the welfare-oriented Work Incentive Program (WIN), even though they represented 90 percent of adult recipients of Aid to Families with Dependent Children (AFDC) (U.S. Department of Labor and Department of Health, Education, and Welfare 1978:20, table 2; 12).

Various factors, including the unavailability of adequate child care, account for the relatively low level of female enrollment in these programs. National statistics prepared by the Department of Health, Education, and Welfare in 1970 showed that about 10 percent of AFDC recipients were not referred to WIN because of the lack of child care and that 6 percent of those referred were turned back for reasons of unavailable child care (U.S. Department of Health, Education, and Welfare 1970: 113-114, 180, table 10). Eight years later, a supervisor of a WIN office still identified the unmet need for child care as perhaps the primary reason why women were less likely than men to be assigned to job training (U.S. Commission on Civil Rights 1979:15).

Lack of child care or inadequate child care restricts women from participating in federally supported education programs. Even though women constitute a majority of participants in programs supported under the Adult Education Act, child-care problems appear to be limiting their ability to enter and to complete such programs (U.S. DHEW 1979:19, table 4). Women of prime child-rearing age (16 to 34) are about 52 percent of all enrollees in that age group, while women 35 years of age and above are about 61 percent of enrollees in the group.[11]

Many participants have said the reason they left the program before completion was because of child care. Data from the National Center for Educational Statistics show that during 1976, some 36 percent of enrollees withdrew before finishing, and 4 percent of these--some 22,957 individuals--cited the unavailability of child care as the chief reason (U.S. DHEW 1979:30-31, table 10).

Child care is also a crucial barrier to the participation of women in programs supported by the Vocational Education Act. Enrollment data for 1970 reveal that women were proportionately underrepresented in postsecondary and adult programs; i.e., they were not undertaking advanced training or preparation for jobs as often as men (U.S. Congress 1975:286). According to Pamela Roby (1979:214) of the Department of Sociology at the University of California's Santa Cruz campus, "the absence of adequate child-care facilities makes it difficult for women to enroll in any advanced education offering, and even more difficult for those women with limited finances."...

It is clear that the unavailability of adequate child care restricts equal opportunity for women in a variety of ways. Given all of these constraints, it is reasonable to ask how extensive the current need for child care is, how it is expected to change over the 1980s, and what amounts and types of child care are needed to increase women's opportunities.

Estimates of day-care need have ranged from one extreme to the other over the past ten years. Some advocates of federally supported child care have claimed that all preschool children not in a licensed center or family day-care home, perhaps as many as seven million, need care (U.S. DHEW 1977). Opponents of federal support point to the increasing number of employed mothers and say that most families make arrangements on their own and no national subsidy is needed (Bruce-Biggs 1977:90-91).

The need for child care is difficult to predict with any precision because it is not a standardized product. The extent and type of out-of-home care that parents need will depend, at any one point in time, on the availability of relatives, on the ages and number of children, on the types of work schedules that they are able to negotiate, and on the price they are able to pay. Moreover, the United States does not have any method for the regular collection of data about child-care need at the local level, although groups in several communities are trying to establish such a procedure.[12]

According to HEW's National Day Care Study, carried out by Abt Associates (1979, vol. 1., p. 2), "in 1978 almost 52 percent of the country's 24.4 million families with children under 13 have a work-related need for some form of day care." Throughout the 1980s that need should continue to increase. According to recent data from the Urban Institute, by 1990 there will be 11 million more women in the labor force, many with young children. "In 1977 there were an estimated 17.1 million preschool children in the United States, of whom 6.4 million (37 percent) had working mothers. By 1990 there will be 23.3 million preschool children. By 1990 there will be 23.3 million preschool children, 10.4 million (about 44 percent) with working mothers" (Hofferth 1979:98-99, table 15). Moreover, an increasing number of these children will be from the families most likely to use day care outside the home--single-parent families and small families, i.e., those without an adolescent to help care for preschoolers (ibid.:102).

As norms about employed mothers continue to change, and with inflation, more women will probably seek to work outside the home when their children are younger--in many cases under 2 and in some cases just a few weeks old. Already the demand for infant care appears to be far outpacing the supply of available centers or family day-care homes (*Washington Post*, Dec. 31, 1979). In San Francisco, for example, the Childcare Switchboard turns away about half of the 250 parents who call each month for infant care. In cities such as Wichita, Kansas, or Washington, D.C., centers that will take infants or toddlers have long waiting lists even before they open (ibid.).

To say there is an enormous need is not to say there is a need for one particular type of child care. Most families use a mixture or "package" of arrangements, combining care by parents or by school with one other regular nonparental arrangement, including day-care centers and nursery schools, licensed and unlicensed family day care providers, baby sitters, relatives, and other informal arrangements (Bane et al. 1979:52). Such packages are often difficult and stressful to construct and can come apart easily. Parents put them together both because of a lack of affordable alternatives and because they put a premium on choosing care that reflects their values and beliefs about child-rearing (Lein 1979:12-14). Meeting future child-care needs requires an expansion of the options available to parents, enabling them to combine work or education more adequately with care for their children at home or out of the home.

The diversity of arrangements needed to increase equal opportunity for women includes the following:

At-home care. Currently, most child care is done by parents, older siblings, or another person in the child's home; this is especially true for children under 3 (Bane et al. 1979:52). Even as the number of women working outside the home increases over the next decade, many will want to continue to have most child care, especially of infants, done at home by themselves, their spouses, or near relatives. To make this child-care need compatible with the goal of equal opportunity, flexible and part-time work options for women and men will be needed in a much broader range and level of jobs than are currently available.

Group day care. Despite the popular image of working mothers leaving their children in day care centers, in which youngsters spend eight to ten hours per day, only 10-15 percent of American families currently use such arrangements (Moore and Hofferth 1979:132-33) [If part-time nursery school care is included, the number of those using group day care is higher (ibid.:134]. Full-day center care is primarily used by two population groups: poor, usually single-parent families, eligible for public subsidy, and upper-middle-class, two-parent families, who tend to use private programs (Rhodes and Moore 1975: vol. 1, p. IV-29, table IV-23; Congressional Budget Office 1978:15, 18-19, table 7). Use of day care centers has approximately doubled over the last decade; in 1978 there were approximately 18,300 licensed day-care centers in the United States serving about 900,000 children (Abt 1979:3). Center programs are increasingly in demand, especially for preschoolers. One recent study indicates that "institutionalized child care arrangements are associated with the lowest report of constraint from employment" (Presser & Baldwin 1980), and *Family Circle*'s 1978 survey reveals that more families would use center care if it were available at an affordable price (Whitbread 1979:102).

Family day care. Care of a child in the home of a nonrelative is an especially flexible arrangement for the care of infants and toddlers or of preschoolers who are in a half-day nursery-school program. According to Presser and Baldwin (1980: table 2), after group day care, family day care is the type least associated with constraints on parental employment. According to Hofferth (1979:109), the 1980s are likely to witness a simultaneous decline in the number of family day-care providers (since many will be seeking other forms of paid employment) and a rise in the need for family day care: "In 1975 there were an estimated 95,000 licensed family day-care homes. However, there may be as many as 950,000 licensed and unlicensed family day care homes. An estimated one million more homes (nonrelative and relative-operated) will be needed by 1990."

Before- and after-school care. Entry of their children into public school has tended to be a watershed for many American mothers; many have waited until their children are in school, which provides child care for a significant part of the day, before they seek or return to paid employment. Indeed, the public school system, through its regular school program, is the largest single supplier of child care for employed parents. While the labor-force participation of mothers of preschool children is approximately 38 percent (Smith 1979:11), for mothers of schoolage children it is over 50 percent and rising (Women's Bureau 1979:32). However, normal school hours are not sufficient to meet the child-care needs of many working mothers, especially if they work full time, and the supply of before- and after-school care does not appear to be adequate to the demand in most parts of the country.

Evening child care. When parents must work late shifts, or when they can only attend school at night because they must work during the day, some form of evening child care is necessary. Many parents in these situations prefer family care, while others prefer some form of reliable center care. Although there are no national figures on the amount of evening care being provided or needed, reports from child-care information and referral services such as San Francisco's Childcare Switchboard indicate that such care is in demand.[13]

Campus child care. Given the unavailability of adequate child care in their own neighborhoods, many women can only enroll in federally supported education programs if there is some form of campus-based or supported child care. So far, however, schools and colleges have had minimal involvement in the support of child care for students. According to a report published by the Department of Labor in 1977, only 132 of 1,200 two-year and technical schools and colleges surveyed by the Center for Women's Opportunities at the American Association of Community and Junior Colleges had on-campus child care facilities (Women's Bureau 1977:32). According to the same study, the National Council on Campus Child Care lists only 750 four-year institutions that operate child-care programs.

In addition to these types of child care, one of the greatest national needs appears to be for information that will help parents to find appropriate child care. According to Edward Zigler, former director of HEW's Office of Child Development, "a major problem with day care is the lack of centralized information to help parents locate existing day care services" (Zigler & Hunsinger 1977:9). Zigler and Hunsinger's analysis is shared by those who advocate and those who oppose federal support for child care and is underscored by a national survey, which found that parents wanted government funds allocated, above all, to a "referral system where parents could get information about screened and qualified people and agencies to provide child care" (Rhodes & Moore 1975:6-14).

Even if the total national need for child care cannot be defined with precision, it appears clear that different types of care are needed. Whether women will be able to enter the labor force or to seek, training and education on an equal footing with men will depend, to a great extent, on the types of care that are available, including those provided or fostered by the federal government...

Notes

1. This is a hypothetical case based on information collected for the Working Family Project, "Work and Family Life," National Institute of Education Project no. 3-3094, Laura Lein, principal investigator.
2. De la Cruz v. Tormey, 582 F.2d 45, 47 (9th Cir. 1978).
3. Telephone interview with Ann Broadwell, attorney for plaintiffs in *De la Cruz v. Tormey*, Legal Aid Society of San Mateo County, Redwood City, Calif., Nov. 15, 1979.
4. Testimony of Kathi Gunlogson, Hearings before the United States Commission on Civil Rights, Chicago, Ill., June 17-19, 1974, vol. 1, p. 16.
5. See, for example, National Organization for Women, NOW Resolution 130, 1970 (National NOW Action Center, 425 13th St., N.W., Suite 1048, Washington, D.C. 20004), p. 23.
6. 125 Cong. Rec. S-77 (daily ed. Jan 15, 1979) (remarks of Sen. Cranston).
7. Interview with Joseph Pleck, program director for Family and Work, Wellesley College Center for Research on Women, Wellesley, Mass., Dec. 19, 1979.
8. Interview with Sheila Kamerman, New York City, Feb. 14, 1980, based upon data in Sheila Kamerman, *Parenting in an Unreponsive Society* (New York: Free Press, 1980).
9. Wendy Cuthbertson, international representative, United Auto Workers, Toronto, Canada, telephone interview, Jan. 25, 1980.
10. Percentages calculated from data in William Barnes, "Target Groups," in National Commission for Manpower Policy, *CETA: An Analysis of the Issues*, Special Report 23 (Washington, D.C.: 1978), p. 79, table 4.
11. Compiled from data in *Adult Basic and Secondary Education Program Statistics*, p. 19, table 4.
12. A national listing is available from Northern California Resource and Referral Network, 320 Judah St., San Francisco, Calif. 94122.
13. Telephone interview with Merle Lawrence, San Francisco Childcare Switchboard, San Francisco, Calif. Apr. 30, 1980.

References

Abbot, Lucille.
1974 "Well, I Passed the Park Today." In Vicki Breitbart (ed.), *The Day Care Book*. New York: Random House.

Abt Associates.
1979 *Children at the Center: Summary Findings and Their Implications*. vol. 1. Prepared for the Day Care Division, Administration for Children, Youth and Families, Office of Human Development Services, U.S. Department of Health, Education and Welfare. Cambridge, Mass.: Abt Associates.

Advisory Committee on Child Development.
1976 *Toward a National Policy for Children and Families*. Washington, D.C.: National Academy of Sciences.

Bane, Mary Jo, et al.
1979 "Childcare Arrangements of Working Parents." *Monthly Labor Review* (Oct.): 50-56.

Barnes, William.
1978 "Target Groups." In *CETA: An Analysis of the Issues*. National Committee for Manpower Policy, Special Report no. 23. Washington, D.C.

Box, Marcy.
1979 *Childcare: A Student Attitudes Survey. A Needs Assessment*. Portland, Ore.: Portland State University, Office of Institutional Research.

Bruce-Biggs, B.
1977 "'Child-Care': The Fiscal Time Bomb." *Public Interest* 49 (Fall):87-102.

Burlage, Dorothy.
1978 "Divorced and Separated Mothers: Combining the Responsibilities of Breadwinning and Childrearing." Ph.D. diss., Harvard University. Mimeo.

Daski, Robert.
1979 "Area Wage Survey Test Focuses on Part-Timers." *Monthly Labor Review* (April).

Hofferth, Sandra.
1979 "The Implications for Child Care." Pp. 97-119 in Ralph E. Smith (ed.), *Women in the Labor Force in 1990.* Washington, D.C.: Urban Institute.

Keniston, Kenneth and the Carnegie Council on Children.
1978 *All Our Children: The American Family Under Pressure.* New York: Harcourt Brace Jovanovich.

Lein, Laura.
1979 "Parental Evaluation of Child Care Alternatives." *Urban and Social Change Review,* vol. 12, no. 1.

Moore, Kirsten, and Sandra Hofferth.
1979 "Women and their Children." Pp. 125-157 in Ralph E. Smith (ed.), *The Subtle Revolution.*

National Commission on Working Women.
1979 *National Survey of Working Women: Perceptions, Problems and Prospects.* Washington, D.C.: National Manpower Institute.

Pleck, Joseph H., Graham Staines, and Linda Lang.
1978 "Work and Family Life: First Reports on Work-Family Interference and Workers' Formal Child-Care Arrangements, from the 1977 Quality of Employment Survey." Prepared for the Office of the Assistant Secretary for Policy, Evaluation and Research, U.S. Department of Labor.

Presser, Harriet B., and Wendy Baldwin.
1980 "Childcare as a Constraint on Employment: Prevalence, Correlates and Bearing on the Work and Fertility Nexus." *American Journal of Sociology* 85, no. 5:1202-13.

Rhodes, Thomas W., and John C. Moore.
1975 *National Childcare Consumer Study: 1975.* Prepared for the Office of Child Development, U.S. Department of Health, Education and Welfare. Washington, D.C.: Unco, Inc.

Roby, Pamela.
1979 "Vocational Education." In Anne Foote Cahn (ed.), *Women in the Labor Force.* New York: Praeger.

Shortlidge, Richard L.
1977 *The Hypothetical Labor Market Response of Black and White Women to a National Program of Free Day Care Centers.* Ohio State University, Center for Human Resources Research. Aug.

Smith, Ralph E.
1978 "The Effect of Hours Rigidity on the Labor Market Status of Women." *Urban and Social Change Review* 11, nos. 1 and 2.
1979 "The Movement of Women in the Labor Force." Pp. 1-29 in Ralph E. Smith (ed.), *The Subtle Revolution.* Washington, D.C.: Urban Institute.

Sreedhar, Kathy.
1979 "My Life as a Single Parent." *Radcliffe Quarterly* (Dec. 20).

U.S., Commission on Civil Rights.
1979 *Women--Still in Poverty.*

U.S., Congress, Congressional Budget Office.
1978 *Children and Preschool: Options for Federal Support.* Washington, D.C.

U.S. Congress, House Subcommittee on Elementary, Secondary and Vocational Education.

1975 *Sex Discrimination and Sex Stereotyping in Vocational Education.* 94th Congress, 1st Session.

U.S. Department of Health, Education and Welfare.

1970 "Services to AFDC Families." In U.S. Department of Labor and Department of Health, Education and Welfare, *Report on the Work Incentive Program.*

1977 *The Challenge of Child Day Care Needs and Improved Federal and State Approaches to Day Care Standard Setting and Enforcement*, by Lela B. Costin and others. Washington, D.C.: Office of the Assistant Secretary for Planning and Evaluation. March.

1979 *Adult Basic and Secondary Education Program Statistics, Fiscal Year 1976.* Washington, D.C.: Office of the Assistant Secretary for Education

U.S., Department of Labor and Department of Health, Education and Welfare.

1978 *WIN: 1968-1978: A Report at 10 Years.*

U.S., Office of the President.

1978 *Employment and Training Report.*

Waldman, Elizabeth, et al.

1979 "Working Mothers in the 1970s: A Look at the Statistics." *Monthly Labor Review* (Oct.):39-49.

Washington Post.

1978 "Woman Trooper Fired." (Dec. 30):37.

1979 "Job Trends Spur Need for Infant Day Care Centers." (Dec. 31).

Westinghouse Learning Corporation.

1971 *Day Care Survey 1970: Summary Report and Basic Analysis.* Report presented to the Office of Economic Opportunity.

Whitbread, Jane.

1979 "Who's Taking Care of the Children?" *Family Circle* (Feb. 20):88.

Women's Bureau, U.S., Department of Labor.

1978 "Twenty Facts on Women Workers."

1979 *Community Solutions for Child Care.* Ed. Dana Friedman.

Woolsey, Suzanne.

1977 "Pied Piper Politics and the Child Care Debate." *Daedalus*, vol. 106, no. 2.

The Working Family Project.

1974 *Final Report: Work and Family Life.* Laura Lein, principal investigator. Cambridge, Mass.: Center for the Study of Public Policy.

Zigler, Edward, and Susan Hunsinger.

1977 "Bringing Up Day Care." *American Psychological Association Monitor*, vol. 8, no. 43.

10. THE SYMMETRICAL FAMILY

Kathleen Newland

Progress toward a new, egalitarian division of labor in the world of paid employment is undercut by the persistence of the old, unequal division of domestic labor. Sociologist Rita Liljeström (1978) has suggested that today's working woman is caught in a time lag between two waves of social change: the first swept away the acceptability of discrimination in formal employment; the second will dissolve discrimination on the home front. Hers is a hopeful formulation, for it endows the succession of events with an inevitability that many overworked women now have cause to doubt.

Part of their doubt stems from a deep ambivalence on the part of governments toward the role of women in society, which is both derived from and reflected in widespread individual ambivalence. The principle that women should be free to work outside the home--and should be free of discrimination when they do--is accepted by most governments. But the idea that women are the guardians of the home and the primary nurturers of children is deeply ingrained in family laws and labor codes throughout the world.

Employers are bound to give women short shrift if they can assume correctly that women will normally be the parents to leave their jobs, even if only temporarily, to care for young children; that they will be the ones to take time off when children fall sick; that they will refuse overtime work because of household responsibilities; that they will relocate when their spouses are transferred to other jobs. These assumptions inevitably prejudice women's standing in the labor force. Governments aggravate the problem when they attempt to make it easier for women to fit the assumptions rather than making it easier for men and women to share family responsibilities.

There is a double standard for women workers: it asserts that their conditions of work should permit them to fulfill all the obligations of their traditional role while taking on a whole new set of obligations associated with formal employment. It also stoutly maintains that women should not be forced to work outside the home--a bit of wishful thinking that is manifestly unfair to women who must work to support themselves. The double standard is also unfair to men, who are never offered the choice--however fanciful--of not working outside the home.

A 1975 memorandum on equal treatment for male and female workers issued by the European Commission (1980) for its nine member governments illustrates the prevalent official ambivalence toward women's roles. On the one hand it embraced the objective of ending the "all too frequent disequilibrium in employment, promotion opportunities and working conditions"; on the other, it recommended "the introduction of more flexible hours to allow for female workers' family responsibilities."

A number of measures commonly offered as solutions to the problems of women's dual role actually reinforce the traditional division of labor. Increased availability of part-time work and flexible hours are commonly presented as aids to working women. Similarly, child care is almost always presented as a "woman's issue." Both, when seen as benefits for women, reinforce the assumptions that women carry the major responsibility for home and children and that their economic roles are secondary.

Attempts to solve the conflict between workplace and family that focus exclusively on women's roles entrench discrimination against women in the labor force. Many countries have labor laws that are meant to protect women from overwork and preserve their ability to meet family responsibilities. East Germany, for example, gives working mothers one day of paid leave per month so that they can attend to housework and child care; women with several children are entitled to shorter working hours and longer holidays with no reduction in pay (Commission on the Status of Women 1980). There is no question that women benefit from measures of this kind in the short run, but the benefits are a poor substitute for genuine equality in work and family life. The long-term effect is to freeze women in secondary jobs, for employers will continue to prefer workers who can measure up to a full-time standard.

In a tight labor market, special provisions for women workers may undercut their ability to compete for jobs on an equal footing with men. David Chaplin (1967) has documented the sharp drop in female industrial employment in Peru that occurred when special benefits for women workers were introduced in 1959. He found that some textile factories did not hire any new female workers after the new benefits were introduced entitling women to seventy-two days of maternity leave at 70 percent salary. The reforms also limited women's workweek to forty-five hours but obliged employers to pay women for the standard forty-eight-hour week. As a result, women became more expensive to hire than men, and many employers virtually stopped hiring them.

The negative impact of the Peruvian reforms could have been at least partially overcome by transferring the cost of the benefits from individual employers to the social welfare system, so that employers would not have had such a strong incentive to stop hiring women workers. The discriminatory effect could have been further reduced if leave had been available equally to fathers and mothers, and if the reduction of the work week to allow for family responsibilities had been applied regardless of sex.

The reconciliation of work and family responsibilities is not just a woman's issue. But very few governments have begun to address this question in a way that would enable men and women to participate equally in both employment and family life. Of those that have, Sweden's is probably the most comprehensive program. The tax system adopted by the Swedish Government in 1970 considers the personal incomes of all adults without reference to family status. Previously a husband and wife were taxed together, and the higher tax payments of the two-income family effectively devalued the wife's earnings. The reforms also made the income tax more steeply progressive, so that two incomes have become more and more of a necessity for the average family (Liljeström 1978).

In 1974, parenthood insurance, one of the most progressive elements of Swedish family policy, was introduced. The insurance allows parents nine months' leave upon the birth of a child, to be apportioned between the mother and father as they see fit. While receiving 90 percent of their regular salary, either parent can choose to stay away from work for one long period or several short ones. Alternatively, the leave can be prorated so that parents can shorten their workdays to half- or three-quarter-time while the child is young. Parents not gainfully employed at the time of a birth are entitled to an allowance in lieu of salary. Up to ten additional days of leave per year are available if the mother or father needs to stay home to care for a sick child. A 1979 revision of the system gives parents of children under the age of 8 the right to work a six-hour day, though in this case the reduced time is not compensated (Liljeström 1978; *Transatlantic Perspectives* 1980).

The tax and insurance measures in Sweden are components of a general policy to encourage and facilitate greater involvement of women in the labor force and greater involvement of men in family life. Other important elements of the strategy include an expansion of public child care and educational facilities (though these are still unable to accommodate all eligible children), a conscious effort to break down occupational segregation, and a steady reduction of salary differentials between male and female workers (Sandberg 1975). All of these measures operate in the context of a strong full-employment policy.

The results of the Swedish experiment have been equivocal. The number of women leaving the labor force after having children went down markedly during the seventies--only 13 percent of working women who had first children between 1975 and 1977 stopped working outside the home, compared with 29 percent from 1970 to 1972. But the number of men who took advantage of the parental insurance grew very slowly. Currently only 10 to 12 percent of fathers take time off from work to look after their children. A more traditional solution to the double day is still common in Sweden: 45 percent of the employed women work part-time in order to cope with family responsibilities (Gustafsson 1979).

Although Sweden has made the most far-reaching effort to reconcile family policy with employment policy and to encourage the development of the symmetrical family, other governments have implemented measures compatible with these goals. France and East Germany, for example, have set up nearly universal systems of pre-school care for children over 3 years of age, as well as substantial facilities for the care of younger children. France and Norway both allow fathers as well as mothers to take leave upon the birth or illness of a child (*Transatlantic Perspectives* 1980).

Clearly, the division of labor within a private household can be influenced by public policy only up to a certain point. It remains a privately determined matter, a subject for communication and negotiation between the man and woman directly involved. The role of the state is important, but limited. It must try to ensure that people have adequate resources to provide for their own needs and those of their dependents; it must acknowledge the social and economic contributions of all productive people without prejudice; and it must set the framework for equality between the sexes by removing all obstacles to equal opportunity in the labor force and the household. The latter requires broadened definitions of men's as well as women's roles. The assumption that women are superior parents is no more justified than is the assumption that men are superior breadwinners.

Perhaps the most effective thing a government can do to encourage equality in private life is to enforce equality in the public sphere of paid employment. Studies from many different countries show that the women who enjoy the greatest equality in their personal relationships with men are those who are closest to their mates in education, occupational prestige, and earnings. If women continue to be cast in secondary roles in the labor force, it will seem natural for them to shoulder most of the responsibility at home. Women's longer hours of housework are often viewed by both them and their mates as justifiable compensation for their smaller financial contributions to the family. If this economic obstacle to equality can be removed, other seemingly immovable cultural obstacles may, over time, yield with surprising grace.

References

Chaplin, David.
1967 *The Peruvian Industrial Labor Force*, Princeton, N.J.: Princeton University Press.

Commission of the European Communities.
1980 "Equal Opportunity for Working Women," *European File*, Brussels, April.

Commission on the Status of Women of the United Nations Economic and Social Council.
1980 "Report of the Secretary-General." 28th Session, Vienna, February 25 - March 5, 1980.

"Europe's Innovative Family Policies."
1980 *Transatlantic Perspectives*, March.

Gustafsson, Siv.
1979 "Women and Work in Sweden." *Working Life in Sweden.*

Liljeström, Rita.
1978 "Integration of Family Policy and Labor Market Policy in Sweden," *Social Change in Sweden*, December.

Sandberg, Elisabet.
1975 *Equality Is the Goal.* Stockholm: Swedish Institute.

11. WORKING WIVES AND MOTHERS: What Happens to Family Life?

Sar A. Levitan and Richard S. Belous

American families seem to be besieged from all sides. Divorce rates are climbing; marriage is being postponed, if not rejected; fertility rates are falling; increasing numbers of children are being raised only by their mothers, either because of divorce or because their parents were never married; and wives and mothers in record numbers are rushing out of the home into the labor market. What is the effect of these occurrences on the institution of the family? Does the "economic independence" of working women influence their decisions to either begin or end a marriage or to rear children? Too frequently, the changing work patterns of women are confused with causing the deterioration of family life. Careful analysis of family-related data show that although American families are changing, they are not eroding.

The fact that women are working in record numbers is not a new phenomenon. What has changed are the conditions and places in which they work. Many tasks which were once performed inside the home are now the source of jobs held by women outside the home. World War II stands as a major breaking point in female work patterns. The war effort's high demand for labor and patriotic fervor induced many women to join the labor force, boosting the size of the female work force by 57 percent during the war. Some analysts predicted that after the war family work patterns would return to the previous norm. They reasoned that rising productivity and economic growth would continue to boost income earned by husbands, thus reducing the need for another check and inducing wives to return to their homes. This, of course, did not happen, as economists failed to consider the nonpecuniary attractions of work and the appetite for more income.

Since World War II, American households have shown a strong propensity to increase their consumption of goods and services. Many wives joined the workforce to finance these upward consumption patterns. Like the mechanical rabbit leading the greyhounds around the racetrack, these aspirations have consistently stayed ahead of rising productivity, often requiring another paycheck in the chase for the "good life." With inflationary pressures and slow growth in productivity during the 1970s and early 1980s leading to sluggish gains and even

Reprinted from *Monthly Labor Review* (September 1981):26-30.

occasional declines in real earnings, another check became necessary to maintain the standard of living, or growing consumption expectations, to which the families had become accustomed. By 1980, three of five families had at least two household members in the labor force--in most cases, the husband and wife.

Work, Marriage, and Motherhood

Some futurologists have assumed that the vast upsurge of women in the work force may portend a rejection of marriage. Many women, according to this hypothesis, would rather work than marry. This "independence effect" would reduce the probability that women would marry as they are better able to support themselves. The converse of this concern is that the prospects of becoming a multi-paycheck household could encourage marriages. Data show that economic downturns tend to postpone marriage because the parties cannot afford to establish a family or are concerned about rainy days ahead. As the economy rebounds and prospects improve for employment, financial security, and advancement, the number of marriages also rises. In the past, only the earnings and financial prospects of the man counted in this part of the marriage decision. Now, however, the earnings ability of a woman can make her more attractive as a marriage partner--a modern version of the old-fashioned dowry.

Coincident with the increase in women working outside the home is the increase in divorce rates. Yet, it may be wrong to jump to any simple cause-and-effect conclusions. The impact of a wife's work on divorce is no less cloudy than its impact on marriage decisions. The realization that she can be a good provider may increase the chances that a working wife will choose divorce over an unsatisfactory marriage. But the reverse is equally plausible. Tensions grounded in financial problems often play a key role in ending a marriage. Given high unemployment, inflationary problems, and slow growth in real earnings, a working wife can increase household income and relieve some of these pressing financial burdens. By raising a family's standard of living, a working wife may bolster her family's financial and emotional stability.

Psychological factors also should be considered. For example, a wife blocked from a career outside the home may feel caged or shackled in the house--a situation some have dramatically likened to a pressure cooker with no safety valve to release the steam. She may view her only choice as seeking a divorce. On the other hand, if she can find fulfillment through work outside the home, work and marriage can go together to create a stronger and more stable union.

Also, a major part of women's inequality in marriage has been due to the fact that, in most cases, men have remained the main breadwinners. With higher earnings capacity and status occupations outside of the home comes the capacity to wield power within the family. A working wife may rob a husband of being the master of the house. Depending upon how the couple reacts to these new conditions, it could create a stronger equal partnership or it could create new insecurities.

Given these conflicting and diverse factors that may have bearing on divorce, statistical demonstration showing a direct positive relationship between divorce and a wife working is unattainable. Often studies have reached the conclusion that families in which the wife is working are no more likely to separate or divorce than households in which only the husband is in the labor force.

The relationship between the expanding female workforce and reduced fertility rates appears to be clearer. With advances in family planning, a majority of wives have managed to combine motherhood with work. The entry of women into the workforce has not led to a vast increase in childlessness among married couples, but has led to a lower fertility rate among working wives when other social and economic factors are taken into consideration. Yet some reservation may be appropriate. In West Germany, for example, fertility rates of the native population during the 1970s have declined even more than in the United States, but with a smaller increase in female labor force participation.

Coping with family-related duties. The wife's responsibilities outside the home have not filtered back into a major reallocation of responsibilities within the family. Within the rising costs of household help, the option to pay another person to do the housework is beyond the means of the vast majority. Also, there are limits as to the chores that can be passed on to the friendly neighborhood supermarket clerk or appliance seller. Even more than in the office or factory, too many household chores cannot be mechanized. Work-sharing by other members of the family remains largely a hope. The working wife and mother is, therefore, left to her devices to cope as wage or salary earner and unpaid houseworker.

When the number of hours a working wife labors outside the home are added to the time spent on household chores, some studies have concluded that most working wives wind up laboring more hours per week than their husbands. Rough estimates based on data from the late 1960s and early 1970s indicated that a wife may average sixty-five hours on her combined jobs inside and outside the home (assuming that she holds a full-time job in the labor market). This exceeds the average time husbands spent working on the job and in the home by about eight hours per week. However, a more recent study based on data from the mid-1970s indicates that married women labored about the same total hours in their combined jobs as men--roughly sixty hours per week. There has been only a very small increase in the hours of housework done by married men, still under three hours per week, or one-sixth the time spent by working wives (Hofferth & Moore 1979:113-15; Stafford 1980:57-58). It is difficult to make accurate estimates of time use by men and women, but it appears that there still exists a significant sexual division of labor even if total hours worked may be becoming equal for many married men and women.

Just as pathologies within labor markets--such as sexual discrimination--have been slow in changing, so will home adjustments to the new realities of both husband and wife working outside. For example, while most men are just starting to become involved in household responsibilities, this trend soon may be the single largest impact on families associated with wives entering the labor force. In the absence of social upheavals, the slow evolution is toward family work roles based more on equality and less on sexual stereotypes. Many working wives appear to be assuming a larger role in making family-related decisions than nonworking wives with no earnings, but again, change has been slow. Yet, there seem to have been some changes in sharing responsibility and authority.

No Turning Back

If the survival of the family depends on women returning to the home to become full-time housewives and mothers, the institution's future existence is indeed fragile. There has been no decline in the career aspirations of women, and continued progress in family planning, bedroom technology, and household management will let more women become both wives and mothers as well as workers outside of the home. As the potential rewards and work opportunities for women expand, the psychic and economic attractions in the marketplace are likely to exert even greater pull.

With inflationary pressures and slow growth in productivity leading to sluggish gains and even occasional declines in real earnings, more families will depend on two wage earners just to make ends meet or to finance a higher standard of living. Women in the workforce, including the majority of married women, are in the labor force to stay, and this is not a new phenomenon. It was only with the rise of the industrial revolution--and then only when it was in full swing and immigrants supplied adequate and cheap labor--that wives were viewed as full-time mothers. The current American family has a long way to go before it fully adjusts to these new and shifting work patterns. The greatest changes will be the reallocation of work responsibilities within households. A decrease of chores allocated along traditional sexist lines coupled with women sharing more effectively in the family decision-making process are the primary adjustments that will be made. These changes--unlike fads which come and go--will probably have some of the deepest and most lasting effects on the family institution and on American society. Instead of dissolution, they offer real opportunities for improved, more stable, and richer lives within families.

Going It Alone

It appears that female-headed families will remain a significant phenomenon on the American scene. Such families, despite feminist advances, are still more likely to be poor and to experience sustained economic hardship. Trying to be family head, mother, and full-time member of the labor force has been a difficult challenge for most women. Working women who head households are at an even greater disadvantage [in the marketplace] than other women.

Single-parent families tend, however, to be a temporary phenomenon. Data on the gross flows of women who become family heads indicate that this condition is for many women only a way station, as they later marry or remarry. Still, the conditions experienced by these women and their children present serious problems covering a wide range of social issues from welfare to labor-market discrimination. Many have found it impossible to pull families out of poverty without government help....

Economic Realities

Of the major differences that exist between households headed by women and those of married couples, distinctions based on income are easiest to quantify. Poverty haunts only one of eleven husband-wife families and one of nine families maintained by men; but one of three families headed by women live in destitution.

Beyond the higher prevalence of poverty, the entire income distribution of families headed by women is lower than that of other kinds of families. In 1979, about four out of five families headed by women had earned incomes under $15,000, compared with three out of ten of all husband-wife families and one out of three families headed by men.

The median income of the families women head is less than half that of husband-wife households. Where dependent children are involved, the median drops to one-third. If a female family head has a child under 6 years, her family income on average is only two-fifths of that for a household headed by a woman with no youngsters.

Coupled with this factor are the younger ages of the women who are heading families. About four out of seven of the children who live in a household headed by a woman have a mother who is under 35 years of age. These younger women, who have a greater chance of having a child, represented 28 percent of all families headed by women in 1970. By 1979, this younger group had grown to represent 37 percent of the families headed by women.

National longitudinal data, which have followed female cohorts for several years, have increased our knowledge about families women head. Data tracking the same women--as they go through a dissolution of husband-wife family and then try making it on their own--give a clearer picture of this dynamic process than information based on cross-sectional estimates. The national longitudinal surveys at Ohio State University included interviews with a nationally representative sample of more than five thousand women under 25 years and 30 to 44 years at the time of the first interview (1967 and 1968, respectively). These women were interviewed annually or biennially, and the data provided a time path of their experiences over ten years. Some of the most important features indicated by longitudinal data concerning families women head are [as follows] (Mott 1979):

Temporary status. There is a large flow of women who move into and out of being heads of families, and few women remain in this condition for an extended period. Over the first five years, the surveys found that as many as 16 percent of all adult women sampled were heading a household. However, only 9 percent were household heads during the entire period: 6 percent of the white women and 21 percent of the black women.

Economic problems. The transition from a husband-wife family to head of a household often creates dire economic problems, which the women who head the new households often cannot solve without outside aid. For the older age cohort, the average household income for white families that experienced this disruption declined by 49 percent over the survey period. While the average income of black families fell by only 38 percent, their income prior to disruption of the family was only about two-thirds of the average for the white households. This same condition is also true for women in the younger age cohort.

Employment patterns. Labor-force patterns of women who experience marital disruption is quite different for whites and blacks for both the younger and older women. When their marriages ended, the older cohort of white wives increased their labor-force participation rate from 58 percent to 70 percent. For black women, just the opposite happened: their rate fell from more than 80 percent to 69 percent. Transition patterns also differ for black and white women concerning their seeking occupational training. When they became family heads, the number of older women who obtained training increased by more than 40 percent for whites but fell by 37 percent for blacks. For younger white women, the labor force participation rate climbed from 51 percent to 68 percent after the disruption. Younger black women, unlike their older counterparts, experienced... [an increase] in participation rates after divorce but it rose much less than that for the young white women--from 46 percent to 53 percent. For younger white women after divorce, the chance of resorting to training increased by 23 percent, while for younger black women it fell by 13 percent.

Even if a female family head lands a job, her earnings are not likely to make up for the income lost because a husband has left. Average per-capita income will decline by 20 percent for white families and 13 percent for black families (Mott & Moore 1978:123-24).

Transfer payments. Families headed by women depend on transfer payments as a major source of income. About 16 percent of all white female heads and 48 percent of black female heads receive public welfare payments. More than 23 percent of the white women who headed families and 19 percent of the black women received social security or disability payments. One-third of the poor white female heads and more than 50 percent of poor black female heads received at least half of their household income from public income-transfer programs. On average, earnings by a female head provided only about one-third of household income for families living in poverty and about three-fifths for those above the poverty line (Shaw 1978:16, 19).

Thus, whatever other advantages a woman perceives in single parenthood over a bad marriage, most families headed by women find the going very rough economically. Even when they combine work with welfare and other transfer payments, many female heads of households can barely life their families out of poverty--and a significant number live below the poverty threshhold.

The word *family*, at one time, evoked a picture of a husband, a wife, and their children living together in one household. Now a variety of cameos surrounds the central picture. None of the cameos, however, portrays the extended family that many analysts had anticipated because they believed a separated woman would return to her parents' or grandparents' household, taking her children with her. An increasing percentage of never-married or formerly married mothers are heading their own households instead of living as a subfamily unit in someone else's household, emphasizing the precarious status of families headed by women. In extended families, a divorced, separated, or never-married mother could count on the financial and social support of other adult family members to help provide for basic needs and ease such problems as child care. Today, if a woman decides, or is forced by circumstances, to separate or divorce, the chances are that she will have to head her own household.

There are some indications that the increase in the single-parent household will not be as swift in the 1980s as it was in the 1960s and 1970s. The view that the woman should seek liberation outside a husband-wife family is not shared by the vast majority of female family heads. Nor is it correct to conclude that those women who remain family heads do so by choice. When questioned, long-term female family heads most often indicated that their current household structure is not their first choice (Lasch 1977:162).

Policy Changes Needed

Social policies can have a significant impact on the work and living decisions of households, even those that are well above the poverty threshold. The federal income tax codes are a prime example: in 1979, the estimated tax liability of 16 million couples exceeded $8 billion, solely because they were married. Even couples with a relatively low family income pay a marriage tax penalty if there are several wage earners in the household. The marriage tax penalty in 1980 for a couple with a combined income of $40,000 was $1,900 (assuming standard deductions), while for a $10,000-a-year couple, the extra tax liability was more than $200. Whatever its equity and costs, there is little evidence that the marriage tax has had a statistically significant impact on marriage, but it may affect work decisions.

Other laws (including social security) affecting family income and work decisions are based on the assumption that the husband would work while the wife became a full-time housewife. Social security laws also assume that, once married, the couples would stay together. One problem with the social security system is that a wife's earnings result in higher total family benefits only if her entitlement exceeds 50 percent of her spouse's benefits. In most cases, the two-earner couple pays far more into the system than a one-earner couple, but receives only a marginal increase in benefits.

Many other social policies are based on family-related assumptions which existed in a bygone age. But American households have become highly pluralistic, and government programs will have to be attuned to the different needs and problems of various types of families. A comprehensive family policy has been impossible to fashion because interested parties cannot agree on even the basic goals. While one policy may seem more dramatic, incremental reform of the existing system may be the most realistic approach to help families during this rough period of transition.

Shifting work roles are altering family life, and changes in living arrangements are having a feedback effect on labor markets. Whether the family is better off because of the changes depends, in large measure, on personal value judgments. Public policies can ease the transition, but such policies should consider that there is no longer one dominant family type. Despite problems, the family remains a resilient institution. Most Americans live in families, and will continue to do so.

References

Hofferth, Sandra L., and Kristin A. Moore.
1979 "Women's Employment and Marriage." In Ralph E. Smith (ed.), *The Subtle Revolution.* Washington, D.C.: Urban Institute.

Lasch, Christopher.
1977 *Haven in a Heartless World: The Family Besieged.* New York: Basic Books.

Mott, Frank L.
1979 *The Socioeconomic Status of Households Headed by Women.* Washington, D.C.: U.S. Government Printing Office.

Mott, Frank L., and Sylvia F. Moore.
1978 "The Causes and Consequences of Marital Breakdown." In Frank L. Mott (ed.), *Women, Work and Family.* Lexington, Mass.: Lexington Books.

Shaw, Liz B.
1978 *Economic Consequences of Marital Disruption.* Columbus: Ohio State University, Center for Human Resources Research.

Stafford, Frank P.
1980 "Women's Use of Time Converging with Men's." *Monthly Labor Review* (Dec.).

12. EMPLOYMENT AND UNEMPLOYMENT: A Report on 1980

Diane Westcott and
Robert W. Bednarzik

Families

Interesting labor-force patterns emerge when workers are grouped according to their position within the family structure. These data show a continual upward movement in the proportion of multi-earner families--that is, two or more workers in a household. Moreover, among husband-wife families in 1980, the proportion in which the husband and wife were both employed (42 percent) exceeded the proportion in which only the husband was employed (36 percent). This phenomenon has occurred only since 1978.

The extent of the impact of joblessness on the family depends upon how many of the unemployed were in families in which someone else was employed. Almost half of all unemployed husbands had no other employed person in their families in 1980; a year earlier, only two-fifths of husband-wife families had this experience. In addition, the percentage of unemployed wives with no other working member almost doubled over the year--from 8.1 to 16.6 percent.

Inflation more than offset wage and salary gains of American workers and their families in 1980. Median weekly earnings of families increased 8 percent between the first 3 quarters of 1979 and the same average period in 1980,[1] to $400; there was, however, an even greater rise in consumer prices, so that the real earnings for the families declined by slightly more than 5 percent over this time period....

Among married couples, the one-earner family experienced the largest drop in real earnings--7.5 percent. The number of such families declined by more than half a million in 1980, with most of the reduction occurring in families in which only the husband worked. The number of families where both husband and wife were wage and salary workers posted a modest increase, reflecting the continuing increases in labor-force participation among married women.

Excerpted from"Employment and Unemployment: A Report on 1980," *Special Labor Force Report 22.* April 1981, pp. 11, 13-15.

The number of families maintained by female wage and salary earners (5.5 million) increased in 1980, as did their median weekly earnings. As with all family groups, however, because of a faster rise in prices, their purchasing power also declined. The median earnings of these families is still very low, $225 a week, compared with $435 for married-couple families and $360 for families maintained by men.

In and Out of the Labor Force

Despite the recession, the civilian labor force continued to grow during 1980, although more slowly than in recent years. This is the usual pattern over the business cycle. Between the fourth quarters of 1979 and 1980, the labor force grew 1.4 million, compared with increases of 2.2 and 2.7 million in 1979 and 1978. Labor-force changes across demographic groups in 1980 were much like the changes that occurred in the last recession: strong growth among women, moderate growth among men, and no growth among teenagers.

At 63.8 percent, the civilian labor-force participation rate was unchanged over the year. In recent years, overall participation has grown almost continuously, primarily because of the pronounced labor-market entry of women. The following shows the participation rates of various demographic groups for selected years of labor-market contraction:

		1971	1975	1980
Total		60.2	61.2	63.8
Teenagers	(16-19 years)	49.7	54.1	56.9
Men	(20 years and over)	82.1	80.3	79.4
Women	(20 years and over)	43.3	46.0	51.4
Never married		68.1	68.7	71.8
Married		41.3	44.8	50.5
Widowed, separated, divorced		39.0	38.8	42.4

More than half of all adult women are now working or seeking work; some 40 million were in the labor force in 1980. Moreover, their share of the labor force, nearly 40 percent in 1980, has continued to grow, while that of adult men and teenagers has fallen. The greatest labor-force increases have occurred among married women. After declining over several years, male participation in the labor force, holding relatively steady following the 1974-75 recession, showed a further drop in 1980, to 79.4 percent. Participation among teenagers, at 56.9 percent, was down slightly from the level of the past few years.

The changing aspects of the labor force are often overlooked in discussions of the national employment situation. Although a majority of workers are attached to the labor force, there is a substantial amount of ebb and flow in the labor force, employment, and unemployment each month. Thus, a deeper understanding of labor-force behavior can be obtained through an examination of gross monthly movements. The flow data show that in 1980, 5 percent of the employed and about 50 percent of the unemployed--more than 8 million workers--changed labor force status each month. Moreover, this count does not include the large number of persons outside the labor force who found jobs or began actively looking for a job over the month (4.5 million), or the unknown number of workers who changed jobs over the month but were tabulated as employed in both months. (CPS flow data indicate only that there was a change in labor-force status between measurements, not that an actual job change occurred.)...

The vast majority of employed men and women who were working in any given month were also found to be employed in the following month. In contrast, the percentage movements out of and into...unemployment each month are sizable. Generally, the changes among male workers are more likely to occur within the labor force between employment and unemployment, while changes among female workers are more likely to involve a period of time outside the labor force.

Interestingly, the outflow of women from the labor force because of home responsibilities has been declining. That is, although women are still more likely to leave the labor force than men, particularly when unemployed, the reason is increasingly less likely to be for traditional family purposes and more likely to be such things as prolonged illness or disability, discouragement over job prospects, or simply retirement from the labor force. Men leaving the labor force are also increasingly likely to cite these same reasons. Indeed, women are becoming more firmly attached to the labor force, as evidenced by the high and climbing percentage that remain employed from one month to the next. Apparently, they are unwilling to give up the income needed to maintain or increase consumption in the wake of rising prices or to leave promising careers to maintain a family on a full-time basis....

Note

1. Median wage and salary earnings adjusted for inflation were not available at the time of this writing.

13. UNEMPLOYMENT AMONG FAMILY MEN: A Ten-Year Longitudinal Study

Martha S. Hill and Mary Corcoran

Typically, unemployment for any one group of individuals is measured over a fairly short period, often no longer than a year. These measurements usually indicate that a relatively small proportion of workers is unemployed during the period studied. Such "snapshots" of unemployment, however, may be consistent with any of several longer term scenarios: observed unemployment could reflect a pattern in which a large proportion of workers spends some time unemployed, but each worker loses only a relatively small fraction of potential total work time; or it could show that a small proportion of workers is unemployed over and over again, with their unemployment accounting for a large fraction of their potential work time, both short term and long term. The distribution and severity of the unemployment burden and the policies appropriate to deal with it are determined by which scenario is indeed the case.

In this article, we present a "moving picture" of unemployment by following the labor market experiences of the same individuals over the ten-year period 1967-76. In this dynamic view we estimate the incidence, duration, and economic costs of unemployment, both annually and cumulatively, over the decade, with a particular focus on how the burden of unemployment is distributed.

This study uses data from the Panel Study of Income Dynamics, an ongoing longitudinal study of more than 5,000 American families begun in 1968. The sample consists of 1,251 men age 35 to 64 in 1976 who were household heads and labor-force participants[1] every year of the 10-year survey period.[2] While such prime-age men have traditionally had lower unemployment rates than other subgroups of workers--the young and women--they constitute a large segment of the labor force, and their unemployment is, therefore, important in the aggregate. Further, they are often the primary earners in their families, so their unemployment is likely to have the strongest effect on family well-being.

Reprinted from *Monthly Labor Review* (November 1979):19-23.

Annual Unemployment Reflects Economy

Despite the well-documented cross-sectional tendency for the unemployment rate to decline with age, the annual unemployment for prime-age men did not fall continuously with time.... Instead, their annual unemployment reflected changes in the overall level of unemployment in the economy, rising dramatically during the recessionary periods 1970-71 and 1974-76. During these recessionary periods, increases in both the incidence and duration of joblessness contributed to the higher unemployment among these workers.

Primarily because of the longer duration of unemployment at these times, mean income losses, both with and without adjustments for unemployment compensation and the taxes otherwise due on forgone earnings, were much higher for those surveyed who were unemployed. For example, in 1967, those who were unemployed averaged 6.9 weeks out of work, with $1,620 (in 1976 dollars) in lost earnings, or $1,176 in lost disposable income. In 1976, when the unemployment rate was about twice as high, those who were unemployed averaged 14.5 weeks out of work, with $4,139 in lost earnings, or $2,870 in lost disposable income (after-tax earnings).

The relative time and money costs of unemployment were high when viewed over a one-year period. Even in 1967--the year with the lowest relative costs--the unemployed men lost more than one-tenth of their expected worktime[3] and expected after-tax earnings;[4] in 1976--the year with the highest relative cost--unemployed men lost 30 percent of their expected work time and 24 percent of their expected after-tax earnings.

Losses Greater over the Long Term

The number unemployed at some time during the decade was three times as large as the number unemployed in 1974, the year with the highest number of jobless. We also found that relative costs for those unemployed were much lower when viewed from a ten-year rather than a one-year perspective. The 38.4 percent of the study sample who were unemployed at some time during the 10 years averaged losses amounting to 5.3 percent of expected ten-year work time and 4.2 percent of expected ten-year after-tax earnings.

While this suggests that unemployment is more pervasive over longer periods, comparisons of percent unemployed also suggest that unemployment is a repetitive occurrence for some workers. Our further investigation supports this contention: while mean relative costs of unemployment over ten years were one-sixth to one-half the size of comparable one-year costs, mean absolute costs were larger for the longer term. Among the unemployed, mean earnings losses were $7,360 (in constant 1976 dollars) and mean disposable income losses were $5,133 during the ten- year period, almost double the mean earnings and disposable income losses in 1976, the year with the largest mean losses for the unemployed. In addition, prime-age men experiencing some unemployment over the longer period averaged three of the ten years with some unemployment.

Profile of the Unemployed

Of the prime-age male workers we studied, blacks, the poor, the less educated, blue-collar workers, and men under age 45 were much more likely than other subgroups to have experienced at least one bout of unemployment between 1967 and 1976. Among those who reported some unemployment, blue-collar workers, workers with less than a high school education, and poor workers also lost considerably large proportions of their expected ten-year work time and after-tax earnings....

A closer look at racial differences revealcd that prime-age black men who headed households were one and one-half times as likely to be unemployed during 1967-76 as were their white counterparts. More than half (53.6 percent) of all blacks surveyed were unemployed sometime during 1967-76, compared with about one-third (37.2 percent) of whites. However, both groups averaged about the same number of weeks unemployed (28.9 and 27.2 weeks) and lost about the same proportion of their expected ten-year after-tax earnings (4.5 and 4.1 percent).

Poor male household heads were also disproportionately subject to unemployment.[5] About two-thirds (68.2 percent) of poor household heads in our sample reported some unemployment between 1967 and 1976, compared with about one-third (37.5 percent) of other household heads. Unlike racial differences, poverty status differences in the average weeks of unemployment and the relative economic costs of unemployment were quite sizable. During 1967-76, poor household heads who were unemployed averaged 45.6 weeks of unemployment and lost 8.5 percent of their expected 10-year disposable earnings, compared with 26.3 weeks and 3.9 percent for other unemployed household heads. Unemployment also appears to have been a more repetitive occurrence for poor household heads: the poor who were unemployed averaged 4 of the ten years with some unemployment, as compared with 2.7 years for those who were not poor.

Blue-collar workers with lower levels of education were more likely to experience repeated unemployment than were white-collar workers or well-educated workers. Unemployed blue-collar workers, on average, experienced unemployment during twice as many years as did unemployed white-collar workers, and this unemployment culminated in a somewhat larger average number of weeks of unemployment over the ten years. Both the number of years and the cumulative weeks of unemployment declined as the level of education of the unemployed workers increased.

Examining factors such as rate, age, occupation, education, and poverty status in a multivariate context, we found that poverty status, occupation, and education each exerted strong and significant independent effects on both the incidence and duration of unemployment over the decade. Age affected only the incidence, and race exerted no independent effect. Whites with comparable levels of education and in similar occupations in similar industries were just as likely as blacks to be unemployed at some time during 1967-76, suggesting that education and type of job may be the keys to racial differences in unemployment incidence among prime-age men who head households and have a long-term labor-force attachment.[6]

Few Bear Greatest Burden

Preliminary analysis showed length of unemployment rather than wages or unemployment compensation to be the dominant component of after-tax income losses from unemployment for both the annual and cumulative data.[7] We investigated the long-run distribution of the unemployment burden by constructing a Lorenz curve depicting the cumulative percentage of total unemployment hours for the prime-age male household heads by the cumulative percentage of the sample, for the years 1967-76. Results indicate that 5 percent of the sample accounted for almost half (46.6 percent) of all the work hours lost by the entire group because of unemployment over the decade. During this period, these men averaged 96 weeks unemployed, or 19.1 percent of their expected ten-year work time, with accompanying average losses of $19,114 in after-tax income, or 15.4 percent of their expected ten-year after-tax earnings.[8] Thus, a small percentage of men accounted for the bulk of the group's unemployment, and their losses were quite substantial.

Moreover, the degree of concentration of unemployment at the family level may well be understated. Analysis of all surveyed household heads and wives indicated that extensive unemployment cumulated within families: in 1975, wives in households where the husband was unemployed for fourteen weeks or more were more likely to be unemployed at least fourteen weeks.[9]

Who were the men who experienced these large losses of work time and money as a result of unemployment?... [U]nemployment over the long term was concentrated among the poor, high-school dropouts, blue-collar workers, and construction workers. While only 1 in 30 of the men who headed households was poor, almost 1 in 8 of the high-unemployment group was poor. And, while only 1 in 10 of the prime-age men who headed households was a construction worker, 4 of 10 of the chronic unemployed were construction workers. Additionally, blue-collar workers and workers with less than a high-school education accounted for about twice as large a proportion of the high unemployment group.

These relationships emerged in a multivariate context as well. Even with controls for other demographic and job characteristics, including the local unemployment rate, workers with fewer than twelve years of school, in poverty, in blue-collar jobs, and in the construction industry were more likely to experience unemployment. However, even though factors such as education, poverty status, and occupation played a role in determining where the burden of unemployment fell most heavily, together they accounted for less than ten percent of the variance in the likelihood of experiencing chronic, substantial unemployment. Thus, we are still far from adequately identifying workers who experience substantial and repeated unemployment.

Questions Remain

Our examination of annual unemployment experiences revealed that, despite the well-documented cross-sectional tendency for the unemployment rate to decline with age, annual unemployment for the workers studied did not fall continuously with time but, instead, moved in phase with changes in the economy-wide level of unemployment. Comparing the annual unemployment experiences with cumulative ten-year unemployment, we found unemployment to be more pervasive in the long run. Finally, among those unemployed, average time and money losses relative to potential total work time and potential income, respectively, were much lower over the long term than in any one-year period.

These averages, however, masked important differences characteristic of unemployment experiences during the decade. Over the long term, two distinct groups of unemployed male household heads emerged. By far, the largest group comprised those workers for whom unemployment was an infrequent occurrence with low relative costs of time and money. The other group was small, experienced extensive and chronic unemployment, and suffered severe losses of time and money, whether measured annually or cumulatively. This group is apparently not being integrated into stable employment even though each of its members has at least a ten-year history of labor-force participation. Why this group accumulated so much unemployment is a question of obvious concern to policy makers. Results of the 1967-76 study show that schooling, occupation, and poverty status (but not race) make some difference, but future research is needed to determine more exact causes of extensive unemployment.

Notes

1. Individuals are defined as "labor-force participants" if they report themselves either working, temporarily laid off, or unemployed/looking for work on the interview date.

   We restricted analysis to household heads, because the Panel Study provides ten years of detailed unemployment and work history data only for household heads. As women who are both household heads and labor-force participants for ten years form only a very small proportion of working women, the analysis was restricted to men. As older men may retire in response to unemployment, only men under age 65 in 1976 were studied. As male household heads under age 25 are not a random sample of all young men, we included only men who were at least 25 in 1968.
2. In the Panel Study, annual work and unemployment data pertain to the year prior to the interview data; consequently, 1967-76 unemployment information applies to individuals interviewed in 1968-77.
3. Expected work time is defined as the sum of employment plus unemployment hours for a given time period. Proportion of work time lost is the ratio of unemployment hours to expected worktime.
4. Proportion of the expected income lost is the ratio of lost disposable income to expected after-tax labor income. Lost disposable income = {(Hourly wage) x (Hours employed) x (1-Average tax rate)} - unemployment compensation. Expected after-tax labor income = {Reported labor income + (Hourly wage x Hours unemployed) x (1-Average tax rate)}.
5. We determined "poor" by computing the ratio of ten-year family income to one-year family needs. Family needs were calculated using the Orshansky index. Whenever the income-to-needs ratio was less than 1.25, we defined a household head as "poor". One

might argue that our analysis is circular, as unemployment might push people into poverty. However, of the 110 poor in the sample of prime-age male household heads, only 3 would have attained ten-year family income/needs ratios of 1.25 or greater if they had received their usual earnings when unemployed.

6. These results should not be generalized to race differences between all men. Among youths, for instance, many of whom are not household heads, there is an extremely large difference in unemployment rates by race.
7. We separated after-tax income losses due to unemployment into three components: unemployment time, after-tax wage, and fraction of after-tax earnings' losses recovered through unemployment compensation. Both in 1976 and 1967-76 the variance in unemployment time accounted for much more of the variance in after-tax income losses than did the variance in the other two components of these income losses.
8. Interestingly, these workers constituted a larger fraction of the unemployed in any one year than of the unemployed over the decade. The three-quarters of this group who were unemployed in 1976 comprised 38.3 percent of the 1976 unemployed, whereas the entire group accounted for only 13.0 percent of the 1967-76 unemployed.
9. In 1975, 2.6 percent of households in the Panel Study included a wife with fourteen weeks or more of unemployment, and 6.3 percent included a head with fourteen weeks or more of unemployment. If the head's and wife's likelihood of exposure to extensive unemployment were statistically independent, we would expect to find 0.164 percent ((.026) x (.063) = .00164)) of all households with both the head and wife unemployed at least fourteen weeks. We found, however, that in 0.4 percent of the households, both the head and wife were unemployed at least fourteen weeks in 1975. This observed percentage was significantly larger (with 99 percent confidence) than the expected percentage. This cumulative unemployment may, of course, result from the wife entering the labor force as a result of her husband being unemployed for a protracted period.

14. TEENAGE UNEMPLOYMENT

Gerald Jaynes and Glenn C. Loury

One of the most severe problems associated with poverty in female-headed household is the large incidence of youth unemployment stemming directly from these families. There are two aspects of this problem. In the short run we should like to provide more employment and income for these youths to alleviate the immediate problem. In the longer run, since it is well known that youths coming from low-income families tend to make up more than their proportion of low-income adults and family heads in the succeeding generation, policies must be developed that will enable these youths to obtain employment adequate to sustain a decent living standard when they become adults. This cannot be accomplished without providing incentives for students to remain in school and to perform as best they can while there. We shall discuss the short-term problem first, but that discussion will indicate a close relationship between both issues.

Unemployment figures verify that teenage unemployment is one of the most important problems facing the nation. For example, teenagers in the late 1970s, while comprising about one-tenth of the labor force, accounted for one-quarter of the unemployed. In particular, black teenage unemployment exceeded 30 percent throughout the 1970s, is now closer to 50 percent, and makes up a tremendous portion of the urban unemployed. However, policy discussions of teenage unemployment have been misguided. Unemployment and the disappointing labor-market experiences of teenagers of school age are not the important social disease many would have us believe, but a major symptom of the most important social malady, the poverty of urban black and other minority families who cannot provide basic necessities or any luxuries for their teenage offspring. Put more simply, how much of a problem would teenage unemployment be if all household heads had a decent income?... Teenagers are notorious for their habits of entering and exiting from the labor force after short spells of employment. Their weak attachment to the labor force is often criticized. Would we have it otherwise? A strong attachment would almost certainly involve an even weaker attachment to school achievement than already exists in most urban areas.

Reprinted from "Urban Unemployment" in *Urban Policy Issues.* A report prepared under a cooperative agreement between the Joint Center for Political Studies and the U.S. Department of Housing and Urban Development, Washington, D.C. 1981, pp. 58-63.

The complete burden of high teenage unemployment is often blamed on the minimum wage. Why hire a 17-year-old at three dollars an hour they argue, when you can get a more experienced and stable adult for the same price? Without the minimum wage, employers might prefer three 17-year-olds at one dollar an hour each, to one three dollar adult. In addition, it is argued that employers would be more likely to provide training to teenagers if they could be hired at subminimum wage rates. We are extremely dubious of the efficacy *and* social desirability of this last assertion. Few training opportunities are provided to individuals earning three dollars an hour precisely because labor turnover is high at such low wages (irrespective of the worker's age). In addition, training opportunities leading to attractive careers occur in firms that have unionized labor with entry rates fixed far above a three-dollar wage and/or require minimum education levels that can demand wages exceeding three dollars. It is highly unlikely that an end to minimum-wage legislation is going to result in a greatly increased supply to private-sector employment with *good training* opportunities for teenagers at one-dollar wages. But perhaps, even more importantly, do we really want five one-dollar-wage teenagers with little or no family responsibilities displacing heads of families earning five dollars an hour?

Historically, minimum-wage legislation was aimed precisely at the fact that adults attempting to support families were faced with the competition of cheap child labor. Minimum-wage legislation not only raised the wages of families, but in lowering labor-market opportunities for youths, it made their continuation in school an attractive alternative. Teenagers are one special group with special problems, but in attacking their problems, we do not want to exacerbate the more fundamental problem by treating only a symptom. These objectives do not, however, make an insurmountable objection to reforming minimum-wage legislation. A judiciously chosen subminimum wage for teenagers only, if restricted to specific employment sectors, may actually displace few adult heads of families. To see why, let us examine the political economy of the minimum wage.

It is important to realize that an employer's perception of a worker's value may involve subjective factors, and need not always be correct. It is a reasonable presumption, however, that employers seek to maximize their profits from business activity. Otherwise they would not survive competition from rival businessmen. This being so, were an employer to learn that he had misperceived the worth of a worker, who could after all be profitably employed, he would feel remorse at the lost opportunity. That is, a profit-maximizing employer is interested in accurately forecasting a prospective worker's worth. He will adjust that forecast as new information about the worker becomes available to him. A "good" worker, from such an employer's point of view, is one whose characteristics (education, work history and recommendations, "attitude" and social bearing) inspire confidence in his performance. This confidence is based upon past observation showing how these characteristics correlate with performance. The employer is thus willing to pay a relatively high wage for a "good" worker, since he can do so and still expect to profit from the transaction.

In a competitive labor market a worker will be offered a wage just equal to the employers' best estimate of that worker's worth. This *offered* wage will be low or high depending upon what the worker's characteristics imply about his likely productivity.

Another factor affecting the wage offered to a worker of given characteristics is the level of business activity in the employer's line of commerce. If demand for the employer's product is low, then no matter how attractive an additional worker may appear, the employer will be constrained in offering employment at a high wage by the anticipation that he will not be able to sell the additional output which that worker would create. Thus a worker's offered wage depends upon how attractive his credentials are to employers, and upon how "tight" is the local labor market in which he seeks employment. Presumably there always exists some wage rate (possibly negative!) at which an employer would be willing to hire any worker.

The worker, on the other hand, will not willingly work at any wage. If the wage offered a worker is too low, compared to what the worker believes to be the value of alternative use of his time, then he will not accept the offer. The alternatives for a worker include continued search for employment, the enjoyment of leisure and receipt of income support payments, or further pursuit of training before entering the labor market. Each worker then will (implicitly) have in his mind a certain *asking wage*, the least for which he will consider working. This asking wage will be higher, the greater are the worker's employment alternatives. The greater is the worker's value of leisure, the higher is the level of income support available to the worker should he remain without work.

Given this framework, it follows that a worker is unemployed whenever his asking wage is greater than his offered wage from the employers he encounters in his search for work. If the worker remains unemployed for a protracted period of time, his asking wage would presumably decline. If business conditions were to improve substantially, then the wage offered by employers to a worker of given characteristics would increase. Similarly, if the worker altered his characteristics by acquiring further training, his offered wage would increase. Thus, the typical worker's unemployment stems partly from the fact that his asking wage is "too high" (relative to the available options), and partly from the fact that his offered wage is too low. The relative importance of these two factors in explaining unemployment in any specific population depends upon the characteristics of workers in that population, and the nature of the local labor market which that population faces.

For central-city low-income populations the unemployment problem is quite serious. The phenomenon is especially pronounced among younger nonwhite workers. These people often have little or no experience, few marketable skills, and low educational achievement. *They therefore face relatively low offered wages.* Yet, since employment is the only avenue to experience and frequently the critical factor in the adolescence to adulthood transition, protracted unemployment for people in this population can be very costly, both to them and to society. Thus, it would be in the interest of members of this population to seek work even at the relatively low wages offered, unless available transfer payments or illegal earnings were greater than the offered wage. That is, one might expect members of the young urban poor population to have relatively low asking wages, so long as transfers and illegal opportunities were not too great. Thus, the fact that offered wages are low does not explain the unemployment of this group.

Federal minimum-wage legislation is a major impediment to workers with low offered and asking wages finding employment. The reason is that an effective wage floor forces all asking wages to be at least as great as the minimum. Any worker worth less than that minimum to an employer will thus not be hired. Those workers willing to work for less and employable at lower wages, but not profitable to employ at the minimum wage, will go unemployed. However, it is true that workers whose asking wage is below the minimum but whom employers would be willing to pay the minimum or more, will gain from the institution of a wage floor. Thus, the major beneficiaries among low-wage workers should be those with the characteristics most favored by employers (i.e., those with the highest offered wages).

To the extent that employers regard race, or "ghetto culture," as detrimental characteristics associated with poor productivity, urban nonwhites will have lower offered wages, and thus will bear the brunt of the unemployment fostered by minimum-wage legislation. Indeed, statistical analysis reveals that, historically, increases in the minimum wage have not been associated with an improved relative position of those lowest in the economic hierarchy. Increases in the minimum have also not been associated with reduced inequality between whites and nonwhites.

There are several reasons why we might expect the effects of the minimum wage to differ by race. As argued above, for sectors of the labor market affected by the minimum, economic theory suggests that wages will be increased and employment reduced, relative to what would prevail absent the minimum wage. In general a circumstance of excess supply will prevail in the covered sectors for low-wage workers, permitting employers some latitude in choosing among those seeking work. If employers are inclined to discriminate among jobseekers by race, and/or if black workers are on average less productive than whites in the affected low-wage markets, then blacks will bear a relatively greater share of the unemployment in these markets. Indeed, the unemployment rate for teenage black workers has consistently been more than twice that among white youth in recent years, with no more than one-half of this difference explained by divergent individual characteristics among workers in the two groups.

Another factor of importance here is that the earnings incidence of the minimum wage will differ substantially between covered and uncovered sectors. Time series evidence suggests that an increase in the minimum induces movement of workers into the uncovered sectors, and a consequent reduction in wages there. Racial differences in the distribution of workers between covered and uncovered sectors within an industry or among industries with varying degrees of coverage will thus induce racial differences in the earnings effect of an increase in the minimum. For example, between 1972 and 1977, according to the Current Population Survey, the average percent covered in industry of employment for workers 25 years and older is 82.0 percent for white males, 78.8 percent for black males, 72.4 percent for white women and 44.5 percent for black women. To measure such possible differences in the effect of the minimum on earnings by race, one could estimate annual earnings equations on individual data disaggregated by age, sex, and race.

Elsewhere one of us has undertaken this estimation. We found that an increase of 10 percent in the level of the (coverage weighted) federal minimum wage was associated with a reduction of 3.3 percent in the annual earning of black male workers ages 16-19. White males in the same age group were unaffected, though white males ages 20-24 seemed to enjoy an increase of 1.7 percent in annual earnings for the same 10 percent increase in the minimum.

Another problem with the minimum wage as a policy for helping the urban poor is that low-wage workers are frequently not from poor families. Teenagers and housewives from middle-class families working part time are major beneficiaries of the minimum wage. For example, the median *family* income of teenagers earning the minimum wage in 1973 was above the median family income of all families in the population. In the research project mentioned above we have attempted to determine how a hypothetical increase in the minimum wage would affect the earnings of families, by race and position in the overall income distribution. We imagined that in 1976 the minimum had been increased by 20 percent, and then used our statistical equations to estimate the effect on family earnings. The results were quite striking, in that they indicated that an increase in the minimum has a much greater impact on white family earnings than black family earnings. According to our calculations,...a hypothetical 20 percent increase in the minimum raises white family earnings by a little more than 1 percent on average, while *the gain for blacks is only one-fifth as large.* There is a large disparity in black and white gains for two-person and four-person families as well as at all earnings levels within a given family size. However, the differences between blacks and whites at the very bottom of the earnings distributions are uniformly higher than those at the top. The percentage gain for all white families in first quintile (i.e., the lowest fifth of the family income distribution) is over 33 times larger than that for blacks, while the percentage gain for those at the top is only 4 times as large. This pattern holds for two-person and four-person families as well.

...[I]ncreasing the minimum is not an egalitarian policy from the point of view of raising the earnings of low-income families relative to other groups. The figures for all families shows that higher income families gain absolutely more from changes in the minimum, that the middle group gains more in percentage terms compared to both high and low earnings families, and that higher earnings groups benefit relative to the lower earnings categories. The relative gains of the highest black quintile are almost 10 times the relative gains for the lowest black quintile... The patterns within family groups of a given size is somewhat more complicated. For two-person black families, those in the fourth and fifth quintiles benefit the most. For four-person white families, those in the first and second quintiles experience the largest gains. There is no pattern for four-person black families, while two-person white families conform to that for all families.

Thus, it is our view that the minimum wage at current levels is probably not a policy in the best interest of the urban poor. They bear more than their share of the unemployment which it generates, and share less than proportionately in the benefits of higher wages. We suggest that some consideration be given to experimenting with a reduced or eliminated minimum for young urban workers. This could be tried in a particular locality for a couple of years to see if the employment prospects of the hard core unemployed are improved. While it is clear that big labor will oppose such efforts, this only illustrates the fact that the interests of labor and of central-city low-income populations do not always coincide. The value of the old coalition may not be worth the costs any more, if the interest of poor central-city nonwhites is to be served....

Current governmental policies are inadequate in many ways, but in particular they fail to enforce an incentive structure for minority urban workers that is consistent with a market economy. Most social scientists agree that during the historical period of latent racial discrimination nonwhites were for the most part relegated to an inferior position in a two-tiered society that provided little *opportunity* or incentives for viable economic growth. Many current public-sector programs unintentionally maintain this two-tiered stratification of society because they are perceived as special dispensations for minorities and therefore emit signals of inferiority to the wider public. Any public programs instituted for the urban poor, if they are to promote viable economic advancement must ultimately provide the recipients with complete access to the private sector and therefore must produce competitive graduates with no tint of inferiority about them.

One method of providing incentives for youths to remain in school is to involve the schools in student employment activities either directly through a special type of public-sector employment and/or indirectly by validating private-sector student employment. Consider the public-sector approach first. Throughout the last decade or so Federal funds have been channeled through local governments during short periods such as summer employment programs. Suppose that similar funds were channeled through: (a) local school systems upon a continuing basis throughout the year. Eligibility for student work participation should be tied to: (b) enrollment in school upon a continuing basis.

Other eligibility requirements such as satisfactory school performance should be examined before a detailed proposal is made. For example, we do not want to limit jobs to only outstanding students, but job eligibility might require satisfactory educational progress similar to eligibility requirements for participation in athletics. Students could work as tutors, library aids, clerical staff, and in other service capacities. There is much room for creativity in designing useful jobs and this end of the program might best be done by local school parent groups. This is not intended to include programs that allocate students to private firms for part of the school day where they do menial tasks, developing neither educational nor job skills. We are against programs that give up on our youth by taking them out of school under the rubric of vocational training that often fails to train.

If these jobs are channeled through the school systems they will not compete with private-sector jobs and this allows us to address an important budgetary problem. If teenagers are willing to work for less than the minimum wage there is no reason why *school-packaged employment programs* should be constrained to pay that wage. If students are willing to work for two dollars an hour, let them do so. With a given budget more jobs of longer duration and a more equitable distribution of income could be achieved. If it proved infeasible to pay subminimum wages, the available jobs could be expanded by specific limits upon the maximum number of hours worked. The entire cost of the program could be kept within limits by allowing local governments to designate school districts which must qualify based upon criteria similar to those in the UJEZ [Urban Jobs and Enterprise Zone] proposal. A small experimental program might be the best way to introduce and test this idea.

Another method of introducing a subminimum wage for teenagers while maintaining the student status would be to make satisfactory performance in school an eligibility requirement for all teenagers seeking employment under the program. Suppose again that the social security tax were eliminated for all *qualified* members of this age group. To be qualified a teenager would have to be issued a card by his school. Eligibility requirements could be constructed along the lines discussed in the school public-sector program above. Teenagers need not participate, but the reduced social security tax would both increase take-home pay and reduce the cost to the employer. Thus not only would eligible teenagers make more money when employed, they would have a greater chance of finding a job. It cannot be doubted that this would provide a stimulus for remaining in school and performing scholastically in order to receive an employment card. Graduates from secondary school could remain eligible for a period of time, say until the age of 21. The bulk of the paperwork involved in enforcing the provisions of the program, restriction to eligible students, etc., could be placed upon the school systems (local government) and the state or federal government.

IV

THE ECONOMIC STATUS OF FAMILIES:

Income Maintenance and Social Welfare over the Life Cycle

Government policies ranging from tax laws to unemployment compensation programs have an impact on the economic well-being of families. In this section the emphasis is on policies directed toward those traditionally considered to need assistance--the poor, the young, the aging, and the disabled.

A historical look at the development of American policies and programs to provide income security helps explain many of the contradictions and inadequacies so evident today. The U.S. approach to providing income security differs considerably from that adopted by some European countries, reflecting contrasts in their underlying philosophies and values, as was discussed in Part I. American policies have been designed primarily to assist the "deserving poor," an orientation especially embraced by the Reagan administration, which is directing social programs toward the "truly needy," a much narrower focus than adopted by previous administrations.

Using such an approach, policy makers design income maintenance programs to provide "minimum standards of income, goods and services only for those whose incomes fall below a minimum level considered necessary for survival" (Smeeding & Garfinkel 1980:41). An alternative approach is to have universal programs, i.e., paid to everyone regardless of their income level. European policies have tended to benefit all families, not just those in need, reflecting the belief that an adequate standard of living is a "right." U.S. policy tends to be directed primarily toward the poor and those considered unable to care for themselves--children, the elderly, the ill, and the disabled (Morris 1979:39).

In Chapter 15, "Promoting the Welfare of Americans," the roots of current government policy are traced to the New Deal, when the Social Security Act of 1935 introduced two types of income security programs: public welfare and social insurance programs. These programs have been modified and expanded, but the basic distinctions between the two types have largely survived. For example, programs like those under the Comprehensive Employment and Training Act (CETA) were devised to promote opportunity for eligible recipients. The Food Stamp program was introduced to enable recipients to purchase essentials. However, in the absence of widespread agreement about reform, no unified system to replace this array of programs has been enacted. "Promoting the Welfare of Americans" outlines several proposals: a guaranteed minimum income, general assistance, and guaranteed jobs. Proposals to provide a minimum income level to poor families have failed to gain widespread acceptance.

Several of the chapters on poverty and social welfare in this section were written before President Reagan took office and can be contrasted with Chapter 17, by Joe, which analyzes the impact of the current administration's cuts on poor families. "Promoting the Welfare of Americans," excerpted from a report by the President's Commission for a National Agenda for the Eighties, presents a somewhat optimistic outlook on prospects for improving the economic well-being of all Americans in the future. A panel analyzed the purposes, philosophy, and deficiencies of the American welfare system and emphasized the need for reform. It favored replacing AFDC, food stamps and general assistance with one overall income maintenance program. The viewpoint and concerns expressed in the report, especially about the equity and adequacy of programs, reflect the goals of administrations in the 1960s and 1970s which seemed to be moving toward a guaranteed minimum income program. Such reform is unlikely now, given the current economic and political climate in this country. The chapters by Joe and by Pearce and McAdoo present pessimistic assessments of chances for eliminating poverty, a pessimism confirmed by recent statistics.

Social insurance programs to provide income security include Social Security, Workers' Compensation, and unemployment compensation. Eligibility and benefits for these programs are determined by past contributions through employment and an identifiable problem like "old age, death of spouse, disability, and unemployment" (Danziger & Plotnick 1981:132). Benefits are considered "earned," and no income or means test is applied to determine eligibility. Policy issues that relate to Social Security will be considered later in this section.

Public Welfare Programs

The Social Security Act initiated a welfare system for the aged, blind, and disabled (which became the Supplemental Security Income program in 1974) and a program of Aid to Dependent Children, later retitled Aid to Families with Dependent Children (AFDC). This latter program was intended to benefit children in families whose male head was ill or disabled (Lynn 1980:218). Introduced to assist "the deserving poor," these programs are still looked upon by many as charity. Strong beliefs that poverty, especially among the able-bodied, stems from individual deficiencies rather than from societal conditions have led to the exclusion of men considered employable (and their families if in the same household) from many programs.

Although conceived originally as a small program for those not receiving assistance under any other social insurance program, AFDC and related programs have grown in numbers of recipients covered, costs, and proportion of the federal budget. Outlays for AFDC increased substantially during the 1950s and 1960s with the rapid growth in families headed by women. AFDC costs would be even higher if all those eligible applied for benefits. Many women on public assistance receive no support for themselves or their children from absent spouses, as Pearce and McAdoo indicate.

Today's recipients of AFDC cash payments may be eligible for additional in-kind benefits, including food stamps, housing assistance, and Medicaid. Such in-kind benefits and services often receive greater public support than cash payments do. They are preferred when recipients' right to assistance does not seem clearcut to large or influential segments in society. Those who think that recipients cannot be trusted to make intelligent decisions about money also prefer in-kind benefits. Moreover, Blaydon and Stack (1977:6) and Lynn (1980) suggest that strong pressures for such benefits come from service-providers with a vested interest in expanded programs.

The Face of Poverty

Who are the poor? (The poverty level for a nonfarm family of 4 in 1980 was set at $8,414.) They are disproportionately female and members of racial minorities, as several chapters in this section indicate. In the past, the elderly comprised a large proportion of poor households. However, government transfers keep an estimated 45 percent of these households out of poverty. Households headed by women have not fared as well. One reason lies in the fact that Social Security payments are indexed to the cost of living; public assistance payments are not and have not kept pace with inflation (Danziger & Plotnick 1981:134). However, for reasons which will become apparent in the discussion of Social Security, many old women still do not have adequate incomes.

The economic problems of women are the focus of the chapter by Pearce and McAdoo. It was written before the Reagan administration's policies had taken effect, with a recent postscript added. Read in conjunction with the chapter by Joe, the report shows how the worst features of AFDC have been emphasized, making it even more difficult today for poor women who head households to improve their economic status. Pearce and McAdoo argue that there are dual welfare systems, just as there are dual labor markets, with women and minorities disproportionately concentrated in the secondary sectors of both. They discuss the barriers that prevent poor women, especially minority women, from obtaining training and jobs that provide more than a poverty-level income. Chapter 9, "Equal Opportunity and the Need for Child Care," assessed other constraints faced by low-income women.

Criticisms of Income Maintenance and Social Welfare Policies

Issues of neutrality and equity. The chapter "Promoting the Welfare of Americans" outlines an array of criticisms directed toward social welfare programs and policies. These include concerns about equity and neutrality. Although there is considerable agreement across a broad political spectrum that federal cash and in-kind transfer programs have reduced the extent of poverty, the costs have been high. In fiscal 1981, benefit payments to individuals accounted for 48.2 percent of the federal budget (Palmer & Mills 1982:65). Moreover, since the majority of the previously poor owe their improved status to transfer payments rather than to employment income, benefit reductions return many to poverty, as Joe indicates. The extent of poverty in this country increased from 13.2 percent of the population in 1980 to 14.0 percent in 1981, the highest figure since 1967 (Palmer & Sawhill 1982:19).

Apart from cost, one objection to these social programs is that they favor certain family and living arrangements over others. Many income maintenance and tax policies were designed to preserve the traditional nuclear family structure and to ensure family stability, but often had the opposite effect. AFDC regulations denied aid to households with an able-bodied father present until the

1960s, when the states were given the option of including families with unemployed fathers. Less than one-half have done so. Consequently, the program has been charged with fostering "divorce, separation and desertion" (Blaydon & Stack 1977). Pearce and McAdoo comment on this issue in "Women and Children: Alone and in Poverty."

New workers unable to find jobs, the working poor, and families with able-bodied male heads have received less support than other groups -- for example, the blind and disabled (Lynn 1980:218). As the chapter by Joe illustrates, the working poor are hardest hit by current and proposed cuts in AFDC and related programs. Issues of fairness also arise because some families and individuals receive assistance but others who are just as needy do not. Families in the same circumstances who live in different states receive different cash payments, as the chapter by Joe makes clear.

Some policy analysts favor a neutral family policy, but an attempt to be fair to one group may have unfavorable or unintended impacts. For example, policies designed to recognize that a single-parent family often lacks the income-generating potential of a two-parent one might encourage family dissolution. Pronatalist policies that give greater benefits or tax credits to large families are considered unfair to single individuals and childless couples.

The fairness of other government programs is questioned too. Perhaps the most frequently heard complaint about the tax laws concerns the "marriage penalty" which means that working couples pay higher taxes than their unmarried counterparts do. To solve this problem a new tax bill lowers the tax rate for dual-earner married couples. Tax policies tend to favor the well-to-do, and recent tax reductions and budget cuts increase this effect. A recent Congressional Budget Office (1982: ii, iii) analysis of the impact of the tax and benefit reductions enacted in 1981 concluded that "gains from federal tax reductions rise substantially with income" and that "reductions in federal benefit payments for individuals will be greatest for households with incomes below $10,000." For example, households with incomes over $80,000 will pay on average about $15,000 less in taxes in 1983, compared to about $120 less for households with incomes under $10,000.

Work incentives and the goal of economic independence. An important goal of income maintenance programs for the poor has been to foster economic independence by helping recipients to enter the labor force or improve their earning ability (See Pearce and McAdoo's evaluation of their success). Few programs have adequate job training provisions so that recipients can become self-supporting. With the Comprehensive Employment and Training Act (CETA) being phased out, job training possibilities are scarce. No new large-scale jobs programs have been introduced, despite high unemployment rates.

Although programs like AFDC increasingly include language about the necessity for recipients to obtain employment, they are often criticized for discouraging work effort. Benefits in income-tested programs decrease sharply as earnings from employment rise. This work disincentive has been increased by changes introduced by the Reagan administration. Joe analyzes how families of the working poor may be worse off when adults work.

Some state and local authorities have imposed workfare requirements on public assistance recipients. This punitive component of programs may satisfy those who believe that assistance has to be earned, but it does not help poor people acquire the skills needed for economic independence. Furthermore, although many Americans believe that welfare recipients do not want to work, many already do as Joe indicates. They do not earn sufficient income to support themselves and their families.

Social Security: A System in Need of Change

Social insurance programs consist of old age insurance (including survivors' and dependents' benefits), Medicare, and Supplemental Security Income (SSI) which benefits those whose incomes fall below the poverty level despite Social Security and other income sources (Smeeding & Garfinkel 1980:4). Benefits are financed through payroll taxes paid equally by employers and workers (Gordon 1979:225). Since 1979, a worker's past earnings have been indexed and then averaged so that benefits automatically increase to reflect rises in the cost of living. This provision is now being reconsidered because of the costs to government. Future increases may be delayed.

Recent changes in family composition and roles have led to recommendations that the Social Security system be modified. Criticism of the system revolves largely around equity issues: fairness to women vs. men, to married vs. divorced individuals, to single vs. married individuals, and to one-earner vs. two-earner couples. These concerns reflect the substantial increases in dual-income couples and the high rates of divorce and remarriage. The treatment of women as the economic dependents of men is another aspect of the system that is criticized.

Although the original proposal covered only individual workers, the system quickly was changed to include benefits for dependents. The differential treatment of men and women exists because Social Security was designed to meet the needs of traditional families with males in the labor force and females as full-time homemakers. Since home production was unpaid, it was labeled "nonwork" and considered without monetary value (Department of Justice 1979:6-7). Consequently, a pension system developed which generally ignored non-working women (Department of Justice 1979:15). This assumption, that wives are economically dependent on their spouses ignores the value of the homemaker's contribution to the family and also leads to inequitable treatment of dual-earner couples.

The spouse of a retired worker is entitled to benefits equal to 50 percent of the spouse's benefits. However, employed wives who themselves are entitled to benefits receive whichever of the two amounts is larger. Similarly, when a worker dies, a spouse is entitled to survivors' benefits--either the decreased's or his/her own, whichever is higher. Therefore, the spouse who earns the smaller amount is duplicating benefits rather than adding to the couple's total lifetime income.

Chapter 19, "Men and Women: Changing Roles and Social Security," is excerpted from a study by the Social Security Administration with assistance from the Department of Justice Task Force on Sex Discrimination and several other groups. The two proposals for reform to meet equity and adequacy considerations explored in this study were: earnings sharing and a double-decker benefit structure. Recent *Social Security Bulletin* articles (Ling 1982; Reno & Rader 1982) have analyzed the current and projected future benefits of individuals and two-worker couples. Reno and Rader (1982) expect a growing proportion of married women to become insured for benefits in their own right. They also estimate that the highest average benefits will be paid to couples in which the wife would be dually entitled; the lowest, to couples in which the wife would receive a spouse benefit only.

A recent change recognizes the prevalence of divorce. Divorced wives who do not remarry now receive the same benefits as if they were still married, provided the marriage lasted ten years. Moreover, the benefits paid to current spouses are unaffected by these payments (Gordon 1979:226). However, divorced homemakers who do not remarry receive low benefits, especially while the ex-husband is alive. No distinction is made between those divorced when they have many years of potential worklife ahead of them and those divorced in their later years, who may have few marketable skills. Even if these older women successfully enter (or reenter) the labor force, they probably will not amass substantial benefits in their own right and they cannot add the benefits they acquire onto their benefits as divorced spouses (ibid.:228).

Dual-earner couples receive fewer benefits relative to the Social Security taxes paid than do single-earner couples. Despite paying considerably higher taxes, they are entitled to no more in benefits than a single-earner couple with the same lifetime income receives (Gordon 1979:228). Furthermore, the survivor in a dual-earner marriage is likely to receive even lower benefits than does the survivor of a single-earner marriage. At the same time, single workers are penalized. Even though single and married workers are taxed at the same rate, married workers receive higher benefits because spouses also receive payments.

Policy proposals for changes in the system differ according to the aspect considered most unacceptable and, sometimes, the critic's views of marriage and family. Those who believe women should be considered individuals in their own right, not economic dependents of men, propose that pension rights be vested in the individual. Others, who want to strengthen the traditional family, recommend Social Security benefits for homemakers to encourage them to stay home to raise children. President Carter's Advisory Committee for Women recommended that proposals for including homemakers in unemployment compensation, disability insurance, and Social Security be studied. These provisions reflect the recognition of marriage as an economic partnership.

Those who stress equality recommend that earnings be shared so that benefit claims built up during a marriage would be divided equally between spouses. Advantages to this approach are that homemakers would have an individually vested claim and, at the same time, a couple's total earnings would be used to compute benefits, even if one spouse had a pattern of irregular labor force participation. As Gordon (1979:255) points out, a shared-earnings plan is "the most neutral policy regarding labor force participation decisions of married women." This alternative is discussed in Chapter 19, "Men and Women: Changing Roles and Social Security."

Although changes in the Social Security system could prevent many future inequities, they will do little to improve the economic status of very old women today. Chapter 18, "Policy Options for Older Women" emphasizes the plight of older women, especially the very old. Societal views about women as economic dependents, discrimination against women workers, and the inadequate treatment of women in both public and private pensions combine to place many of the oldest in poverty or near poverty. Major recommendations are to improve pension benefits for women, to encourage employment opportunities for older women, and to improve programs and services for older persons. The report was prepared before the Reagan administration took office and prospects for implementing the recommendations are not encouraging.

The Reagan administration's primary goal with regard to Social Security is to ensure the soundness of the system. Consequently, its actions are likely to result in decreased benefits for recipients in the future. The recommendations of the panel appointed to study the system, which have been adopted, will have this effect, as well as delaying cost-of-living increases for recipients.

What a Difference a Decade Makes: Policy in the '80s

Income maintenance and social welfare represent areas in which the Reagan administration has made a distinct break with the past. In part, these changes substitute primary concerns with efficiency and cost containment for the concerns about the equity and adequacy of programs prominent since the "War on Poverty" and "Great Society" programs of the 1960s and early 1970s. As Morris (1979:49, 58) noted, the principles of the 1930s continued to guide programs into the 1960s and 1970s. Efforts were directed toward improving benefits and helping the disadvantaged to improve their economic status through a wide array of educational, job training, and public sector employment programs.

The current administration's policies reflect its philosophy about what government should and should not do. It has greatly narrowed and even seems to reject the concept of entitlement, which has led to expanded benefits for the poor, elderly, and disabled. Eligibility for many programs is being redefined in an attempt to limit benefits to "the truly needy," defined loosely as those who literally would starve without assistance.

The emphasis on containing costs has led to substantial curtailing of social welfare programs, including AFDC, food stamps, job training, Medicaid, and child nutrition and health programs. However, attempts to decrease expenditures for Social Security have not been successful, largely because of protests by well-organized groups and the unwillingness of politicians to take such unpopular action in an election year. This issue will be dealt with in 1983, when attempts to institute reforms will be made.

Meanwhile, the burden is falling most heavily on the poor. Joe's analysis of the Reagan administration's public assistance cuts shows how the situation of poor families has become more precarious. Work disincentives, one of the most damaging aspects of the recent changes, make it difficult, if not impossible, for recipients to move gradually toward economic independence. Children may suffer the most from the changes in public assistance and in health, nutrition, and educational programs, and many will be locked into poverty as adults. The opportunity structure for both adults and children has been considerably diminished with the elimination of many War-on-Poverty programs discussed in Chapter 15, "Promoting the Welfare of Americans."

The chapters by Pearce and McAdoo and by Joe leave the impression that the chances have decreased for disadvantaged families to move out of poverty. The situation for such families may worsen. Recent research (Smeeding 1982) indicating that the number of persons considered poor would decrease if in-kind transfer payments were counted as income could be used to justify further cuts in entitlement programs. A second detrimental change would occur if AFDC were turned over to the states, as President Reagan has proposed. Such a shift would increase the inequities so graphically illustrated in Joe's chapter. The federal government assumed responsibility for welfare in the first place because the state programs were so inequitable.

Furthermore, with budget deficits soaring, additional cuts in social programs are likely. Some past cuts are beginning to hit home now, as many states facing their own budget crises are unable to make up for federal fund losses. Many families will begin to suffer from the effects of decreased funds at both the federal and state levels which, in turn, will affect the ability of local governments to maintain current program and service levels.

References

Blaydon, Colin C., and Carol B. Stack.

1977 "Income Support Policies and the Family." Working Paper. Center for the Study of the Family and State, Institute of Policy Sciences and Public Affairs, Duke University.

Congressional Budget Office.

1982 "Effects of Tax and Benefit Reductions Enacted in 1981 for Households in Different Income Categories." Special Study prepared by the Staff of the Human Resources and Community Development Division and the Tax Analysis Division. Pursuant to the Separate Requests of Senator Ernest F. Hollings and Chairman James R. Jones. Feb.

Danziger, Sheldon, and Robert Plotnick.

1981 "Income Maintenance Programs and the Pursuit of Income Security." *Annals of the American Academy of Political and Social Science* (Jan.):130-52.

Gordon, Nancy M.
1979 "Institutional Responses: The Social Security System." Pp. 223-255 in Ralph E. Smith (ed.), *The Subtle Revolution: Women at Work.* Washington, D.C.: Urban Institute.

Lingg, Barbara A.
1982 "Social Security Benefits of Female Retired Workers and Two-Worker Couples." *Social Security Bulletin* 45, 2 (Feb.):3-24.

Lynn, Laurence E., Jr.
1980 "Fiscal and Organizational Constraints on United States Family Policy." Pp. 199-230 in Joan Aldous and Wilfried Dumon (eds.), *The Politics and Programs of Family Policy: United States and European Perspectives.* Notre Dame, Indiana and Leuven, Belgium: University of Notre Dame Press and Leuven University Press.

Morris, Robert.
1979 *Social Policy of the American Welfare State: An Introduction to Policy Analysis.* New York: Harper and Row.

Palmer, John L., and Gregory Mills.
1982 "Budget Policy." Pp. 59-95 in John L. Palmer and Isabel V. Sawhill (eds.), *The Reagan Experiment.* Washington, D.C.: Urban Institute.

Palmer, John L., and Isabel V. Sawhill.
1982 "Perspectives on the Reagan Experiment." Pp. 1-28 in Palmer and Sawhill (1982).

Reno, Virginia, and Anne Dee Rader.
1982 "Benefits for Individual Retired Workers and Couples Now Approaching Retirement Age." *Social Security Bulletin* 45, no. 2 (Feb.):25-31.

Smeeding, Timothy M.
1982 "Alternative Methods of Valuing Selected In-Kind Transfer Benefits." U.S. Bureau of the Census. Washington, D.C.: U.S. Government Printing Office.

Smeeding, Timothy M., and Irwin Garfinkel.
1980 "New Directions for Income Transfer Programs," *Monthly Labor Review* (Feb.):41-45.

U.S. Department of Justice, Task Force on Sex Discrimination, Civil Rights Division.
1979 *The Pension Game: The American Pension System from the Viewpoint of the Average Woman.* Washington, D.C.: U.S. Government Printing Office.

Suggested Additional Readings

Beckerman, Wilfred, et al.
1979 *Poverty and the Impact of Income Maintenance Programmes in Four Developed Countries: Case Studies of Australia, Belgium, Norway, and Great Britain.* Geneva: International Labour Office.

Foner, Anne, and Karen Schwab.
1981 *Aging and Retirement.* Monterey, Cal.: Brooks/Cole.

Garfinkel, Irwin (ed.).
1982 *Income-Tested Transfer Programs: The Case For and Against.* New York: Academic Press.

Hudson, Robert B.
1981 *The Aging in Politics: Process and Policy.* Springfield, Ill.: Charles C Thomas.

Piven, Frances Fox, and Richard W. Cloward.
1971 *Regulating the Poor: The Functions of Public Welfare.* New York: Random House.

15. PROMOTING THE WELFARE OF AMERICANS IN THE 1980s

President's Commission for a National Agenda for the Eighties

The present public welfare system consists of layer upon layer of outdated, sometimes redundant, programs. The bureaucratic complexity of the system helps to defeat its object: many persons in need do not receive adequate assistance.

Some of the needs overlooked by the public systems are supplied by private charities and other nonprofit organizations, whose contributions are, and will continue to be, vital to the public good. Nevertheless, the design and implementation of public welfare programs clearly require significant improvement. The Panel is of the opinion that this can best be accomplished by replacing the current maze of programs with a minimum security income.

It cannot be denied that the multiplicity of programs in place today embodies an approach that has not been entirely successful. Poverty persists in America--official estimates placed the number of the poor at 25 million in 1976. This figure comes from Bureau of the Census estimates of how many people have incomes below the official poverty standard. The standard is derived by computing the cost of a "temporary, low budget, nutritious diet" and multiplying that result by a constant chosen to represent the amount of income a family should spend on food. The official poverty standard is modest; in 1978 the poverty level for a typical urban family of four was $6,665 (Bureau of the Census 1978:15).

Some experts dispute the official statistics because the value of such programs as food stamps and Medicaid is not included. By the most optimistic estimates, one with which this Panel has serious disagreements, 8 million Americans remain poor.

The poor suffer real hardship. Often they do not get enough to eat, and they experience more than their share of sickness. Those poor families that manage to

---

Reprinted from Chapter 3 of the President's Commission for a National Agenda for the Eighties, *Government and the Advancement of Social Justice: Health, Welfare, Education, and Civil Rights in the Eighties.* Washington: U.S. Government Printing Office, 1980, pp. 55-71.

obtain welfare face a harsh existence. An Illinois family on welfare, for example, receives about $500 a month. If $215 is spent for shelter and $149 is used to purchase food, only $136 remains to cover the cost of clothing, household supplies, and everything else. Those who fail to obtain welfare live even more debilitating lives.[1]

Poverty and Social Expenditures

The American poor are not randomly distributed. Women account for about two-thirds of the adult poor, and nonwhites are more than twice as likely to be poor as are whites. In fact, almost 16 percent of all nonwhite families were poor in 1976. Government programs do aid nonwhites; but they actually benefit whites more than nonwhites (Pearce 1978; U.S. Commission on Civil Rights 1978; Congressional Budget Office 1977).

The incidence of poverty also varies by region. Recent data show that the South has twice as many poor people as do the North Central states, even after welfare and Social Security benefits are paid (Congressional Budget Office 1977:16).

More disturbing than this persistence of poverty along sexual, racial, and regional lines are recent trends in income levels. Between 1968 and 1972 real income per household rose only 1.7 percent, and the number of families placed in poverty began to increase. Between 1972 and 1976, this trend was exacerbated; real income per household actually dropped 5.0 percent (Danziger & Plotnick 1980).

It has been argued that the eradication of poverty is an unreasonable goal, one that does not belong on an agenda for the 1980s. The poorest of poor Americans, after all, lives well by world standards. In addition, some analysts think that the nation already spends too much on social welfare, and that the creation of a large welfare establishment has unintentionally erected barriers that prevent people from rising above poverty. The nation, in this view, may have reached the limit of its ability to do good.

The United States does spend a great deal of money for social purposes. Between 1960 and 1975, social welfare expenditures more than quadrupled to $1,319 dollars per capita.[2] Expenditures that fall more strictly under the heading of welfare have increased at an even greater rate, rising from $34 per capita in 1950 to approximately $187 in 1975. Some $394 billion, a figure equivalent to 19.3 percent of the gross national product (GNP), were spent on social welfare in 1978. In 1965 this share was 11.5 percent.

Social welfare expenditures reached a peak of 20.4 percent of the gross national product in 1975. Their share of the gross national product and of total government spending has declined since 1976. The real rate of growth in social welfare expenditures declined to 2.5 percent by 1979 (Social Security 1980). Because of inflation and other factors that constrain the federal budget, this decline in the growth of social welfare expenditures will probably continue; only a severe recession will arrest the trend.

The Institutional Setting

The only rationale for the existing welfare system is historical. Each program represents a small piece of history, embodying a politically acceptable approach to a particular problem at the time of the program's creation. There are at least five distinct types of welfare programs, each of which reflects a different approach to aiding the poor or ending poverty. Briefly described, the five types of programs are designed to:

- Aid members of the "deserving poor";
- Define minimum standards;
- Insure against loss of income;
- Support the purchase of essentials; and
- Provide, or promote, opportunity.

Today's system is an uncoordinated collection of past efforts to accomplish not one end, but many.

Aid to the "deserving poor." In the oldest kind of program, the government aids those members of the community who are unable to care for themselves: the very young, the very old, and the disabled. The traditional means of helping such dependent persons was to place them under the care of a family or of the community itself.

In time, institutions such as orphanages and poor farms began to replace this informal system. By 1900, states permitted counties to provide cash grants to the deserving poor. Reliance on local governments to provide aid to the poor ended with the passage of the Social Security Act in 1935, when Congress authorized federal aid to the states for grants to the needy elderly, the blind, and dependent children.

The creation of these federal public assistance categories marked the beginning of what is now called welfare. The basic approach was inherited from the earlier state laws. If a person could show that he was elderly, blind, or a dependent child, and if he could demonstrate need, then he received a cash payment from the local authorities. The federal government paid a portion of the local government's expenses.

With the entry of the federal government into the field of welfare, the informality and flexibility characteristic of local arrangements gave way to rigid categories mandated at the federal level. This approach offered the benefit of what experts call target efficiency--it reached only the poor--but it left gaps in coverage. One had to be more than poor to receive government aid; one had to belong to the "deserving poor," to be old, young, blind, or permanently and totally disabled.

Definition of minimum standards. Another type of welfare program, one that defined minimum standards, began during the Progressive Era at the turn of the century. Progressive reformers advocated, and saw passed, protective labor legislation that set minimum standards for working conditions. Typical laws of this kind included child labor laws, maximum hours and minimum wage requirements, safety standards, and workers' compensation laws.

These laws answered perceived needs of the Progressive Era. It should be recalled that women were discouraged from working in those years, and that many Americans were concerned about the disruptions caused by rapid immigration. Conditions differ today. No longer does the nation wish to exclude women or those of foreign origin from the labor force. No longer is there a strict distinction between occupational and nonoccupational problems; no longer does the government limit itself to promulgating social welfare standards, instead taking an active role in maintaining incomes and in protecting people against the risk of sickness. Despite these circumstantial changes, the turn-of-the-century program of minimum standards endures as an American approach to social welfare.

This "standards of decency" approach is beneficial in some respects; however, it has the drawback of sometimes substituting the wish for the deed, particularly in the case of minimum wages. Mandating minimum wages does not ensure that everyone will receive them; it may mean instead that employers choose not to hire those workers whose productivity fails to merit the minimum wage. Ironically, it is the young, the disabled, and the members of minority groups--precisely those whom society seeks to protect through minimum wage legislation--who may suffer by that wage's existence.

Social insurance. A third type of welfare program, government insurance against loss of income, owes its origin to the passage of the Social Security Act in 1935. The act created an old-age insurance program; its reach has since been broadened to include survivors' insurance (1939), disability insurance (1956), and health insurance for the elderly (1965). As a result, a program that cost $23.5 million in 1940 now costs $9 billion (in current dollars) and reaches 3.5 million people each month.

Unemployment compensation, or temporary payments to workers laid off from their jobs, also began in 1935 with the passage of the Social Security Act. This program differed from Social Security in that it was run by the states instead of the federal government. Such program details as which workers were eligible for benefits and the number of weeks they could receive benefits varied greatly from state to state. From a national perspective, the unemployment compensation program, like Social Security, has expanded greatly; the program cost $500 million in 1939 and $17 billion in 1975 [in current dollars] (Hamermesh 1979).

President Roosevelt, in describing Social Security and unemployment compensation, and federal officials, in administering the programs, took pains not to connect the words "welfare" and "social insurance." Social security was portrayed as a reliable government insurance program to which all Americans paid premiums and from which all Americans received benefits. These benefits came to people as a matter of right, and the program provided money to rich and poor alike. Programs for the poor, officials believed, made poor programs.

Both Social Security and unemployment insurance, however, contained what could be seen as welfare elements. To deal with the problem of paying everyone adequate benefits, for instance, planners allowed low-wage earners a higher rate of return on their Social Security and unemployment compensation premiums than high-wage earners.

Social Security possessed the additional feature of taking money from workers and giving it to the elderly and disabled. Under the original design of the program, a worker and his employer deposited money in a Social Security account; the worker was to receive it back with interest upon his retirement. In an effort to broaden coverage, raise benefits, and lower payroll taxes, Congress altered the system so that it could be run on a pay-as-you-go basis. After 1939, current workers and their employers paid for the current group of retirees and disabled workers.

The insurance analogy helped to establish Social Security and enabled the program to grow. The very size and success of the program, in turn, produced demands that it do more than insure against loss of income, that it help to deal with some of America's welfare problems. As a public assistance vehicle, however, Social Security was flawed. First, the program failed to reach people outside the labor force who had no income to insure. Second, it developed funding problems that were related to its special feature of relying upon employment and employee contributions. Benefit levels were increased faster than were payroll taxes; this led to occasional shortages in the fund that was used to pay the benefits. (When the postwar generation retires after 2010, this problem will become severe.) Finally, a program built upon the social assumptions of the 1930s contained many outdated elements by the 1980s. Divorced women, for example, received less than did married women.

Aid to purchase essentials. The intent of a fourth type of government program is to ensure that participants are able to purchase certain essential goods and services, such as food or medical care. Food stamps, for example, may in their modern form be traced to an unsuccessful New Deal experiment and a Kennedy administration program of 1961.

The food stamp program was extended to the entire nation by Congress in 1964, but it experienced only modest growth until late in the decade (McDonald 1973). The food stamp program expanded rapidly between 1968 and 1971 for two reasons. First, themes sounded by the Robert Kennedy campaign and by civil rights activists and other reformers made the existence of hunger in an otherwise affluent society unacceptable. Something had to be done to feed the poor quickly, and the food stamp program was conveniently at hand, ready for increased appropriations. Second, members of the Nixon administration and others who favored simplifying the welfare system saw in food stamps an approach that provided the poor with essentials and could be--in fact, was--administered at the local level. Conservative and liberal members of Congress, able to agree on little else, compromised on the expansion of food stamps. In a series of amendments, benefit levels were increased, uniform eligibility standards were promulgated, and all counties were required to have a program. One authority has called the expansion of food stamps "the most important change in public welfare policy since the passage of the Social Security Act in 1935."[3] The growth of Medicaid, a program that enabled the poor to purchase medical care, matched that of food stamps.

These programs fill real needs, and help to remedy gaps in the American welfare system. Still, these essential purchase programs raise the question of whether the government knows better than the individual what it is good for him [or her] to have. Essential purchase aid, in short, owes more to political expediency than to rational planning.

Promotion of opportunity. The four classes of welfare programs already discussed involve maintaining the needy. A fifth kind of government aid attempts to raise the poor above poverty by education, rehabilitation, provision of a special social service, or placement in a job.

Welfare programs featuring such government sponsorship of expanded opportunity originated in the 1920s when the benefits of rehabilitation were recognized: instead of allowing a person to become a welfare recipient, he could be trained, counselled, or cured to become a productive citizen. This transformation was doubly attractive, for it contributed to the public as well as the individual good. Among the programs that followed this approach were vocational education and vocational rehabilitation.

These efforts were not meant to include large numbers of people. Each program worked selectively, concentrating on a few clients, and all were run by the casework principle. Vocational rehabilitation, for example, was a painstaking process of direct interviews between a disabled client and a counselor. Each counselor could handle only 75 to 100 cases at any one time; coupled with the small number of counselors, this constraint severely limited the number of people the program could serve. As the counselors were forced to choose among clients, they often selected the most promising clients, those who needed the least help. Rehabilitation programs, therefore, served the mildly impaired and not the severely disabled.

Government efforts to improve opportunity suffered from the fact that they were only as strong as the economy. Almost all of the programs took as their object the eventual placement of their clients into the general labor market. In times of high employment, such as the 1920s, the approach worked relatively well; in hard times the approach almost always failed. These programs, then, failed to deal with the distress caused by recession or depression.

After World War II, an increase in the welfare rolls and an emerging belief that the nation had the means to end poverty prompted a new interest in government promotion of opportunity. The problems of the older programs were forgotten as the nation launched a new series of programs. In 1962, a well-known Congressional supporter spoke of a "realistic program which will pay dividend on every dollar invested. It can move some persons off the assistance rolls entirely, enable others to attain a high degree of self-confidence and independence, encourage children to grow strong in mind and body."[4] Two years later, President Johnson (1965:988) announced the start of the War on Poverty by observing, "We are not content to accept the endless growth of relief rolls or welfare rolls. We want to offer the forgotten fifth of our people opportunity and not doles."

Although the optimism engendered by this hopeful rhetoric faded, a large social service establishment remained. In addition to the programs begun in the 1920s, many states offered a full range of supplementary services, often including day care, family planning, and special transportation programs. In fiscal year 1979, in fact, federal spending for social services amounted to nearly $2.6 billion (General Accounting Office 1980).

Despite its shortcomings, government promotion of opportunity continues to be a politically attractive means of aiding the poor. Conservative politicians have supported it as an alternative to public assistance, one that is expected to reduce government spending in the long run. Liberal politicians have regarded the strategy as one way of increasing vital social services. Members of both groups like the implicit idea of a permanent solution, through jobs, to the welfare problem.

The most recent example of this type of welfare program is the Comprehensive Employment and Training Act (CETA) of 1974. This consolidation of federal manpower programs includes social services for adults who are the victims of structural unemployment. In addition, CETA authorizes the Secretary of Labor to provide special services to such groups as native Americans, migrant and seasonal farmworkers, displaced homemakers, the handicapped, persons of limited English-speaking ability, offenders, older workers, and public assistance recipients. Half-buried under layers of confusing regulations and dense jargon, government promotion of opportunity remains an important type of U.S. welfare program.

Inherited Problems

There are, then, not one but at least five types of government welfare programs. The nation also maintains a large number of private charities, and from an individual's point of view, the result is often confusion. For example, a recently widowed mother of several children, one of whom is disabled, may now apply to seven federal programs for aid. In a typical jurisdiction, she will have to go to at least four different offices, fill out at least five different forms, and answer some three hundred separate questions. The programs may treat the information obtained from these forms differently; the value of the same car, for example, is almost sure to differ from program to program. Fourteen hundred pieces of information may be needed just to determine accurately the level of the woman's income. This illustration underscores the 1974 finding of a Congressional subcommittee: Instead of forming a coordinated network...our... income maintenance programs are an assortment of fragmented efforts that distribute income to various persons for various purposes, sometimes on conflicting terms and with unforeseen results" (Joint Economic Committee 1974).

Despite pleas for simplification, the separate tactics of government aid to the "deserving poor," definition of minimum standards, insurance against loss of income, aid to purchase essentials, and promotion of opportunity all contribute to the present American welfare system. This system is, in effect, a catalogue of historical approaches to social welfare; it features the very oldest as well as the very newest ideas. Attempts to reform the current set of welfare programs must relieve the confusion caused by the persistence of programs long after the time of their enactment.

...

Adequacy, Equity, Efficiency

Many of the problems of AFDC and the other programs of the U.S. social welfare system concern the three goals of a modern welfare system--equity, adequacy, and efficiency. Ideally, the nation's welfare programs should treat similar people in a similar manner, [according to] the concept of equity. It should provide benefits that give all households an income above the poverty level, the goal of adequacy, and it should contain incentives to substitute work for welfare wherever possible, the target of efficiency. The present system meets none of these criteria.

The system fails to meet the goal of equity in part because the programs classify people according to the original "deserving poor" categories. As a Congressional subcommittee noted, "with few exceptions, people are only more or less employable, not employable or unemployable" (Joint Economic Committee 1974). This modern truth suggests that the "deserving poor" approach to welfare creates fundamental inequities. An able-bodied person of working age who has neither children nor job skills can be poor; so can a 59-year-old man whose health is breaking down. Neither of these people qualifies for federal assistance, but others in similar circumstances, who have children or are a few years older, do qualify.

Sometimes the requirements of the programs produce social pathologies that compound the system's inequities. To use a pointed example, a Minnesota mother of three could receive AFDC, Medicaid, and food stamps until her income reached $8,000 a year. A Minnesota father who remained with his family and worked full-time at a low wage disqualified his family for aid, regardless of need. In 1972, according to a congressional subcommittee, a man who worked for $2.00 an hour could increase the annual income of his family (a wife and two children) by an average of $2,158 if he deserted them (Joint Economic Committee 1974). The system in these cases rewarded one family over another, and many would argue that it rewarded the wrong family.

Because welfare benefits cannot be given to everyone, an income level beyond which aid is terminated is established. This threshold, or notch, produces inequities. If a person who earns $19 is entitled to Medicaid, but someone who earns $20 is not, severe problems result. By making $1 less, the first person gains benefits worth a great deal; he begins by making less money and ends by having the use of more money than the second person. The second person may decide that he will be better off if he works less. A welfare system with sharp notches, therefore, produces inefficiencies as well as inequities.

The persistence of poverty testifies to the fact that the goal of adequate benefits is not being met. Some people who qualify for benefits fail to receive them; others live in the twenty-four states where benefits from AFDC and food stamps amounted to less than three-quarters of the poverty line in 1977. Still others reside in states with comparatively high welfare benefits that have not been adjusted for inflation and have consequently become less than adequate.

The welfare system fails to meet the goals of adequacy, equity, and efficiency. Once programs are in place they tend to stay in place, long after the conditions that created them, and the needs to which they should respond, have changed. These observations argue for the need to create a coherent welfare system.

A Systematic Approach

The events of the past twenty years may be seen as the maturing of the social welfare system. In a mature system, coverage ceases to be limited to a small and select group; a far greater percentage of the poor benefits from social programs. Work incentives become important as programs reach beyond the "deserving poor" and begin to affect labor force participants. Receipt of multiple benefits becomes more common. By these criteria, the social welfare programs of the past 20 years have begun to function systematically. This tendency would be far greater if the interactions and common effects of programs were carefully considered during the planning process.

A number of schemes for such reform of the system have recently received public attention. Many plans rely upon the idea of a negative income tax, an idea that followed from the observation that welfare programs penalize work. If a person who earns a dollar loses a dollar in welfare benefits, he has little incentive to work, because there is, in effect, a tax of 100 percent on his earnings. To remedy the problem, he must be allowed to keep a certain percentage of his earnings. In fact, federal officials have long tried to create work incentives within individual programs, but the results of these experiments have been unsatisfactory.

The negative income tax. If a universal negative income tax were adopted, all families would receive the guarantee of a minimum cash benefit and pay a tax of less than 100 percent on earnings. Suppose there were a guaranteed benefit of $2,000 and a 50 percent tax rate on earnings. A family with no earnings would receive the guarantee of $2,000 from the government. A family that earned $2,000 would receive the guarantee and keep half of its earnings; the guarantee of $2,000 and the after-tax earnings of $1,000 and total $3,000, so the government would give $1,000 to this family. A family that earned $4,000 would receive the guarantee and retain $2,000 in earnings, for a total of $4,000; this family would neither receive money from the government nor owe the government money.

In the 1970s the negative income tax moved from the realm of idea to the status of a serious congressional proposal with the introduction of the Nixon administration's Family Assistance Plan (FAP). The Family Assistance Plan contained a proposal to provide a federal minimum cash payment to all families with dependent children; the AFDC program would have been eliminated. The bill containing the Family Assistance Plan was not passed, but it was followed by a series of proposals that used the negative income tax idea. In 1974 the Income Supplement Program proposal appeared; this was a negative income tax scheme that would have replaced food stamps, AFDC, and welfare programs for the elderly and disabled. Later in the decade, the Joint Economic Committee's Subcommittee on Fiscal Policy recommended a negative income tax after 3 years of study (Joint Economic Committee 1974).

Although the negative income tax failed to gain congressional passage, those programs that were created followed the general principles of a negative income tax. Amendments to the food stamp program transformed it into a guaranteed income, payable in food stamps, and Supplemental Security Income created a guaranteed annual income for the elderly and the disabled. Administrative control over the traditional welfare categories (the aged, the blind, and the disabled) was transferred from the states to the federal government. In 1974, when the Supplemental Security Income exemplified a creative blend of new ideas and old traditions. These programs follow two of the traditional American approaches to welfare, aid to the "deserving poor" and aid to purchase essentials; at the same time, they incorporate new ideas about work incentives and efficient administration associated with negative income tax schemes.

Obstacles to comprehensive reform. The more ambitious aspects of the negative income tax proposals, such as a guaranteed income for the working poor, failed partly because they demanded sacrifices from groups that fare relatively well under existing programs, such as veterans of foreign wars and the blind. Welfare programs that accommodate such special interests retained their appeal because they concentrated benefits upon a readily identifiable group, a seemingly sensible tactic in a small welfare system. Under modern conditions, this practice blocks systematic reform by creating groups that have nothing to gain from such reform.

The negative income tax proposals also failed because legislators had few opportunities to acquire a comprehensive view of the social welfare system. Committee structures helped to lock legislators into a program-by-program view of social policy. Control over income maintenance, for example, was divided among more than sixty Congressional committees and subcommittees in 1980.[5] This circumstance helped to reinforce legislators' natural loyalties to programs they had helped to design or to pass, loyalties that are abandoned only reluctantly.

More than political and structural considerations prevented the passage of a negative income tax; there were also serious questions related to cost. Locked within the arithmetic were difficult social choices. Providing adequate benefits just for the poor requires setting high tax rates on additional income earned by the poor (the marginal tax rate). On the other hand, these high tax rates discourage people from working.

If the marginal tax rate were lowered, the income level at which the government would continue to pay benefits would rise. Halving the tax rate doubles this break-even point, and doubling the break-even point would bring welfare payments to many families not considered poor. Congress showed great reluctance to take this action. In addition, if benefits were available at the income levels earned by the greatest number of families, the number of families on welfare and the costs of welfare programs would both increase greatly.

Results from social experiments suggested potential problems. Attempts to simulate the effects of a negative income tax in Seattle and Denver led to the finding that the negative income tax decreased the number of hours worked, particularly by wives in two-parent families. This phenomenon was the result, in part, of broadening welfare coverage to some groups who were previously excluded. Secure in their new income, some people chose to reduce the number of hours they worked (U.S. Department of Health, Education and Welfare 1978).

Acceptance of the principles of the negative income tax was nevertheless common among welfare reformers by the end of the 1970s. There was widespread agreement that welfare coverage should be expanded, benefits made more equitable, and work incentives improved. The expansion of the food stamps program and the passage of supplemental security income indicated wider acceptance of the tenets, it not all the implications, of a negative income tax.

Guaranteed jobs. By the late 1970s, a new approach to large-scale reform of the welfare system emerged: the concept of a guaranteed job. The poor were to be divided into two groups, one of which was expected to work. Mothers of dependent children, the disabled, and the elderly were not expected to work; they would receive a relatively high guaranteed income. Those who were expected to work would receive a lower guarantee and the opportunity to raise themselves above poverty by means of a guaranteed job. Some of the proposals, such as the Carter administration's program for better jobs and income included an eight-week screening period during which the applicant would receive help in looking for a job in the private sector.... [The applicant unable to find one] would be given either a public service job or a government-subsidized job with a private employer. One source of such employment would be an expanded CETA program.

Although this new idea has much to recommend it, it also presents problems and uncertainties. No one knows if the nation has the ability to find or create jobs for all who want to work. More than a million new jobs may be required, a substantial number of which would be in the public sector. During a severe recession, the numbers of jobs needed would rise, and these jobs may cost the government more than cash payments would. Special social services for mothers of children older than 6, such as after-school programs, may have to be offered, and these services are costly. In addition, no one knows if the recipients would remain in these jobs, move on to private employment, or, indeed, come to work. Wage levels will play a crucial role in this respect. Wages, which cannot be set lower than the minimum wage, may draw many people out of private-sector jobs.

Finally, there remains the vexing problem of separating those who are expected to work from those who are not expected to work. Simple guidelines may apply to families with dependent children, but defining who is disabled has always been difficult. Disability programs have experienced great growth partly because no objective criteria for defining "disability" exist. Often programs rely on impairments, such as the loss of a limb, as the criteria by which to make judgments, and may unfairly relegate many productive people to the disabled category.

General assistance. Some have urged the creation of a means-tested general assistance program under which any person who could demonstrate poverty would receive a flat payment. This approach, explored in various forms by conservative thinkers since the 1950s, has the virtues of directing aid to the poor and reducing total expenditures.

The most recent such proposal would provide federal block grants to the states for the purpose of making welfare payments. Each state would receive the same amount of money that it presently receives for AFDC. States would then be responsible for any cost increases and for any expansions of the program they chose to undertake, and would retain any savings that they were able to effect (Carleson 1980).

Because these plans depend on a caseworker's services, they are frequently both costly and inefficient. The block grant proposal will also perpetuate the disparities that exist in the levels of state welfare payments. States with low benefits would continue to pay low benefits; in fact, they would be rewarded for providing low benefits.

In summary, then, a number of welfare reform proposals have appeared in the past decade. The negative income tax would eliminate some existing programs, substituting an income guarantee and a tax on earnings that would supply incentives to work. Another, the work-and-welfare proposal, would attempt to substitute work and wages for government cash payments. Still another would broaden coverage under a traditional public assistance format. All of these proposals involve thinking about welfare as a comprehensive system rather than as a collection of scattered programs.

Conclusion

At this point the discussion of welfare should be summarized and some conclusions drawn.

Poverty persists in America despite a large array of welfare programs that take at least five distinct approaches to the problem. The system itself consists of layer upon layer of programs. These programs are difficult to enact; they tend to remain in place for a long time, resulting in a system with too many programs that nonetheless leaves many people in need without adequate help.

Changed conditions in the 1980s will make the need for system reform more urgent. The median age of the population will continue to rise, and public attention will shift from the problems of dependent children to those faced by the elderly. In all likelihood, the pressures on the social budget will become more severe. Inflation will continue to affect the economy, and the poor, adversely. Without substantial reform, the welfare system will simply become more of an anachronism, more out of touch with modern problems and needs.

The Panel believes that many types of programs (such as those that set minimum standards, offer aid to purchase essentials, and help the "deserving poor") are no longer as important as they once were. Now the system must work toward providing all Americans, and particularly those Americans with incomes below the poverty line, with a modicum of security.

Income maintenance therefore must take precedence over other welfare goals, even such important goals as employment training and aid to the disadvantaged. The Panel believes that it should be the national policy to seek an end to poverty through the provision of a minimum security income for all Americans, and that this should be affirmed through legislation.

In placing paramount importance on the goal of income maintenance, the Panel does not mean to slight the problems of civil rights, health care, and education. Each of these concerns is addressed elsewhere in this report. This recommendation is based on a simple observation: of all the things the poor desire, they want money most of all, for money enables them to purchase health care, education, and other social services.

Furthermore, testimony before this Commission and other evidence suggest convincingly that income maintenance is a proper function of the federal government. The experience of the 1970s bears out this judgment. Under the rubric of the New Federalism, efforts were made to strengthen local decisionmaking. In the process of sorting out the government's functions, however, the proponents of the New Federalism decided that programs that transferred money from the government to individuals should be administered by the federal government. The Panel agrees with this assessment.

Local governments, for their part, have an important role to play in the provision of social services. People who live in troubled communities know the problems of those communities best, and they deserve a say in how the community deploys its resources to solve those problems. Local governments and private, nonprofit, voluntary charities have worked together closely in the past; the government's provision of a minimum income will free private charity to do its beneficent work.

The private sector must also be prepared to accept responsibility if the nation is to reach its goal of providing a minimum security income for all Americans. Jobs in the private marketplace are the best solution to the problems of welfare. It remains for the government only to secure the essentials of life to its citizens.

The Panel therefore favors the creation of a minimum security income with a guarantee set initially at three-quarters of the poverty line and a 50 percent tax on earnings. This new program would replace Aid to Families with Dependent Children, food stamps, and the general assistance programs. The Supplemental Security Income program would make additional grants to the elderly and disabled in order to bring the income of those groups up to the poverty line.

Many of the objections to this plan will concern its cost. In all likelihood, welfare costs would rise, at least in the first years of the plan. The plan would raise benefits levels in many states, and it would expand welfare coverage. Estimates prepared for this Commission place the additional cost of the minimum security income program to the federal government at $15 billion to $20 billion.[6]

Although the plan would cost a great deal, its advantages outweigh its disadvantages. The plan would end many of the problems created by an incremental approach to welfare and ensure that the welfare system functioned coherently. No longer would the state of Alabama pay an average of $37 to each welfare recipient and the state of Hawaii pay an average of $115, a difference far in excess of the relative costs of living. The plan would establish an incentive for those on welfare to work by lowering the tax on their earnings. It would end the incentive for poor families to separate, and it would go far toward eliminating the burden that the welfare system now places on women.

The plan also offers the government many potential savings. Significant reform of Social Security could occur. States could devote more of their budgets to social services, for they would no longer carry the burden of paying a share of AFDC costs as well as the entire cost of general assistance. In fact, the welfare system could be cleared of much of its clutter and confusion, and private charities could play an expanded role. All of these developments would produce cost savings.

Commissioner Juanita Kreps recently expressed the Panel's views on welfare reform in an eloquent manner. "Eliminating poverty is affordable," she said. "What we cannot afford is its persistent devastation of the human spirit." Twenty years after the beginning of the War on Poverty, the insight remains timely.

Notes

1. President's Commission for a National Agenda for the Eighties, Hearings in Chicago Ill., July 22, 1980, transcript. Testimony of the Public Welfare Coalition for a Humane Public Aid Program in Illinois.

2. The term "social welfare" as used here includes social insurance, public aid, health and medical programs, veterans' programs, education, and housing. Figures are given in current dollars.
3. President's Commission, Hearings, testimony of Richard Nathan.
4. Senator Ribicoff, as quoted in Gilbert Steiner, *Social Insecurity: The Politics of Welfare* (Chicago, 1966), p. 39. The senator is referring to the Public Welfare Amendments of 1962.
5. President's Commission, Hearings, testimony of Senator Durenberger; "U.S. Income Security System Needs Leadership, Policy and Effective Management."
6. Cost estimates were prepared for the Commission by the Urban Institute.

References

Bureau of the Census, U.S. Department of Commerce.
1978 *Current Population Reports.* Series P-60, no. 115. Washington, D.C.

Carleson, Robert B.
1980 "The Alternatives: True Reform or Federalization." *Commonsense* 3:13-23.

Congressional Budget Office.
1977 *Poverty Status of Families Under Alternative Definitions of Income.* Background Paper 19. Washington D.C.: U.S. Government Printing Office.

Danziger, Sheldon, and Robert Plotnick.
1980 "Has the War on Poverty Been Won?" Paper delivered at the Second Annual Middlebury College Conference on Economic Issues, Middlebury, Vt., April.

Hamermesh, Daniel S.
1977 *Jobless Pay and the Economy.* Baltimore: Johns Hopkins press.

MacDonald, Maurice.
1973 *Food Stamps and Income Maintenance.* New York: Academic Press.

Pearce, Diana.
1978 "The Feminization of Poverty: Women, Work and Welfare." *Urban and Social Change Review,* 11 (Feb.):28-36.

Johnson, Lyndon B.
1965 "Remarks upon Signing the Economic Opportunity Act, August 20, 1964." *Public Papers of the Presidents 1963-64.* vol. 2. Washington, D.C.

U.S. Commission on Civil Rights.
1978 *Social Indicators of Equality for Minorities and Women.* Washington, D.C.: U.S. Commission on Civil Rights.

U.S. Congress, General Accounting Office.
1980 "U.S. Income Security System Needs Leadership, Policy, and Effective Management." Washington, D.C.

U.S. Congress, Joint Economic Committee, Subcommittee on Fiscal Policy.
1974 "Income Security for Americans: Recommendations of the Public Welfare Study." Washington, D.C.

U.S. Department of Health and Human Services, Social Security Administration, Office of Research and Statistics.
1978 "Social Welfare Expenditures, Fiscal Year 1978." Research and statistics note.

U.S. Department of Health, Education and Welfare.
1978 *Summary Report: Seattle, Denver Income Maintenance Experiment.* Washington, D.C.
1979 "Monthly Benefit Statistics." Washington, D.C.

16. WOMEN AND CHILDREN: Alone and in Poverty

Diana Pearce and Harriette McAdoo

Two out of three poor adults are women (Census, Social Indicators III 1980). Moreover, families headed by women raising young children are experiencing a steady decline in their economic status. Why are we experiencing this "feminization of poverty"? (Pearce 1978.) What is the role of social welfare programs and policies and what could be the impact of policy on the poverty faced by women? These questions will be addressed in a discussion focusing on the following themes:

- ☐ The decade of the seventies was characterized by a double trend: More of the poor were women, and more women, especially those heading families with minor children, became poor.
- ☐ The unusual amount of stress poor women experience exacts a toll on their physical and emotional health. Informal support systems are important, yet they cannot replace a lack of tangible resources. Adequate income is essential for improved well-being.
- ☐ The causes of women's poverty are different from those of men's poverty. For example, after a divorce, mothers must often bear the economic as well as emotional responsibility of child-rearing, a burden that often impoverishes the family. U.S. welfare policies do not work for women because they have been based on the "male pauper" model of poverty and do not take account of the special nature of women's poverty.
- ☐ Women who are members of ethnic minority groups are more likely to suffer the curse of poverty.
- ☐ Social welfare efforts to reduce welfare dependency and poverty among women are blunted by societal ambivalence toward economic and social independence of women, as well as concerns about maintaining marital stability.

- ☐ Inappropriate theories of the causes of poverty and inconsistent policies and goals designed to alleviate it have led to the development of a dual welfare system, divided according to gender and race.

  This process combines with the dual labor market to reinforce economic inequality. Those in the secondary sphere of the labor market, who are increasingly and disproportionately women and minorities, find themselves locked into a combination of welfare and marginal work that can be best characterized as a "workhouse without walls" (Pearce 1978:35).
- ☐ To alleviate women's poverty, social welfare policy must focus on two crucial areas: (1) the services, particularly quality day care, that are essential for wage-earning mothers; and (2) the structures and practices that bar women from jobs now held by men with similar education, skills and experience in the labor force.[1]

American society can reverse the trend toward increased impoverishment of women only by building a social welfare policy that takes into account the distinct nature of women's poverty.

The Feminization of Poverty

Although the number of poor families changed little between 1969 and 1978, its composition shifted dramatically. The number of families with male heads (a group that includes families with a husband and wife as well as male-only families) dropped from 3.2 to 2.6 million, while the number headed by poor women with minor children increased by one-third, from 1.8 to 2.7 million. Today more than half of the total number of poor families are maintained by women.

Families with female heads have a poverty rate six times that of male-headed families (31.4 percent vs. 5.3 percent;...). When race is taken into account, the poverty rate also increases so that minority families supported by women have even higher rates. More than half of the families with female heads live in poverty, and 40 percent of all black children are poor.

The most recently reported median income for Hispanic families was $12,570. In 1980, the median income for white families nationwide was $21,521 and $11,648 for black families. In contrast the median income for white single mothers was $9933 and $6907 for black single mothers (Glick 1981). Black single mothers had income that was only 69.5 percent of that of the white mothers.... The median income of single mothers was much lower than that of two-parent families. White mothers had a median income that was only 38 percent of the median income of two-parent white families; similarly, the income of Hispanic mothers was 38 percent of average Hispanic family income; and the income of black mothers was 40 percent of black family income (Glick 1981).

The '70s saw an even greater shift among black families, as the decrease in poor households headed by black males--from 630,000 to 410,000--was far exceeded by the increase in poor families headed by black females, from 740,000 to 1.2 million. Among families of Spanish origin, about 12 percent of the male-headed and over 50 percent of the female-headed families were poor (...data from Census, Series P-60 1980).

Some of the trends within groups...may appear to be contradictory. For example, though income of individual blacks has increased, black family income has decreased in relation to that of non-blacks (Farley 1977). This is because the number of black families with multiple earners is decreasing, and a rising proportion of black families are headed by women.

The number of black families with multiple earners fell by 15 percent, while that of Hispanic families increased by 13 percent. At the same time, white families with only one earner declined 25 percent (*Status of Children, Youth and Families* 1979). The largest change, however, is in the category of families with no earners. While the proportions of Hispanic and white families without an adult earner increased by 29 percent and 34 percent, respectively, the proportion of black families in this category increased by 50 percent during the decade of the seventies (*Status of Children* 1979). There has been a marked decline in the proportion of poor families in all groups.The recent recession and the present economic uncertainty have forced many more families into poverty.

...

Adolescent women. Gender and minority status constitute especially acute problems for teenagers. Teenage mothers enjoy little economic mobility; many never earn more than they did at age 16, while the earning curves for men continue to rise during their early and middle years.[2] Young adults born in the "baby boom" after World War II have been confronted with overcrowded schools and a depressed economy. Demographers see this group of children as having a profound impact on our society. Their sheer numbers have trapped them into a permanent disadvantaged status. They caused overcrowding in schools and colleges throughout the United States, resulting in massive building programs for schools that now stand empty.

These young people then entered a shrinking labor market, and their rate of entry into the job market was six times that of the previous generation. The negative impact of this baby boom generation was temporarily delayed when many of its members were sent to college and thousands were sent to Vietnam. But now, young adults, even members of the traditionally privileged class, face a bleak future. The minority teenager has become a permanent member of the underclass whose prospects are worse now than they were for any group during the Great Depression (Jones 1980).

Transitions in family structure. The major transitions have been the increase of impoverished women and children due to divorce and out-of-wedlock births, rather than from widowhood. The dissolution rate of marriages is almost exactly what it was a century ago, about 34.5 per 1000 marriages per year. But the major cause of dissolution has changed. A century ago divorce accounted for only 3.5 percent of all dissolutions. Even as late as 1951, more than half of the female-headed households were headed by widows. Today widows head less than one-third of such households.

While many of today's widows are older than those of a century ago, more women who head households now are young mothers with young children to support. The transitions are accelerating, for the number of divorces have tripled in the past twenty years. Between 1970 and 1980, the percentage of female householders, with children under 18, had increased by 82 percent in all families and 92 percent in black families (Glick 1981). Not only will fewer female-headed households be headed by widows raising young children, but more families will be experiencing marital disruption...[because of] divorce which has doubled since 1963. Two out of every five marriages in the United States end in divorce, and the figures are higher for teenage marriages. The most recent data indicate that 50 percent of all children can expect to live in one-parent homes for a significant part of their lives (*Status of Children* 1979).

The proportion of female householders with children increased from 11 percent to 18 percent between 1970 and 1980; and from 30 percent to 44 percent for black female householders and their families (Glick 1981). Single parents whose spouses were absent (because of military service, job responsibilities, illness or jail) increased by 24 percent and those who were separated increased by 29 percent. The number of widows increased by 15 percent (*Status of Children* 1978). However, there is a racial difference in the meaning of this status. Single white women tend to marry, or marry a second time. Black women, however, tend to remain single, in part because of the excess of black females compared to males at the ages when most people marry.

Out-of-wedlock births tend to trap mother and child into poverty. The number of single parents who were never married has soared 109 percent chiefly because of teenage pregnancy. These births can push three generations of a family into poverty, because a wage earner is lost as an additional dependent child is added to the family.

*Financial supports in female-headed families....*The typical outcome of a marital breakup in a family with children is that the man becomes single, while the woman becomes a single parent. Unlike widows whose economic loss has been made less devastating by Social Security, including Supplemental Security Income (SSI) and Old Age Survivor Disability Insurance (OASDI), other groups of single parents rarely find private and public transfers sufficient to make up the deficit.

A national survey in 1975 found that only 25 percent of those eligible actually received child support, and that 60 percent of those who did, received less that $1500 (Schulman 1981). These awards tend to be low, in part because they are based on the needs of two-parent families with no child day-care costs, and in part because judges permit the absent parent to deduct the cost of maintaining his household--including the costs of time payments on cars, recreation and entertainment--from what he would pay as child support. The result is that half the fathers who did pay support were contributing less than 10 percent of their income.

In the group of single families that result from divorce, black women fared worst in terms of child-support payments. Child-support payments were awarded by the court to 71 percent of the white women, 44 percent of the Hispanic women, and only 29 percent of the black women. The level of support payments showed the same pattern: The white mother was awarded $2800; the Hispanic mother, $1320; and the black mother $1290.

Poorly educated women are less likely to receive alimony, child support or maintenance payments (Census, Series P-23 1978). Less than half of the 12 million divorced women received property following divorce, but in 1979 the median value of property received was only $4650 (*Marriage and Divorce Today* 1980).

For the 1.4 million mothers who have never been married, the situation is extremely bleak. Only 8 percent were slated to receive support, and only 5 percent ever received any payments (*Marriage and Divorce Today* 1980).

For women who rely on public transfer payments, the picture is equally dismal. Depending on the state, welfare payments range from 49 to 96 percent of the poverty level (Levitan, 1980). The average family payment in 1977 was $241 per month.... The real value of the average welfare payment, accounting for inflation and the declining size of recipient households, has decreased by approximately 20 percent in the last decade (Unpublished memorandum).... Female-headed families that were maintained on non-employed income averaged $5314 in 1978, while all female-headed families averaged $10,689.

These amounts stand in stark contrast to the average income for families headed by men (including husband-wife families), which was $21,703 (*Characteristics of the Population*). While death halts the "private transfer," or sharing of income from husband to wife, divorce or desertion has virtually the same effect on a woman's economic status. The woman whose former partner is still alive is likely to be more devastated economically than a widow, whose plight is addressed through Social Security and other assistance programs.

Aid to Families with Dependent Children (AFDC) originally grew out of concern about the damage the loss of a father would be to the family, yet today there is virtually no sanction, either legal or informal, against the father who contributes little or nothing for the support of his offspring. Nor, where fathers cannot or will not pay, is the attempt to ameliorate the poverty of the mothers and children even minimally adequate.

Stress, Poverty and the Single Mother

The most vulnerable aspect of the female-headed home with minor children is finances. All families of all races experienced a loss of real income between 1973 and 1978 (*Status of Children* 1979). The lower income of black families, and specifically of black female-headed families, placed many at or below the poverty level.... To meet even the most minimal developmental needs of children and mothers, the family support system must be augmented by external resources. Since not all single mothers function with a kin-help network, their support needs must be augmented by community-based programs.

Research has shown that single-parent mothers experience a level of stress significantly higher than that experienced by other groups. Within the single-parent mother population, those who have never been married experience even greater strain. Their children, often the result of out-of-wedlock teenage pregnancies, are born into the most precarious mother-child units in our society. Several authors have detailed the unfavorable physical, emotional and social impact of teenage pregnancy (Hambridge 1974; Lane, 1973; Dravits & Smith 1973).

The ecology of the black family predisposes it to continuous stress, in addition to the normal developmental strains experienced by all families. Despite the cultural preference for meeting crises and family needs within the extended kin-help network and then through friends, families may often experience a level of stress and lowered personal satisfaction that forces them to seek assistance from the wider community.

Even when they were well above the poverty level, single mothers in one study experienced significantly more tension than those who were married (McAdoo 1978).

The stress experienced by low-income mothers is occasioned by crises as well as ongoing conditions--especially insufficient money to meet basic human needs. On a checklist of ninety-one life events requiring change and readjustment, most community surveys have shown that individuals experience an average of two such events a year (Dohrenwend 1973). In contrast, mothers in a Boston study of forty-three black and white low-income women reported an average of fourteen such events during the past two years (Bell 1979). Though their lives included violent and emotionally exhausting events, the lack of money took greatest toll on their mental and physical health. Depression levels were high in these women living in high-density, high-crime urban areas.

A later study showed that working-class single mothers who were employed but still earned salaries that placed them just above the poverty level, were under extreme stress caused by finances, housing concerns, and problems at work, in that order (McAdoo, 1980). Many felt that they were underpaid but wanted to work because, as one woman stated, she had once been on welfare and that was "the worst experience in my life." Safe, dependable and affordable/subsidized child day care was needed. Mothers tended to be particularly bothered by the conflicting demands of motherhood, employment and their social and private lives.

Extended family help patterns. One of the strongest black and ethnic-minority cultural patterns is extensive help systems. The family's effective environment is composed of a network of relatives, friends and neighbors that provide emotional support and economic supplements and, most important, protects the family's integrity from assault by external forces.

Viewing the higher proportion of one-parent families as unstable ignores the extended family adaptation bonds (Hamilton 1971). Many groups maintain a strong extended family system despite mobility (Sussman 1974). Only recently have researchers begun to recognize similar patterns in black families. Functionality of the home is positively related to the parent's ability to manipulate the American economic system. The black extended family has demonstrated that it is a source of strength and a protection against isolation in the larger society (Hills 1971).

The degree of kin interaction is often overlooked in research studies that focus only on structural features. There is a need to determine the norms and values of family interaction and to examine how the process related to the forces shaping it (Staples 1973). The kinship network is more than an extension of family relationships (Farber 1971). It can be considered a system of social relationships derived from birth and marriage and pertaining to an individual's place in society. The major activity of the kin network is the exchange of material and nonmaterial help. Friends and relatives often support the mother's activities outside the home, but they may not attempt to intervene as a family member might do. They also care for the children when the mother must be alone or when she attempts to establish a social life.

The use of social networks has been shown to be important to the functioning of successful single parents (Barry 1979: 65-73). In one study, the support system and proven coping patterns of single Puerto Rican mothers were found to be most important to maintaining their stability. Their support structures were composed of their relatives (usually their mothers and sisters), boyfriends or former husbands, neighbors and religious beliefs. Ability to control their own fertility and the ability to participate in community affairs and advanced education were most helpful.

Of course, inherent in any support is a degree of reciprocity. These informal supports are often the only means of survival for a mother working outside the home. Not all mothers live near relatives or desire to be totally dependent upon kin. The ties they form with other mothers and close friends increase their ability to cope with the stress of their multiple roles.

Many tactics are used to increase the number of individuals who share in the reciprocal obligations. Enlarging the circle of persons who may be called upon in cases of need beyond the household increases the security of the individual. The "friend-network" can be considered a kind of community, a social world outside of the single parent's home (Weiss 1979).

While often emotionally supportive, the extended family can provide only limited financial help to a poor family in poverty, for kin networks are not responsible for creating or alleviating poverty itself.

Causes and Cures for Poverty: Men vs. Women

Women are poor for different reasons than men are poor. This is not to say that needy women and men do not ever share poverty-causing characteristics; in fact, many women are poor because their husbands are poor. But, increasingly, many women are poor "in their own right," and yet we know very little about female poverty.

...

Men generally do not become poor because of divorce, sex-role socialization, sexism or, of course, pregnancy. Indeed, some may lift themselves out of poverty by the same means that plunge women into it: The same divorce that frees a man from the financial burdens of a family may result in poverty for his ex-wife and children.

Distinct reasons for the poverty among women can be traced back to two sources. First, in American culture *women continue to carry the major burden of childrearing*. This sex-role socialization has many ramifications. For example, women tend to make career choices that anticipate that they will interrupt their participation in the labor force to bear children, and a woman is the parent who wins child custody in the overwhelming majority of cases (Grossman 1978). The second major source of poverty among women is the kind of opportunities, or more accurately, the limited opportunities available to women in the labor market. Occupational segregation, sex discrimination and sexual harassment combine to limit both income and mobility for women workers (Blaxall & Reagan 1976).

The interaction of these two sources is illustrated by society's view of child care and child care workers. Since childrearing is primarily a female responsibility, it is virtually only women who do child care work, whether in their homes or in child day care centers. Day care is considered a woman's expense, either because she has custody or it is viewed as an expense incurred because the mother is working outside the home. Furthermore, because many women earn substantially less than men, child day-care workers earn very low wages. It should be noted that if day-care expenses were subtracted from the incomes of women who work outside the home, there would be substantially more households headed by women in poverty.

Thus the two fundamental sources of female poverty combine to keep women in an economic "ghetto." When these factors interact with minority status and youth there is even greater likelihood of being poor.

Poverty among men, by contrast, is often seen as the consequence of joblessness, and therefore it is concluded that the cure for poverty is a job.... For most poor men, the "ball game" is overcoming barriers to employment. Most men who work can support themselves and their families. In one study, less than 5 percent of families with children and a male wage-earner were in poverty (*Characteristics of the Population* 1978).

But many women cannot, by themselves, support themselves and their families. Women who work outside the home full-time, year-round, earn only 59 percent of what men earn (*Characteristics of the Population* 1978). Particularly for those poor women, who are generally lower than average in skills and education, getting a job is not a panacea. Since the woman with a college education earns less on the average than a man with an eighth-grade education, the opportunity for a woman with an eighth-grade education to earn a "living wage" is considerably limited (*The Earnings Gap* 1979).

Poverty among hundreds of thousands of women already working underlines the failure of the "job" solution. Of the mothers working outside the home who headed households with children less than 18 years old in 1978, more than one-quarter had incomes below the poverty level (*Characteristics of the Population* 1978). Even among those currently on welfare, a substantial portion are also in the labor force (about 24 percent), while of those who are long-term recipients of AFDC, one-half have been employed within the past year.[3] In other words, even a full-time job does not provide a route out of poverty for women with the same certainty that it does for most men who are poor.

Why does the "job" solution not work for women? First, occupational segregation confines women to job "ghettoes" where the pay is low and the mobility is little or nonexistent. The latest data suggest that this concentration and segregation do not seem to be declining (Blau & Hendricks 1979).

Second, those women who manage to avoid female job ghettoes encounter sex discrimination in salaries, promotions, benefits and/or sexual harassment. Breaching admissions barriers of previously male-dominated (often, white-male dominated) occupations and professions does not bring immediate and full equal opportunity.

These difficulties are exacerbated if the women involved are minority as well. The experience of women who have sought jobs outside of traditionally female occupations parallels that of the small number of black children who attended white schools in the South under "freedom of choice" desegregation plans. In both instances, the newcomers encountered harassment, social isolation, and denigration of their personal integrity and motivation.

Given that a job often does not alleviate poverty for women, nor enable them to leave welfare, what has been the response of the welfare system? In brief, it has been to continue its obsession with the question of work incentives, and to develop programs that deal with barriers to employment often experienced by *men*--lack of job search skills, experience in the labor force or job training--while ignoring the special problems women face, such as segregation, sex discrimination, and sexual harassment. The lack of child day-care and appropriate job-training also complicates the problems of mothers with young children. In other words, the welfare system continues to push the recipient--who is almost always a woman--to go to work outside the home, even if employment neither lifts her from poverty nor frees her from welfare.

Welfare programs force women into the labor market and reinforce their economic disadvantages in a number of ways.

In the decade of the seventies, several programs, most notably the Work Incentive Program (WIN), were transformed in a way that decreased their effectiveness for women. These changes included de-emphasizing vocational and on-the-job training in favor of direct job placement, particularly in jobs created by the Comprehensive Employment and Training Act (CETA). In addition, some services, particularly child care and transportation, were decreased. It is not surprising, therefore, that although men represented only 26 percent of the WIN registrants, they accounted for over one-third of those who secured unsubsidized jobs. Many women who are potentially eligible for the WIN program have been exempted because they have a child under 6 years old, are needed in the home as a caretaker, or are aged, ill or disabled. Child care, of course, is not provided as part of the program itself; likewise, although 90 percent of the women in CETA have children, these programs also fail to provide child care. In short, if they do not fit the "male pauper" model, then they do not fit the program (Unpublished memorandum).

CETA programs, although not usually targeted as "welfare" programs, were designed not only to serve women equally, but also to overcome "sex-stereotyping" in occupational assignment. However, inequality and sex-stereotyping were not eliminated in these programs. In one case, a woman CETA participant sued her program because she had been offered the choice of secretarial or cooking class. When she sought to transfer to a computer repair class, she was refused. At the same time, a male student in the secretarial class was allowed to transfer (Bachrach 1981).

Several evaluations of CETA and WIN have indicated that women, minorities, and youth have been underserved, both in comparison to their proportion in the population and in proportion to their registration in the program (Baumer et al. 1979). Particularly where the training programs have been in occupations traditionally dominated by males, few women have participated (Comptroller General 1980).

Sometimes women and men receive different forms of training. Women receive small stipends or "work experience" at the minimum wage, while men receive public service jobs which are full time and pay $8,000 per year and up (Baumer et al. 1979)....

Inconsistencies in social welfare policy may reflect the general ambivalence in American society about the role and status of women. Enabling women to become "primary" earners is not yet a societal goal. While it has become increasingly acceptable and even expected that a woman will work outside the home, it is also expected that her job will be secondary both to her husband's job (the husband still being the "primary" earner) and to her home and family responsibilities. The stability of the marriage is often considered endangered if the woman earns more than her spouse. Yet more and more women are becoming displaced homemakers and/or heads of their own households. For these women, the social role of "secondary" earner is clearly dysfunctional and almost guarantees poverty.

"Female independence" has two components: social independence, that is, heading one's own household; and economic independence, being economically self-sufficient. As for social independence, policy makers have long worried that welfare programs generally, as well as some welfare policies specifically, may inadvertently cause marriages to break up and/or encourage the formation of single-parent households. For example, the development of the Aid to Families with Dependent Children--Unemployed Parent (AFDC-UP) programs in many states was based on the conviction that eligibility for welfare should not be predicated on the unemployed father leaving home. Much concern has also been expressed about the finding that the families in the negative income experiment who received high and guaranteed incomes compared to similar families using the regular welfare programs had significantly higher divorce rates than their counterparts (Bishop 1980).

Certainly social welfare programs should not cause families to break up, nor should they exacerbate the poverty that women and children frequently experience as a result of such break-ups. But there is strong evidence that the role social welfare programs play in family break-ups is not primary. First, the rate of divorce has been rising steadily but dramatically at all income levels. It would be difficult to argue that middle-class families that break up do so for such reasons as incompatibility and unfaithfulness, but [that] poor families do so in order to become eligible for welfare, especially since many of those receiving AFDC were middle-class families before their marriages ended (Mudrick 1978).

Second, one should at least ask what kind of marriage and family life previously existed in the families, such as those in the negative income experiment, for whom a relatively small increment of guaranteed income apparently allowed families to exercise the option of divorce. There is much evidence, for example, that children who are raised in an unhappy but unbroken home sometimes suffer more ill effects (such as low academic achievement and juvenile delinquency) than do children with similar problems in single-parent homes. This is not to suggest that divorce and/or single parenthood are uniformly positive, but rather that an increase in them is a social trend upon which social welfare policies can have relatively little impact. In short, this trend should be treated, at least by public agencies, as a given. To treat it otherwise is to develop, *de facto*, two sets of rules, one for the poor and one for the nonpoor. That is, while the nonpoor are permitted to choose freely among life-styles, the poor are presented with the choice of marriage or poverty (at least for women and children). Contemporary welfare policy may already be forcing such a choice; one of the most often cited reasons for leaving AFDC is marriage.

Social welfare efforts to make poor women self-supporting have frequently enabled them to enter the labor force as only marginal workers. For increasing numbers of women, the presence of even a few dependent children has required combining employment and welfare, concurrently or alternately (Rein & Rainwater 1978).

Dual Welfare Systems, Dual Labor Markets, and Gender Inequality

The concept of the dual labor market has been developed elsewhere (Gordon 1972). This concept divides the labor market into two spheres, the primary and the secondary. Relatively few workers move between the two. The primary sector is characterized by high wages, job security, fringe benefits, opportunities for advancement, a high degree of unionization, and due process in terms of job rights. The secondary sector is characterized by low wages, low security, part-time and seasonal work, few fringe benefits, little protection from arbitrary employer actions, and a low rate of unionization.

The duality in the welfare system complements and supports the inequality in the labor market itself. Over all, the primary sector of welfare seeks to minimize the costs to the individual when the system fails, as when there is high unemployment in a geographically concentrated industry. It seeks to enable workers to move from job to job without impoverishing them or their families.

The secondary welfare sector, on the other hand, seeks to provide only the most minimal support necessary to meet basic needs. It also seeks to subsidize low-wage workers (and through them, low-wage industries) by providing some of the support services, such as health care through Medicaid, found in the fringe benefits of the primary sector.[4]

These very different goals and patterns of services create two worlds differentiated by poverty rates, gender, and race. Men, especially white men, are found disproportionately in the primary sector, while women and minorities are concentrated in the secondary sector. This division forces people to circulate between employment and unemployment within either the primary or the secondary sectors, but not between sectors, thus making permanent the inequality of opportunity and achievement between the two worlds.

In the primary sector, workers enjoy jobs with high pay and good fringe benefits, and if they do lose their jobs they are compensated relatively generously through unemployment compensation and/or union supplementary benefits. In contrast, in the secondary sector, workers find themselves at relatively low-wage jobs with little job security and few fringe benefits. Should they lose their jobs--which happens relatively more frequently than in the primary sector--they may have to turn to public assistance. Indeed, AFDC functions as the poor woman's unemployment compensation.[5]

Because such benefits as health care and child day care are available only to these secondary workers through being "on welfare," many in this sector participate in both the labor market and the welfare system. This is especially true for women, and even more so for minority women. Although theoretically one could work one's way into the primary sector, in reality the secondary welfare and work sectors reinforce each other in a vicious cycle, ensuring that workers in the secondary sector remain there.[6]

The disparity in treatment between the primary and secondary sectors is more than a matter of remuneration or eligibility. It derives from fundamentally different conceptions of men workers and women workers: Men who are disadvantaged by factors such as imports and recessions should be compensated in a way that will facilitate their readjustment, via training, relocation, and further education. That is, they have a "right" to the opportunity of good, self-supporting jobs. In contrast, women who are disadvantaged because of divorce, poor vocational training or preparation, or low education, should be helped--or forced--to take any job and any child day care as quickly as possible, even if the job does not provide them with sufficient income to support themselves.

...

Postscript

Reagan's policies can be viewed as an attempt to unilaterally return to an earlier age, or an idealized version of the time when the poor could be neatly separated into those who could be self-supporting--the able-bodied, almost all of them adult men--and those who could not, through no fault of their own, support themselves. The latter group included the very young and old, the blind, disabled, mentally ill, and those single parents with young children to take care of. At times and even now, the two groups were referred to in moral terms as the undeserving and the deserving poor; and even without the labels, the judgment of society about moral worth is implicit in the levels of benefits, the amount of stigma, and the degree to which benefits are given generously by right or not.

Recently the welfare system, and related programs that provide services to the poor, have recognized that some of those who are dependent on welfare and not able to support themselves may become "able-bodied" and self-supporting through a combination of their own efforts and programs geared to their needs for services (e.g., medical, child care) as well as skill development (job training, education). Work incentive programs, including the "thirty and a third" policy, which allows welfare recipients to retain a portion of their earnings, have created a system that allows recipients to build up work experience, acquire skills, and/or be employed. For some this experience has been a transition to economic independence; for others, handicapped by health problems, large families, low skills, statuses that experience discrimination (being female, minority, non-English-speaking, older), and/or poor geographic location, this policy has permitted them to be partially self-supporting. In short, such work incentive policies, and related training and support services, recognized that some of the poor cannot be self-supporting solely through their own efforts, but with help they can be.

We have critiqued the current structure of welfare because it too often locks a woman into a life of poverty, where income from neither work nor welfare is adequate to her and her family. And we have pointed out that much of the oppressive nature of the system derives from the fact that it ignores the special nature of women's poverty. The changes in policy introduced in the Reagan administration, particularly the virtual elimination of all work incentive programs and policies and their attempted replacement with punitive-style workfare programs, will further lock women into poverty. Even more distressing is the effect it will have on the dual welfare system described above, making it increasingly difficult for the poor to escape the secondary market/system. More and more of the poor are women, the overwhelming majority of whom have young children dependent upon them; they do not clearly fall into the class of "deserving" or "undeserving" poor and instead form a third group. Ironically, as this third group increases, the system is turning its back on them and is converting back to a two-group model.

Two groups are most affected by these changes. Because of the increased likelihood of living in a single parent household sometime during childhood, and the high probability that such a household will be in poverty, as well as the dramatic reduction in poverty rates for the elderly, more and more of those experiencing the budget cuts' effects will be children. And because of the additional effects of race (discrimination, segregation), and the differential pattern of welfare use (more mixing of work and welfare, longer but more partial dependence on welfare), it is estimated that two out of three of those affected by the cuts will be minority families.

There has been an increasing trend towards the feminization of poverty in our society. The effect of the budget cuts is to both exacerbate that trend and lock those families in more or less permanent poverty and welfare dependency. Do we want a society in which a child born to, or subsequently living with, a single parent is doomed to grow up in poverty? Do we want a society that has an underclass of the poor that is overwhelmingly families headed by women and predominantly minority, that is trapped in poverty, that is characterized by increasing isolation and hopelessness, and in which increasing numbers of American's future citizens are born and grow up?

Notes

1. Providing essential support services, particularly day care, for women in the paid labor force may enlarge the pool of jobs. But breaking down artificial barriers of gender, as well as race, may simply alter the composition of the poor. That is, if poverty were "de-sexed" and racially integrated, it might then become apparent that unemployment and poverty are structural problems, and not ones associated with particular groups and individuals (e.g., that there are simply not enough jobs to go around). But the current trend is just the opposite, towards a concentration of poverty among women and minorities. The structure of the American economy may well have taken a very different form by the time poverty is distributed equally between men and women, and between whites and minorities.
2. U. S. Civil Rights Commission, quoted in *Washington Post*, August 2, 1980, p. A2.
3. "Long-term" refers to those who received public assistance for four or more consecutive years out of the last seven; see Rein and Rainwater (1978).
4. There is an incentive for the employer to reinforce this dual welfare/labor market. By hiring mostly women, and paying them low wages and/or firing them in ways so that they use AFDC as unemployment compensation, or as wage supplement, the employer knows they will be minimally supported. But if the employers' former employees utilize unemployment compensation, under most state systems, his contribution to the unemployment compensation is increased. Thus the employer that "uses" AFDC instead of unemployment compensation can pay both low wages and save on the unemployment compensation taxes.

5. Obviously, AFDC disproportionately "benefits" women, including many who are unemployed. But whether unemployment compensation, in terms of numbers and dollars, disproportionately benefits men cannot be determined with the statistics available at this writing. The unavailability of even this basic information testifies to the "gender-blind" nature of welfare policy.
6. Even the Federal Government reinforces the secondary status of women workers. In the program entitled "While Actually Employed" (WAE), which has the ostensible purpose of helping to ease the transition of women returning to the work world, women are "allowed" to work fewer than eight hours per day and to set their own hours. In return, they are paid minimum wage (though many have college degrees); are not paid on federal holidays; and have no vacation, no lunch hour, no health or other "fringe" benefits, no promotional opportunities; and can be fired with one day's notice.

References

Bachrach, Deborah.
1981 "Women in Employment." *Clearinghouse Review.* Feb.

Barry, A.
1979 "A Research Project on Successful Single-Parent Families." *American Journal of Family Therapy* 7 (Fall):65-73.

Baumer, Donald C., C. Van Horn, and M. Marvel.
1979 "Explaining Benefit Distribution in CETA Programs." *Journal of Human Resources* 14, no. 2.

Bell, B., et al.
1979 "Depression and Low-Income Female-Headed Families." *Families Today,* 1. NIMG Science Monograph. Rockville, Md.: U.S. Dept. of Health and Human Services.

Bishop, John.
1980 "Jobs, Cash Transfers and Marital Instability; A Review in Synthesis of the Evidence. *Journal of Human Resources* 15 (Fall).

Blau, Francine D., and Wallace E. Hendricks.
1979 "Occupational Segregation by Sex: Trends and Prospects." *Journal of Human Resources* 14, no. 2.

Blaxall, M., and B. Reagan.
1976 *Women and the Workplace: The Implications of Occupational Segregation.* Chicago: University of Chicago Press.

Bureau of the Census, U. S. Department of Commerce.
1978 "Child Support and Alimony." *Special Study.* Series P-23, No. 106. Washington, D.C.
1980 "Characteristics of the Population Below the Poverty Level: 1978." In *Current Population Reports.* Series P-60, No. 124 (July).
1980 *Social Indicators III.* Washington, D.C.: U.S. Government Printing Office.

"Divorced Women: The Myth of Alimony, Property Settlements and Child Support.
1980 *Marriage and Divorce Today* (Nov. 24).

Dohrenwend, B.
1973 "Social Status and Stressful Life Events." *Journal of Personality and Social Psychology,* 28.

Dravits, J., and S. Smith.
1974 "The Acceptance of a Family Clinic by Recently Delivered Teenagers." *Southern Medical Journal* 67 (July).

Farber, E.
1971 *Kinship and Class.* New York: Basic Books.

Farley, Reynolds.
1977 "Trends in Racial Inequalities: Have the Gains of the 1960's Disappeared in the 1970's ?" *American Sociological Review* 42, no. 2.

Glick, Paul.
1981 "A Demographic Picture of Black Families." In Harriette McAdoo (ed.), *Black Families.* Beverly Hills, Cal.: Sage.

Gordon, David M.
1972 *Theories of Poverty and Unemployment: Orthodox, Radical and Dual Labor Market Perspectives.* Lexington, Mass.: Heath.

Grossman, Allyson.
1978 "Divorced and Separated Women in the Labor Force--An Update." *Monthly Labor Review* (Oct.).

Hamilton, C.
1971 "Just How Unstable Is the Black Family?" *New York Times* (Aug. 1).

Hills, R.
1971 *The Strengths of Black Families.* Chicago: Nelson Hall.

Jones, L.
1980 *America and the Baby Boom Generation.* New York: Coward Books.

Hambridge, W.
1974 "Teen Clinics." *Obstetrics and Gynecology* 43, no. 3.

Lane, M.
1973 "Contraception for Adolescents." *Family Planning Perspectives* 5 (Winter).

Levitan, Sar A.
1980 *Programs in Aid of the Poor for the 1980's.* 4th ed. Baltimore: Johns Hopkins.

McAdoo, H.
1978 "Factors Related to Stability in Upwardly Mobile Black Families." *Journal of Marriage and the Family,* 40, no. 4.
1980 "Role of Black Women in Maintaining Stability and Mobility in Black Families." In L. Rose (ed.), *The Black Woman: Current Research and Theory.* Beverly Hills, Cal.: Sage.

Mudrick, Nancy R.
1978 "The Use of AFDC by Previously High- and Low-Income Households." *Social Service Review* (March).

"Need to Ensure Non-Discrimination in CETA Programs."
1980 Washington D.C: Office of the Comptroller General (June 17). HRD-80-95 (GAO).

Pearce, Diana.
1978 "The Feminization of Poverty: Women, Work and Welfare." *Urban and Social Change Review* (Feb.)

Rein, Martin, and Lee Rainwater.
1978 "Patterns of Welfare Use." *Social Service Review* (Dec.).

Schulman, Joanne.
1981 "Poor Women and Family Law." *Clearinghouse Review* (Feb.).

Sussman, M.
1974 *Sourcebook in Marriage and the Family.* Boston: Houghton Mifflin.

U.S. Department of Health and Human Services.
1979 *The Status of Children, Youth and Families.* Washington, D.C.: USDHHS.

U.S. Department of Labor, Women's Bureau.
1979 *The Earnings Gap Between Women and Men.* Washington, D.C.: U.S. Department of Labor.

Weiss, R.
1979 *Going It Alone: The Family Life and Social Situation of the Single Parent.* New York: Basic Books.

17. THE EFFECTS OF FEDERAL BUDGET CUTS ON FAMILIES IN POVERTY

Tom Joe

Introduction

American citizens know little about the segment of their population that is poor, yet the ranks of the poor continue to swell and the problems related to poverty become more pervasive. The latest Census Bureau report shows that, primarily due to severe economic conditions in 1979, the number of people below the poverty standard (a measure widely recognized to underestimate the number of people in poverty) has risen precipitously. Thirteen percent of the population currently has incomes below the poverty level (set at $8,414 for an urban family of four), a sharp increase over the 1979 level of 11.7 percent. Census data also indicate that a disproportionate number of minority group members live in poverty: 32.5 percent of black and 25.7 percent of Hispanic families. Poverty afflicts persons over 65 disproportionately as well, and the percentage of elderly persons below the poverty line has also risen, from 15.1 percent in 1979 to 15.7 percent in 1980 (Bureau of the Census 1980).

The number of people in poverty declined over the last decade, and this recent increase thus marks a reversal of a trend. Confronted with continued high inflation, unemployment which approaches 9 percent nationally and exceeds 15 percent for minorities, and a decline in economic productivity, low-income individuals and families are the first to suffer economic distress.

Since the 1960s, the stated goals of federal policy have been to reduce and eliminate poverty and to improve the conditions associated with it--that is, poor health and nutrition, inadequate housing, lack of education, limited skills, and limited access to employment opportunities. As a result, over the last two decades government has spent increasing sums of money on income support, food stamps, Medicaid, subsidized housing, manpower, health, social services, and other categorical programs to improve the conditions and life chances of disadvantaged people. It is these public expenditures and, more basically, the public responsibility for these efforts, that are now being called into question. The conditions of people in poverty have changed significantly as public policies and programs serving the poor undergo dramatic revision. These changes reflect a shift in the definition of governmental responsibilities and in public attitudes toward recipients of government programs. No longer is public assistance considered an individual entitlement, and no longer are we providing the poor the recourse to challenge reductions in benefits and pursue political strategies to increase their opportunities for a better life.

The direction of these changes raises important philosophical questions concerning the appropriate role of government and challenges longstanding notions of legal and social rights. Perhaps more immediately alarming, however, is the prospect of families being pushed deeper into poverty, ineligible for public support, unable to find jobs due to worsening economic conditions, and forced to absorb losses in federal, state, and local assistance. The holes in the safety net are widening, and there is evidence of many people falling through, unable to cope with the task of providing the basic necessities of food, clothing, and shelter for themselves and their families.

Characteristics of the Poor and Programs Serving Them

Welfare recipients are among the very poorest of the poor. Statistical data on the characteristics of this population defy the general stereotype of the lazy black mother with twelve children. In 1981, before any federal budget cuts, 3.8 million families received Aid to Families with Dependent Children (AFDC), the basic welfare program in this country. To be eligible for AFDC, one must have children and qualify under the state's income and resource limits. In half of the states, a parent (usually the mother) must be single. In the other half, a two-parent family may be eligible if one parent is unemployed.

The following characteristics of families receiving welfare should be kept in mind when discussing the impact of program changes:

- Approximately 80 percent of AFDC families were headed by women in 1979, compared to only 13.6 percent of all families.
- In 1979 over two-thirds of all welfare recipients (69 percent) were children. Their average age is 12 years.
- Nationally, half of all AFDC families are black. The proportion rises, however, in many states. In both Louisiana and Mississippi, 87 percent of recipients are black. In the District of Columbia, 98 percent are black.
- Over half of the mothers are under age 30, and one-third are under age 25.
- Only one-third have graduated from high school.
- One-quarter of the mothers are in the labor force [14 percent were working, 11 percent were actively seeking work, and 10 percent were registered for the Work Incentive Program (WIN) in 1979]. The most typical occupation for AFDC mothers was some type of service employment such as waitress or housekeeper (Department of Health and Human Services 1979).

The primary programs serving the poor are AFDC, food stamps, energy assistance, and Medicaid. For each of these programs, as well as several others, people become eligible on the basis of a means test which measures their income and resources against a set standard. AFDC is a joint federal-state program in which the federal government sets broad guidelines for the states and pays approximately 55 percent of total expenditures. Each state, however, sets its own benefit levels and eligibility standards by establishing what is called a "standard of need." This standard is determined as the minimum amount of money which the state believes to be necessary for a family to live and is varied according to family size. Not all states, however, pay AFDC benefits up to their standard of need, but pay a lesser amount known as the payment standard. Moreover, the standards themselves are generally far below the poverty level. Each state is also required by federal law to ensure that applicants do not have assets exceeding $1000. A house and one car may be excluded from this amount. If the family passes this assets test, its income is then measured against the state payment standard, after exclusion of a small portion of their income for work-related expenses and child care if the parent works.

In addition to the basic welfare program, several programs also provide needed assistance to the poor. The food stamp program, which dates from 1964, has played a major role in reducing domestic hunger and malnutrition. Food stamps are distributed in the form of coupons to households with incomes under 130 percent of the poverty standard. These households may then use the coupons in grocery stores to purchase food items.

Energy assistance is provided to certain low-income households to help them meet the rising costs of fuel. Begun in 1979, this program was enacted when energy prices first became exorbitant and Congress realized that many low-income households could no longer afford to heat their homes adequately. Under the Home Energy Assistance Acts of 1980 and 1981, the federal government makes payments to the states. Each state decides how it will in turn allocate these monies among its needy households. In some cases payments are made directly to energy suppliers; in other cases, directly to individual households. Eligibility levels and payment standards are set by each state and vary widely.

The Medicaid program is jointly financed by the federal and state governments, with the federal share ranging from 50 to 78 percent. It is administered by the state within broad federal guidelines. Medicaid provides health care coverage to low-income persons through reimbursements from the federal and state governments to health care providers. All recipients under AFDC and Supplemental Security Income (SSI) are automatically eligible for Medicaid coverage. The "medically needy" also are eligible for Medicaid, at the state's option. This group is defined by each state, but in general includes those individuals who may have sufficient income to pay for their basic living expenses, but not enough income to pay for their medical care.

Inadequacy of Benefits before the Cuts

AFDC, which provides cash payments to needy families with dependent children and food stamps, established to ensure adequate nutrition for the poor, are the two programs that help provide the basic necessities of food, clothing and shelter to low-income families. The benefits provided by these programs prior to

1980 were bare minimums and often failed to provide families with even a subsistence standard of living. AFDC benefits, for example, are rarely sufficient to cover even basic shelter costs. Twenty-one states pay a maximum monthly AFDC benefit of less than $300 for a three-person family with no other income, an amount significantly below the federally-established 1981 poverty standard of $589 per month. The lowest benefit states, Mississippi, Texas, Alabama, and Tennessee pay a *maximum* of only $96, $118, $118, and $122 per month respectively for three-person families to cover basic living costs. The real value of these already inadequate AFDC benefits has been further eroded by inflation over the past several years. A study conducted by the Department of Health and Human Services found that AFDC recipients have experienced a 19 percent decline in the value of average real benefits between 1969 and 1979 (Kasten & Todd 1980).

Food stamp benefits, based on a minimum amount of money needed to obtain adequate nutrition according to the Thrifty Food Plan, provide a maximum of $183 per month for a three-person family. This amount translates into 67 cents per person per meal.

The combined income provided by AFDC and food stamps does not equal the poverty level in any state except Alaska. In 1981, twelve states provided combined benefit levels which were less than 65 percent of the poverty level, and in over half of the states combined benefit levels did not even equal 75 percent of the poverty standard. Mothers with two children in the lowest benefit states, Mississippi, Texas, Alabama and Tennessee, were faced with paying for all food, clothing, shelter and utilities on combined AFDC, food stamp, and energy assistance benefits of only $287, $306, $307 and $322 per month respectively, *before* any cuts were enacted.

Compounding the effects of inadequate benefits on the poor are major gaps in coverage that leave certain groups of people ineligible for public assistance. Only the food stamp program provides assistance on a regular basis to all needy Americans, regardless of family composition. AFDC is limited to single parents with children in twenty-six states; twenty-four states include two-parent families, but only if one parent is unemployed. Thus, two-parent families in twenty-six states and low-income single individuals and childless couples in all states are not eligible for AFDC and must rely on more restricted general assistance funds provided by state and local governments and food stamps provided by the federal government.

In many states, a mother currently working at sub-minimum wages is ineligible for AFDC payments. For example, a mother working for $2.66 per hour (which is $0.70 below the current minimum wage) in South Carolina does not qualify for AFDC and thus is forced to raise her two children on gross earnings of $400 per month, plus food stamps. After deducting payroll taxes and any child-care or transportation expenses, her monthly disposable income is between $200 and $300, yet she is still ineligible for AFDC and therefore Medicaid as well. Families whose personal property exceeds the assets limit are also ineligible for AFDC and food stamps, even though their disposable income may be within the eligibility guidelines of the state. As can be seen, even AFDC and food stamps fail to cover a significant percentage of poor people in this country.

Effects of FY 1982 and Proposed FY 1983 Cuts

In the Omnibus Budget Reconciliation Act of 1981, Congress enacted sweeping changes in the basic welfare programs serving the poor. The administration has proposed another round of cuts in its fiscal year 1983 budget. In attempting to determine how these program changes will affect low-income families, it is necessary to look closely at the income levels of these families before and after budget cuts are made. Discussion of multibillion dollar national budget figures has tended to obscure the reality of the effects of these cuts on individuals. Too often, the types of detailed eligibility and benefit changes proposed seem technical and abstract. As a result, they may not receive attention from more than a handful of policy makers and they certainly cannot be scrutinized or debated by the people whom they most affect. To counteract this, we have attempted to show the impact of federal budget cuts on average families. The combined 1982 and proposed 1983 cuts will affect two groups distinguishable for purposes of discussion: those who must depend totally on government assistance and those receiving assistance who also work. The effects on each group are described below.

1. *Hurting the "truly needy".* In all areas of the country, the FY 1983 budget proposals affecting AFDC, food stamps, energy assistance, Medicaid and housing assistance programs would move people who are already poor even deeper into poverty. These proposals will lower the incomes of 14 million of the nation's neediest individuals: people who have no other source of income, a population comprised of children, the disabled, the elderly, and mothers unable to work.

Although drastic in many respects, the FY 1982 AFDC revisions did not cut the AFDC and food stamp benefits of AFDC mothers unable to work. However, several changes enacted in other programs in 1982 did reduce their incomes. These include the following:

- Non-working families living in public housing were required to pay a larger portion of their incomes for rent.
- Cuts in Medicaid in FY 1982 forced some states to decrease the scope of health care services available to families.

While these cuts cannot be quantified easily in terms of average dollars lost to those relying totally on public assistance, they, in combination, significantly weakened the ability of many low-income households to provide for basic necessities in FY 1982.

FY 1983 proposals will further decrease the incomes of families who are not working. First, the grants of all AFDC families will be reduced. This new provision effectively eliminates any benefit of the energy assistance program for

AFDC recipients. Food stamp benefits will also be reduced up to $5.25 for each $10 of energy assistance received. Furthermore, a change in the formula by which food stamp benefits are calculated reduces the amount of benefits to all recipients of the program. Furthermore, a change reduces benefits of earned or unearned income by 35 percent, instead of by 30 percent as in the past.

In every state, these provisions reduce the disposable incomes of AFDC recipients unable to work, as shown in Table 17.1. Reductions are highest for families living in states with high energy costs. In Connecticut, for example, a family with no income other than AFDC, food stamps, and energy assistance, will have its disposable income reduced from 96 percent of the poverty level in 1981 to 86 percent in 1983. In Minnesota, a similar family's income drops from 97 percent of the poverty level in 1981 to 89 percent in 1983. In southern states with low energy assistance benefits, the drop in disposable income is smaller, but AFDC families are already at income levels far lower than the national average. In Alabama, for example, the income of a non-working AFDC family of three will drop from 52 percent to 51 percent of the poverty level; at these income levels, even a 1 percent loss is significant. On average across the nation, non-working AFDC families will have their incomes reduced from 76 percent of the poverty level to 72 percent.

Nationwide, AFDC families with no earnings in 1981 received an average of $450 in monthly benefits, an amount which was not changed by the Budget Reconciliation Act for FY 1982. The proposed 1983 changes, however, would leave these families with only $423 per month, an average drop of $27. In Colorado, for example, a family of three with no other income would have its combined AFDC, food stamp, and energy assistance benefits reduced from $478 to $435, a loss of $33; in South Dakota, a similar family's income will drop from $478 to $441, a loss of $37. Because these families have no other sources of income and must rely entirely on these benefits to pay for food, shelter, and other necessities of life, the average $27 per month reduction nationwide is more dramatic than it first appears.

Numerous other cuts in addition to the AFDC and food stamp cuts shown in Table 17.1 deplete the disposable income of the neediest families under the FY 1983 proposals. Cuts in Medicaid and housing programs are likely to have a particularly severe effect on the poor. Moreover, the cumulative effects of the AFDC, food stamp, Medicaid, and energy assistance cuts will reduce a typical AFDC family's income by approximately $42: $27 on average nationwide from AFDC, food stamps, and energy assistance, and at least $10 to $20 per month from Medicaid cuts. This sum represents a 10 percent decrease in total income based on the national average shown in Table 17.1 of $423 per month. Cuts in housing assistance are not quantified but will further deplete the incomes of people dependent on public assistance.

A final point worth noting is that minority AFDC recipients will be particularly affected by the cuts. Although blacks comprise approximately half of the AFDC caseload nationwide, they are concentrated in states with the lowest benefits. In the thirteen states where black families comprise at least 60 percent of the caseload, the average total monthly disposable income from AFDC, food stamps, and energy assistance is $354--that is, only 60 percent of the federally-established poverty standard. The average income in those states where black families comprise 10 percent or less of the AFDC caseload, is considerably higher: $451 or 78 percent of the poverty level. The inequities existing in the current welfare system are thus widened and further entrenched by the FY 1982 changes and the FY 1983 proposals.

2. *Penalizing the working poor.* According to the 1980 Census, half of the over six million families below the poverty level worked at least part of the year. Approximately 16 percent of the AFDC caseload (600,000 families) and 17 percent of those receiving food stamps (4.9 million persons) work at any given time.

It is these low-income families trying to work themselves out of poverty are hit hardest by the FY 1982 changes and FY 1983 budget provisions. The disposable incomes of working AFDC families, in particular, will be significantly reduced, and the financial incentives for these families to work are reduced in all and entirely eliminated in many states. Low-wage employment will be even less profitable than welfare in many states.

The working poor are hurt by these FY 1982 and FY 1983 changes as well as by several additional provisions targeted to working families. In 1982, for example, the benefit disregard for AFDC working parents was eliminated after the parent has been working for four months. The benefit disregard is an amount of money disregarded when calculating AFDC or food stamp benefits, thereby increasing the benefit. The 1983 proposals would also eliminate the earnings disregard in calculating food stamp benefits. In the past, 20 percent of earnings was disregarded, which has in effect, raised the food stamp benefit by that amount.

As Table 17.2 shows, the incomes of AFDC families with average earnings were reduced from an average of 101 percent of the poverty standard in 1981 to 81 percent in 1982 as a result of the Budget Reconciliation Act. Incomes of working AFDC families would be reduced further to 73 percent of the poverty standard by the FY 1983 proposals, a cumulative income drop over the two years of 28 percentage points.

In several states the reductions in income are particularly dramatic for the working poor. Recipient families with average earnings in California, for example, will find their disposable incomes drop from $758 to $479 per month, a decrease of $279. This reduction in their monthly income translates into a drop from 129 percent of the poverty standard to 81 percent. In other words, the decision to work throws the family back into poverty. In Georgia, a comparable family's income drops from $453 to $437 per month. This decrease of $106 moves this family from 77 percent of the federal poverty standard to only 59 percent. Prior to these changes, AFDC families with average wages in twenty-nine states were able to raise their incomes to the poverty level or slightly above by working. After the 1982 cuts, no state had average AFDC earners above the poverty level; and under the proposed FY 1983 changes, no average earner in any state would have a disposable income above 85 percent of the poverty standard. The effect on currently-working families with children is a permanent, non-reversible reduction in income of up to 37 percent, even if their work effort remains the same as before the cuts. By reducing the disposable incomes of working AFDC families, the FY 1983 proposals reduce the incentives for AFDC families to enter the work force, and for currently working families to increase their work effort.

Table 17.3 shows the differences in disposable income available to an AFDC parent who chooses to work at the average earning level for that state and the disposable income available to a parent choosing not to work. Several points are worth noting:

- A parent with average earnings receives a higher disposable income by choosing not to work in the following twenty-four states:

Arizona	Louisiana	New York
California	Massachusetts	Ohio
Colorado	Michigan	Rhode Island
Connecticut	Minnesota	Utah
Georgia	Montana	Vermont
Illinois	Nebraska	Washington
Iowa	New Hampshire	Wisconsin
Kansas	New Jersey	Wyoming

- In California, for example, an AFDC mother working at the minimum wage would have $82 less in disposable income than if she did not work at all.
- In the eight states below, a parent gains less than $20 per month by working:

Florida	Pennsylvania
New Mexico	South Dakota
Oklahoma	Virginia
Oregon	West Virginia

For example, in Florida, an AFDC family with average earnings would have only $10 more per month in disposable income than one not working.

- In only four states will an AFDC parent with average earnings have substantially more in disposable income--at least $100--than if the parent were not working. These states are Arkansas, Mississippi, South Carolina, and Tennessee. The comparatively larger gains in disposable incomes in these states result from the fact that AFDC recipients in these states have relatively high earnings, whereas AFDC benefits are very low. Prior to the Budget Reconciliation Act, however, AFDC families in all but five states increased their disposable incomes by at least $100 per month by working at average earning levels.

The elimination of financial incentives to work, in fact the creation of financial disincentives, can be illustrated even more vividly through the concept of the "marginal benefit reduction rate." This is the rate at which a recipient's benefits are reduced as earned income increases. Historically, the nation's income maintenance programs have allowed recipients who work to keep some portion of their earned income to maintain financial incentives to work. If a recipient's benefits are reduced by $0.50 for every dollar earned, the program is said to have a 50 percent marginal benefit reduction rate. If the benefits are reduced by $0.75 for every dollar earned, this program is said to have a benefit reduction rate of 75 percent. In this latter example, the recipient's disposable income increases by only $0.25 for every dollar she/he earns.

The appropriate marginal benefit reduction rate has been the subject of much debate. Past efforts to reform welfare programs have tried to arrive at a rate high enough to reduce public subsidies as a recipient's earnings rose, but not so high as to eliminate financial incentives to work. Some analysts believe that a benefit reduction rate above 50 percent no longer preserves full work incentives. (Interestingly, the maximum rate for the federal income tax is 50 percent.) At this level, a recipient's disposable income is increased by half of the amount of his/her earned income.

Prior to passage of the Budget Reconciliation Act, the minimum cumulative benefit reduction rate for working AFDC families receiving AFDC, food stamps, energy assistance and the earned income tax credit (EITC) was at least 63 percent in all but four states. In other words, a family's benefits were reduced by at least $.63 for every dollar earned, giving it at most an additional $.37 of disposable income. The FY 1982 changes and the FY 1983 proposals raise the cumulative marginal benefit reduction rate high enough to destroy any financial incentive to work for many AFDC working families.

Low-wage earners are penalized in all states under the FY 1983 proposals. In Washington, for example, the cumulative benefit reduction rate rises as high as 130 percent for workers earning $525 per month. At this level of earnings a working family's disposable income would be $51 less than if it relied solely on welfare benefits. In Louisiana, the rate reaches 103 percent on earnings of up to $225 per month, so that a family is $8 per month worse off by working than by not working. In Georgia, workers with incomes under $200 per month actually lose $7 per month of disposable income compared to a similar family with no wage-earners. In all states these extraordinarily high cumulative benefit reduction rates that would result from the FY 1983 budget proposals are on top of rates already increased sharply by the Budget Reconciliation Act. For all states, the minimum cumulative benefit reduction rate is 94 percent in FY 1982. In FY 1983, the minimum average rate will be 99 percent if the administration's proposed budget is enacted by Congress.

Benefit reduction rates at these levels clearly discourage work effort and may prevent many recipients from seeking work altogether. Parents with low skills and no work experience, who might move into the work force gradually by accepting low wages or part-time work, would lose money if they worked. At best, families would increase disposable income negligibly; at worst, they actually would lose money. While many parents may continue to work for non-financial reasons, those who decline jobs can hardly be criticized since parents seeking better lives for their children cannot be expected to opt for lower incomes, given a choice.

In addition to basic benefit reductions, many families will lose their Medicaid benefits as a result of federal AFDC budget cuts. In thirty-two states and the District of Columbia, working AFDC families with average earnings would no longer be eligible for AFDC benefits under the proposed FY 1983 budget. These states are:

Alabama*	Kentucky	Oklahoma
Arkansas	Maryland	Oregon*
Connecticut	Massachusetts	Pennsylvania
Delaware*	Minnesota	South Carolina*
District of Columbia	Mississippi*	South Dakota*
Florida*	Missouri*	Tennessee
Georgia*	Nebraska	Texas*
Idaho*	New Jersey*	Vermont
Illinois	New Mexico*	Virginia
Indiana*	North Carolina	West Virginia
Iowa*	North Dakota	Wisconsin

Working AFDC parents in these thirty-two states and the District of Columbia comprise 62 percent of all AFDC working parents.

In the 15 states marked with an asterisk (*), AFDC families also would automatically lose their Medicaid benefits one month after losing AFDC benefits.[1] These states provide no Medicaid coverage for the "medically needy." Under current law, Medicaid benefits can be retained for four months following termination from AFDC; the FY 1983 proposals reduce this period to one month.

The loss of Medicaid benefits constitutes a large decrease in a family's resources and thus creates an additional disincentive to work. In large families or families with members requiring extended medical attention, medical care is expensive and insurance protection recipients in low-wage jobs is rarely sufficient. Thus, even in those states where an AFDC parent working at average wages does secure a small net gain in disposable income, the loss of Medicaid coverage is likely to more than offset this gain. In these cases, the working AFDC parent may feel compelled to reduce her/his work effort.

Effects on Children and Youth

Perhaps the most severe effects of these budget cuts are on children in low-income families. These cuts discussed in this chapter comprise only a part of the withdrawn assistance for needy children and youth. The cuts in basic income assistance programs combined with cuts in child health programs, community medical care programs, day care, and Title XX, which all provide essential service supports to disadvantaged children, effectively revoke the nation's commitment to support and assistance for children in poverty. These changes seem especially short-sighted. At a time when the U.S. infant mortality rate at last is approaching that of other industrialized nations, programs for maternal and child health care and child health clinics are being curtailed. At a time when research indicates that prenatal, neonatal, and infant health care are the most significant determinants of later well-being, proposals are being made to reduce supplemental food and other nutritional programs for children.

Youth aged 16 to 21 are also primary victims of the cuts. Whereas, the FY 1982 provisions eliminated AFDC payments for youth ages 18 to 21, the FY 1983 proposals further lower eligibility to 16 years. These provisions deny benefits to young people who most need them: children between 16 and 21 attending high schools, post-secondary colleges, vocational or technical schools. Moreover, despite unemployment rates in excess of 15 percent for all youth and 40 percent for minority youth, cut-backs are proposed in grants and loan programs for vocational training, remedial education, and higher education. As jobs become scarcer, education and training become even more essential for achieving economic self-sufficiency.

To eliminate intergenerational poverty, children of poor families must have the full opportunity to obtain education and skills. Retaining grant and loan programs and benefits for students through age 21 to allow them to complete their education can make the difference between long-term dependence and future productivity. By striking so deeply at the welfare of poor children, these cuts guarantee a legacy of health and social problems. Yet no attempt has been made to weigh the benefits derived from these programs against the cost savings predicted to result from their cancellation. The result is short-sighted both in economic and social terms. The FY 1983 budget proposals represent a significant reduction in the nation's investment in its children's development at those very points--early childhood and adolescence--when we know it can yield results.

Cost Implications of the Work Disincentives

If an AFDC mother finds it beneficial to reduce her work effort, the federal cost savings anticipated in the FY 1983 proposed budget for AFDC and food stamps are not likely to materialize. For example, in FY 1981, the federal government paid $143 in AFDC benefits and $40 in food stamps, a total of $183, to a working AFDC family with average earnings in New York. If this mother decides to depend totally on welfare to receive $40 more per month in disposable income, federal government costs for that family rise to $288.50 per month--$204.50 in AFDC and $84 in food stamp payments. This represents an increase in federal costs of $105.50 per month for one family. Nationwide, federal costs would rise from an average of $189.80 to $279.40 if working mothers go on welfare full time in 1983.

Recent Congressional Budget Office (CBO) analysis indicates that AFDC mothers' work effort will be reduced. A CBO (1982:126) analysis of the 1983 budget proposals contends that AFDC recipients will reduce their work effort because of the AFDC cuts enacted last year. Specifically, CBO now estimates that one-third of the 188,000 AFDC working families eliminated from the program last year will leave their jobs to go back on welfare. Accordingly, CBO now estimates that in FY 1983 and succeeding years, the AFDC changes in the 1981 Budget Reconciliation Act will save about $350 million per year less than projected by the administration. Furthermore, this CBO estimate pertains only to reduced work effort by those eliminated from AFDC and does not include the fiscal impact that results when non-working AFDC mothers decline jobs or when those working part-time choose not to increase their work effort. CBO also has not yet quantified the fiscal effects of further reductions in work effort from new proposals in the FY 1983 budget.

Conclusion

Cuts in basic welfare benefits, food stamps, and energy assistance serve to lock low-income workers into poverty by making it more profitable for the majority of recipient parents to remain unemployed. Under former AFDC rules, a family could raise its income by working, even though cash assistance supplementations were decreased. Movement out of poverty was slow and often gradual, but gains in income accruing from work provided incentives for families to continue to increase their earnings and to stay in the labor force. The latest data on these families show that half of all families receiving welfare do so for less than one year. Under the FY 1982 changes and 1983 proposals, these incentives vanish. If recipients work and remain on welfare, they often have less income than if they do not work at all. If recipients earn enough to go off welfare, under the new rules they may also lose Medicaid benefits and are unlikely to have sufficient funds to replace them on their own.

As public policy, this reversal of incentives toward not working is clearly counterproductive. The work effort of these families "on the edge" between financial self-sufficiency and full economic dependence should be supported, not undercut. The costs to the public of providing them with additional income through small AFDC supplements or food stamps are low compared to the high returns from preventing greater dependency and increasing economic productivity. By fundamentally altering the incentives and opportunities available to these families, the administration is significantly reducing the likelihood that they will be able to work their way out of poverty.

For years there has been wide agreement that our array of social welfare programs is inadequate. The system is confusing to policy makers and recipients alike. It perpetuates inequities across states and distributes benefits unevenly among similar groups of disadvantaged persons. It reflects a series of uncoordinated initiatives rather than a coherent policy toward the nation's poor. Yet, as a result of federal and state efforts to improve the system over the years, it had become reasonably responsive to people in dire need. In many states, it also had adopted to the often rapidly changing work status of low-income families. When family income was adequate to provide basic necessities, families went off the welfare rolls; but income supplementation was provided when necessary. Thus, at least a minimal financial incentive to work was maintained. For many low-income workers forced to take seasonal, part-time, and/or minimum wage jobs, this system made the difference between total dependence and labor force participation that, while sporadic, continued over time.

These latest proposals alter the structure of this stop-gap system and reduce the likelihood that low-income families can move gradually out of poverty. A welfare system, universally considered unsatisfactory, will become even less flexible, less transitional in nature, and more likely to entrap low-income families permanently in poverty. These cuts seem to be based on the assumption that income assistance programs should be only for the permanently dependent, and that financial incentives for work should not be part of the system's structure. Intentionally or not, this administration has proposed changes which could make welfare dependence a more permanent condition for many families. Therefore, the most serious effect of this new welfare structure will be a long-term one. Instead of breaking the cycle of intergenerational dependence--a goal of every attempt to reform public assistance, whether launched by conservatives or liberals, Republicans or Democrats--the new provisions may actually promote it.

The damage done to the incentive structures of the public assistance program under these proposals will take time to undo. The historical development of income maintenance programs provides ample evidence that such changes often persist for years. In future policy and budget debates, it is critical that the long term effects of these changes on the opportunities of low income parents and their children be given much more careful consideration.

Note

1. In addition to these 15, five other states do not provide Medicaid coverage to the medically needy. In these 20 states, Medicaid coverage is restricted to those on AFDC or SSI.

References

Bureau of the Census, U.S. Department of Commerce.
1980 "Money Income and Poverty Status of Families and Persons in the U.S.: 1980." *Current Population Reports*, Series P-60, No. 127. (Advance data from the March 1981 Current Population Survey)

Congressional Budget Office.
1982 *An Analysis of the President's Budgetary Proposals for Fiscal Year 1983.* Washington, D.C.: U.S. Government Printing Office. Feb.

Kasten, Richard A., and John E. Todd.
1980 *Transfer Recipients and the Poor during the 1970's.* Prepared for the Second Research Conference of the Association of Public Policy Analysis and Management. October.

U.S. Department of Health and Human Services, Social Security Administration, Office of Policy, Office of Research and Statistics.
n.d. *1979 Recipient Characteristics Study: Part 1: Demographic and Program Statistics.*

TABLE 17.1

EFFECT OF BUDGET RECONCILIATION ACT AND FY 1983 BUDGET PROPOSALS ON MONTHLY DISPOSABLE INCOME* AND POVERTY STATUS** OF AFDC NON-WORKING FAMILIES

	Prior to Budget Reconciliation Act		Current Law		FY 1983 Proposals	
	Disposable Income	Percent of poverty	Disposable Income	Percent of poverty	Disposable Income	Percent of poverty
ALABAMA	$307	52%	$307	52%	$301	51%
ARIZONA	$370	63%	$370	63%	$363	62%
ARKANSAS	$311	53%	$311	53%	$305	52%
CALIFORNIA	$584	99%	$584	99%	$561	95%
COLORADO	$468	79%	$468	79%	$435	74%
CONNECTICUT	$563	96%	$563	96%	$509	86%
DELAWARE	$438	74%	$438	74%	$405	69%
DISTRICT OF COL.	$450	76%	$450	76%	$427	72%
FLORIDA	$377	64%	$377	64%	$368	62%
GEORGIA	$362	61%	$362	61%	$351	60%
IDAHO	$466	79%	$466	79%	$436	74%
ILLINOIS	$449	76%	$449	76%	$428	73%
INDIANA	$419	71%	$419	71%	$398	68%
IOWA	$505	86%	$505	86%	$466	79%
KANSAS	$467	79%	$467	79%	$445	76%
KENTUCKY	$376	64%	$376	64%	$354	60%
LOUISIANA	$366	62%	$366	62%	$356	60%
MAINE	$462	78%	$462	78%	$428	73%
MARYLAND	$432	73%	$432	73%	$408	69%
MASSACHUSETTS	$518	88%	$518	88%	$478	81%
MICHIGAN	$513	87%	$513	87%	$489	83%
MINNESOTA	$573	97%	$573	97%	$522	89%
MISSISSIPPI	$287	49%	$287	49%	$279	47%
MISSOURI	$409	69%	$409	69%	$393	67%
MONTANA	$472	80%	$472	80%	$431	73%
NEBRASKA	$500	85%	$500	85%	$460	78%
NEW HAMPSHIRE	$505	86%	$505	86%	$457	78%
NEW JERSEY	$500	85%	$500	85%	$466	79%
NEW MEXICO	$417	71%	$417	71%	$393	67%
NEW YORK	$537	91%	$537	91%	$508	86%
NORTH CAROLINA	$369	63%	$369	63%	$357	61%
NORTH DAKOTA	$525	89%	$525	89%	$464	79%
OHIO	$422	72%	$422	72%	$403	68%
OKLAHOMA	$434	74%	$434	74%	$415	70%
OREGON	$462	78%	$462	78%	$441	75%
PENNSYLVANIA	$465	79%	$465	79%	$439	74%
RHODE ISLAND	$567	96%	$567	96%	$526	89%
SOUTH CAROLINA	$334	57%	$334	57%	$316	54%
SOUTH DAKOTA	$478	81%	$478	81%	$441	75%
TENNESSEE	$322	55%	$322	55%	$305	52%
TEXAS	$306	52%	$306	52%	$301	51%
UTAH	$503	85%	$503	85%	$471	80%
VERMONT	$596	101%	$596	101%	$542	92%
VIRGINIA	$417	71%	$417	71%	$398	68%
WASHINGTON	$551	94%	$551	94%	$518	88%
WEST VIRGINIA	$380	65%	$380	65%	$366	62%
WISCONSIN	$579	98%	$579	98%	$539	92%
WYOMING	$471	80%	$471	80%	$437	74%
AVERAGE	$450	76%	$450	76%	$423	72%

* Disposable Income Figures for each state represent the monthly AFDC, food stamps, and energy assistance benefits that would be paid to a non-working AFDC family of three.

** Poverty status is expressed in terms of monthly disposable income divided by the federally-established 1980 poverty level for a family of three, or $589 per month.

TABLE 17.2

EFFECT OF BUDGET RECONCILIATION ACT AND FY 1983 BUDGET PROPOSALS ON MONTHLY DISPOSABLE INCOME* AND POVERTY STATUS** OF AFDC WORKING FAMILIES

	Prior to Budget Reconciliation Act		Current Law		FY 1983 Proposals	
	Disposable Income	Percent of poverty	Disposable Income	Percent of poverty	Disposable Income	Percent of poverty
ALABAMA	$406	69%	$365	62%	$347	59%
ARIZONA	$449	76%	$374	63%	$355	60%
ARKANSAS	$464	79%	$454	77%	$420	71%
CALIFORNIA	$758	129%	$537	91%	$479	81%
COLORADO	$601	102%	$477	81%	$424	72%
CONNECTICUT	$731	124%	$534	91%	$470	80%
DELAWARE	$589	100%	$480	82%	$438	74%
DISTRICT OF COL.	$616	104%	$499	85%	$453	77%
FLORIDA	$491	83%	$402	68%	$377	64%
GEORGIA	$453	77%	$368	62%	$347	59%
IDAHO	$634	108%	$512	87%	$460	78%
ILLINOIS	$590	100%	$459	78%	$420	71%
INDIANA	$564	96%	$463	79%	$426	72%
IOWA	$664	113%	$501	85%	$450	76%
KANSAS	$612	104%	$478	81%	$433	73%
KENTUCKY	$522	89%	$470	80%	$432	73%
LOUISIANA	$449	76%	$371	63%	$349	59%
MAINE	$649	110%	$526	89%	$464	79%
MARYLAND	$590	100%	$485	82%	$443	75%
MASSACHUSETTS	$685	116%	$511	87%	$459	78%
MICHIGAN	$675	114%	$532	90%	$482	82%
MINNESOTA	$742	126%	$537	91%	$472	80%
MISSISSIPPI	$504	85%	$442	75%	$410	70%
MISSOURI	$570	97%	$483	82%	$442	75%
MONTANA	$566	96%	$478	81%	$423	72%
NEBRASKA	$656	111%	$498	85%	$447	76%
NEW HAMPSHIRE	$649	110%	$515	87%	$444	75%
NEW JERSEY	$661	112%	$497	84%	$451	77%
NEW MEXICO	$546	93%	$439	75%	$406	69%
NEW YORK	$703	119%	$525	89%	$468	79%
NORTH CAROLINA	$504	86%	$441	75%	$410	70%
NORTH DAKOTA	$684	116%	$521	88%	$464	79%
OHIO	$543	92%	$430	73%	$393	67%
OKLAHOMA	$587	100%	$468	79%	$430	73%
OREGON	$628	107%	$496	84%	$451	77%
PENNSYLVANIA	$631	107%	$501	85%	$455	77%
RHODE ISLAND	$720	122%	$567	96%	$502	85%
SOUTH CAROLINA	$495	84%	$453	77%	$418	71%
SOUTH DAKOTA	$633	107%	$489	83%	$445	75%
TENNESSEE	$456	77%	$438	74%	$405	69%
TEXAS	$409	69%	$372	63%	$353	60%
UTAH	$629	107%	$511	87%	$460	78%
VERMONT	$768	130%	$543	92%	$478	81%
VIRGINIA	$549	93%	$439	75%	$407	69%
WASHINGTON	$713	121%	$545	93%	$485	82%
WEST VIRGINIA	$493	84%	$404	69%	$378	64%
WISCONSIN	$750	127%	$537	91%	$467	79%
WYOMING	$593	101%	$479	81%	$426	72%
AVERAGE	$595	101%	$476	81%	$432	73%

* Disposable Income Figures for each state represent the sum of monthly earnings plus AFDC, food stamps, and energy assistance benefits for a working AFDC family of three, assuming average earnings for AFDC families in that state.

** Poverty status is expressed in terms of monthly disposable income divided by the federally-established 1981 poverty level for a family of three, or $589 per month.

TABLE 17.3

THE EFFECT OF EMPLOYMENT ON THE MONTHLY DISPOSABLE INCOME* OF AFDC FAMILIES: COMPARISON OF FY 1981, FY 1982, AND FY 1983

	FY 1981 Prior to Budget Reconciliation Act			FY 1982 Current Law			FY 1983 Budget Proposals		
	DISPOSABLE INCOME			DISPOSABLE INCOME			DISPOSABLE INCOME		
	Non-Working Parent	Working Parent	Difference**	Non-Working Parent	Working Parent	Difference**	Non-Working Parent	Working Parent	Difference**
ALABAMA	$307	$406	$ 99	$307	$365	$ 59	$301	$347	$ 46
ARIZONA	370	449	79	370	374	4	363	355	−8
ARKANSAS	311	464	154	311	454	144	305	420	115
CALIFORNIA	584	758	174	584	537	−47	561	479	−82
COLORADO	468	601	133	468	477	9	435	424	−11
CONNECTICUT	563	731	168	563	534	−29	509	470	−40
DELAWARE	438	589	151	438	480	42	405	438	33
DIST. OF COLUMBIA	450	616	166	450	499	49	427	453	26
FLORIDA	377	491	114	377	402	25	368	377	10
GEORGIA	362	453	91	362	368	6	351	347	−4
IDAHO	466	634	168	466	512	46	436	460	24
ILLINOIS	449	590	141	449	459	10	428	420	−8
INDIANA	419	564	144	419	463	44	398	426	29
IOWA	505	664	159	505	501	−4	466	450	−16
KANSAS	467	612	145	467	478	10	445	433	−13
KENTUCKY	376	522	147	376	470	94	354	432	78
LOUISIANA	366	449	83	366	371	5	356	349	−7
MAINE	462	649	187	462	526	64	428	464	37
MARYLAND	432	590	158	432	485	54	408	443	35
MASSACHUSETTS	518	685	167	518	511	−6	478	459	−19
MICHIGAN	513	675	162	513	532	19	489	482	−6
MINNESOTA	573	742	169	573	537	−36	522	472	−50
MISSISSIPPI	287	504	216	287	442	154	279	410	131
MISSOURI	409	570	161	409	483	74	393	442	49
MONTANA	472	566	94	472	478	6	431	423	−8
NEBRASKA	500	656	156	500	498	−2	460	447	−12
NEW HAMPSHIRE	505	649	145	505	515	10	457	444	−13
NEW JERSEY	500	661	162	500	497	−3	466	451	−15
NEW MEXICO	417	546	129	417	439	22	393	406	13
NEW YORK	537	703	166	537	525	−12	508	468	−40
NORTH CAROLINA	369	504	135	369	441	72	357	410	53
NORTH DAKOTA	525	684	159	525	521	−4	464	464	0
OHIO	422	543	121	422	430	8	403	393	−10
OKLAHOMA	434	587	152	434	468	34	415	430	15
OREGON	462	628	166	462	496	33	441	451	10
PENNSYLVANIA	465	631	166	465	501	36	439	455	16
RHODE ISLAND	567	720	152	567	567	0	526	502	−24
SOUTH CAROLINA	334	495	161	334	453	119	316	418	102
SOUTH DAKOTA	478	633	155	478	489	12	441	445	4
TENNESSEE	322	456	134	322	438	116	305	405	100
TEXAS	306	409	104	306	372	66	301	353	52
UTAH	503	629	126	503	511	9	471	460	−11
VERMONT	596	768	172	596	543	−53	542	478	−64
VIRGINIA	417	549	132	417	439	22	398	407	10
WASHINGTON	551	713	161	551	545	−6	518	485	−33
WEST VIRGINIA	380	493	112	380	404	24	366	378	12
WISCONSIN	579	750	171	579	537	−42	539	467	−72
WYOMING	471	593	122	471	479	8	437	426	−10
US AVERAGE	$450	$595	$146	$450	$476	$ 26	$423	$432	$ 9

*Disposable income figures shown for each state represent the sum of earnings, AFDC, Food Stamps, EITC, and energy assistance benefits for either a working or non-working family in that state. Earnings are calculated based on the average earnings for an AFDC family in that state.

**All numbers do not add due to rouding.

18. POLICY OPTIONS FOR OLDER WOMEN

The Women's Studies Program and Policy Center at George Washington University in conjunction with The Women's Research and Education Institute of the Congresswoman's Caucus

Policy makers have already made a major commitment to the elderly through federal policy. In programmatic terms 134 federal programs benefiting the aging under the jurisdiction of forty-nine congressional committees and subcommittees have been identified. In addition, there are other programs initiated by state and local governments, as well as by private institutions. In budgetary terms, it has been estimated that total expenditures for the aging and their survivors now constitute 25 percent of the federal budget and future increases are anticipated (Binstock 1978:57).

The demographic data in this paper demonstrate a significant change in the aging population: the number of older people is increasing rapidly, the greatest increase is among the oldest of the old, and the majority of the elderly are women.

The data also reveal significant differences between older women and men in marital status, living arrangements, and economic status. While the federal government has achieved considerable success in providing economic security for the aging, a disproportionate number of older women remain close to the poverty level. Many of these women are widows who live alone.

By every economic measure, women are more deprived in their later years than are men. This is a most significant fact when the numerical importance of unmarried women 65 and over and the predominance of women at the oldest ages are taken into account. The limited economic security experienced in old age by such women is the result of their longer life expectancy, the lifetime impact of limited employment opportunity, society's assumption of women's economic dependency, and the bias against women both as workers and as dependents that is imbedded in public and private pension systems.

Reprinted from *Older Women: The Economics of Aging* January 1981, pp. 27-33.

Furthermore, while all those living on fixed incomes have been affected adversely by the high inflation rate of the 1970s, the poorest and the oldest, both groups in which women predominate, have been most severely affected. The costs of necessities, such as food, housing, and health care have exceeded the general rate of cost increases and consequently, consume growing portions of the incomes of those elderly with the least resources--elderly women (Data Resources 1980:Ch. 4).

In response to demographic changes and rising economic pressures, older women are rapidly emerging as a significant group politically. A higher proportion of older people tend to register and vote than do younger people but because of the numerical dominance of women among the elderly, there are more women voters in this group. In the 1978 congressional election, almost 7 million women 65 and over voted, casting 1 million more votes than did men of the same age. Furthermore, older people are becoming more highly organized than formerly. Established organizations, such as the National Association of Retired Persons and the National Council of Senior Citizens, report expanding memberships, which are predominantly female. They also note an increasing intensity of activism related to retirement income issues.... [T]wo new national advocacy organizations specifically for older women, the Older Women's League and the National Action Forum for Older Women, ...[have recently been formed] to press for social and legislative reforms of benefit to older women. As a result, older women can no longer be easily dismissed or neglected, because they comprise a large, well-organized constituency and are becoming a potent political force.

To address the needs of older women, changes in public policy can be made in programs that serve those who are presently among the elderly. Changes must also be made in policies affecting women at earlier life stages in order to adequately meet the needs of future cohorts of the aged. The policy options that follow present only a few and very general suggestions for study and action. More specific policy options will be developed at a later date.

1. To Develop Comprehensive Data

- ☐ Older women, as a group, have been typically subsumed under the general category of "women" without regard to age or under the category of "elderly" without regard to sex. The invisibility of older women in current statistical descriptions results from the use of broad age categories (e.g. 25 to 64 years, 65 and over, and 35 and over) and the unavailability of comparable gender-based data across age, marital status, living arrangements, income, race and ethnicity classifications. These factors, interacting with each other, have important implications for the economic status of the aging and consequently for sound public policy. While the data available on older people is improving in both quantity and quality, development of even more extensive data that takes factors into account reflecting the heterogeneity of the aging population is strongly recommended.

2. To Promote Public Awareness

- Effective public policy must be based on public awareness of the facts and the development of consensus. Broad-based discussion is necessary to dispel myths and to examine carefully the actual economic status of the aging population. The public particularly needs to understand the functioning of present income maintenance systems and the impact of proposed changes on those of different sexes, ages, races, ethnic groups, and marital status. For maximum effectiveness, such discussion should cut across traditional socioeconomic barriers to include policymakers, the aging, women, and younger people. Women's organizations are one of the most appropriate agents to spearhead such public dialogue in order to build an informed constituency for action. Continuing involvement in education and action programs, particularly of the aging and women, is vital since their interests converge and joint advocacy will benefit both groups.

3. To Insure Income Adequacy

Since widowhood and divorce cause loss of income more often to older women than to older men, support systems should be designed to aid this population. There are at present several proposals for reform of the public and private pension coverage that would adapt these programs to the needs of contemporary women. For example, the Department of Health and Human Services (HHS) experts on Social Security are now advocating that earnings of a married couple be considered equally vested in both members of the marriage, with both husband and wife entitled to one-half of the earnings record vested in either member of the marriage. In addition, consideration should be given to the fact that while changes in current private pension laws might involve increased costs and reduced benefits for some, such changes would nevertheless have a relatively greater impact on women's well-being as retired workers. While it is beyond the scope of this paper to examine the technical details of the various proposals now under consideration, some aspects are of particular interest.

A. Public Pensions

- Civil Service Retirement law has been changed by the Congress so that divorced spouses can claim a pro rata share of husbands' retirement benefits. The divorced spouse, however, must prove in court that she should receive some share of her husband's retirement, and state law should allow this form of entitlement in its divorce settlements. Many states do not currently allow divorced wives to claim retirement benefits.
- The Social Security Advisory Council has recommended that the Social Security law be changed so that a spouse's earnings record would be split between the two spouses at the time of divorce in any marriage that has lasted ten years, thus protecting the implicit claim of the wife who had contributed to family well-being while her husband earned the larger share of its income.

- ☐ The council has also recommended that the Social Security law be changed so that a widow would continue to receive 100 percent of total combined benefits (her husband's plus her dependent's benefit) after her husband's death, instead of the two-thirds of the total combined benefits (survivor's entitlement) that widows currently receive.
- ☐ Since wages are an important source of income for women over 65, especially unmarried women and black women, Social Security disincentives to employment may harm these women by limiting the income they can earn without suffering a reduction in Social Security benefits. It is unclear at this point what the financial trade-off would be between continuing Social Security payments to employed older women and paying for federal programs to aid older women who were discouraged from earning wages to supplement Social Security payments. Research needs to be done to ascertain the relative cost of these expenditures.

B. *Private Pensions*

- ☐ The Presidential Commission on Pension Policy is considering a policy that would set a mandatory level of private pension coverage and allow employer portability of the pension after one year's coverage.
- ☐ Pension systems should allow not only portability, but also earlier vesting of pension rights and cumulative vesting of pension rights. In light of the current pattern of women's labor force participation, these are especially important changes, although they would also benefit male workers. Women still have higher labor force participation rates in the 20 to 24-year-old cohort than do men, and pension vesting should begin before age 25, the level at which it is currently mandated. Women also still have more discontinuous labor force participation than do men, which means that a system allowing cumulative vesting over the course of the work life would be especially beneficial and would more accurately reflect women's total labor force participation during a lifetime.
- ☐ It is often assumed that, because more women are now active participants in the labor force, they will receive much greater benefits in the future from work-related pension programs. While this may be the case, all evidence indicates that the patterns of women's employment still differ from those of men in terms of full-time, long term commitment to the labor force that the majority of women remain clustered in the predominantly female occupations that have traditionally provided low status and low pay, and that a significant gap between the wages of men and women remains. Current efforts to develop pay equity for men and women merit attention and encouragement in order to raise the level of benefits secured by working women in the future.

4. To Encourage Employment

Although popular thinking holds that most older people are eager for retirement, it is obvious that many older women, particularly those who are displaced homemakers, require employment for economic survival. For women who have remained out of the labor force for a number of years because of family responsibilities, employment is often difficult to secure because of their age, lack of recent work experience, and lack of credit awarded for skills developed as a homemaker or community volunteer. Suggestions to facilitate the employment of older women follow.

- Through public education programs, the heterogeneity and employability of the older population needs to be emphasized and negative stereotypes eliminated. The vitality, experience, and motivation that an older person can bring to the employment situation is often as great as or greater than that of a younger worker.
- Efforts should be made to dispel the image of the older person solely as a resource for volunteer assistance. While voluntary involvement in community affairs can be productive for both the older individual and the community, for economic reasons older women and men may require paid employment fully as much as a younger person and should be perceived as an asset to the labor force.
- Some existing programs have dual purposes and dual benefits. Such programs as Senior Companions, Foster Grandparents, Green Thumb, and Home Health Aides meet vital community needs and in addition, provide needed employment opportunities for older persons. These programs merit expansion.
- More counseling and retraining programs for older people are needed so that they can secure employment. As a target population most needing assistance, older women seeking employment would produce immediate benefits and improve their economic status in their later years. Such counseling and retraining should be realistic and closely related to available opportunities in the current labor market. Training should also include information on translating skills derived from work in the home or community into marketable skills. Specific measures suggested are an employment and training bill, adapted to the needs of older women, which would be similar to the G.I. bill and provide entitlement for employment training. Also, tax credits might be utilized to assist those older women seeking re-entry to the labor market with the education expenses involved in their retraining.
- The federally supported system of educational scholarships and financial aid needs to be examined to ascertain whether or not it facilitates the participation of mature people in the educational system in preparation for employment. This includes examining the effects of current regulations on attendance by part-time students, on attendance by those with less familiarity with formal education whose test scores may be lower than those of conventional students, and on attendance by those, especially women, whose

total family incomes are high even though the wife may not have access to much of the total income.

- Flexibility in the work place with flextime, job sharing and other part-time options is desirable for all workers and is of special importance in facilitating the employment of older workers.
- Training programs like CETA provide a suitable mechanism for employment training and should be expanded to include more older workers. While current training programs for women emphasize employment in nontraditional career fields that offer them the potential for upward mobility, the fact that such an emphasis may not be desirable nor advantageous for older women should be recognized. Women, who are older and anxious to obtain employment to meet their immediate financial needs, may indeed prefer employment in a more traditional field, such as health care, which is related to their previous experience and most appropriate to their needs.
- The most popular job creation proposal is to change Medicare provisions to allow payments for "home care" of the elderly in addition to current payments for institutional care. The Department of HHS is currently running a demonstration project to ascertain whether or not home care payments would, in fact, lead to Medicare recipients being removed from institutional care to be cared for at home. Should the study indicate that this tradeoff is made, then presumably the funds to pay for home care and home care workers would come from reduced payments for institutional care. In this way, new employment opportunities as home care workers would become available for older women.
- Although age discrimination is a major impediment to women's employment, they rarely use existing age discrimination legislation. Women's organizations could play a central role in publicizing this legislation, sensitizing older women to the dynamics of age discrimination, and supporting their claims for redress.

5. To Improve Service Program Design and Delivery

- Service programs which assist older persons may be an important income supplement. Several basic principles should be kept in mind in designing such programs.

  A. Public policy should recognize the physical, social and economic differential existing among people categorized as aging and design such services appropriately.

  B. Every effort should be made to encourage inter-generational services and programs rather than continuing the isolation and age segregation experienced by many of the elderly.

  C. Public policy should encourage actions by local agencies and organizations to provide services in environments which are familiar and comfortable for older people.

  D. All programs and services should enhance the independence of the individual, rather than increasing dependence.

- At present, many elderly are not benefiting from public programs designed for them. Efforts are being made to coordinate the many Federal programs serving the aging but they remain fragmented and access is complicated. More publicity and effective outreach efforts are needed in order to inform and involve the elderly, who may be among the most isolated in the population, of services and programs that can be of assistance to them.
- Transportation is critical to dispel the isolation of older persons and to provide access to service programs. Many do not own their own cars and must rely on public transportation. While the lack of transportation impacts heavily on both the urban and rural elderly, it is the rural elderly who are most severely affected. These people, who may be among the most isolated and needy, consequently benefit least from public programs, particularly health care, nutrition, legal and other service programs.
- Because the elderly are a diverse group and many may be reluctant to accept government assistance or unable to cope with bureaucracy, it is important to present information and programs in a clear manner designed to increase their acceptability. More programs and delivery systems should be incorporated into community centers and churches which are known to and trusted by the aging constituency. Racial and ethnic differences must also be accommodated.
- The demographic fact of the predominance of women among the aging population suggests that both government agencies and private organizations should be encouraged to examine the impact of all programs on older women to ascertain if the particular needs of this group are being met. It is also of great importance that a large number of those involved in program planning and service delivery be representative of older women.

* * *

Currently, the negative stereotypes and implications of aging discourage discussion and realistic assessment. In fiscal and social terms, the aging are frequently portrayed as "a burden." The complex issues involved in equitable and adequate public programs for the aging almost defy objective analysis and will continue to do so until the antipathy to aging is addressed.

Dr. Robert Butler, director of the National Institute on Aging, has observed that it is vital to deal effectively with the problems of aging, for these relate directly to "our futures and our future selves." Despite each person's reluctance to accept the effects of aging, the numbers are rising and the public costs are escalating. Also, the changing ratios of the elderly in relation to active workers in the labor force raise serious questions about who shall bear these costs.

Whatever level of costs is chosen by society, this study focuses attention on the needs and inequities faced by a specific and numerically dominant segment of the aging population, namely women. The majority status of women among the aging population implies that aging is a women's issue. However, in terms of the equitable distribution of resources among the aging, facing old age and responding to its needs is a major social issue.

References

Binstock, Robert H.
1978 "Federal Policy toward the Aging--Its Inadequacies and Its Policies." In National Journal, *The Economics of Aging: The Economic, Political, and Social Implications of Growing Old in America*. Washington, D.C.: Government Research Corp.

Data Resources, Inc.
1980 *Inflation and the Elderly*. Washington, D.C.: National Retired Teachers Association / Association for Retired Persons.

19. MEN AND WOMEN: Changing Roles and Social Security

U.S. Department of Health, Education and Welfare

Under the Social Security Amendments of 1977 (P.L. 95-216), the Congress required the Secretary of Health, Education and Welfare, in consultation with the Department of Justice Task Force on Sex Discrimination, to study and prepare a report on proposals to eliminate dependency as a factor in entitlement to Social Security spouse's benefits and to eliminate sex discrimination under the Social Security program.

When the Social Security program was established in 1935, basic protection was provided for workers in the jobs that were covered under Social Security. In 1939, before Social Security benefits were first paid, supplementary protection was provided for workers' wives and widows as dependents. This method of providing protection reflected a pattern of family relationships in American society-- lifelong marriages in which women were solely homemakers and men provided economic support--that was much more common then than today.

The traditional rules of lifelong homemaker and lifelong paid worker are no longer as typical: rather, there is a growing diversity of roles. The labor-force participation of married women had grown from 17 percent in 1940 to about 47 percent in 1977 and is expected to continue to grow. Although more married women are working, the majority do not work when their children are very young. In 1977, 39 percent of married women under age 55 with pre-school-age children who were living with their husbands were in the paid labor force.

The increase in the divorce rate also has contributed to the growing diversity of family roles and work patterns since many divorced women must work to support themselves or their families. The ratio of divorces to marriages increased from one in six in 1940 to one in two in 1975. The marriages of one in three women age 26 to 40 are expected to end in divorce.

For a variety of reasons, many more married women are working but no typical pattern of lifetime roles is emerging. Some married women are lifetime homemakers, some are paid workers throughout their lives, and others combine these two roles.

Reprinted from *Social Security Bulletin*, 42 (May 1979):25-32.

There also have been changes in the way society in general thinks about the role of women and in the way women view themselves. There is a growing perception that married women should not be treated as dependents under Social Security because so many of them work in paid jobs and are not financially dependent on their husbands. Women are increasingly recognized as equal partners in marriage, which is viewed as an interdependent economic relationship where each spouse renders services of an economic value to the family. And women generally view themselves as having a choice of careers--working in paid employment, working as unpaid homemakers, or both.

As a result of these changes in society, interest has grown in the way women are treated under the Social Security program. A central issue is whether the system of dependent's benefits designed decades ago adequately serves today's society. The present Social Security structure works best in the case of a lifelong married couple where one spouse is a lifelong paid worker and the other is a lifelong homemaker. Many believe that Social Security should be changed so that it accommodates the diversity of roles and work patterns of men and women in today's society.

In addition to the issue of the dependency basis of benefits, a number of other important Social Security issues are discussed...the fairness of treatment of couples when both spouses work, and the adequacy of protection for divorced people, disabled homemakers, widows, etc....

The report explores two comprehensive options for dealing with the issues that arise from the present system of providing dependent's benefits. The two options are earnings sharing and establishment of a new double-decker benefit structure for the Social Security program.

This report is intended to focus public debate on concerns about the way Social Security relates to the present complex and diversified structure of American society and on various options to deal with these concerns. The report contains no recommendations for legislative changes: such recommendations would be premature at this time. Extensive public debate of the issues and options is necessary before any consensus can be reached on what changes might be desirable. In addition, the options discussed are complex and will require further refinement and study before their precise effects on the protection of various groups, and on other public and private income maintenance programs, are fully known.

ISSUES

Most of the issues that have been raised pivot on the fact that married women generally have Social Security protection as dependents of their husbands. Under the current program, a married woman can receive benefits as a dependent wife or widow (or ex-wife) of a covered worker; she can also receive benefits as a covered worker in her own right, but she cannot receive both benefits in full. If she is entitled to both a worker's benefit and a dependent's benefit, she receives an amount equal to the higher of the two benefits--that is, she receives her worker's benefit plus the amount, if any, by which the spouse's benefit exceeds the worker's benefit...

The concerns about the Social Security protection of women relate to the fundamental goals of the system which are to provide benefits that are adequate to meet important social needs and at the same time are equitably distributed among different categories of beneficiaries and contributors to the program. In many cases, the goals of adequacy and equity are inconsistent; program changes that improve adequacy may reduce equity and vice-versa. This tension has been with the system since its inception, and the appropriate balance between these two goals is often a source of controversy.

The issues that have been identified are fundamentally tied to the Social Security program's twin goals of adequacy and equity and the conflicts between them. Reducing inequities for women workers while providing adequate protection for women with little paid work history will involve striking a new balance between the adequacy and equity of the Social Security system.

Adequacy Concerns

One area of concern arises from gaps and inadequacies in the protection provided for homemakers and dependent spouses. Homemaker or child-care activities may preclude or reduce participation of married women in the paid labor force therefore preventing them from obtaining primary protection as workers. Also, since dependent's benefits are based on a proportion of the worker's benefits and are only payable under certain conditions, homemakers may have inadequate protection under Social Security. These concerns include:

- ☐ Married women workers get substantially lower benefits than men workers both because they frequently spend time out of the paid labor force (or work part time) to perform homemaker or child-care activities and because average wages for women are lower than for men.
- ☐ The divorced wife's benefit of 50 percent of the worker's benefit is often not adequate to support a divorced homemaker living alone. A divorced person has no Social Security protection based on the marriage if it lasted less than 10 years....
- ☐ Widowed homemakers under age 60 cannot receive benefits unless they are either at least age 50 and disabled or are caring for children. Many widows have no Social Security protection during a period when they may face difficulty entering or reentering the labor force.
- ☐ Women working in the home have gaps in disability protection. Benefits are not provided for disabled homemakers or their children if the homemaker has no recent attachment to the paid work force. Widows who become disabled under age 50 do not have disability protection.
- ☐ Aged widows frequently remain on the benefit rolls for many years; they often do not have resources to supplement their Social Security benefits, may live in poverty, and may need additional protection.

Equity Concerns

A second area of concern centers on the equity of benefits between one- and two-earner couples and married and single workers. These concerns include:

- □ ...Married women may find that the Social Security protection they earn as workers may duplicate, rather than add to, the protection they already have as spouses.
- □ Some two-earner couples are concerned that benefits are often higher for couples where one spouse earned all (or most) of the income than for couples where both spouses had earnings even though their total family earnings are the same.
- □ Since benefits are payable to dependents, married workers receive greater protection under Social Security than single workers, even though both pay Social Security taxes at the same rate; single workers may view this situation as inequitable.

COMPREHENSIVE OPTIONS

...Under earnings sharing, 50 percent of the total annual earnings of the couple would be credited to each spouse's individual earnings record. The benefits for each spouse would be based on one-half of the couple's earnings during years of marriage and on individual earnings while unmarried. The idea underlying earnings sharing is that each spouse is an equal partner in marriage and each--whether a worker in paid employment or an unpaid homemaker--should have equal credit for total family earnings. This idea implies, then, that each should have equal protection in his or her own right rather than as a dependent of the other spouse.

Under a double-decker plan a new two-tier benefit system would be established. A flat-dollar benefit (tier I) would be payable to everyone, regardless of earnings, who met certain requirements. In addition, an earnings-related benefit (tier II) would be payable on the basis of earnings from employment covered under Social Security. Certain features of the earnings sharing option would be incorporated in the provisions for tier II to deal more comprehensively with the issues....

In designing the options, arbitrary decisions were frequently necessary to estimate costs. In general, the options were designed with the idea that a new benefit system should result in costs that would approximate long-range costs under present law. Because of these cost constraints, when benefits were increased in some areas, reductions were provided in other areas. Further, to hold down costs, benefits for one- and two-earner couples were equalized by reducing benefits for one-earner couples rather than by raising benefits for two-earner couples.

The estimated long-range (75-year) cost of the earnings-sharing option comes very close to approximating long-range costs under present law. This option is estimated to decrease long-range costs by an average of 0.06 percent of taxable payroll.[1] (If applied to 1979 taxable payroll, 0.06 percent would represent savings of $0.6 billion over present law.)

The long-range costs of the double-decker plan are highly dependent on how the benefits are adjusted to keep pace with rising wages or prices. Under various assumptions for adjusting the benefits the estimated long-range cost of the double-decker plan would range from a cost of 0.50 percent of taxable payroll ($5 billion if applied to 1979 taxable payroll) to a savings of 1.86 percent of taxable payroll ($19 billion if applied to 1979 taxable payroll). The long-range cost of the double-decker plan could closely approximate present law costs by changing the way the tier I benefit is adjusted for changes in economic conditions or by making other changes in the plan....

Option #1: Earnings Sharing

Under earnings sharing, a couple's annual earnings would be divided equally between them for the years they were married for purposes of computing retirement benefits. The earnings would be divided when the couple divorced or when one spouse reached age 62. This would entitle each spouse to a primary benefit which would replace aged dependent spouse's and surviving spouse's benefits provided under present law.

The basic earnings-sharing idea has been modified in certain respects in order to pay benefits that are somewhat comparable to present law benefits. The modifications are:

1. When one spouse dies, the survivor would be credited with 80 percent of the total annual earnings of the couple during the marriage, but not less than 100 percent of the earnings of the higher earner.
2. For purposes of benefits for young survivors--children and young surviving spouses caring for children--earnings would not be transferred between the spouses with regard to a marriage in effect at the time of death. Benefits for young survivors would be based on any earnings credits the deceased person had from paid work (while unmarried or during a current marriage), plus any credits acquired as a result of a prior marriage terminated by death or divorce.
3. For purposes of disability benefits, earnings would not be shared with regard to a marriage still in effect at the time of disability. Disability benefits would be based on any earnings credits the disabled person had from paid work (while unmarried or during the current marriage), plus any credits acquired from a prior marriage.

Option #1 also includes certain features that are not essential to earnings sharing. These features are included to illustrate one way of dealing comprehensively with the concerns that have been raised or to limit the cost of the option to roughly that of present law. For example, benefits would be payable to surviving mothers and fathers only until the youngest child reaches age

7, rather than age 18 as under present law. To make up partially for this benefit loss, an adjustment benefit equal to 100 percent of the deceased spouse's benefit would be payable for one year following the death of the spouse. This benefit would be paid regardless of whether there are any children in the family eligible for benefits.

Response to issues. Following is a list of the ways earnings sharing would respond to the issues discussed previously.

1. *Low benefits for women workers who spend time out of the paid labor force in child-care and homemaking activities.* The plan would not reduce the number of years used to compute average earnings but would improve the protection of married women through sharing of earnings during a marriage.
2. *Gaps in protection for divorced women.* The sharing, upon divorce, of earnings during a marriage would help prevent gaps in protection for divorced women; each spouse would have protection in his or her own right.
3. *Aged widows may need additional protection.* Inheritance of earnings credits would substantially improve protection for many survivors of two-earner couples with lifelong marriages; benefits for the survivors of one-earner couples would not vary substantially from present law.
4. *Benefits are not provided for nondisabled surviving spouses under age 60 unless they are caring for children.* Persons widowed before retirement age would receive an adjustment benefit for one year. Protection would be reduced for some widowed persons under age 60 who do not have children under age 7 in their care. (Under present law widows can receive benefits if they have a child under age 17 in their care.) Under the earnings-sharing option, only the one-year adjustment benefit would be paid to surviving spouses who do not have a child under age 7 in their care. Aged surviving spouses could not get benefits (other than the adjustment benefit) until age 62, rather than age 60 as under present law.
5. *Some married women workers do not meet the recency-of-work test to qualify for disability benefits.* Earnings credits acquired due to death of a spouse or divorce would help some divorced and widowed women to meet the recency-of-work test.
6. *Benefits are not provided for disabled homemakers.* This option would not provide disability protection for married homemakers.
7. *Benefits are not provided for disabled widows and widowers under age 50.* Surviving spouses would acquire earnings credits that would count toward disability protection in their own right at any age.
8. *Benefits are not provided for survivors of deceased homemakers.* This option would not provide protection for the survivors of married homemakers who died. Divorced and widowed homemakers would acquire earnings credits that would count toward protection for their survivors.

9. *Benefits of married women as paid workers largely duplicate their benefits as dependents.* Each spouse would get a benefit based on his or her earnings while single, and earnings credits acquired as a result of marriage.
10. *Different benefit amounts may be paid to married couples with the same total average earnings.* Retired couples (in a lifelong marriage) with the same total average earnings would receive the same total benefits.
11. *Different benefit amounts may be paid to the survivors of married couples with the same total average earnings.* The difference in benefits for survivors of one- and two-earner couples would be reduced but not eliminated.
12. *Married workers have greater* Social Secur*ity protection than single workers.* Elimination of dependent spouse's benefits would decrease the difference in protection of married workers compared to single workers under present law.

Major Effects of Earnings Sharing

Effects on retired people. Retirement benefits would be the same for lifelong married couples with the same total average earnings. Benefits would be reduced for one-earner couples; the benefit of the higher-earning spouse would be less than under present law and the benefit of the lower-earning spouse would be higher. For most couples in which no dependent spouse's benefit would be payable under present law, there would be no change in benefit amounts. Assuming a lifelong marriage, each spouse would receive the same benefit amount.

Under the 50-50 sharing of earnings at divorce, the lower-earnings spouse would have greater protection and the higher-earnings spouse would have lower protection than under present law. The amount of change would depend on the duration of the marriage and the level of earnings, if any, of each spouse both during and after the marriage.

Benefits equal to 50 percent of the retired person's basic benefit would be paid to children and young spouses caring for children under age 7 (or disabled). The same maximum limit on family benefits would apply that applies under present law.

Effects on survivors. The surviving spouse would inherit 80 percent of the total annual earnings of the couple during the marriage, but not less than 100 percent of the earnings of the higher-earning spouse. Survivors of two-earner couples (with lifelong marriages) would generally get higher benefits than under present law. Benefits for survivors of one-earner couples would generally be about the same as under present law--they could exceed benefits for survivors of two-earner couples with the same total average earnings, although by less than under present law.

Protection would be reduced for surviving spouses with a child in their care as follows: (1) No benefits would be paid unless the child were under age 7 (rather than under age 18 as under present law); and (2) the benefit amount would be 50 percent of the worker's basic benefit (rather than 75 percent as under present law).

This modification of present law was included to reduce costs, to reduce the payment of benefits to spouses as dependents, and to channel benefits more directly to children. Since the labor-force participation of women increases substantially when they do not have pre-school-age children, there may be less need to provide a monthly benefit for such women.

An adjustment benefit equal to 100 percent of the deceased spouse's basic benefit would be provided for the year for surviving spouses under age 62 to help meet the special needs of homemakers widowed before old age.

Dependent's benefits would not be paid to widows and widowers age 60 and 61 or to disabled widows and widowers aged 50-60, but they would qualify for an adjustment benefit; such people might have disability protection in their own right based on inherited earnings credits.

The benefit for a surviving child under age 18 or disabled would be 100 percent of the deceased person's basic benefit (rather than 75 percent as under present law). Where there is more than one surviving child in a family, the total benefits to the children would be equal to 100 percent of the worker's basic benefit for the child plus 50 percent of the worker's basic benefits for each additional child. Each child would get an equal share of the total.

Earnings during a marriage still in effect at the time one spouse dies would not be shared (or inherited) for purposes of paying benefits to young survivors. As a result, when a lifelong-married homemaker dies, her surviving children would not receive benefits. However, divorced or widowed homemakers could become insured for benefits as a result of earnings sharing at divorce or inheriting earnings at death.

Effects on disabled people. Benefits for a disabled earner would be roughly the same as present law benefits. Benefits would be based on the person's own earnings, taking into account earnings shared with a spouse during a prior marriage or credits acquired due to the death of a spouse.

Disabled lifelong homemakers could be eligible for disability protection only on the basis of earnings credits acquired as a result of divorce or death of a prior spouse; earnings of a spouse in a current marriage could not be counted.

Although the present survivor's benefits for disabled widows and widowers would be eliminated, widowed homemakers might qualify for disability benefits on the basis of earnings credits inherited when their spouses died. The disability benefits would be payable at any age (not only between age 50-60 as under present law).

Disability protection for lower-paid or non-paid divorced spouses would be improved as the result of the 50-50 split of earnings at divorce. Disability protection for divorced people who were the higher (or sole) earner would be reduced due to the 50-50 split of earnings.

The provisions for children and spouses with children in their care would be the same as for dependents of retired earners.

Option #2: Double-Decker Benefit Structure

Under the double-decker option, each U.S. resident would have retirement, survivors, and disability protection. This universal protection would be the first tier of a two-tier system. Tier I would be a flat-dollar payment of $122 for U.S. residents beginning at age 65 (or upon disability). Reduced benefits would be paid as early as age 62. Tier II would be a benefit equal to 30 percent of a person's average earnings in covered employment. Tier II benefits would be payable as early as age 62 (reduced if taken before age 65). The benefit for an aged or disabled worker would be equal to the sum of a tier I and a tier II benefit.

Under the double-decker option, the adequacy and equity elements of the program would be separated--tier I generally would provide the social adequacy element and tier II the equity element. Dealing with the goals of adequacy and equity with separate benefit tiers should make it easier for the public to understand the underlying principles and for policy makers to develop proposals to fulfill specific goals.

A number of the features of this option are not an integral part of a basic double-decker system but were included to improve the protection of specific groups of persons. Such features include the 50-50 split of earnings at divorce, the inheritance of earnings by a surviving spouse for purposes of computing tier II benefits, and the provision of an adjustment benefit to a surviving spouse at any age. These features of the plan are generally the same as those under earnings sharing although the benefit amounts would be somewhat different due to the different benefit structure.

Response to issues. Following is a list of the ways the double-decker option would respond to the issues discussed previously.

1. *Low benefits for women workers who spend time out of the paid labor force in child-care and homemaking activities.* The plan would not reduce the number of years used to compute average earnings for tier II benefit purposes, but it would improve protection for some women workers by providing for a split of earnings upon divorce and inheritance of earnings credits from a deceased spouse.
2. *Gaps in protection for divorced women.* Aged or disabled divorced persons would get a tier I benefit; divorced persons would get earnings credits for tier II purposes equal to half of the couple's annual earnings during their marriage.
3. *Aged widows may need additional protection.* Aged or disabled widowed persons would get a tier I benefit; inheritance of earnings credits for tier II purposes would improve protection for many widows.
4. *Benefits are not provided for nondisabled surviving spouses under age 60 unless they are caring for children.* Persons widowed before retirement age would receive an adjustment benefit for one year. Protection would be reduced for some widowed persons under age 60 who do not have

children under age 7 in their care. (Under present law widows can receive benefits if they have a child under age 18 in their care.) Under the double-decker option, only the one-year adjustment benefit would be paid to surviving spouses who do not have children under age 7 in their care. Aged surviving spouses could not get benefits (other than the adjustment benefit) until age 62, rather than age 60 as under present law.

5. *Some married women workers do not meet the recency-of-work test to qualify for disability benefits.* There would be no insured status requirements to qualify for disability benefits under either test.
6. *Benefits are not provided for disabled homemakers.* Disabled homemakers could receive a tier I benefit. If they acquired any earnings credits, they could also get a tier II benefit.
7. *Benefits are not provided for disabled widows and widowers under age 50.* Disabled widows would receive full tier I benefits at any age plus tier II benefits based on earnings credits acquired as a result of their own paid work or from prior marriages.
8. *Benefits are not provided for survivors of deceased homemakers.* Survivors of deceased homemakers could receive tier I benefits plus any tier II benefits based on individual earnings and earnings credits acquired due to prior marriages.
9. *Benefits of married women as paid workers largely duplicate their benefits as dependents.* Each aged or disabled person would get a tier I benefit in his or her own right, plus a tier II benefit if he or she had earnings credits.
10. *Different benefit amounts may be paid to married couples with the same total average earnings.* Retired couples with the same total average earnings would receive the same total benefits.
11. *Different benefit amounts may be paid to the survivors of married couples with the same total average earnings.* The difference in benefits for survivors of one- and two-earner couples would be reduced but not eliminated.
12. *Married workers have greater* Social Secur*ity protection than single workers.* Elimination of dependent spouse's benefits would decrease the advantage of married workers under present law.

Major Effects of Double-Decker Plan

Effects on retired people. Older people who are not eligible for any Social Security benefits under present law would get a tier I benefit. If they had any covered earnings, they would also get a tier II benefit even if they were not insured for benefits under present law. Benefit amounts would be lower than under present law for one-earner couples (except at very low earnings levels where they would be higher). Benefits for two-earner couples would not vary significantly from present law (except at very low earnings levels where they would be higher).

A homemaker spouse would get a tier I benefit in his or her own right instead of a dependent spouse's benefit as under present law. Tier I benefits would be higher than dependent spouse's benefits under present law in cases where the primary earner was low paid and lower in all others.

As under earnings sharing, earnings credits for each year of the marriage would be split 50-50 upon divorce. The effects on protection would be similar under both options although the benefit amounts involved would be different.

Benefits would be paid to children and young spouses caring for entitled children of retired workers under the same conditions as under earnings sharing but the benefit amounts would be different. Each would get a tier I benefit of $122. This would be more than present law benefits at average earnings levels of about $420 and below, and less than present law benefits at higher levels.

A relatively small number of children and young spouses would qualify for benefits that they would not qualify for under present law because the retired person had not worked in jobs covered under Social Security.

Family benefits would be subject to a maximum family benefit of 250 percent of the tier I benefit--$305--plus a tier II benefit. The maximum family benefit would be lower than under present law at average earnings levels of about $530 or more; at lower levels there would be an increase.

Effects on survivors. Surviving spouses would inherit earnings as described under earnings sharing. Benefits for the survivor of a one-earner couple with a lifelong marriage would not vary substantially from present law benefits except that benefits would be higher than under present law at very high earnings levels.

Benefits for survivors of a lifelong marriage where both spouses had worked would be higher than under present law; benefits would increase the most where each spouse had the same amount of earnings.

Benefits would be payable to surviving spouses with children in their care under the same conditions as under earnings sharing. The amount would be a tier I benefit, which would be payable regardless of whether the deceased person had ever worked in covered employment.

A one-year adjustment benefit would be provided for a surviving spouse under age 62. The amount would be 100 percent of the tier II benefit, which would be computed based on all the earnings credits of the deceased person - including earnings credits acquired from any prior marriage - plus the actual earnings of the person during a marriage that had not terminated prior to death. This benefit would be paid in addition to any benefit payable because of caring for an entitled child.

Dependent's benefits would not be paid to widows and widowers age 60 and 61; they would qualify for a one-year adjustment benefit.

The benefits for a surviving child would be a tier I benefit plus a tier II benefit. Where there is more than one surviving child in a family, the total benefit to the children would be a tier I benefit for each child, plus one tier II benefit for the family. Each child would get an equal share of the total.

The level of dependent's benefits payable to a surviving family compared to present law would vary substantially depending on: (1) the deceased person's average lifetime earnings level, (2) whether or not an adjustment benefit is payable, and (3) whether or not there is an entitled child under age 7, so that mother's or father's benefits would be payable.

Effects on disabled people. Disability benefits would be payable to everyone who meets the applicable definition of disability; there would be no insured status requirement.[2] The benefits would be a tier I benefit; if the disabled person had earnings credits as a result of his or her own earnings or due to divorce or death of a spouse, tier II benefits would be payable as well.

Benefits payable to a disabled worker would bear roughly the same relationship to present law benefits as would retirement benefits.

Benefits would be payable to disabled homemakers who had not worked in covered employment. (They would also get Medicare protection if they were entitled to disability benefits for twenty-four consecutive months.)

Disabled widows and widowers of any age could get tier I and tier II disability benefits, not just those age 50-60 as under present law. The benefit amount would generally be higher than present law since there would be no reduction based on age at entitlement.

Disabled divorced spouses would qualify for a tier I benefit, plus a tier II benefit based on their own earnings and on earnings credits acquired at the time of divorce. If a disabled person who was divorced was the higher earner, his or her benefits could be much lower than under present law depending on the level of earnings of the spouses and the length of the marriage. A divorced person who was the lower earner would generally get higher benefits.

The provisions for children and young spouses caring for children of disabled persons would be the same as those for dependents of retired workers.

Notes

1. Long-range costs are expressed as a percentage of taxable payroll. The cost or saving of a provision represents the average amount over a 75-year period by which the combined employee-employer Social Security tax rate would have to be raised or lowered to leave the Social Security trust funds in the same financial position.
2. If the recency-of-work test under present law were not met without the inclusion of earnings credits acquired due to death or divorce of a spouse, the stricter definition of disability applicable to disabled widows and widowers under present law would apply.

V

HOUSING AND COMMUNITY

Housing Needs

Federal government policies have had an important impact on how Americans live. Since the passage of the Housing Act of 1937, the rationale for government involvement in housing has been: (1) "to provide decent housing for the poor" and (2) "to increase homeownership among American families" (Weicher 1980:3-4). By encouraging homeownership, government has stimulated construction and raised the level of economic activity.

Homeownership grew not only because of government policies like FHA mortgages and tax incentives for homeownership, but also as a response to economic growth in the years after World War II. In recent years, owning a home has been a hedge against inflation and the increase in dual-earner couples has made more families able to afford a home (U.S. Department of Housing and Urban Development 1980:4-1). About two-thirds of all households own their own homes.

Now, however, high interest rates and rapidly increasing new home prices make it more difficult for families, especially first-time buyers, to afford a home. The type of property owned is changing too, with condominiums, cooperatives and mobile homes becoming more prevalent. Consequently, there is a growing gap in income and other social characteristics between homeowners and renters, with incomes of owners rising more rapidly. As Chapter 20, from *Housing Our Families* indicates, renters are increasingly concentrated among low-income households, given the advantages of homeownership for middle and upper-income households. The growth in single-person households, smaller families, and divorce has contributed to these trends.

Renters have less choice in apartments and houses, except in the luxury market. From 1970 to 1978, rental stock grew only half as fast as owner-occupied stock. Shifts in available housing and increased costs of both owning and renting, combined with changes in household composition, leave certain families hard-pressed to find adequate housing and forced to spend a larger proportion of their incomes on rent. Some groups are especially disadvantaged in their search:

> [B]eing a member of a non-white minority household, a female-headed household, or a large household substantially increases one's chances of being poorly housed. Moreover, households with black, Hispanic, or female heads are less likely to own their own homes than the average household and are more likely to spend over 25 percent of their incomes for adequate, uncrowded housing [U.S. Department of Housing and Urban Development 1980:1-1].

Several chapters in this part focus primarily on these households. Chapter 20 considers existing and future housing needs in the light of changes in family composition, suggesting a growing mismatch unless new policies are introduced. The problems of female-headed households, and those with children, are emphasized. Conversion of schools and other buildings is suggested to increase the supply of rental housing, especially for large or extended families. Ways of meeting the housing and community needs of dual-earner families with children are also discussed.

Discrimination against families with children affects households regardless of their size, marital status, or race. However, research indicates that female-headed and minority households are most affected, suggesting that such discrimination often masks other prejudices. Public housing is the only option for many low-income women and children. Chapter 21, "Where Do You Live?" presents a mother's impressions of, and reactions to, living in a low-income project, adding first-hand experience to the research and policy analyses of previous chapters.

Female-headed households have special problems. In many ways they are households in transition, reorganizing after divorce or separation. Many will become traditional husband-wife families in the future, since about 71 percent of divorced women remarry within five years. However, 30 percent of the divorced mothers must restructure their families more or less permanently (U.S. Department of Housing and Urban Development 1980:3-4). Decent housing presents a severe problem for single mothers whose incomes are greatly reduced after divorce or separation.

Single parents often want to stay in the same neighborhood to maintain continuity in their children's lives. It is also important for them to be near work, child-care services, and support networks. Discrimination against renting to families with children may limit their choices. Unable to meet all their requirements, single-parent families often make several moves after divorce (Weiss 1979). Upper-middle-income women and their children are most likely to remain in the same (usually single-family) home, despite the drop in income. Single-parent, white-collar families may stay in the same neighborhood after divorce, but move from a single-family home to a less desirable apartment. The majority of blue-collar and working-class women move after divorce. Their decisions are influenced by the dependability of alimony and child support payments, location of relatives, and community ties (Department of Housing and Urban Development 1980:3-4). Poor families frequently have no choice other than public housing, with all the limitations described by Francis.

Housing Our Families (1980:3-6) asks whether government should develop policy to assist single parents during this one- to five-year transition period when stress and financial problems are greatest: "What is essential then is that compassionate housing policies recognize the legitimate aspirations of families, whether two-parent, one-parent, or in transition." Such a development wil not occur under the current administration, which is curtailing existing programs.

Barriers to adequate housing. Despite government housing programs, many Americans do not live in adequate or affordable units. Barriers posed by discrimination or zoning laws limit their choices. Some families face multiple and overlapping constraints. A large, single-parent black family with young children may be discriminated against as minority group members (despite laws to the contrary), as a female-headed family, as a large family, and as a household with young children. Black and Hispanic households tend to be larger than average and are more frequently extended families. However, large units are scarce and some communities or property owners limit units to "nuclear families."

A "nontraditional" household may find that a community's zoning laws prohibit unrelated individuals from buying homes and/or that mortgage financing is difficult. Single parents or displaced homemakers who seek to economize by combining households may be similarly affected.

In central cities, poor minority households may be victims of "gentrification," in which low-income tenants are displaced from sound housing which is later renovated and rented or sold to more affluent households (U.S. Department of Housing and Urban Development 1979). This change increases the city's tax base, but decreases housing for low- and moderate-income households. It also imposes hardships on uprooted residents, especially those in their later years, who must adjust to unexpected and unwanted changes in their lives.

Other constraints come from discrimination in mortgage lending, redlining, and snob zoning. Property owners create additional barriers when they limit rentals to adults only. Other households are unable to obtain mortgages on homes in neighborhoods which lenders have "redlined." A report for HUD examined illegal discrimination by urban mortgage lenders and explored the extent of redlining (Schafer & Ladd 1980:Summary, 2). The researchers found limited evidence of discrimination based on sex or marital status in New York and California, the two states studied. Interestingly, lenders seemed to discriminate against male-only applicants and against unmarried or separated applicants, but not on a widespread basis against female-only applicants. On the other hand, discrimination based on race was prevalent in both areas. There was evidence, too, that older applicants were treated less favorably than younger ones, especially with regard to modifying loans. Red-lining occurred, often in older or largely minority neighborhoods (ibid.:40-41).

Zoning and land-use regulations affect housing choices in many ways. Even policies like rent controls, designed to improve housing availability, may actually shrink housing options. State and local regulations, like snob zoning, limit multi-family housing for low- and moderate-income households in suburbs. Suburban areas may approve subsidized housing only for the elderly, to avoid the cost of building schools and other facilities for families with children--and to keep out "undesirable elements." They also may impose one-acre or larger minimums on housing lots to keep out multi-family or moderately-priced single-family homes. On the other hand, some states, like Massachusetts, already have anti-snob-zoning laws.

Federal housing assistance programs. To achieve its goal of providing housing for poor and low-income families, the federal government subsidizes housing for more than 3.2 million lower-income households. It also insures or guarantees homes purchased by 7.9 million households (Weicher 1980:2). However, one estimate is that as many as 18 million families need some kind of assistance: 6 million families live in substandard housing, 10 million spend more than one-quarter of their income on housing, and an additional 2 million live in crowded units (Clay 1982:11). The worst housing historically has been in the South and in rural areas.

Policies and programs to provide housing for the poor have undergone numerous changes in direction over the past few decades. In the 1950s and early 1960s, urban renewal--often called "urban removal"--resulted in the demolition or withdrawal from the market of almost 250,000 family units. These were replaced by 60,00 dwelling units, only one-third for low-income families (Morris 1979:101). Moreover, until about the mid-1960s, policy makers showed little concern for the social effects of government programs that destroyed stable communities and disrupted the lives of residents. The role that policy played in maintaining or increasing segregation by race and income was ignored. Pruitt-Igoe, a mammoth high-rise apartment complex in St. Louis, was hailed as a model for public housing when it was built in the 1950s. But it came to symbolize all that was wrong with federal policy and was demolished in 1972 as a "mistake." In recent years, policy has shifted to subsidizing private homebuilders to provide low-income housing, with the emphasis on low-density units scattered throughout communities.

Who benefits from federal housing programs? Public housing and rent supplements serve a high proportion of minority and large households. New Section 8 units serve the highest proportion of single-parent and elderly households. Existing Section 8 housing serves smaller households and single-parent families. There are more minority and fewer elderly participants in existing than in new Section 8 units. However, many elderly persons live in housing built especially for them. The groups served most frequently by four HUD programs (all types of Section 8, public housing, rent supplements, and Section 236) are single-parent families with four or more children and very low-income families, followed by single-parent families with one to three children. Non-elderly one- and two-person households without children are eligible for only 10 percent of the public housing and Section 8 units. Households of unrelated individuals for the most part are ineligible for public housing or for Section 8 assistance.

Homeowner programs serve a high proportion of relatively young and small families, as well as some single persons. Minority and female-headed families are relatively well represented among participants in five HUD ownership programs (U.S. Department of Housing and Urban Development 1980:7-1 to 7-11). In addition, federal government policies, such as those that permit tax deductions, credits and exclusions, aid homeowners. Depreciation allowances and other provisions decrease the cost of homeownership or housing development for individuals and businesses.

Families and Community

Housing policies and programs have a direct impact on how families live, but other government policies also affect their quality of life. When families choose a place to live, they consider not only housing but also neighborhood facilities, services, accessibility, and other characteristics. The range and availability of community services may be important. Families with children or older members may consider community health and day-care facilities, or centers for older residents, which offer hot meals and recreational activities to be essential. Federal policies and funds help determine the nature and extent of such services. The U.S. government has played a much less active role in shaping the character of communities than have governments of countries like Sweden which have emphasized planned communities.

In this country, private development has led to suburban sprawl and lack of emphasis on services, especially mass transit. Such planning decisions remain largely in the hands of state and local authorities. Moreover, the integration of income and racial groups has not been a major thrust of federal policy. In contrast, residents in planned Swedish suburbs come from a range of income groups and those with subsidies who live alongside others who pay full rents. Such communities have a range of dwelling units from high-rise to single family homes as well as social services, shopping, and other facilities.[1]

When seeking a place to live, families weigh a variety of factors. Household composition and economic status play important roles in ordering priorities. A dual-income couple with no children may want to live in a location that offers necessary services and amenities within a reasonable distance from work. They may be willing to allocate a large portion of their combined incomes for housing that meets these criteria. If they choose a large metropolitan center where costs and vacancy rates limit their choice of rental units, they may decide to purchase a condominium or cooperative. Such housing or community characteristics as space and the quality of schools may be most important to a traditional nuclear family. As we have seen, households in transition have their own list of important community attributes, while families with elderly or handicapped members may give highest consideration to accessibility of the dwelling unit for wheel chair occupants and convenience to needed services.

Housing arrangements for older persons are varied. Some live with family members, as Chapter 23 indicates. Others live with their counterparts (see Chapter 27 in Part VI). Maggie Kuhn of the Gray Panthers advocates age-integrated communal living in which older individuals share housing with younger people. There is fierce debate over the most advantageous arrangements for older people. Age-segregated private and subsidized complexes are widespread. They have been called "ghettoes for the elderly," but at least some residents have voluntarily chosen this environment over other options. Some favor "granny annexes" to permit older people to live near, but independent of, their families. Tissue and McCoy (see Chapter 22) studied how a permanent income increase affected the living arrangements of older singles when they were transferred from public assistance to the Supplemental Security Income (SSI) program in 1974. Moderate increases in income did not make a significant difference in their living arrangements. Health status was a major factor in determining whether or not individuals lived alone.

Chapter 23, by Finch and Groves, is especially important because it shows how government programs and regulations may work at cross purposes. Families who care for ill, disabled, or elderly members receive little aid, despite the shift in policy from favoring institutionalization to community care in both England and the United States. In this country, Medicare and Medicaid policies penalize families that provide home care for relatives. For example, Medicare "prohibits payment for services otherwise covered if they were rendered by family or household members," since "these services will be presented gratis in any event" (National Senior Citizens Law Center 1980:114-15). That assumption is incorrect for women who must give up paid employment to provide care with little or no compensation. Policies in both countries also work against payments for care when older persons live with unrelated individuals, forcing some into institutions. The Reagan administration has indicated that it will ease some regulations concerning home care. The authors raise important questions about how community care for relatives will affect the work and family lives of women. Many will suffer emotional and financial costs if they leave the labor force. Moreover, Chapter 23 underscores the need for community services like respite care and supports to ease the strains on families who provide constant care.

For many families today, employment opportunities are a crucial determinant of their well-being. The impact of unemployment on individuals and their families was considered in Part III. In this section, the problem is analyzed from the larger perspective of the community. High unemployment, combined with major job losses from plant closings or difficulties in industries like autos and steel, leave some communities with unemployment rates well above the national average.

Buss and Redburn studied the impact of plant closings on workers and their families in Youngstown, Ohio. In Chapter 24, they describe how the community tried to cope with massive unemployment and to minimize its harmful effects on workers and their families. They show that human service agencies were unprepared to plan and institute programs to meet worker needs. Rayman and Liem (1982:1121) reported on a study of unemployment in Hartford, which came to a similar conclusion: workers were not aware of community agencies that could assist them and, at the same time, "social service providers, unions and companies were uniformly unresponsive to the needs of this group." As in Youngstown, unemployed workers and their families in Hartford sought help primarily from close relatives.

Federal policies to deal with this issue are few. In contrast, some European countries provide migration and other assistance to unemployed workers (President's Commission 1980:59-61). In a concluding section of Chapter 24, Buss and Redburn recommend a broad set of policies that local, state, and federal authorities might adopt to minimize the adverse economic effects of plant closings on a community and its inhabitants. With unemployment high in many communities, innovative programs and policies to revitalize older industrialized areas are urgently needed.

Unemployment is extremely high in inner-city areas, especially among black teenagers, whose unemployment rate is almost 50 percent. In the past, the federal government under Presidents Kennedy and Johnson devised a range of programs to improve the lives of residents in poor neighborhoods. These programs were introduced after it became clear that housing policies that concentrated poor families in high-rise apartments in low-income neighborhoods had increased segregation and created additional social and economic problems for residents. Moreover, there was growing national support for assisting the poor and disadvantaged. The War-on-Poverty and Great-Society programs of the 1960s were designed to attain these policy goals. By the middle of the 1970s, however, control of the programs had begun to shift from the federal to the local level with block grants, and the priority previously given to low-income areas was often lost. With the Reagan administration, the few remaining programs have been further gutted. In its urban and housing policies, as in other policy areas, allocations for the poor have been significantly reduced.

Current policy directions. Unlike previous administrations, the Reagan administration has not espoused the goal of providing decent housing for all Americans. Instead, it wants to reduce the number of those receiving subsidized housing assistance by 300,000 persons by 1985 (Schellhardt 1981:4). Those who continue to receive rent subsidies will be required to allocate a larger share of their annual income to housing--30 percent rather than the more usual 20 to 25 percent. Moreover, for the first time since 1937, the federal government does not have a public housing construction program (Guenther 1982:33). No new construction or rehabilitation program has been proposed to replace the Section 8 program, which has expired. Overall, the Reagan administration's total housing budget for the 1982 fiscal year was only $18.1 billion whereas the Carter administration had proposed a $28.8 billion budget (Daniels 1982:8E). Further cuts in funds for fiscal 1983 mean that existing housing will deteriorate further.

The current administration has been slow to introduce its own policies in this area. In its first interim report, the President's Housing Commission set forth some basic principles: achieving fiscal responsibility and monetary stability, encouraging free and deregulated markets, reliance on the private sector, "enlightened federalism with minimal government intrusion," and programs directed toward people not structures ("Emerging Reagan Housing Policy" 1982:A5). Its major recommendation was for "consumer-oriented assistance payments" or housing vouchers instead of construction. Eligibility would be confined to those with very low incomes, primarily those paying 50 percent or more for housing, or those being displaced. Thus, many working poor would be eliminated.

The United States already has experimented with housing vouchers (see U.S. Department of Housing and Urban Development 1978; Struyk & Bendick 1981; Bradbury & Downs 1981). Vouchers have advantages for government: they cost less than construction or rehabilitation; they do not commit federal resources on a long-term basis; and they do not impose national standards or objectives on local government (DeGiovanni & Brooks 1982). However, the program has obvious limitations. It assumes that housing quality is not a serious problem and that rental units are not in short supply. Moreover, it does not encourage rehabilitation of existing substandard units. Finally, since it is not an entitlement program, many who live in substandard housing would not qualify for assistance.

In March of 1982, President Reagan introduced his major urban policy initiative, urban enterprise zones. He called the concept the direct opposite of Model Cities programs which relied on government subsidies and "central planning" (Raines 1982:A1, B5). Instead, the program will use the market to solve urban problems and will rely on private sector institutions. Tax rollbacks, tax credits for hiring the disadvantaged, and reduced government regulations are the incentives to be offered business. Criteria for eligibility have not been set, but areas with a poverty rate of 20 percent or more and an unemployment rate one and one-half times the national average would be considered. Rural as well as urban areas would be eligible. Up to twenty-five areas could be so designated in each of the three years of the program. State and local governments would be required to contribute through "tax relief, regulation relief, improved neighborhod services, and neighborhood organizations," as well as job training and minority business assistance ("President's Message" 1982:B8). The President has called the proposal his administration's main program to deal with black unemployment. However, no action on it had been taken by the beginning of 1983, although the president mentioned the program again in his State of the Union Message.

Is there a clear purpose in the action or inaction of this administration? In analyzing its housing policy, Struyk and colleagues (1982:414) summarized the Reagan administration's priorities as a "dramatic reduction in housing assistance, cuts in community development and credit programs, and expansion of subsidies to homeowners." It does not intend to increase the number of households receiving assistance. A further result of budget and program changes is that "housing policy is being tilted further to serve middle- and upper-income Americans" (ibid.). These actions are consistent with the reductions in assistance to poor and low-income families made in other policy areas discussed in this book.

Note

1. For a comparison of an American suburb, Levittown, Pennsylvania, and a Swedish one, Vällingby, see Popenoe (1977). Also see Genovese (1975) for a critical look at some of the newer planned suburbs around Stockholm.

References

Bradbury, Kathleen, and Anthony Downs.
1981 *Do Housing Allowances Work?* Washington, D.C.: Brookings Institution

Clay, Phillip.
1982 "Community Development and Housing." Pp. 1-17 in *Urban Policy Issues.* A report prepared under a cooperative agreement between The Joint Center for Political Studies and the U.S. Department of Housing and Urban Development. Washington, D.C.

Daniels, Lee A.
1982 "Housing-Aid Cuts Affect Poor Individually and Collectively." *New York Times* (Jan. 3):8E.

DeGiovanni Frank, and Mary Brooks.
1982 "Housing Vouchers: The Shape of Aid to Come." *City Limits* (Jan.):A10-A14.

"The Emerging Reagan Housing Policy: A Summary of Recommendations from the
1982 President's Housing Commission." *City Limits* (Jan.):A5-A7.

Genovese, Rosalie G.
1975 "Social Factors in Planning New Suburbs: The Swedish Example." *Sociological Symposium* (Spring):53-61.

Guenther, Robert.
1982 "Outlook in Low-Cost-Housing Is Gloomy as Programs Expire." *Wall Street Journal* (Dec. 8):33.

Morris, Robert.
1979 *Social Policy of the American Welfare State: An Introduction to Policy Analysis.* New York: Harper & Row.

National Senior Citizens Law Center.
1980 "The Family and the Elderly." Pp. 113-118 in *Families: Aging and Changing.* Hearings before the Select Committee on Aging, House of Representatives, Ninety-Sixth Congress, Second Session. June 4. Committee Pub. no. 96-242. Washington, D.C.: U.S. Government Printing Office.

Popenoe, David.
1977 *The Suburban Environment: Sweden and the United States.* Chicago: University of Chicago Press.

President's Commission for a National Agenda for the Eighties.
1980 *Urban America in the Eighties: Perspectives and Prospects. Report of the Panel on Policies and Prospects for Metropolitan and Nonmetropolitan America.* Washington, D.C.: U.S. Government Printing Office.

"President's Message to Congress on Urban Enterprise Zones"-- Excerpt.
1982 *New York Times* (March 24):B8.

Raines, Howell.
1982 "Reagan Offers Enterprise Zones Plan for Urban Revitalization." *New York Times* (March 24):A1, B8.

Rayman, Paula, and Ramsay Liem.
1982 "Health and Social Costs of Unemployment. Research and Policy Considerations." *American Psychologist*, 37:1116-23.

Schafer, Robert, and Helen F. Ladd.
1980 *Equal Credit Opportunity: Accessibility to Mortgage Funds by Women and Minorities.* 2 vols. and Summary. Washington, D.C.: U.S. Department of Housing and Urban Development, Office of Policy Development and Research. May.

Schellhardt, Timothy D.
1981 "Reagan Seeks to Cut 300,000 Americans from Fiscal '85 Subsidized Housing Rolls." *Wall Street Journal* (Dec. 24):4.

Struyk, Raymond J., and Marc Bendick, Jr. (eds.)
1981 *Housing Vouchers for the Poor: Lessons from a National Experiment.* Washington, D.C.: Urban Institute.

Struyk, Raymond J., John A. Tucillo, and James P. Zais.
1982 "Housing and Community Development." Pp. 393-417 in John L. Palmer and Isabel V. Sawhill (eds.), *The Reagan Experiment: An Examination of Economic and Social Policies under the Reagan Administration.* Washington, D.C.: Urban Institute.

U.S. Department of Housing and Urban Development, Office of Policy Development and Research.
1978 *A Summary Report of Current Findings from the Experimental Housing Allowance Program.* Washington, D.C.: HUD. April.
1979 *Displacement Report.* Washington, D.C.: HUD. February.
1980 *Housing Our Families.* Washington, D.C.: U.S. Government Printing Office. August.

U.S. General Accounting Office.
1979 *Rental Housing: A National Problem that Needs Immediate Attention.* Washington, D.C.: U.S. General Accounting Office.

Weicher, John C.
1980 *Housing, Federal Policies and Programs.* Washington, D.C.: American Enterprise Institute.

Weiss, Robert S.
1979 "Housing for Single Parents." *Policy Studies,* 8 (special issue no. 1):241-48.

Suggested Additional Readings

Caplow, Theodore, et al.
1982 *Middletown and Families: Fifty Years of Change and Continuity.* Minneapolis: University of Minnesota Press.

Gondor, John, and Steve Gordon.
1979 *The Housing Needs of "Nontraditional" Households.* Bulletin of the Community and Economic Development Task Force of the Urban Consortium. Washington, D.C.: U.S. Government Printing Office.

National Research Council.
1982 *Critical Issues for National Urban Policy: A Reconnaissance and Agenda for Further Study.* First Annual Report of the Committee on National Urban Policy. Washington, D.C.: National Academy Press.

Stack, Carole B.
1975 *All Our Kin: Strategies for Survival in a Black Community.* New York: Harper and Row.

20. HOUSING OUR FAMILIES: Policy and Research Options for the Future

U.S. Department of Housing and Urban Development

Most American families are adequately housed but problems remain which can create difficulties for families with children. As with all types of households, income is a major factor in a family's ability to command housing services. Thus poor families with children--and especially minority and female-headed families, which are disproportionately represented among the poor--are likely to be inadequately housed, to be overcrowded, and to pay burdensome amounts of the limited incomes for housing. Family size also affects a family's housing fortunes because large families are much more likely to live in inadequate housing.

In large part, as a result of the rapid inflation of the last decade, the rental market has been "skimmed" of many of its higher-income households as more and more have moved into homeownership. The perverse impact of inflation on the rental market has been intensified by its effect on tax incentives for homeowners, the largest housing "program" by far. The already sizable tax advantage of owning versus renting has greatly increased as inflation has moved households into ever higher marginal tax brackets. The increasing tax savings on each dollar of deductions for mortgage interest and property taxes are more valuable, the higher the income bracket of the homeowner. Simultaneously, entry into homeownership has become more difficult for lower-income households, who are barred from homeownership by rising house prices, mortgage interest costs, and downpayments.

At the same time, as a consequence of demographic trends, dramatic shifts in the composition of households have resulted in proportionately more households headed by women and proportionately fewer households with children.

When families with children are unable to afford to own their own homes, they must now compete with single persons and childless couples for rental housing in a market that has grown more slowly than homeownership. Complicating matters even more are the growth of rental policies that exclude or restrict children. It is not clear to what extent these rental practices are an economic response to shifts in demand or to what extent they are society's

---

Reprinted from U.S. Department of Housing and Urban Development, Office of Policy Development and Research, *Housing Our Families*. Washington, D.C.: U.S. Government Printing Office, 1980, pp. 8-1 to 8-4.

response to changing perceptions about children or working mothers. Nor are there any good measures of the inconvenience, frustration or pain suffered by individual families and family members as a result of these practices. What is clear is that the housing options for many families are limited because they have children and that in some localities these families may be excluded from a significant share of the existing rental market. These worrisome changes intensify the usual desire to know the future.

It goes without saying that we cannot predict the future with any certainty. But we can examine trends and, basing projections on stated assumptions, attempt to anticipate what housing needs might look like a decade hence.

The Joint Center for Urban Studies of Harvard/MIT has developed for HUD a series of projections based on the continuation of recent patterns of family formation and housing consumption. These projections show that between 1975 and 1990, there will be an increase of between 20 to 25 million households. Most of this increase will be in households without children, but, there will also be an increase in the number of households with children. This latter increase of about 6 million will be almost evenly split between married couples and single-parent families. Most of the single-parent families will be headed by women.[1]

Homeownership will increase among the married and remain relatively fixed among female-headed families. But among renters in 1980, the 4.3 to 4.4 million families headed by women will account for 43 to 50 percent of all renter families with children, whereas in 1975 they accounted for only 30.5 percent.

These families headed by women will be competing with 28 to 30 million other renter households for the same housing. And over two-thirds of their competitors will not have children. On the one hand, increasingly smaller proportions of the nation's households will need family housing, yet that very fact could turn against them and result in a housing market more heavily weighted to the demands of the childless. Moreover, because larger proportions of families with children will be headed by women--who, as we have seen, are less able than others to afford adequate housing--the options of many families with children may be increasingly limited.

These are not predictions, but they do illustrate what could occur in the next ten years. The issues of affordable housing and choice for families with children in the rental market are likely to remain on the public agenda for the foreseeable future.

A crucial question then is what direction should future policy take: Are new legislative initiatives called for? Should HUD's own programs be altered? Is there an appropriate role for voluntary cooperation between the suppliers of housing and fair-housing groups? Because of the complexity of the issues and the lack of definitive research on many conditions limiting housing choice, no one specific policy initiative suggests itself as the solution for the coming decades. We hope the information in this report will stimulate a debate that will take proper account of the needs of families with children. Our goal at this point is to lay out some of the options that might be considered in that debate.

[Elsewhere in this report is documented]...for the first time the scope of exclusionary and restrictive rental practices across the Nation. We now know that although these practices may be more common in certain regions of the country than in others, the extent of the problem is significant enough to create a high national average. All types of renter families with children--regardless of income, race, or sex of head--are likely to encounter some of these restrictions. Our data also suggest that the emotional and economic costs of restrictive practices affect different types of families in different ways.[2]

Because the housing problems of families result from an interplay among rental practices, the increased burden of housing costs, and household demographics, appropriate solutions necessarily range to issues beyond restrictive policies. Many options that appear at first glance as almost ideal solutions, often have drawbacks. We cannot make those intricate balancing decisions here, but we hope our discussion of the various statutory, supply, and programmatic options will facilitate the process.

Protective Laws

Restrictive rental practices are the most visible way that freedom of choice is curtailed, and...the issue of statutory protection for families with children is already a current focus of activity in some states and localities. Some groups also advocate that the federal government move in this direction as well.

The advantage of statutory change is that it makes a very clear statement regarding society's commitment to its children. In a period when there has been what some would consider an excessive emphasis on individual self-fulfillment, statements regarding the collective interest in the next generation may be particularly valuable. Such statements can help to alter both behavior and attitudes. On the other hand, the very process of enacting such legislation could intensify conflict among the various groups concerned with specific rights. Moreover, laws which grant rights do not necessarily create the means by which these rights can be realized. Too often enforcement mechanisms are ineffective. Additionally, such laws do not get to an underlying source of the problem: a tight rental market. And perversely, a possible side-effect of protection might be to add a further disincentive to new construction. This is by no means a certain outcome, however, and careful evaluation of local impacts in communities that already have ordinances prohibiting discrimination against families with children would give us greater insight into the benefits and effects of such legislation.

Supply Incentives--Rental Housing

Modifying supply incentives does not provide direct relief to families in immediate distress, but if the available rental stock could be increased through appropriate incentives, families would obtain long--term relief. Supply incentives could focus on either the construction of new multifamily units or the more effective use of the existing stock. New construction has traditionally been the most appealing option, and given the lag in new construction..., specific proposals designed to stimulate construction are particularly important. One option that Congress is now considering would provide shallow subsidies on mortgages for newly constructed rental housing for moderate-income families.

Some amount of new construction will be always be necessary, but rising costs and concerns over shrinking resources may very well preclude new construction adequate to meet anticipated needs. If this happens, more innovative utilization of existing dwellings might have to be considered more seriously than in the past. Can we open up that portion of the rental stock currently unavailable to families with children? Can we modify structures to better suit the needs of large and extended families?

At this point we do have some idea of the motivation behind the resistance to housing families with children. We do know that managers who do not rent to families with children *think* that their maintenance costs will be greater if their tenants include children. The National Neighbors roundtable recently held in Dallas indicated that managers feel their costs will be particularly high when families with children do not include a full-time homemaker. Since we have no data to support any of these perceptions, we need systematic empirical research to determine the actual costs associated with renting units to these families. If children do increase costs, consideration might be given to devising appropriate incentives to compensate owners for their loss. Currently, landlords typically respond to their expectations of higher costs by simply refusing to rent to families with children.

Even if research indicated that actual costs are not greater, it may still be necessary to provide economic incentives that would serve as a countervailing force to the prejudices and stereotypes that do exist concerning children. (However, our data on renter attitudes suggests that negative views about living near children are less prevalent than "popular wisdom" would hold.)

Clearly, the impact of supply incentives would not be limited solely to the existing housing stock. In fact our data on the high frequency of restrictive practices in newly constructed units suggest that, in the absence of intervention or special incentives, new construction may not yield a substantial increase in the number of units available to families with children.

Another possibility for increasing the supply of family housing would be incentives to investors, coupled with favorable financial arrangements, to convert unused public and private structures to rental housing for families with children. Such incentives would increase the available housing stock while alleviating the national problem of unused and under-utilized school facilities. All unused schools, for example, may not lend themselves to conversion, but with innovative architectural design many will. The pre-existing recreational facilities in schools may make conversion easier and increase the desirability of such units for families with children.

These conversion incentives might also apply to the conversion of small units in multifamily dwellings to units appropriate for large and extended families or the "reconversion" of what were once single-family dwellings to units appropriate for large families. Since new large-family units are most costly to construct, modifying existing dwellings may be a less costly way to provide large family units.

Increasing the supply of rental units available to families with children is an important avenue to pursue. But supply in itself may not be enough, because the application of occupancy standards may disqualify families with children from living in units for which they would seem to be eligible. (The data do not indicate whether these standards derive from local housing codes, managers' policies, or HUD guidelines. Additional research is needed on the precise interface between these components because their net effect is to severely restrict the housing options of families with children.) The challenge is to have standards that prevent excessive overcrowding, without denying families housing opportunities.

HUD Programs

HUD's Section 8 programs apply standards intended to prevent overcrowding and to ensure that excessive under-occupancy does not occur. Waivers are granted to allow some flexibility. In practice, however, when standards are waived, waivers occur typically in the direction of under-occupancy rather than over-occupancy. Perhaps in a tight rental market standards may need to be re-evaluated or relaxed to allow more people to live in a unit.

There are other areas in which HUD could make appropriate programmatic or administrative adjustments that might increase the supply of HUD-assisted housing for families or at least make the available supply more accessible to persons eligible for HUD programs. These include:

- examining HUD site selection procedures;
- creating incentives for PHAs to help families, particularly large families, find housing under the Section 8 existing program;
- streamlining paperwork to encourage greater landlord participation;
- reaching out to greater numbers of landlords to encourage their participation;
- encouraging local flexibility in extending the search time for certificate holders in tight rental markets;
- counseling tenants more actively.

Any of the various options that have been outlined here could modify existing programs in ways that are helpful to families with children. However, it is important to bear in mind that the ability of subsidized programs, in particular Section 8, to help families is heavily shaped by the private market. For instance, certificate holders in the Section 8 existing program are likely to have their search process constrained by whatever restrictive practices exist in the private market....[N]ew monies are going into Section 8 rather than public housing. While there have been recent improvements in the representation of families with children in the Section 8 new program, it is crucial that we continue to monitor HAPs to ensure that commitments to families with children are realized.

Homeownership

We have been focusing on increasing the supply of rental housing for families with children. But the other major alternative for meeting their needs is to increase their opportunities to own their own homes. If larger proportions of families with children could own their own homes, the overall impact of restrictive rental practices would be minimized and more families would have achieved the American "dream." Additionally, homeownership might make available to large families the larger units they need.

Because rising housing costs have made homeownership increasingly difficult even for many middle-income families, several new policies supportive of homeownership are now either under HUD's active consideration or are actually being implemented. One option being developed within HUD would fund a demonstration program to provide assistance to a broader range of households.

In place as of 1980, we now have a new version of the Graduated Payment Mortgage program, which is targeted to lower income, first-time homebuyers. The program reduces the downpayment requirements of the previous Graduated Payment Mortgage, while simultaneously keeping initial payments low.

In addition to facilitating the entry of families into the homeownership market, consideration also might be given to helping families who are already homeowners to maintain that status. Extension to all homeownership programs of counseling for homeowners who encounter problems would be a very simple, yet effective, method for facilitating this goal.

Housing and Social Services

With regard to the problems of families in transition. Can policies be designed to minimize the impact of housing burdens during crucial transitional years, and thereby reduce the number of involuntary housing moves?

Existing HUD programs might develop outreach programs tailored to the needs of those families who are eligible. Housing subsidies and/or appropriate counseling services during the crucial two- to three-year period following a transition would permit these families to adapt successfully to their changed family circumstances and possibly decrease the likelihood of dependency in future years.

In recognition of the special needs of single-parent families, the Volunteers of America of Los Angeles pioneered in 1970 the Maud Booth Family Center, a program of stabilizing services that includes low-cost housing, child care, specialized counseling, and vocational guidance. Warren Village in Denver, Colorado, in operation since 1974, also provides residential units and on-site support services.

Future policy planning might consider replicating such efforts, perhaps within HUD's own public housing program. Because many female-headed households are already located within public housing, the provision, within the project, of appropriate family services such as family counseling, child care, and employment counseling might be a useful way of providing needed help while promoting upward mobility. Moreover, the physical security within such projects might be enhanced if the members of the families in need were receiving appropriate support services. Such focused housing and service programs might also prevent many of the families that become users of HUD housing programs from becoming permanently dependent on subsidies.

Housing and Family Composition

If future policy is to meet the needs of the coming generation, it is crucial that the fundamental changes in family composition be taken into account. But we must also remember that basic compositional changes are not limited to the growth of single-headed households. They also include the revolutionary growth in the number of dual-earner households. Although our projections do not include such households, we can reasonably infer from projections on the labor-force participation of married women that the proportion of dual-earner households will increase significantly in the coming decade. Whereas in 1978 50 percent of married women ages 16-54 with a husband present and children under 18 participated in the labor force, 64 percent of these women are projected to be in the labor force in 1990.[3]

As an initial step toward ensuring that HUD programs are sensitive to different kinds of families, HUD programs and administrative procedures need to be reviewed to assess whether they take account of family composition. For instance, current income eligibility standards for subsidized housing do not consider the labor force status of the adult members of the household. If they have the same total income, a four-person family with both parents in the labor force will face the same eligibility criteria as a four-person family with only one parent working full-time outside the home, despite the fact that the first family will have less "effective" income. (The dual-earner family will have to purchase services provided by the unpaid homemaker and may have to pay additional employment-related transportation costs.)

Though dual-earner households typically do not experience the burdens of housing costs to the same degree as single-headed households, the two types of households may share many other housing needs that should be considered by planners. For instance, the problems many of these families appear to be having in juggling the responsibilities of family and work bring to the fore an issue of long-standing--the relationship between location of housing, work, and service and recreational facilities. It might be argued that the disjunctions of our basic living environments cause much of the stress and strain experienced by today's families. The challenge is to facilitate the meshing of housing with these other needs that can be crucial to healthy family life.

The relationships within our physical environments also need rethinking. For instance, play space for children that assumes a full-time single caretaker may be neither adequate nor safe for children of working parents. More research on the housing needs and preferences of single-parent and dual-earner families is desirable. This research should address the characteristics of the housing itself as well as its location and the availability of social services and other public services.

We have presented some of the policy and research questions that are raised by the changing composition of our nation's families. Our hope is that the response to the initial discussion will lead to more refined proposals and ideas. Because of the increased diversity of families, careful thought and dialogue are essential if housing policy is to be responsive to actual needs. We will also need to become more conscious of the ways in which policies themselves shape family life. The convening of the White House Conference on Families represents the crucial first step in creating this new consciousness about families and the role of government. Hopefully our efforts to discuss housing within its broader social context will continue that process.

No, we cannot know the future, but we can ask questions that are sensitive to changing needs. In particular, in a period when fewer and fewer families include children, we may well need to give greater recognition to the fact that children are our future.

Notes

1. John Pitkin and George Masnik, "Projections of Housing Consumption in the U.S. 1980-2000 by a Cohort Method," Annual Housing Survey Study #9, Office of Policy Development and Research, U.S. Department of Housing and Urban Development includes six different projections. The more expansionary of the projections presented here assumes the continuation of housing consumption trends observed for the different age groups in the period from 1970 to 1975, while the more conservative one is based on the continuation of housing consumption trends from 1960 to 1970. Both projections assume medium marriage and fertility rates.
2. Future research should systematically analyze whether the stresses and tensions that result from these practices vary by the composition of the household. For instance, one might hypothesize that the problems would be greatest in families where the only parent is employed full time and least severe in families with two parents, only one of whom is employed full time.
3. Computed from data in Ralph E. Smith, *Women in the Labor Force in 1990* (Washington, D.C.: Urban Institute, 1979).

21. WHERE DO YOU LIVE? Women in the Landscape of Poverty

Pat Theresa Francis

Living without men or money, low-income women have been prime targets of scorn and mistrust. Rejecting or failing to achieve everything society has taught them to want, single mothers have been viewed as women with nothing to lose, and nobody to keep them in line. As such, they pose a certain danger to the established order. Their isolation and segregation in housing projects are ways of confining that threat, and exiling them for the crime of living without men.

These shoddy, demoralizing environments, designed and built specifically to contain poor people, are called "government subsidized housing." Although such projects are not new or uniquely American, they have proliferated in cities across the country in the past 20 years. The development of low-income housing has been part of the illustration of progress we've seen since World War II, during which time increased lip-service has been paid to inequalities based on race, sex, and class. However, despite the rhetoric and the numerous programs designed to alleviate the inequalities, 1978 found more women and Blacks living below the poverty level than those counted in 1968.

The housing projects themselves did much to sustain this illusion of progress. Freshly painted, well-lit, and often quite spacious, the new developments that were a large part of urban renewal campaigns undertaken in the sixties were quickly filled with tenants while others signed waiting lists hoping to get in. However, these schemes like many other programs reinforced the psychological oppression of poverty. Their standardized building types easily identified them as "projects" and their bad reputations began to flourish almost before the tenants moved in.

Poor families moving into the developments are given a further class branding, as if anyone who is poor in America is likely to forget it. A low-income woman is not only reminded of her status by the things she lacks, but she must identify herself by it, often several times a day. She must identify herself as poor when she goes into the supermarket and uses her food stamps, when she takes her children to the doctor with a Medicaid card, and, if she lives in low-income housing, whenever she gives her address. Her children, as well, must be identified as poor as soon as they enter the first grade and learn to answer that most basic question, "Where do you live?"

Reprinted from *Heresies 11*, vol. 3, no. 3 (1981), pp. 10-11 by permission of the author.

Ostracism and identification are only two of the ways the projects psychologically oppress their inhabitants. Physically, the projects are not designed to accommodate privacy or comfort to any appreciable degree. In most projects the ordinary sounds of daily living are audible through the walls, and one family's quarrels or celebrations intrude disruptively on the lives of neighbors. Thus, the police are called more often than in the suburbs, or in apartment complexes with better acoustic design, adding to the notion that the project is a "bad neighborhood."

Other signs indicating that subsidized housing is designed to contain a criminal or "delinquent" element include the excess of lighting in parking and play areas. In the apartment where I live it is never dark (even with the shades drawn and heavy curtains on the windows) because the many bright globes of light that stud the project create an unnatural daylight that penetrates into all the apartments. Though there have been no murders or rapes, and few burglaries in the five years I've lived here, and I consider it to be a relatively safe neighborhood, it was obviously designed in anticipation of the crimes the planners expected the low-income community to commit. I am reminded of the writer who was shocked to find a similar absence of night in the Soweto ghetto, and compared its psychological abuse to Nazi concentration camps, where bright lights also simulated an eternal daylight.

But perhaps the most significant psychological factor of life in the projects is that the poor, who have little control over many aspects of their lives as it is, suffer a further loss of control of their children to this environment. As soon as the children leave their apartments, they are part of the neighborhood, a world that has its own laws and hierarchies (often based on physical strength and "toughness"). It is one in which parents/mothers have little power. Since the children are crowded into small play areas, there is little opportunity to choose playmates for one's children, or to keep them from influences or knowledge they are not yet prepared for. Unlike children in most affluent neighborhoods, poor children generally have little opportunity to leave their projects at all, due to the same economic conditions that put them there in the first place.

Often the close proximity of buildings to the play areas discourages active games such as baseball, which might cause windows to be broken. In fact, in one project I visited in Boston recently, ball playing of any kind was expressly prohibited, and signs stating that were posted on every building. What is most disturbing about this is not that children are denied the space and opportunity for the active play they need, but that they are being subtly punished for their parents' low-income status, and taught to view their own natural exuberance and energy as a negative force by the design of the buildings and layout of the grounds.

Constructed as cheaply and quickly as possible, the projects are quite simply not built to last. This, too adversely affects the morale of the inhabitants, who find that the poor-quality fixtures need replacing sooner than they should, usually at the tenant's expense. I am reminded of the children's story "The Three Little

Pigs," in which the pig in the brick house has an evident psychological advantage over the one in the straw house. Likewise, human inhabitants of a clearly impermanent environment must be reminded daily of their particular vulnerabilities. Yet, when the projects show signs of wear, it is not the architects or builders who are called to task. It is the tenants who are blamed for failing to keep up the property, fueling theories that hold the poor responsible for their own misfortunes.

Women, of course, are not the only inhabitants of subsidized housing, though female heads of households frequently lease one-half to two-thirds of the apartments in a development. For them the psychological impact of life in the project can be more devastating than it is for male residents. Since nearly all the women in projects are mothers, often without cars or the means to secure childcare, they do not have the freedom to leave the project for extended periods of time. They spend most of their hours inside their apartments or in the neighborhood, with few releases for pent-up frustration, and little opportunity to gain another perspective on their situation. Obviously, this can only exacerbate the sense of isolation and powerlessness that accompanies poverty. Without outside stimulation and extensive contact with women exploring other options, women find projects in their own lives and what they perceive as their choices increasingly narrowed.

In outlining the disadvantages inherent in subsidized housing, I do not mean to deny their advantage, which is real and needed economic help. However, there are ways to subsidize housing which are not stigmatizing and subtly punitive. Instead of being herded into projects, a low-income family can choose a reasonably priced apartment and have their rent subsidized in the same way it would be in the development. At this time this kind of help is very limited. Some families wait for years for their name to come up on a waiting list. In the meantime rules may be changed making them ineligible, the list may be scrapped, and the family then accepts their life in the project and does not seek an alternative.

At this time there are only individual answers to the challenges of living in an environment built for poverty, and, as women, we have come to mistrust individual answers that make tokens of a few while effecting no real change. It is for us to remember that poverty is very much a feminist issue, not only because the majority of the poor are women, but also because many of the tactics used to repress the poor are also used on women, whatever their economic class. The weapons may be wielded differently, but they are of the same arsenal and can only be countered through the awareness of the "underclass," whether that term is defined by race, economic status, or sex.

22. INCOME AND LIVING ARRANGEMENTS AMONG POOR AGED SINGLES

Thomas Tissue and John L. McCoy.

The living arrangements of the nation's elderly poor are often determined by income. Cross-sectional--that is, point-in-time--surveys show that the poorest aged reside in shared households more often than elderly persons with higher incomes. Moreover, the steady and substantial increase in the real income of old people over the past several decades has been accompanied by an impressive rise in the proportion of single-person households among the aged.

On the other hand, comparatively little is known about the effect of altering people's income after they have become old and poor. Is household composition determined by habit and noneconomic factors at this late date, or will significant numbers of the unmarried elderly poor actually change their living arrangements if their income goes up or down? This article addresses that question with data gathered in a large, two-stage panel survey of the nation's public assistance recipients. It presents findings on their living arrangements in late 1973, discusses the concomitants of living alone and with others at that time, summarizes the changes in living arrangements and income that occurred over a twelve-month period, and examines the effect of income change upon individual decisions to set up (and give up) a home of one's own in later life. The article concludes by discussing the probable outcome of future increase in means-tested benefits for the aged poor.

Background

All other things being equal, old persons seem to prefer living alone in their own homes to sharing a place with their grown children or other family members. Young persons do not plan to live with their children when they themselves grow old, and younger heads of households quite often reject the notion that aged parents should move in with their adult sons and daughters. The preferred arrangement appears to be "intimacy at a distance"--living within easy visiting range of friends and relatives but in a home of one's own.

Reprinted from *Social Security Bulletin* 44, 4 (April 1981):3-12.

The complaints about shared households are familiar ones. Older persons say that they feel useless, unwanted, or just in the way. The division of authority and responsibility for household operation is difficult, at best, when an older woman moves in with her grown daughter or daughter-in-law, and close and prolonged contact with small children can tax the affections of even the fondest grandparent. Worst of all perhaps, shared households in old age may constitute a public admission of dependency. As Hess and Waring (1978:305) point out, the current generation of old persons consists of men and women who "have internalized the great American virtues of independence and self-reliance and consider making a home with an adult child only as a last resort."

In view of the problems associated with joint households and the professed lack of enthusiasm for them, why do so many old persons share a home with someone else? Loneliness, recent bereavement, and filial affection must play some part, but considerations of money and health seem paramount. Generally, people can stretch their income by living together in one large household instead of several small ones. The larger unit produces important economies of scale with respect to food and shelter costs, provides a form of insurance against temporary interruptions in personal income, and often guarantees access to a shared pool of appliances and other household amenities that is beyond the resources of a single family member living alone. Furthermore, combined households practice income and resource sharing that usually improves the financial welfare of the added member at the expense of the primary unit. Thus, low-income older persons have a clear economic incentive for sharing the home of others, particularly if the others are better off financially.

For the frail and sick, a combined household is both an assurance that someone will be on hand in case of a medical emergency as well as a continuing source of routine care and assistance with the chores of daily living. These themes--money and health--appear repeatedly in the discussion of old persons' living arrangements. As expected, the poor and the sick live in the home of relatives more frequently than do healthier, financially secure old persons.

Over the past several decades, the rate at which unmarried old persons live with relatives has declined appreciably. For never married, divorced-separated, and widowed women over age 65, the proportion living with relatives dropped from 58 percent in 1940 to 29 percent in 1970 (Kobrin 1976:136). Between 1940 and 1970 was, of course, a historical period in which the Social Security system grew to maturity and a time of rapidly expanding means-tested welfare programs for older persons. The effect on the income of the aged was considerable. The elderly experienced a 38 percent increase in real income over the period 1952-72 (Warlick 1979). During the 1960s the incidence of poverty among the aged dropped by 30 percent.

The joint emergence of these two trends--increased personal income and increased rates of single-person households among the aged--did not go unnoticed. Orshansky (1966:32) observed that, "...more and more people, particularly women, are being enabled to maintain a household in their old age because they now have some income." Rivlin (1975:5) asserts that, "Rising incomes, including transfers, have enabled Americans to increase their consumption of a luxury good--the luxury of living apart from their relatives," while Lampman (1974:72) flatly concludes, "...there can be no doubt that Social Security and public assistance benefits have enabled old people and women heading families to live and be counted separately as low-income households." Taussig (1972:376-86) goes so far as to suggest that the Social Security program enjoys the support of workers not because it will some day provide old-age benefits to them but because it relieves them of the responsibility to share homes and incomes with their aged parents today.

There is, in short, an extensive literature that attests to the importance of personal income in determining how and with whom older persons live. That money matters seems indisputable by now. Equally clear, however, is the fact that very little is known about the way households are formed and dissolved in old age and the specific circumstances under which income exerts its influence on these decisions. Previous research does not help much in predicting whether or not income manipulation will produce a demonstrable change in household composition within a particular population of low-income elderly. It is fairly certain that the living arrangements of the poor were never dictated solely by their poverty. The elderly poor suffer a great many disadvantages and handicaps beyond low income. Compared with other old people, they are not only poorer but sicker too. There is no guarantee that raising their income will permit very many of them to establish homes of their own--making them richer does not make them healthier or better able to care for themselves.

Neither is it absolutely clear that declining poverty rates for old people were the sole or even the major reason for the upswing in single-person households over the past few decades. Expansion of the income-transfer programs was not the only event of that historical period. Previous studies have identified major demographic trends that manifest themselves in a sharp increase in the number of old people relative to the number of adult children with whom they might live (Bane 1976; Kobrin 1976:127-38). Glick (1979:301-9) notes that today's aged were born into families that typically produced five children, but the next generation had only three, while those of childbearing age now are likely to have just two. It seems fair to hypothesize that changes in the nation's age structure, life expectancies, and levels of functional capacity, for example, also accounted for the shifts in living arrangements so often attributed to economic factors.

There is reason to suspect that the household choices of old persons are influenced by available income. But there is little direct evidence with which to confirm the suspicion, particularly as it relates to the change in living arrangements that can be induced by income manipulation alone.

Survey Data

The financial circumstances of a great many old persons changed abruptly on January 1, 1974. Those receiving old-age assistance were transferred en masse to a new Federal income-maintenance program called supplemental security income (SSI). Operated by the Social Security Administration, SSI introduced nationally uniform eligibility criteria, standard administrative procedures, and a guaranteed minimum income for all eligible persons. For recipients in states with the lowest welfare payment standards, the shift to SSI was sure to produce substantial income improvement immediately.

As part of a larger study of SSI's impact on its prospective clientele, Bureau of the Census enumerators conducted lengthy personal interviews with 5,192 aged welfare recipients during the last three months of 1973. These interviews emphasized income and assets but also gathered detailed information on household composition, health, housing, diet, and social activity. They provide a rich body of data for describing the circumstances of aged welfare recipients immediately before their transfer to SSI. Followup interviews were completed with 4,599 (89 percent) of the initial cohort during October, November, and December of 1974. Of the original sample, 308 died in the year following the first interviews, 205 were institutionalized, and 80 were "lost" for miscellaneous reasons such as failure to locate and refusals to be reinterviewed. The same questions were asked in 1974, in addition to questions pertaining specifically to SSI. The analysis that follows is based on the responses of 3,305 aged persons who were receiving public assistance in 1973, *and* not living with a spouse in 1973, *and* successfully reinterviewed in 1974. Thus, it excludes married persons and those who failed to complete both interviews....[1]

Living Arrangements in 1973

Examined separately, the 1973 data confirm most of the conventional wisdom as it pertains to living arrangements in old age. Roughly 60 percent of the unmarried sample was living alone at the time of the 1973 interview. Of those sharing a home, the majority did so with one or more of their adult children. The demographic correlates of living arrangements were quite similar to those identified in Chevan and Korson's (1972:45-53) analysis of widows. Compared with the aged in shared accommodations, people who lived alone were younger and better educated.... They were also more likely to be male, white, childless, and residing in urban areas. Although all of these differences are significant at the 0.01 level, the percentage point differences are typically modest. Widowhood per se was not associated with living arrangement. Widows and widowers lived alone at virtually the same rate as divorced, separated, and never married persons.

Aged welfare recipients are more frail and physically infirm than most of the old people in this country (McCoy & Brown, 1978:14-26). Within the welfare population, however, some recipients were better able to care for themselves than others. As anticipated, the self-care capacity of those in solitary living arrangements were clearly superior to persons living with others.... They were better equipped to do their own grocery shopping, prepare their own meals, wash their own clothes, do light housework, and take care of themselves when ill with a minor illness. Those in shared accommodations were consistently less able to deal with these basic tasks of daily living without regular assistance from others.

Those who lived alone also maintained a more active social life.... Greater numbers of them belonged to formally organized clubs or lodges and to informal social groups that visited or went on outings from time to time. They also maintained higher rates of contact with persons in the immediate neighborhood as well as with friends who did not live nearby. They did not, however, see relatives or entertain visitors in the home any more frequently than did older singles in shared households. The latter were not uniformly reclusive, but they did occupy a comparatively narrow sphere of social involvement and interaction. Persons who lived with others did not seem to get out very often.

The income hypothesis is borne out too. Aged singles living alone enjoyed a clear financial advantage over those living with others. Their average monthly cash income was dreadfully low ($157) when judged by any objective standard, but it was still higher than that available to persons who shared a home ($135). If the needs and income of others in the household are disregarded, it is apparent that the vast majority of the unmarried aged in shared homes would have fallen below the official poverty line if they had tried to live alone on the income available to them personally. Their individual poverty rate was appreciably higher--by 10 percentage points--than that of aged recipients who maintained a separate home.... Cash income, of course, is not the only benchmark for assessing financial security. Henretta and Campbell (1978:1204-23) argue for the inclusion of net worth in the analysis of economic status in later life. As they point out, the level of living available to old persons is not merely a function of income but is also influenced by the amount of their liquid assets and the ownership of property that can be mortgaged or sold. On both counts, older recipients who lived alone were better off than those living with others. They were more likely to own the homes in which they lived and to have assets (exclusive of the home) with cash value greater than zero.

In one sense, there is nothing startling in the discovery that functional capacity and financial security were associated with the household choices of old persons. That is, after all, the conclusion that has emerged from countless studies of later life. What seems important is that these variables are so consistently related to household composition in a sample that exludes almost everyone who is aging comfortably. Among the poor and the sick, it is still the poorest and the sickest who most often turn up in shared households.

Do combined households actually deliver the economic and material benefits so often claimed for them? The 1973 survey data indicate that they do. In developing the concept of the "hidden poor," Orshansky (1967:177-231) identifies a group of older persons with extremely low personal income. These persons do not appear in the official poverty counts, however, because they live in households that are not poor as a whole.... Although 81 percent of the aged in shared households were poor when their own income was matched against their individual poverty thresholds, just 40 percent were living in households whose combined income fell below the poverty standard appropriate to the larger unit. Compared with older recipients living alone, those in combined households were poorer individually but much less likely to live in poor households.

The obvious advantage to be gained from sharing the income of other household members is that it is much cheaper to live that way. Persons living alone were considerably more likely to be spending half or more of their income for food and shelter than were old persons who shared homes with others. And those in shared homes seemed to be living better. Their houses appeared to have been superior structurally, at least in regard to hot and cold running water and the provision of unshared access to a kitchen and bathroom facilities. They enjoyed greater access to various appliances and consumer amenities too. Their homes were more likely to include a television set, washing machine, refrigerator, and telephone. Unexpectedly, quality of diet was not associated with living arrangement. Daily diets were evaluated according to Department of Agriculture criteria (Feaster 1972). Application of the minimum recommended daily diet standard to the food consumption reports of the survey respondents yields virtually identical results for both groups.

Change in Income and Living Arrangements, 1973-74

No one became wealthy after being transferred to the SSI program, but most people experienced a net improvement in their financial condition. Even after adjusting for an 11 percent inflation rate during the study period, two-thirds of the aged singles received a higher monthly income in 1974 than in the preceding years.[2] Real income rose $19 per month for the average recipient living alone in 1973. Those living with others at the time of the first interview experienced a mean individual increase of $22 per month. Quite a few persons received income advances appreciably larger than the average. Actual monthly purchasing power increased by $50 or more for one in six survey respondents.

Because 1973 income was so low, dollar increases of this amount produced major proportional gains in monthly income for a large number of recipients.... [R]eal income increases of 40 percent or more were not uncommon in either segment of the sample. It should be noted that there were losers as well as gainers. In evaluating the impact of SSI on its larger transferred caseload, Schieber (1978:18-43) found that some SSI transfers lost money in an absolute sense and many of them failed to increase their income at a rate sufficient to match inflation. Within the present sample, roughly 5 percent suffered real income declines of 20 percent or more during the year.

There was virtually no net change in living arrangements during the study period.... In 1973, 58 percent of the full sample was living alone. A year later the same proportion (58 percent) lived by themselves. That is not to say that nothing happened during the year. Nearly 7 percent of those who had lived alone initially were in shared households at the second interview. About half of them (3.2 percent) had left their former home to move in with others; the remainder (3.3 percent) were still in their 1973 homes but other people had moved in with them. The experience of recipients who had begun in shared homes was almost a mirror image of that reported above. They became one-person households at nearly the same rate (8.4 percent) at which the others shifted to joint living arrangements. And, as before, about half of that change could be attributed to a move on the part of the recipients themselves: 3.9 percent left a shared home to find their own place but 4.5 percent just stayed behind while everyone else moved out.

Effects of Income Change

The data show that income manipulation leads to change in living arrangements over the course of a year, but only for certain kinds of changes and not always in the anticipated fashion. Failure to confirm a simple, unilinear income hypothesis is not surprising. Recent studies have concluded that poor persons do not suddenly begin to act, think, and live like their wealthier peers simply because their income is adjusted upwards. In some cases, a reverse effect is observed. Elesh and Lefcowitz (1977:401) found that the New Jersey-Pennsylvania Negative Income Tax Experiment, "...had no effects on either our measures of health or on our measures of utilization of health care." The Seattle-Denver Income Maintenance Experiment appears to have increased rather than decreased the rates of unemployment and geographic mobility among experimental subjects, and though the level of psychological distress remained about the same for most persons, "...several groups did respond to an experimental treatment and it was always with significantly increased distress" (Hannon et al., 1978:612). Working with data from the same project, it was discovered that certain kinds of marriages were stabilized by income increases, but that overall "...income maintenance treatments substantially raised rates of marital dissolution" (Thoits & Hannon 1979:612). It would appear that more can be learned about poor persons' behavioral responses to income adjustment as it occurs in the real world.

In the recent analysis, functional capacity or health is the most important determinant of change in living arrangements. If recipients cannot take care of themselves, they have little choice but to move in with someone else or convince someone to move in with them. The luxury of living alone is reserved for those who can meet the physical demands of independence....

Income change and age were the only other variables to achieve significance in more than one logit model. The rest turned up as important predictors of change only once (race, sex, parental status, housing quality, home ownership, social participation) or not at all (education, urban-rural residence, diet quality, assets). It seems reasonable to conclude that most of these point-in-time correlates of living arrangements in old age play a very minor role in the short run. These factors may have influenced the household choices made in the past but it is quite clear that functional health, age, and income change were more important predictors of household change during the study period.

In examining the four independent routes to change in living arrangements, it is relatively easy to interpret recipient initiated change--moving in with others or moving out of the home--as a function of individual strengths and weaknesses. Giving up a home of one's own to move in with others is closely associated with the survival needs of the recipient. Extreme old age, social isolation, and physical helplessness combine to force the individual into the home of another. The fact that income change plays no appreciable role in this process is interesting but not startling. Equally plausible is the finding that comparative youth, physical self-sufficiency, and increased income allow persons in shared households to move out and maintain homes of their own. These factors do not compel people to leave shared households but they certainly make it easier to indulge a preference for solitary living.

One has less confidence in the interpretation of change initiated by others. Half of the changes in living arrangements occurred among recipients who did little themselves--other people moved into or out of their homes but the survey recipients just stayed put. Although the self-care variable was consistent, the other correlates of change were seldom those anticipated. Why, for instance, do other people move into the homes of younger recipients whose income increased over the year? It is difficult to imagine that income advances to the magnitude that SSI delivered would attract very many people for purely venal reasons, but the possibility cannot be discounted entirely. Is it true that others move out of the recipient's owned home because the home lacks modern conveniences, and why does this general form of household disaggregation occur most frequently for whites? Answers to these kinds of questions are possible only if detailed information is available on the status, needs, and preferences of the "others," as well as the aged individual. Although each of the four paths to household change requires some degree of participation or consent from both parties, "others-initiated" change is the most difficult to explain or interpret using data on the older person only.

As a guide to policy, the study offers useful conclusions regarding the effects that can be anticipated from raising the income of the elderly poor in the future. The transfer of aged public assistance recipients to SSI provided the opportunity to examine income change that was imposed arbitrarily and abruptly across the nation, that was permanent rather than experimental, that was varied in amount, and that was about as large an overall increase as can be expected in the near future, given the economic and political realities of the time. In short, these data are ideally suited for predicting the behavioral outcomes that would result from future liberalization of the basic SSI benefit standard.

Overall, it seems unlikely that moderate, across-the-board increases in SSI benefits will ever have a major effect on the living arrangements of aged recipients. Large numbers of them are simply too old and frail to consider independent living situations, no matter how large their income. Neither does it seem reasonable to suppose that great numbers of the aged at these income levels will choose to spend a benefit increase for privacy, or independence rather than for clothing, better food, entertainment, or other amenities routinely forgone for purely financial reasons. Income increase in these amounts should have its principal effect on the living arrangements of old persons who are healthier than most SSI recipients and who have fewer unmet needs to start with.

Finally, it may not make sense to assume that very many old persons, rich or poor, will suddenly change their living arrangements simply because their income goes up while everything else stays the same. It seems more reasonable to suppose that income increase dictates few changes but does define the range of solutions that are possible when other circumstances force a decision. From this perspective, increased income is not a powerful independent stimulus for change but is instead a resource that enables one to achieve a satisfactory solution when the children finally leave home, the spouse dies, the building goes condominium, the grandchildren prove too boisterous, or it just becomes obvious that one person does not need an entire house to himself or herself any longer. For aged SSI recipients, whose median age is 75 years, it seems likely that most of these issues were faced and resolved long ago.

Notes

1. For details of the survey and the sampling procedures, see Erma Barron, "Survey Design, Estimation Procedures and Sampling Variability" (SLIAD Report no. 5), Social Security Administration, 1978; Thomas Tissue, "The Survey of Low-Income Aged and Disabled: An Introduction" (SLIAD Report no. 1), *Social Security Bulletin*, February 1977, pp. 3-11.
2. To offset inflation, 1974 income was converted to constant 1973 dollars (that is, multiplied by 0.9) before comparing it with 1973 income. Increase in absolute or nominal income was, of course, much larger than real increase. For persons living alone, mean monthly income rose for $157 to $191 and for those living with others it increased from $135 to $176.

References

Bane, Mary Jo.
1976 *Here to Stay: American Families in the Twentieth Century*. New York: Basic Books.

Chevan, Albert, and J. Henry Korson.
1972 "The Widowed Who Lived Alone: An Examination of Social and Demographic Factors." *Social Forces* (Sept.):45-53.

Elesh, David, and M. Jack Lefcowitz.
1977 "The Effects of the New Jersey-Pennsylvania Negative Income Tax Experiment on Health and Health Care Utilization." *Journal of Health and Social Behavior* (Dec.).

Feaster, Gerald.
1972 *Impact of the Expanded Food and Nutrition Education Program on Low Income Families.* Agricultural Report no. 220. Economic Research Service, U.S. Department of Agriculture. Feb.

Glick, Paul C.
1979 "The Future Marital Status and Living Arrangements of the Elderly." *Gerontologist* (June):301-09.

Hannon, Michael; Nancy Brandon Tuma, and Lyle P. Groenevald.
1978 "Income and Independence Effects on Marital Dissolution: Results from the Seattle and Denver Income Maintenance Experiments." *American Journal of Sociology* (Nov.).

Henretta, John C., and Richard T. Campbell.
1978 "Net Worth as an Aspect of Status." *American Journal of Sociology* (March): 1204-23.

Hess, Beth B., and Joan Waring.
1978 "Changing Patterns of Aging and Family Bonds in Later Life." *Family Coordinator* (Oct.).

Kobrin, Frances.
1976 "The Fall in Household Size and the Rise of the Primary Individual in the United States." *Demography* (Feb.).

Lampman, Robert.
1974 "What Does It Do for the Poor--A New Test for National Policy." *Public Interest* (Winter).

McCoy, John L., and David L. Brown.
1978 "Health Status among Low-Income Elderly Persons: Rural-Urban Differences" (SLIAD Report no. 4). *Social Security Bulletin* (June):14-26.

Orshansky, Mollie.
1966 "Recounting the Poor--A Five-Year Review." *Social Security Bulletin* (April).
1967 "Counting the Poor before and after Federal Income-Support Programs." Pp. 177-231 in Congress of the United States, Joint Economic Committee, *Old Age Income Assurance Part II: The Aged Population and Retirement Income Programs.* Washington, D.C.: U.S. Government Printing Office.

Rivlin, Alice.
1975 "Income Distribution: Can Economists Help?" *American Economic Review* (May).

Schieber, Sylvester.
1978 "First Year Impact of SSI on the Economic Status of 1973 Adult Assistance Population" (SLIAD Report no. 2). *Social Security Bulletin* (Feb.):18-43.

Taussig, Michael.
1972 "Long Run Consequences of Income Maintenance Reform" Pp. 376-386 in Kenneth Boulding and Martin Pfaff (eds.), *Redistribution to the Rich and the Poor*. Belmont, Cal.: Wadsworth.

Thoits, Peggy, and Michael Hannon.
1979 "Income and Psychological Distress: The Impact of an Income Maintenance Experiment." *Journal of Health and Social Behavior* (June).

Warlick, Jennifer.
1979 "The Relationship of the Supplemental Security Income Program and Living Arrangements of the Low-Income Elderly." Paper presented at the annual meeting of the National Conference on Social Welfare. August.

23. CURRENT COMMUNITY CARE POLICIES IN BRITAIN: Some Implications for Women

Janet Finch and Dulcie Groves

Since the Second World War, British state welfare policies concerning the care of dependent groups in the population, such as the frail elderly and the physically and mentally handicapped, have increasingly incorporated a commitment to notions of "community care." Such notions have been fostered by successive governments of differing political persuasions, and the term "community care" has gradually changed its meaning in the process. The overriding commitment, however, has been to the development of apparently enlightened and humane alternatives to certain forms of residential care which trace their ancestry back to the "institutional care" provided in the workhouses, lunatic asylums and orphanages of the nineteenth century.

This chapter seeks to explain the emergence of these "community care" policies and to examine their implications for women. Over the past two decades, it has become customary for the great majority of adult women who do not have very young children to engage in paid work, without which a substantial number of households would be in poverty. At the same time, welfare policies for the elderly and handicapped have increasingly implied reliance upon women as the providers of care, especially in the home. This consequence has seldom been acknowledged, partly because the meaning of "community care" has been unclear and partly because women's caring in the home has been regarded as "natural" and therefore as presenting no particular problems to policy makers. Thus, it is useful to understand how community care policies have developed in Britain and what the phrase "community care" really means, from the perspective of women.

The Evolution Of Commmunity Care

The concept of "community care" can only be fully understood in relation to residential care. The two have been viewed as alternative modes of providing for the needs of dependent groups, with community care increasingly being perceived and promoted as the more desirable goal. Thus, community care policies have grown up in the shadow of reactions against residential care.

Current community care policies have their origins in postwar "welfare state" legislation, and also in mid-1950s concern for the care of increasing numbers of elderly people and for the care of the mentally ill and handicapped (Jones, Brown & Bradshaw 1978: ch. 7). In the 1960s, increasing evidence was amassed that pointed to the undesirability of large residential institutions for any dependent group. The case against such institutions was made mainly on grounds of their physical unsuitability for modern forms of treatment and their encouragement of authoritarian attitudes among staff. There were certain documented and well-publicized instances of ill-treatment of residents. Large residential facilities were seen as incorporating an organizational system which so structured people's lives as to "institutionalize" them, so that they could not manage in the outside world.[1]

In the light of this kind of evidence, a "community care" alternative began to look very attractive--but what did it mean? As Jones et al. put it

> To the politician, "community care" is a useful piece of rhetoric; to the sociologist, it is a useful stick to beat institutional care with; to the civil servant; it is a cheap alternative to residential care which can be passed on to the local authorities for action--or inaction; to the visionary, it is a dream of the new society in which people really do care; to social services departments, it is a nightmare of heightened public expectations and inadequate resources to meet them. We are only just beginning to find out what it means to the old, the chronic sick and handicapped [Jones et al. 1978:114].

"Community care" was in fact developed as a concept that could cater to all tastes. Hence, its meaning must be examined very carefully in relation to specific policy contexts. When this is done, it usually becomes clear not only that the meanings attributed to "community care" are ill defined and vary considerably in different discussions, but also that many of the assumptions upon which "community care" rests are never spelled out or held up for critical scrutiny. For instance, there are unexamined assumptions about how "care" can be provided in "the community." Although unexamined, these assumptions nevertheless seem to point fairly clearly to women as the providers of front-line care. This can be illustrated by focusing upon one important change in meaning, which can be identified historically.

Although the various meanings attributed to "community care" can and do co-exist at any given time, a very important distinction can be made between care "in" the community and care "by" the community. This distinction was first made by Michael Bayley (1973), and since then it has been influential in discussions about community care. Care "in" the community may simply mean that an individual lives away from a large residential institution; whereas care "by" the community implies some active involvement in the caring by individuals or groups living in the vicinity.[2] Using Bayley's distinction at its simplest, it can be argued that most early discussions of community care (in the 1960s especially) assumed care "in" the community rather than anything more. As previously noted, a strong case was made at this stage against large residential institutions but this case did not necessarily imply a total rejection of residential care. It could just as easily imply the development of a different type of residential institutions: smaller units, modern facilities, located in "ordinary" surroundings, and run in less bureaucratic and authoritarian ways. Many of the early community care policies promoted this type of development, that is, care "in" the community (Finch & Groves 1980). The crucial difference between these and many of the later policies is that care "in" the community accepts the continuing need for a fairly high level of residential provision, funded collectively through the state.

Increasingly in the 1970s, community care policies came to imply care "by" the community as well as in it; that is, "the community" came to be seen not only as the *location* for caring, but also as a *resource* for caring. As will be seen later, this is an important shift from the point of view of women, because if elderly and handicapped persons who would otherwise have been in residential institutions are to be cared for "at home," some person or persons must be found who will undertake the daily (and sometimes hourly) tasks that the dependent persons cannot perform for themselves. Although the nature of those tasks vary considerably with the degree of disability or handicap, *anyone* who would otherwise have been in residential care for this reason needs, by definition, a considerable amount of assistance. Who then is to provide the kind of front-line caring that in residential institutions would be done by paid staff such as care assistants? The answer given--often implied rather than explicitly stated--is that it will be relatives (where available) assisted by some combination of friends or neighbors, perhaps supplemented from time to time by volunteers not previously known to the dependent person.

So it can be seen that one important implication of the shift from care "in" the community to care "by" the community is the abandoning of the assumption that the state will fund the provision of care for elderly, disabled, or handicapped citizens. Care "by" the community embodies the intention that most of such care is to be provided on an unpaid basis and that, at most, the state will "orchestrate" such care (Jenkin 1981). This is no accident, since the shift in the meaning of "community care" has occurred at a time when governments in Britain, both Labour and Conservative, have been seeking to reduce public expenditure and therefore to find "low cost solutions" in social service provision (Finch & Groves 1980). In this situation, community care appears to offer a very convenient strategy, since not only is it a way of cutting costs, but it also can be presented as the preferred option for dependent people, on quite other grounds. "There is little doubt about the benefits to be gained from providing for people's needs in a flexible way which maintains their links with ordinary life, family and friends, wherever possible" (DHSS 1981:47).

The government document from which this quotation is taken, unlike its predecessors, recognizes not only that home-based care is usually only possible where there is an unpaid contribution by family and friends, but also that community care is not necessarily cheaper than care in an institution, if account is taken of the full range of support services necessary to make the burden of unpaid front-line carers tolerable (ibid.:21).

A further boost to the idea that community care should mean care "by" the community has come from the recent interest of some academics and practitioners in the use of so-called informal care networks in social service provision. This interest was importantly stimulated by American work on the topic, especially Collins and Pancoast (1976). In the form in which it has been taken up in Britain, the argument, in brief, runs that a concentration upon services provided by the state and by formally organized voluntary bodies overlooks the important fact that much care for dependent individuals is *already* being undertaken by family, friends, and neighbors, often completely unknown to formal agencies. This fact, it is argued, should be taken into account in planning social service provision, which should in fact embrace all three "sectors"--the statutory, the voluntary and the informal. Given that state funding cannot go on expanding, statutory agencies should--instead of ignoring informal caring networks--seek to support and strengthen them, and only step in with their own residual provisions when such networks fail (see Hadley & McGrath 1980; Hadley & Hatch 1981).

The drift in the meaning of "community care," and its reflection in policy making and service provision, has highly significant implications for women. These derive not only from actual reductions in state-funded provision, but also from the meanings implicit in the very phrase "community care." The very word "care" implies female activity since, especially in family settings, women traditionally are assumed to be the natural carers (Finch & Groves 1980). The associations of personal warmth implied by the word "*care*" rather obscure the fact that the activities implied can actually be very hard *work*. As Parker (1981:17) points out, "'Care' also describes the actual work of looking after those who, temporarily or permanently, cannot do for themselves. It comprises such things as feeding, washing, lifting, cleaning up for the incontinent, protecting, and comforting."

Equally, the term "community" also demands some scrutiny. When used in the phrase "community care," it again appears to evoke images of warmth and consideration for individuals. As Titmuss (1968:104) put it, it "conjures up a sense of human kindness, essentially personal and comforting." Titmuss warns that this can be very dangerous if it means that patterns of social life which certain people might like to exist are assumed actually to exist already. Such a warning is very pertinent in relation to care "by" the community, since it is difficult to find solid evidence that "caring" services do pass between individuals simply on the basis of locality, except in rather special circumstances. As Abrams (1977, 1980) has shown, where they do exist, such services are likely to be exchanges on the basis of kinship, race, ethnicity, or religion, but hardly ever on the basis of mere physical proximity. It is probably also true that wherever such "neighboring" does take place, again it is primarily a female activity.

Thus, an examination of what is actually meant by the phrase "community care" suggests that the imagery invoked points to women as the main providers of care, and this indeed seems to be true in practice. As we have shown elsewhere (Finch & Groves 1980), the processes through which this occurs can be seen as a double equation: community care means care by the family, and in practice that means by female relatives. The way is opened up for the operation of this equation by the shift from care "in" the community to care "by" the community, and is further strengthened by the concentration on informal networks as providing care. Simply because all such policies rely upon *unpaid* labor as the basis of service provision, women are far more likely than men to become unpaid carers. This happens for two reasons. First, despite increases in female employment and male unemployment, women are still far more likely than men to be at home full time or part time (OPCS 1981:ch. 5) and therefore are available to undertake the daily work of caring. Second, women are socialized to be carers, whereas men are not: undertaking the domestic and personal tasks necessary to keep a dependent person "at home" can easily be regarded as a natural extension of a woman's role in the family. In this context, recent enthusiasm on the part of politicians both in Britain and the United States for supporting "the family" and the development of family policies can be seen as potentially having extremely conservative implications. Such policies can very easily become a vehicle for easing more and more women out of the labor market and back into the home as full-time domestic workers where they provide, at very low cost to the public purse, a range of caring services for dependent children and adults.

Therefore, while the idea of community care originally was seen--and to some extent still is--as an exercise in developing humane alternatives to the less desirable features of institutional care, it has increasingly also become a vehicle (whether intended or not) through which women's unpaid labor is incorporated into social service provision.

Women and Community Care

We have argued that "community care" policies can be seen as having the effect of pulling women back into the home to act as unpaid carers for their handicapped and infirm relatives or friends. But are women really as available for this home-based caring as such policies imply? And if they do provide such care, what are the costs to the women themselves? The following section examines these questions on the basis of the British evidence. Broadly, we will argue that a combination of demographic, economic, and cultural factors should lead us to question whether there will be a ready supply of willing female carers; we also argue that those women who do act in such a capacity often do so at considerable cost to themselves--not least, financial cost. We will explore these issues by looking first at some demographic trends, then at trends in the employment of women, and finally at the financial costs of caring.

Certain trends in the composition of the British population have significantly affected both the numbers of dependent adults requiring care and the potential supply of unpaid female carers. In particular, the numbers of elderly people (especially the very old) increased by 1.8 million between 1961 and 1976 (OPCS 1978:6, Table 1.4), and a further slight increase of those aged 75-84 is expected by the end of the century. Thus, there are increased numbers of elderly people likely to need some form of care. Meanwhile, the supply of potential carers has decreased. Although marriage rates have increased in Britain until recently, smaller families have become the norm. There are fewer childless marriages, and many fewer large families (Rimmer 1981:23). Thus, there are likely to be fewer family members potentially available to care for the handicapped and elderly, though more families are likely to have three or even four generations alive at the same time (Rimmer 1981: 12). Further, the supply of single daughters--the group who traditionally have been seen as particularly appropriate carers--has been considerably reduced by the shifting balance between the sexes in the younger adult cohorts of the population, so that since 1961 men have outnumbered women in the under-44 age groups (ibid. 1981:13, Table 2). This sex ratio has contributed to a very high marriage rate, especially for women. The present generation of middle-aged women contains a very small proportion of "never married."

A further complicating factor in the supply of potential carers arises from increasing rates of divorce and remarriage. About one in four marriages in Britain now ends in divorce, of which 60 percent involve dependent children (Rimmer 1981:36). The substantial increase in divorce that has occurred since the early 1970s has certain implications for community care. For instance, increasing numbers of people in the future will have step-relationships generated by remarriage. It remains to be seen what effects this will have on the obligations and availability of family members with regard to the care of frail and handicapped relatives. Mothers commonly have day-to-day custody of dependent children, while fathers have access. This again is likely to have long-term implications for parent-child relationships and family obligations.

The "availability" of women as carers is affected not only by the demographic composition of the population but also by women's participation in the labor market. In order to take on responsibility for the "front line" care of a handicapped or frail elderly person, the carer needs to be at home most of the time. With the exception of the very limited number of jobs that can actually be done at home, this means usually that the carer cannot be in paid work, certainly not on a full-time basis.

Any policy that sees women as a useful source of low-cost care must conveniently ignore the fact that the majority of adult women in Britain engage in paid employment and that many contribute substantially to the household budget. The 1979 General Household Survey shows that married women have high rates of economic activity. Fifty-nine percent of women between 25 and 34 were working or available for paid work, 70 percent of women between 35 and 44, 69 percent of those between 45 and 54, and 57 percent of those between 55 and 59 were in paid work. Non-married women characteristically work full time if economically active, while married women typically work part time where there are dependent children in the household. If women are in paid work, they cannot also be full-time carers.

Is the assumption made that they will give up work whenever relatives' needs dictate? Obviously, where a woman has sole or major responsibility for the provision of household income, giving up work is a very serious matter, especially in a situation of high unemployment which may make later reentry to the labor market difficult if not impossible. Withdrawal from paid work can also entail loss of occupational pension rights. It has become evident that the earnings of married women constitute a crucial component of the household budget, without which many more families would live in poverty (Hamill 1976). Although it remains true that women earn less on average than men, nevertheless, given a situation in which women give up paid work in order to "care," the loss of earnings can be relatively substantial and, in some cases, catastrophic.

One obvious compromise would be a policy that allowed substantial financial assistance from public resources for anyone who cares for a handicapped or infirm person, especially if such caring precludes paid work. In Britain, such financial assistance is minimal, and in the case of many women it is nonexistent. There is one social security benefit--the invalid care allowance--designated especially for those who give up paid employment in order to care for a very handicapped person for at least 35 hours a week. The person being cared for also must qualify for a benefit called the "attendance allowance," which is a discretionary weekly payment available to those who are so severely handicapped as to need attendance by day, night (for which a lower-rate benefit is payable), or both day and night (which attracts a higher-rate benefit). Many handicapped people fail to qualify for the attendance allowance, though there is a high rate of success on appeal to a legal tribunal. In any case, the handicap must have existed for six months before the attendance allowance is payable at all (Bradshaw & Lawton 1980). At 1981 prices, the invalid care allowance was payable at the rate of £17.75 per week, with an additional £10.65 for a wife or adult dependent and £7.70 for each child. Dependent children also qualified for a child benefit at £5.25 per week. If "topped up" to the level of supplementary benefit, this gives a total of £22.50 for a single adult and £13.90 for an adult dependent. Nothing extra is obtainable for child dependents. When the invalid care allowance was first introduced in 1975 the "target" beneficiaries were single women who had given up work to care, though men were also made eligible. However, the eligibility was strictly confined to those caring for close relatives. In June 1981 entitlement to invalid care allowance was extended to all men caring for nonrelatives, but only noncohabiting single women were to be eligible, whether caring for relatives or friends.

Thus it can be seen that financial support from public funds for those who actually make "community care" policies possible is hardly generous. From the point of view of women, however, the most important point about it is that large numbers of carers are excluded even from this meager provision. The invalid care allowance is not available to married women or to those who are "cohabiting," i.e., deemed to be living as married. Nor is it available to widows drawing a state widow's pension equal in amount to the benefit or to divorced women receiving a like amount of maintenance from their exhusbands. Therefore, very few women are qualified to receive it. This exclusion of most women is neither an oversight nor even an isolated aberration, but an entirely consistent part of the British social security system, in which married and cohabiting women are considered to be the financial dependents of men, that is, husbands or the men they are deemed to be living with. Conversely, the concept of the male breadwinner remains "deeply embedded" in the social security system, as Hilary Land (1978) has convincingly shown. Thus, married and cohabiting women cannot get the invalid care allowance, nor can they apply for "supplementary benefit," which is roughly the British equivalent of "public assistance." It is possible for a single (non-cohabiting) woman or any man to apply for "supplementary benefit" in addition to the invalid care allowance, if there are no other financial resources or if she/he is waiting for the person being cared for to complete the six-months qualifying period for the attendance allowance which itself is the key to receipt of an invalid care allowance. The exclusion of major categories of women from these benefits means that the vast majority of women carers are eligible for no financial support whatsoever from public resources, even if they actually have given up paid work in order to provide care for a handicapped or infirm person.

Conclusion

The content of this paper raises a number of important policy issues which cannot be dealt with fully here. Different readers will address themselves selectively to these issues according to their own perspectives: some may want to focus on the inequity of the exclusion of the majority of women from financial provision for carers; others may be concerned about the rights of elderly and handicapped people to be cared for as they choose; we ourselves have taken up the issues of denial of equal opportunities implicit in the assumption that women will undertake unpaid care rather than paid work (Finch & Groves 1980).

Whatever the focus on specific policy issues, the underlying analysis presented in this paper is pertinent. We have shown that women are subject to being pulled--or often, perhaps, to being pushed--in two quite different directions. Social, economic, and cultural features of contemporary life increasingly draw women into the labor market, and by their own choice in the majority of cases. But "community care" policies run counter to this, and effectively attempt to push women back into unpaid labor in their own homes.

Thus, apparently humane and enlightened policies concerning the elderly and handicapped have consequences--whether intended or not--which are anything but benign for the women likely to be identified as their potential carers. However desirable community care policies may be on other grounds (and we have not attempted to evaluate that here) their effect is to subject women to pressures that may well run counter to their other needs and wishes. If women submit to these pressures they may experience, among other things, considerable material hardship.

This effect is made likely by the crucial shift of meaning from care "in" the community to care "by" the community. Once "the community" comes to be seen as a resource for caring, not merely as a location for caring, community care policies are set on the path of reliance upon unpaid labor. Women are the likely providers of such labor because of the strong cultural tradition that it is "natural" for them to undertake precisely the kind of activities involved in caring for an elderly or handicapped person. This is reinforced by the assumption (embodied in public law) that most women will be financially dependent upon a man and thus not really in need of paid work--the assumption of dependency being turned into a reality in part through the rules governing entitlement to state benefits.

The issues identified here are, of course, part of wider social processes endorsing women's dependency on men and designating them as carers for the young, the old and the infirm. As we have demonstrated, such processes can be reinforced by public policies that appear to be about something else entirely. Concepts such as "community care" and "natural helping networks" imply a warmth and humanity which seem difficult to resist, and may indeed have much to commend them on other grounds. But their meanings should be carefully questioned, and their applications thoroughly examined. If that is done, it may very well be found that their vagueness actually conceals a version of the widely believed (and widely questioned) assertion that woman's place is in the home.[3]

Notes

1. See Jones, Brown, and Bradshaw (1978), ch. 7, for a summary of the arguments for and against residential care and community care.
2. Bayley's discussion is based on a study in Sheffield of mentally handicapped children and adults living outside residential institutions. His aim is to suggest ways of developing care "by" the community, so that "community care" does not turn out to mean that "members of the community, untrained and unaided, should be left to get on with it" (Bayley, 1973:343).
3. This chapter is based on the authors' work on various aspects of community care policies in Britain, and their implications for women. Fuller treatment of the issues discussed here, including issues of entitlement to the invalid care allowance, can be found in Finch and Groves (1980, 1982, 1983).

References

Abrams, Philip.

1977 "Community Care: Some Research Problems and Priorities." *Policy and Politics*, 6:125-51.

1980 "Social Change, Social Networks and Neighborhood Care." *Social Work Service* (Feb.):12-23.

Bayley, Michael.

1973 *Mental Handicap and Community Care.* London: Routledge & Kegan Paul.

Bradshaw, Jonathan, and Dorothy Lawton.

1980 "An Examination of Equity in the Administration of the Attendance Allowance." *Policy and Politics*, 8:39-54.

Collins, A. H., and D. L. Pancoast.

1976 *Natural Helping Networks: A Strategy for Prevention.* New York: National Association of Social Workers.

Department of Health and Social Security.

1981 *Care in Action.* London: Her Majesty's Stationery Office.

Finch, Janet, and Dulcie Groves.

1980 "Community Care and the Family: A Case for Equal Opportunities?" *Journal of Social Policy*, 9:487-511.

1982 "By Women for Women: Caring for the Frail Elderly." *Women's Studies International* Forum, 5:427-38.

Finch, Janet, and Dulcie Groves (eds.)

1983 *A Labour of Love: Women, Work and Caring.* London: Routledge & Kegan Paul. Forthcoming.

Hadley, Roger, and Stephen Hatch.

1981 *Social Welfare and the Failure of the State.* London: Allen and Unwin.

Hadley, Roger, and Morag McGrath (eds.).

1980 *Going Local: Neighborhood Social Services.* London: National Council for Voluntary Organisations.

Hamill, Lynne.

1976 *Wives as Sole and Joint Breadwinners.* Economic Advisors Office, DHHS. London: Her Majesty's Stationery Office.

Jenkin, Patrick, Secretary of State for Social Services.

1981 "Trumpet Volunteers." *The Guardian.* Jan. 21.

Jones, Kathleen, John Brown, and Jonathan Bradshaw.

1978 *Issues in Social Policy.* London: Routledge & Kegan Paul.

Land, Hilary.

1978 "Who Cares for the Family?" *Journal of Social Policy* 7:257-84.

Office of Population, Censuses and Surveys.

1978 *Demographic Review* 1977. Series DR no. 1. London: Her Majesty's Stationery Office.

1981 *General Household Survey 1979.* Series GHS no. 9. London: Her Majesty's Stationery Office.

Parker, Roy.

1981 "Tending and Social Policy." Pp. 7-32 in E. M. Goldberg and S. Hatch (eds.). *A New Look at the Personal Social Services.* London: Policy Studies Institute.

Rimmer, Lesley.

1981 *Families in Focus.* London: Study Commission on the Family.

Titmuss, Richard.

1968 *Commitment to Welfare.* London: Allen & Unwin.

24. DEVELOPING A COMMUNITY RESPONSE TO A PLANT CLOSING

Terry F. Buss and F. Stevens Redburn

In October 1977, the directors of the Lykes Corporation, owners since 1969 of the Youngstown Sheet and Tube Company, announced the closing of its huge Campbell Works facilities near Youngstown, Ohio, and began laying off over 4,000 workers. Thus began a sequence of mill closings that has permanently eliminated over 10,000 jobs in one metropolitan area in less than three years (see Buss & Redburn 1983; Buss et al. 1983). Communities like Youngstown are, unfortunately, not unique (see Redburn & Buss 1982). Indeed, many communities in the industrial Northeast and Midwest have had similar experiences. Other regions will experience closings in the future.

In spite of the nation's vast collective experience with devastating plant closings, two ironies persist. The first is that even in the fact of predictable, inevitable closings, few communities organize themselves to develop an effective response to meet the needs of workers or of the larger community. This failure is particularly costly in view of the scarce, meager resources possessed by some communities to deal with economic crisis. The second is that there does not exist, on any level, public policies to guide and assist communities in preparing for, responding to, and recovering from the impacts of closings. The result of this is that chaos reigns in some communities, and valuable human and capital resources are wasted. It is hoped that case studies of this sort will help focus attention on the problem of plant closings and will offer suggestions for the development of a public policy.

In this chapter we will first describe some of the ways in which workers and their families typically responded to the Youngstown shutdown. We will then examine the responses of human services agencies intended to help workers and others affected to deal with the presumed effects of sudden job loss. By considering the needs generated by the crisis, it is possible to judge the appropriateness and effectiveness of the local human services system's response to the crisis and to suggest social policies for dealing with mass unemployment at the local, state, and federal levels.

Coping Processes

In the crisis of mass unemployment, most workers do not experience a need for life-sustaining necessities. Unemployment compensation, pensions, or finding a job reduce the threat to physical well-being. Nevertheless, many face emotional stresses beyond their previous experience. A worker has worked all his life in the mills. Perhaps he cannot retire, or his skills are not transferable to other jobs, or he is in poor health because of working conditions. He may have children in college or parochial schools and a mortgage on his home. For most of his life he has had a middle-class income. There may be little in his personal experience that would guide him to an appropriate response.

Several case studies based on actual experiences among the unemployed may serve to illustrate the wide range of positive and negative individual responses to job loss.

Case 1: *John Edwards*
Employed by Youngstown Sheet and Tube Company, 1967-1977
Age: 34
Spouse: Mary, married 1970
Children: two daughters

John Edwards had worked for Lykes for over twelve years as a crane operator. John was president of his local union and editor of the local union newspaper. Both as president and as editor, John established himself as a fair, although tough, union boss. He was respected by his fellow workers and company managers. John's union activities were conducted on his own time, with only his expenses compensated by the union. He had to work full time in the mills. John felt that he could make a significant contribution to labor-management relations in the mills, but at Lykes he would rise no further than worker. John decided to get a college degree in his spare time, of which he had very little. He estimated that a college degree would require six or seven years to complete while he worked full time and ran his union. Nevertheless he persisted.

In February 1980, John was told that his department in the mill was shutting down. This forced John to search for another job--something he had never done before. Instead of searching for a blue-collar job, John decided to apply for high level labor-management positions in steel mills in the area. Much to his surprise, he landed a job as a labor relations representative in a large steel firm, making one and one-third his laborer's salary. The firm was impressed by John's handling of his union, as well as by his efforts to obtain a degree. The firm not only hired John, but also is paying the tuition for the remainder of his education.

John certainly was not an average worker with average skills and ability. He felt after a while that working in the mills thwarted his potential. John might have worked his way out of the mills, had they not closed; but, the closing gave John a reason to seek to implement higher goals, which he was able to realize. In his new job, he feels he is making a major contribution to labor-management relations in the steel industry.

Case 2: *Gil Reeves*
Employed by Youngstown Sheet and Tube Company, 1963-1977
Age: 58
Spouse: Myra, married 1962
Children: two daughters and a son

Myra said that since Gil's layoff more than a year earlier, he had become gradually more depressed and moody. Even though he was always looking for work, each job rejection became more difficult for him to accept. Myra believed that her husband's joblessness and reduced income added to existing problems within the family. At about this time, they separated and she took the children to West Virginia where her parents live.

Case 3: *George Kendik*
Employed by Youngstown Sheet and Tube Company, 1946-1977
Age: 52
Spouse: Carolyn, married 1963
Children: one daughter and one son

George spent thirty-one years at Youngstown Sheet and Tube as a production foreman. It was the center of his social life. Although hard hit financially by the loss of his job, he and his wife, Carolyn, were not deeply in debt and had money saved. Emotionally, however, George was devastated. He could not leave the house for weeks and was unable to discuss the situation with friends. Not until several months later did he feel ready to look for work. He then found work in a state liquor store at considerably reduced income and benefits. He still feels cheated and deceived; he blames the company for doing nothing to aid him after the layoff. Now when he meets his old friends, he finds it hard to communicate. He says that the glue that held them together for so many years has become weak and unbinding.

Case 4: *Tom Cinelli*
Employed by Youngstown Sheet and Tube Company, 1971-1977
Age: 26
Spouse: Betty, married 1977
Children: one son

Tom's unemployment benefits stopped in April 1979, after he completed a publicly funded drafting design course. By mid-1979, Tom and Betty were close to bankruptcy. Two-thirds of Tom's $500 monthly income was spent on rent and utilities. They were ineligible for food stamps because their income was considered too high. They could not afford medication for Betty's and her son's chronic sinus conditions. A year later, Tom was still without work and the couple had divorced. Betty feels the layoff hurt their marriage but does not blame the divorce on that alone. She now has a part-time job in a local grocery store.

Aside from the central task for most workers--finding or preparing for new jobs--how did most respond? We can begin by noting what they did not do. First, very few workers engaged in collective action, either through the unions or other political organizations. Despite substantial and prolonged efforts by a coalition of community leaders to engage them in the campaign to reopen the mills under community-worker ownership, a majority took no part in rallies, letter writing, or other political action to influence federal and state decisions on subsidies for this purpose (Buss & Hofstetter 1981).

Second, only a small minority of terminated workers made any use of formal human services, including those established under an emergency state grant to the community mental health program. For instance, of the over 4,000 affected workers, less than 2 percent had contact with the community mental health centers during the year following the closing. Also, a "drop-in" mental health counseling center in the union hall, operated throughout 1978, was visited by only twenty-two workers. Although terminated workers were significantly more likely than non-terminated workers to report contacts with any of forty-six principal local human services agencies, the overall level of contact is surprisingly low, less than one contact per individual.

To the extent that workers relied on others for help in handling their personal crises, they turned for extra help to informal networks of social support. However, terminated workers were less likely than nonterminated workers to have asked for extra help from friends, neighbors, and coworkers. In fact, the lending agency was the only potential helper from which the terminated workers sought assistance more frequently than did nonterminated workers. Under stress, workers did not see the need, or were reluctant to ask, for help from others--especially from those they knew best.

Such evidence suggests that most workers coped with the crisis individually rather than collectively and often withdrew from social contact rather than reaching out to others. Individual efforts to cope independently with a personal crisis are not necessarily less functional than efforts that involve reliance or dependence on others, but unemployed or prematurely retired persons can benefit by turning to others for counsel or emotional support.

Human Services Response

A major potential resource for helping workers find such ways of coping more effectively with the stresses of job loss was the complex of formal human services agencies in the community. Their leaders were not only willing but anxious to respond to needs generated by massive unemployment. Yet, as will be shown, their efforts were unsuccessful. When over 4,000 workers lost their jobs with little warning, Youngstown's human service delivery system was caught by surprise. Subsequent responses demonstrated that it was ill-prepared to respond to the crisis of mass unemployment.

Emergency mental health grant. The Youngstown community's effort to mount a response took two directions. The first responses were precipitated by a state grant to a community mental health agency serving Mahoning County, the area most affected by the closing. The mental health center received $150,000 to provide "emergency" service to terminated workers and their families. With this new capacity, the center established new programs aimed at the terminated workers. In addition, small portions of the grant were passed through to a credit counseling agency and an emergency telephone information and referral service to meet anticipated increases in demands for service due to the crisis among the center's new programs: a drop-in center was established in one local union hall, to act as a referral point for persons who needed assistance and might otherwise not enter the services system and to provide advocates to assist workers in obtaining needed services. A full-time mental health staff worker, based at the drop-in center, was to provide "outreach" contact with union leaders and maintain communications among all service providers. A community outreach/organization effort was mounted to bring together experts and interested persons in attempts to lessen the problems produced by the steel crisis. Community education was to inform and attract potential clients to the agency and gain and maintain community support. Finally, agency coordination/in-service training for other local service agencies was to upgrade professional skills of staff workers. In addition, the center's hours of operation were extended to seventy hours a week.

Despite high visibility and varied outreach efforts, there was little worker response to this or to other formal helping efforts. During the first year after the emergency grant, forty-nine former Youngstown Sheet and Tube workers or their spouses, and thirty-four men and women from families who had a member still working at Youngstown Sheet and Tube used the agency's services. The agency's figures indicate that, of 4,100 laid-off workers, less than 2 percent visited the agency. In fact, families associated with other mills in the area (Republic Steel Corporation and U. S. Steel) used the services almost as much as those from Youngstown Sheet and Tube.

It is unlikely that the union hall was a good location for contacting many workers, independent of whatever social stigma was attached to mental health service. As one mental health staffworker, whose father had been laid off from the mills during an earlier economic crisis period, explained: "The last place my dad would go when he was laid off was, very simply, the union hall, 'cause those were the people who didn't protect his job and he had paid them $20 a month to do that. He wanted no part of that. When he went back to work, they were great people."

Seventy percent of both terminated and nonterminated workers said they found it hard to ask others for help." More than 60 percent believed "grown people should stand on their own two feet," rather than "depending on someone else sometimes." More terminated workers (33 percent) were bothered by seeing the government spend tax dollars on the unemployed than were the nonterminated (23 percent). Likewise, more nonterminated workers said it was easy to ask for help (32 percent) and sometimes be dependent (37 percent) than did terminated workers (26 percent and 30 percent). A comparison of the attitudes held by the two groups suggests that job loss may reinforce, rather than diminish, the desire to be self-reliant.

Community planning process. Simultaneously, a second direction was taken by the community in developing a system-wide human services response. Youngstown State University's Center for Urban Studies, supported by a grant from the Ohio Board of Regents, brought together most of the involved community human services planners and administrators and for a year assisted them in thinking through the nature of the community's need and the kinds of human services programs appropriate for this crisis (Buss & Redburn 1980). From that process emerged a consensus on goals for action to meet the needs generated by the crisis. These twenty goals--set by leaders of the human services system itself--provide one comprehensive, concrete set of standards against which to judge the system's performance. Here are some examples:

Services

Goal: A stabilization training package will be developed.

Subgoals:

A. To assist unemployed persons to meet their financial obligations
B. To assist unemployed persons to have and follow a personal/family financial plan.
C. To assist unemployed persons to have the necessary legal knowledge to cope with unemployment and job search.
D. To help insure that unemployed persons will act within the law.

Goal: A unique preventive family counseling program will be developed.

Subgoals:

A. To help unemployed persons recognize predictable social stress indicators.
B. To help unemployed persons to use peer support groups and local community groups, as well as social service agencies to cope with symptoms of social stress.
C. To help unemployed persons to identify and practice ways to anticipate and counteract damaging consequences of social stress.
D. To help unemployed persons to avoid serious social stress consequences.

Goals: human service awareness should be encouraged in order to prevent future employment crises.

Subgoals:

A. A preretirement program will be made available to private sector companies.
B. A prelayoff program will be developed and available to each company.
C. All employed persons should know what benefits are available in the event of layoff or retirement.
D. Company management, community leaders, and other decision makers should act consistently with knowledge of the effects of closings/layoffs on the total economic/social picture.

Financial Needs

Goal: There will be a health insurance alternative for the over 1,700 unemployed steelworkers who have lost their group coverage.

Goal: A social service deferred payment system for both short-term and long-term credit will be devised and implemented.

Goal: A program to protect mortgages will be developed in cooperation with banking institutions.

Six months after these goals were set--and more than a year after the layoffs began--some of the group who had set and tried to implement these goals were asked whether each was "already accomplished," "badly needed," "possibly useful," or "not necessary." None of the twenty was seen by a majority as accomplished. Our own review of progress through 1980 showed that virtually nothing had been done to achieve these human services goals--or to meet similar needs created by the wave of new mill closings in 1980, which eliminated an additional 5,000 jobs.

Assessing the Human Services Response

To evaluate the community's human services response through its array of formal helping agencies, it is necessary both to assess the appropriateness and effectiveness of what was done and to note what was not done to meet the needs of affected workers.

On the one hand, workers displayed little evidence of trauma or breakdown of the type typically treated by crisis-oriented mental health and other social services agencies. On the other hand, it is apparent that workers had widely varying experiences and demonstrated varying levels of ability to cope. Some managed the stresses of job loss and unemployment gracefully or even creatively, discovering opportunities in crisis. Others, either from bad luck or a lack of personal capacity, handled stress in destructive or unhelpful ways. Those who were unemployed for long periods appeared to have the most difficulty. If the objective is to help workers manage their personal crises in ways that are beneficial rather than destructive, then many of the helping strategies appropriate to the workers' needs fall into the category of "primary prevention," as defined by community mental health professionals (Catalano & Dooley 1980).

The steel crisis response illustrates the difficulty of developing effective programs of prevention and of reaching people with problems less severe than those generally classified as pathologies or "breakdowns." In-depth discussions with local mental health administrators produced a portrait of people frustrated and floundering. They were surprised by the lack of response to their efforts to reach workers through media publicity, mass meetings, the union hall walk-in center, and other means.

Our own investigation indicates why this is likely to be the case. What little academic research exists on plant closings and their social and psychological effects is virtually silent on the design of outreach or human services programs of this sort (Catalano & Dooley 1980).

Options not taken. In the absence of preexisting models, the local agencies faced the practical task of spending an emergency grant in a way that was consistent both with their general continuing mandate and with the specific mandate of the grant to meet the mental health needs of workers. The following examples give some idea of the range of options open to them:

1. To reduce stress, the agencies might have used the limited funds to provide small emergency grants to steelworkers with unusual expenses, such as those of an uninsured illness or injury. The short-term financial needs of most workers were met by unemployment insurance and other benefits; however, some suffered severe income losses or built up heavy debts.
2. To reduce stress, the agencies might have organized support groups and informal helping networks among the workers. The feasibility of such networking strategies is suggested by the remarkable sense of group and community among workers, the low rate of relocation or outmigration of laid-off workers after the closing, and the ability of individual workers, up to two years later, to locate and describe job histories of several dozen former coworkers. In these circumstances, gaining the trust and active assistance of a handful of workers in each area of the mill would have put the mental health staff at only one remove from personal contact with every worker in the plant.
3. To reduce stress, human services professionals might have helped to organize collective political or social action by the workers. Any role that a public agency plans in such actions is likely to be controversial. Nevertheless, the Federal Community Action program of the 1960s provides examples of how organized collective responses can produce both material and psychological benefit--especially where powerlessness threatens to produce despair.
4. To increase competence and coping skills, the mental health centers might have developed and conducted education and training programs for the workers. Such programs could have included (a) education, giving workers awareness of the social and psychological as well as the economic consequences of job loss and knowledge of reemployment prospects and available human services; (b) cognitive restructuring to destigmatize job loss and protect self-esteem; and (c) behavior training, providing such coping skills as relaxation, stress avoidance, and skills needed for active efforts to overcome the effects of job loss, including job search skills and new job skills.

When we examine what was done by the agencies to meet the perceived needs of workers, we find no clear-cut strategy. Most effort was devoted to outreach and education, designed to draw workers into existing services programs. In nearly all cases, these programs were oriented toward treatment of individuals who have already demonstrated either temporary or chronic inability to manage problems without professional assistance. Moreover, eligibility limits or fee structures of the programs pose barriers to their use by recently unemployed workers. The inappropriateness of existing human services programs is highlighted by the fact that they could not be used to meet any of the service goals set by the community planning process, a judgment confirmed by the workers' indifference to available services.

Little attention was paid to the delayed secondary wave of impacts on others in the community, and few efforts were made to identify and directly aid those in this group, many of whom have fewer resources and less skill or work experience than the industrial work force first affected. If unemployment is massive in scale and the community has little prospect of replacing the lost jobs, even some highly skilled and experienced workers will remain unemployed for some time. The majority who find replacement work will pass the unemployment burden to others with fewer personal resources. Thus, where a permanent loss of jobs occurs, income maintenance programs are an important component of any intervention strategy aimed at maintaining the quality of life, and they should be extensive and generous enough to protect the many who are not covered by unemployment insurance.

A good deal of evidence suggests that it is difficult to construct human services responses appropriate to economic crisis. A major obstacle is the lack of knowledge and experience--not only at the local level where programs are delivered, but at higher levels of government where programs are designed, funded, and sometimes coordinated. As a nation, we have simply not learned from the plant closings that have periodically plagued our industrial communities: impact studies were not conducted; programs to assist the unemployed were not evaluated; and cumulative knowledge about plant closings has been difficult to assemble and disseminate. A second set of barriers is posed by the existing structure of services, priorities, eligibility, and financing--which does not recognize the particular needs of recently unemployed workers.

What Treatments Are Needed?

It has been established that in Youngstown, the unemployed steelworkers and their families were normal (i.e., typical) people under stress. This stress presumably placed them at risk of developing more serious problems that might require professional treatment. Thus, it is plausible to hypothesize that an early intervention either to relieve stress or to enhance the person's ability to cope with stress would be helpful.

A preventive program that would meet this hypothesized need might or might not involve mental health professionals. It is likely that the greatest benefits will flow from actions that increase the self-esteem, coping skills, and general resources of the affected workers and their families. For instance, training of unemployed workers for roles as information-givers and network-builders--work for which they could be paid and which builds both their capacities and those of former colleagues without implying dependency--might prove a valid, cost-effective technique.

1. *What human services are most needed by terminated workers and their families?*

Some tentative conclusions can be drawn from Youngstown's experience. The apprehension and anxiety accompanying a closing announcement can be reduced by timely and accurate information concerning the company's plans, eligibility for various benefit programs, human services available to workers, and realistic alternative employment possibilities.

An intensive orientation and coping skills program should be offered to all terminated workers at the earliest possible time. Despite their varied coping abilities and personal situations, these workers face similar tasks: of accepting the fact of job loss and its implications, of designing a personal adjustment strategy that maximizes their chances of coming through the crisis well, and of maintaining their own and their families' morale in a disturbing situation. Every worker needs an intensive period and appropriate environment in which systematically to analyze the crisis, work out possible personal solutions, and test these against the perceptions of others. Workers who have experienced and dealt successfully with termination can serve as helpful sounding boards.

Because the abilities of workers and their families to cope with unemployment vary widely and because excessive stress may lead to a variety of problems, many services programs in local human services agencies should be augmented to meet the service needs created by economic crisis. Increased stress due to job loss interacts with a wide variety of preexisting personal problems. A young couple may experience intensified marital problems. An alcoholic may drink more heavily. A depressed spouse may become more withdrawn and passive. An older person forced into early retirement may have difficulty finding creative uses for his energy and consequently may suffer physically and emotionally.

The reluctance of many people to seek help hides the extent and consequences of personal stress produced by job loss and unemployment. Moreover, the capacity of existing agencies to help is limited because (1) their existing case loads absorb most or all of their funding and staff time; and (2) their programs and outreach-intake procedures give priority to those with more severe problems or manifest crises.

Equity questions arise because other individuals in the community with similar levels of need would not be served by a program targeted to a group of newly terminated workers. Increased expenditures will be needed for a wide range of human services but the added funding will not be available in many communities. Therefore, such services should be made available on the basis of relative need, as assessed by the community.

2. *What is the best time and method to reach the maximum number of affected persons with the needed services?*

Many obstacles must be overcome to improve the match between need and service delivery. Corporations should be required by law to provide information needed by public agencies to contact affected workers and to do so as soon as plans for layoffs are final. Ideally, detailed information on every worker's employment experience and skills, interest in further training and education, medical and other personal and household characteristics should--with his or her consent--be placed in a computer file where it can be analyzed to develop an individualized package of diagnostic services and other assistance appropriate to the needs of that worker and his dependents. Such information can be most readily assembled prior to termination, with the cooperation of both management and unions.

An in-plant program of group information sessions and individual counseling should be implemented prior to any terminations, since the best time to reach workers, as a group, is before they leave a shut-down plant permanently. Also, this is a time when the "rumor mill" is likely to generate inaccurate information, and worker anxieties are high.

A central, noninstitutional access point should be created to facilitate access to all community human services. Union sponsorship is one option for avoiding the "agency" image. The Youngstown drop-in center did not escape institutional identification and was not used by workers. Linking such an access point to in-plant counseling and continued contact with workers by union counselors after termination appears to be one workable arrangement.

Already-existing networks of friends and kin should be used for information and referral whenever possible. Recent research has confirmed the importance of informal self-help networks in neighborhoods and communities (Collins & Pancoast 1976; Durman 1976). This network operates in the shadow of the formal system to provide support for individuals in time of need. For instance, a group of terminated workers met regularly for breakfast for several months following the Youngstown closing. Our experience suggests that to meet effectively the needs of terminated workers and their families requires a well-coordinated human services system combined with an effective helping network of the displaced workers, their families, friends and neighbors. Further research is needed to evaluate various methods by which the formal services system can support and not supplant these informal helping networks.

Because all nonretired workers are required to visit state employment services offices regularly in order to receive unemployment compensation, employment services counselors should receive special training and should be mandated to make diagnoses and referrals for problems not directly related to employment. In the Youngstown steel crisis, Ohio Bureau of Employment Services counselors were instructed not to go beyond employment-related counseling, which was provided at the initiative of the worker only. Given present authority and funding, this may have been the proper administrative course.

A representative human services providers' council should be formed to develop and oversee the steps necessary to integrate more effectively the community's services for the unemployed. In the absence of such a council in Youngstown, no one had clear responsibility for creating a joint human services response to the crisis. The failure to create such a collective decision-making structure in the 2-1/2 years following the first layoffs suggests a need for state-level action to foster such organizations.

3. *At the state level, what human service planning should be undertaken in anticipation of future local employment crises, and who should have responsibility for this planning?*

The state level appears to be the appropriate one for planning an explicit human service policy to assist communities in economic crisis. The aims of this policy should be (1) to meet the increased mental health and financial needs of affected workers and their families in the wake of job losses; and (2) to permanently strengthen the human services system in these communities. To these ends, the states should:

a. Identify communities with large, older, and unprofitable industrial facilities to develop estimates of the annual incidence and most probable locations of future closings. Such information is needed both to indicate to these communities the need for contingency planning and to develop estimates of the social cost and increased public expenditures likely to occur. In particular, it will help to identify each state's need for an explicit human services policy for communities in economic crisis.
b. Identify state-level interagency agreements necessary for rapid coordinated response to local economic crisis. The poor coordination of state employment services with those administered by local CETA (Comprehensive Employment and Training Act) prime sponsors and the virtual absence of linkage between these services and other human services underscores this need.
c. Conduct a continuing action research program to identify human service strategies effective in meeting human services needs generated by employment crisis.

4. *What pattern of authority, funding, and accountability will provide better integration and more effective delivery of needed human services to those affected by economic crisis?*

To implement effective human service responses to employment crises at the community level, most states must act to change their current patterns of authority, funding, and accountability. Specifically, the states should:

a. Require by law that companies planning to close major facilities or lay off large numbers of workers provide, at a minimum, an address file of workers to be laid off and provide access to the plant during the period by public agencies for the purpose of providing appropriate information and counseling. Legislation has been proposed in Ohio and other states to require prior notice of plant closings (Blasi & Whyte 1982). Approval of such legislation at the state or federal level is needed to implement the above recommendation. The successful experience of a few communities with pre-layoff counseling and the difficulties of reaching workers once they have been terminated point strongly to the importance of such a legal requirement.

b. Encourage and support local coordinative efforts of human services providers, including common staffing of outreach, diagnosis, referral, and follow-up services and a shared data base on recently terminated workers. This could be expanded eventually to include all unemployed workers. Despite initiatives undertaken at state and local levels throughout the nation to provide better coordination of services to the unemployed and other dependent populations, most local human services systems today are characterized by highly fragmented planning, administration, and service delivery.
c. Conduct independent evaluations of all state-supported programs to meet service needs generated by economic crisis. Formal scientific evaluation of human service programs for communities in crisis is urgent; far too little is known about the needs generated by such crises or how to meet them.
d. Increase funding for human services during periods of employment crisis or continuing high unemployment. However, such increases should not be used simply to supplement staffing of existing programs. It should be clear from the preceding discussion that communities must develop new methods of outreach, new coordinative linkages, and innovative services programs to meet the needs of unemployed workers.

5. *What role should the federal government play in ameliorating the impacts of plant closings on individuals and communities?*

The federal government must ultimately play a limited role in responding to the specific human service needs of individual communities. The cost of subsidizing local service delivery is prohibitive when viewed as a nation-wide problem. In addition, it is not clear what sorts of services should be subsidized in order to meet the needs of the mass unemployed. As this and other research has shown, it may also be the case that traditional services for the laid-off worker are unwanted, underutilized, and unnecessary.

The federal government can play some role in human service delivery, albeit a limited one. The federal government should:

a. Offer emergency funding to distressed communities for the purpose of developing experimental or innovative demonstration programs to serve the unmet needs of the mass unemployed.
b. Support scholarly and practical research on the human impact of plant closings as short- and long-term phenomena, and on the need for different kinds of human services.
c. Collect, evaluate, and disseminate information on the impacts of plant closings and the human service needs of the laid-off worker, so that practitioners in impacted communities can organize an appropriate response.

A more important role for the federal government to play in distressed communities experiencing plant closings involves concentration on developmental programs or policies that foster revitalization and reemployment. Returning to work in a good job seems to obviate the need for human services of the maintenance, intervention or custodial type.

Before outlining an appropriate developmental strategy, it is necessary to understand the nature of the economic crisis of the 1970s-1980s. The United States and most other mature industrial powers are experiencing major transformations of their industrial bases. Many industries in sectors such as steel, autos, rubber, textiles, and others no longer represent viable economic concerns. The laws of economics, therefore, dictate that some must fail. This process of growth and decline, often referred to as the process of "creative destruction," is inevitable.

The process of creative destruction implies the following kinds of government action or inaction (Vaughan 1981):

a. Failing firms should not be heavily subsidized by government to keep them in business. Instead, government resources should be channeled into activities that stimulate the growth of healthy firms and the birth of new enterprises, and into programs that help people directly.
b. Government economic revitalization programs should assist communities in developing the capacity to participate effectively in the economic revitalization process. Programs might include funding for developing community-wide strategies, supporting community-based development organizations, funding self-help groups, etc.
c. A concerted effort to remove impediments or barriers to development should be made. Actions might include revisions of tax codes, streamlining of the regulatory process, reorganization of capital markets, formation of venture capital, removing biases against small businesses, etc.
d. Much of the federal plant-closing legislation (Blasi & Whyte 1982; Harrison & Bluestone 1982) contains provisions which are not consistent with the process of creative destruction. In the long term, this legislation does not seem to benefit either industry or labor. A more careful analysis of the implications of this legislation should be conducted before it is seriously pursued.

The policies above may stimulate the growth of industry, but there remains the problem of matching workers with jobs. This problem of matching is a result of "labor market imperfections"--the allocation of labor to available jobs is inefficient. Part of the problem of matching could be solved by means of public policies that remove the barriers in labor markets in the following ways:

a. By reducing the costs (both individual and public) of linking workers with jobs (e.g., providing relocation allowances to accept other jobs or travel allowances to search for jobs).
b. By increasing the availability of unemployment-related information to workers and employers (e.g., developing regional or national systems for sharing labor market information).
c. By encouraging and supporting workers in retraining efforts in public and private institutions (e.g., make retraining expenses to obtain another job tax deductible, allow workers receiving unemployment to participate in retraining without loss of benefits, etc.). Retraining should not be conducted only to

keep workers occupied (e.g., public works programs), but should be targeted toward the precise needs of industry at a variety of skill levels (e.g., CETA "customized" training programs tailored to specific industries are of this type).

d. By continuing to provide unemployment compensation at present or current levels in order to assist workers in the transition between jobs.
e. By making it easier for persons, especially those who are laid off, to start new, small businesses (e.g., worker cooperatives, worker buyouts, or ownership of viable firms, etc.).

Conclusion

A human services policy meeting the short-term needs generated by plant closings also represents longer-term investment in human resources. The entrepreneurial talents, productive skills, and leadership potential thus protected and increased can be applied to the tasks of rebuilding the local economy and strengthening its political capacity. It is possible to outline a social strategy to aid in revitalizing such communities.

References

Blasi, Joseph R., and William Foote Whyte.
1982 "Worker Ownership and Public Policy." Pp. 177-193 in F. Stevens Redburn and Terry F. Buss (1982).

Buss, Terry F., et al.
1983 *Mass Unemployment: Plant Closings and Community Mental Health.* Beverly Hills: Sage.

Buss, Terry F., and C. Richard Hofstetter.
1981 "Communication, Information and Participation." *Social Science Journal,* 18:81-92.

Buss, Terry F., and F. Stevens Redburn.
1980 "Evaluating Human Service Delivery in the Crisis of Mass Unemployment." *Journal of Health and Human Services Administration* 3:229-50.
1983 *Shutdown: Public Policy for Mass Unemployment.* Albany: SUNY Press.

Catalano, Ralph, and David Dooley.
1980 "Economic Change in Primary Prevention." In Richard H. Price et al. (eds.), *Prevention in Mental Health.* Beverly Hills: Sage Annual Review of Mental Health.

Chapman, A. H.
1964 "Iatrogenic Problems in Psychotherapy." *Psychiatry Digest* (Sept.):23-29.

Collins, A. H., and D. L. Pancoast.
1976 *Natural Helping Networks.* New York: National Association of Social Workers.

Delbecq, Andre L., and Andrew N. Van de Ven.
1971 "A Group Process Model for Problem Identification and Program Planning." *Journal of Applied Behavioral Science* 7 (Fall):466-92.

Durman, Eugene C.
1976 "The Role of Self-Help in Service Provision." *Journal of Applied Behavioral Science* 12, no. 3:433-43..

Gross, Martin L.
1978 *The Psychological Society: A Critical Analysis of Psychiatry, Psychotherapy, Psychoanalysis, and the Psychological Revolution.* New York: Random House.

Hadley, Suzanne W., and Haus H. Strupp.
1976 "Contemporary View of Negative Effects in Psychotherapy." *Archives of General Psychiatry* 33:1291-1302.

Harrison, Bennett and Barry Bluestone.
1982 "The Incidence and Regulation of Plant Closings." Pp. 131-69 in Redburn and Buss (1982).

Luborsky, Lester, Barton Singer, and Lise Luborsky.
1976 "Comparative Studies of Psychotherapies." In Robert C. Spitzer, Donald F. Kline (eds.). *Evaluation of Psychological Therapies.* Baltimore.: Johns Hopkins.

Redburn, F. Stevens, and Terry F. Buss (eds.).
1982 *Public Policies for Distressed Communities.* Lexington, Mass.: Lexington Books.

Rice, A. K.
1970 "Individual, Group and Intergroup Processes." *Human Relations*, 22:565-84.

Taber, Thomas D., Jeffrey T. Walsh, and Robert A. Cook.
1979 "Developing a Community-Based Program for Reducing the Social Impact of a Plant Closing." *The Journal of Applied Behavioral Science*, 15:133-55.

Thompson, J. D.
1967 *Organizations in Action.* New York: McGraw Hill.

Vaughan, Roger J.
1981 *Economic Renewal: A Guide for the Perplexed.* Washington, D.C.: Council of State Planning Agencies.

VI

POLICY ISSUES FOR THE EIGHTIES

Domestic Violence: A Neglected Policy Area

Domestic violence, by no means a new issue, is an area in which policy has been slow to emerge. Yet violence affects all age, income, and educational levels, and occurs among dating and cohabiting couples as well as in families (a brief discussion of child abuse appears in Chapter 7.). Recent studies have found violence fairly prevalent among college students, suggesting that such patterns may persist throughout their lives (Cate 1982). Policies to deal with family violence are needed because it is often intergenerational. Many adult abusers were themselves abused as children, and women and children in the same household may all be abused.

Family violence is a policy issue that highlights the differing viewpoints on government intervention in family life discussed in previous sections of this book. Feelings run high on both sides of the issue:

> Controversy exists concerning the extent to which government should bear a major responsibility for coping with the abuse problem. Those associated with the so-called Moral Majority have steadfastly maintained that abuse cases are family or church matter, not within the province of government. Others claim that it is difficult or even impossible to curb such personal abuse without the intervention of government and laws [Harris 1981:1].

Despite these conflicting viewpoints, three-quarters of the national sample in the Harris survey (1981:1-2) believed that government should take major responsibility for dealing with abuse of children and the emotionally or physically handicapped. Seventy-two percent thought that coping with abuse of the elderly should be a major responsibility of government. A smaller proportion, 62 percent, expressed this opinion with regard to wife abuse.

The Harris poll found that about one in four respondents knew a victim of child or wife abuse and one in six knew an elderly or handicapped victim of abuse. Yet the problem has long been hidden. Victims did not talk about it; medical personnel often did not report it; and law enforcement personnel frequently did not take it seriously. The tradition of "blaming the victim" is strongly associated with wife battering. Moreover, the courts, agencies, and practitioners who deal with the problem frequently define their task in terms of preserving the family rather than helping the victims.

The movement to assist domestic violence victims began at the local level with the opening of shelters in many cities across the country. Policies are being formulated and implemented at the local and state levels. Chapter 25, from the New York State Governor's Task Force on Domestic Violence, shows how one state has proceeded. Since the report was prepared, more than one-half of the recommendations have been completely implemented (Recommendations 1-4, 12, 15, 16, 20) or are close to that stage (Recommendations 5, 6, 9, 14).[1] Progress has already been made toward implementing several of the remaining items (Recommendations 7, 8, 17).

Important actions taken include the passage of the Omnibus Domestic Violence Bill, which accomplished Recommendation #1. Also in 1981, New York became the first state to give the right of counsel to victims seeking orders of protection against relatives. (These protect the petitioner from harassment, intimidation or assault by the person named in the order.) Orders of protection have been expanded to include nonrelatives. Furthermore, the New York State legislature has authorized Family Court judges to order batterers to participate in an educational program, another objective of the task force.

The National Coalition against Domestic Violence, formed by grassroots organizations in 1978, monitors federal activities that have an impact on battered women, as well as assisting member organizations in building state and regional coalitions (Center for Women Policy Studies 1981:4). The issue of family violence will not go away. In periods of economic recession, it tends to increase as unemployment and financial pressures within families mount. With shrinking budgets, shelters may be in a precarious position, since this policy issue has never received high priority.

The Growth in Single and Nontraditional Lifestyles

Numerous policy issues for the current decade stem largely from changes in family and household composition that have been a running theme throughout the book. It is clear that the diversity in family types will continue. The traditional family is unlikely to predominate, despite the wishes of the new right and its attempts to bring back an idealized version of it (see Chapter 1 by Hess in Part I). As Masnick and Bane (1980:110) note, "traditional families are a small minority of all households at any given time." The trends toward declining marriage rates, increased divorce rates, and declining fertility seem likely to persist, although some experts expect a new baby boom soon (Fialka 1982:31, 41). If current trends continue, as many as 30 percent of white women and 20 percent of nonwhite women will not have children.

The 1980 census figures confirm these trends, especially decreases in both household and family size. Average household size in 1980 was 2.75 compared to 3.11 a decade earlier. Several factors contributed to this change. First, the percentage of families headed by a single parent has grown, from 12.3 percent in 1970 to 19.1 percent in 1980. Second, average family size has decreased since 1970. Third, there has been a considerable increase in the number of nonfamily households--people living alone or with nonrelatives--as more young and old are living alone (Herbers 1981:A1, A18).

Young people are choosing a variety of marriage and family types, as well as delaying marriage in favor of singlehood or cohabitation. The lifestyles of individuals born after 1940 may be characterized by "less permanency and less attachment to the conventional accoutrements of nuclear-family living," except for homebuying by the married and unmarried alike (Masnick & Bane 1980:116).

At midlife, many men and women are divorced, separated, or members of blended families which may include children from their current marriage and from the previous marriages of either or both partners. A growing number of women are becoming "displaced homemakers" faced with making new lives for themselves, often on limited incomes. For these and other reasons, some individuals will live with unrelated individuals who consider themselves a family, as described in Chapter 28 by Streib and Hilker, for example. Others will form "cooperative households in which men and women simply share expenses," but lack strong emotional ties to each other (Bernard 1981:56). Adding to the diversity of household types are those composed of two workers and of husbands and wives whose grown children have households of their own.

Three chapters in this part deal with these changes in household composition and living arrangements. Shostak, in Chapter 26, discusses the growing popularity of singlehood and raises important issues of concern to singles. He asks whether they are likely to become a political force in the future, as women and the elderly did in the 1960s and 1970s. His suggestion that singles might form a bloc to advance their interests has important implications for married persons and for families. If successful, singles' efforts may lead to policy changes that are in the opposite direction from those supported by the Moral Majority, New Right and others who favor an emphasis on the "traditional family." (A look back at the Chapter 1 makes this abundantly clear.) The emergence of "single power" would make it unlikely that the forces favoring a cohesive family policy will accomplish their goal. Shostak raises some policy issues of special concern to singles, as well as those relating to contraception and abortion that they share with other adults. If singles become a political force, we will be hearing more about these issues in the future. Shostak explores and assesses the potential for such a movement in the final section of his chapter.

As he points out, singles represent a diverse group. They may not live permanently on their own, but may marry or choose a nonmarital relationship or other alternative lifestyle. Some will be single at various stages in their lives--after divorce or between marriages as well as in their young adult years.

In Sweden the trend toward cohabitation has been so marked that it is considered a social institution today, according to Trost (see Chapter 27). He provides a picture of nonmarital relationships in Sweden and discusses how cohabitation is viewed by the population. He touches on important policy issues, which arise on the death of a partner or the dissolution of the relationship. The status of children born to cohabiting couples is another important policy issue. Such issues are arising more frequently in this country now.

The *Marvin* case in the United States publicized legal issues that accompany the break-up of cohabiting couples. Denmark and Sweden have grappled with such issues as the disposition of nonmarital property for a much longer time. In a recent article, Pedersen (1979) pointed out that in Denmark these issues are complicated by the fact that not all cohabiting arrangements are alike. Whereas in the past couples often lived together in a "trial marriage," today many couples establish a long-term "marriage-like" relationship without formalizing the arrangement. Others may live together for a short period. Sometimes the law tries to distinguish between these two types of relationship so that couples in a long-term relationship are treated like married couples. However, efforts to distinguish between the two types of cohabiting couples involve "quilt raising--the investigation of matters that are essentially private" (Pedersen 1979:125). One way out of this dilemma has been the use of the term "*naermest*" ("closely associated") in some statutes. This and similar terms refer to "a personal connection between persons who may or may not be relations or spouses," making it unnecessary to determine whether or not the relationship is "marriage-like."

In her analysis of public policy in Denmark, Pedersen (1979:127) recommends that it be directed toward (1) abolishing rules and regulations that make it more attractive for people not to marry and (2) providing the public with information about advantages and disadvantages of the different types of union. She warns, however, of "two equally dangerous pitfalls. One is to think that nonmarital relationships are a moral danger and ought to be suppressed. The other is to think that a progressive attitude toward family law must necessarily result in a desire for full equality between married and non-married couples." In the United States, family law is an area that has already undergone significant change in the past decade. If nonmarital relationships achieve the same frequency and acceptance here as in other countries, many more issues will have to be resolved.

It is not the young alone who are experimenting with alternative lifestyles. Although aging individuals increasingly live alone, some are combining their resources, either informally or in programs run by nonprofit organizations. These congregate living arrangements make it possible for older persons to be independent but, at the same time, to have access to special services and the companionship of others. Streib and Hilker (Chapter 28) report on a program in which older persons live together in a communal setting. The authors assess the success of these arrangements and raise some policy issues for consideration. Some of the comments made by residents, especially with regard to requirements for self-sufficiency, are interesting. The extent of interaction among residents in congregate settings varies. In a complex that housed older residents in California, Hochschild (1976:320-36) found many communal aspects to their lives. She used the term "sibling bond" to describe their relationships. Though not a substitute for family, these ties provided residents with a meaningful life independent of their children. They had developed a social network and a sense of community (ibid.:334).

While endorsing communal living, Maggie Kuhn (1980) rejects age-segregated housing for older people in favor of age-integrated "families" in which individuals at various life stages pool their resources and share household and family care tasks. Research indicates that older people differ on whether they prefer to live with others their own age or in environments with a diversity of age and family types (Brody 1980:55).

Individuals and Families with Special Needs

Policy analysts have drawn attention to numerous issues that accompany changes in families and living arrangements. According to Levitan and Belous (1981:188), this pluralism in lifestyles will require "a greater degree of flexibility in public policies to cope with the diverse needs of different household types." Yet policies to assist some families with special needs are lacking and few attempts are being made to address their problems. The dearth of programs and policies for single parents, primarily women, trying to provide adequately for themselves and their families has been emphasized in each section of this book. Their basic needs are economic. With adequately paid employment, women could afford child-care, decent housing, and other necessities. However, as Chapters 16 and 17 demonstrate, too often government programs serve to reinforce or even increase dependency. Teenage mothers especially need assistance. Budget cutbacks in public assistance, job training, and nutrition and related programs will adversely affect these young mothers and their offspring, who start life with sometimes irreversible handicaps.

At the other end of the life cycle, pressing issues need to be addressed. Policies that affect the care of the ill and disabled should be reexamined as many individuals spend fewer years within nuclear family settings. In small dual-worker families, fewer persons in their young and middle adult years will be available to provide constant care for aging or ill members. Women, the traditional caregivers, find this role in conflict with their labor force participation, as Finch and Groves illustrated in Chapter 23.

Since children growing up in single-parent or blended families may have weaker family ties, they may be unwilling to assume the responsibility of personally caring for a stepparent or the parent who did not raise them. Policy makers will have to consider how to meet the needs of aging unmarried or childless individuals, whose numbers may swell in the future.

Although relatively affluent dual-earner families may be able and willing to purchase private nursing and housekeeping services for relatives, those with limited incomes will look to government for services and programs (Masnick & Bane 1980:126). According to Masnick and Bane (ibid.:128), government has played an important but limited role in providing care and support services for dependent individuals. If the trends begun by the Reagan administration are continued and existing government services shrink further, the gap between demand and available services will widen. To decrease deficits, administration policy makers are concentrating on making cuts in Social Security, Medicaid, and Medicare in the FY 84 and later budgets. This emphasis will affect middle-income families who were not touched by previous cuts in social programs and who benefited from some Reagan administration tax policies. Many will join low-income families in falling through the "social safety net."

Informal networks may be called upon to meet some needs as programs and services become increasingly inadequate. Whether married, single, cohabiting, divorced, separated, or widowed, individuals may turn to networks for social support. Such groups may help counter isolation and alienation among those of all ages who are alone. In addition to providing support, networks can serve as referral sources, advocates and crisis-intervention mechanisms.

Chapter 29 by Genovese reviews the types and functions of self-help networks that aid and support families. Given the decreased funding for entitlement and other social programs, families may rely more on networks to help them cope with their needs and crises. Partly to preserve their informal character, policy makers have avoided giving serious consideration to funding self-help networks. However, such networks may offer government a low-cost alternative to services that are being eliminated or that are being called for to meet emerging needs of individuals and families. Such a development would be a mixed blessing, since networks should not be regarded as substitutes for necessary government programs and services, a point made by Finch and Groves in Chapter 23.

Prospects for a Comprehensive Family Policy--Not in the Eighties

Given the changes already discussed, the development of a family policy in this country may be an unrealistic goal at this time. Kamerman and Kahn (1978: 479-500) present arguments for policy oriented to individuals rather than families. First, one-person households represent a rapidly growing household type. As Carolyn Shaw Bell notes, the individual represents the only "entire unit" in society (cited in Kamerman & Kahn 1978:479). Second, families traditionally have perpetuated inequality: "The family undermines much social policy aimed at equalization because families are unequal and are most influential during the early years when children are socialized" (ibid.:498). Finally, since so many societal goals are individual goals, a "people policy" makes sense (ibid.:499).

This approach avoids value judgments that lead to favoring some family forms over others. Those who needed assistance would receive it, regardless of family status. Children in poor families would be aided, whether or not they lived with both parents. Needy adults who did not live with family members would receive the help they needed too.

The pluralism in family composition and lifestyles suggests that groups with widely differing viewpoints about the future of the family are unlikely to reach a consensus on a comprehensive family policy. Steiner's (1981) view is that the fragile coalition of "children's advocates, women's advocates, welfare advocates, senior citizens' advocates, and civil rights advocates" who favor a family policy falls apart when it comes to establishing priorities. Family policy unifies groups only so long as it remains a general concept:

> Competing ideologies--in abortion, pro-choice vs. pro-life; in welfare, more income assistance versus more pressure for self-sufficiency; in foster care, unlimited spending on foster care of poor children versus pressures for permanent placement; in adolescent pregnancy, "secondary prevention" versus primary contraceptive efforts--claim or are thought to be able to "fix" family problems. But the superior validity of one or the other ideology is not established. In none of the family policy issues can it be said that only one side is the pro-family side.... Family policy evokes visions of social programs that will benefit all persons in all families. In some cases, however, the interests of parents and the interests of children do not overlap. In other cases, the interests of some parents and children will not overlap those of their parents and children. Ultimately, advocates for children, for women, for the aged, and for special groups among them will go their separate ways [p. 214].

Attempts to establish a family policy have faltered in the face of recent budget-cutting. In its place have been stepped-up lobbying efforts by advocates and interest groups to keep or increase programs and policies that benefit their own members or constituency. If possibilities for coalitions seem endless, so do potential conflicts. In the process of protecting their interests, however, some groups could work to curb policies to aid families in general or certain types of families. Childless dual-earner couples and singles might unite to oppose being taxed for facilities and services that benefit children, perhaps with support from groups that represent the aging. On the other hand, some singles and married couples are united on the abortion issue. Even within a group, some issues may be divisive, as Shostak points out in this section. The interests of singles at various life-cycle stages may be incompatible.

For these reasons, as well as because of the improbability that new policies or programs to aid families will be introduced at the federal level, the issue of family policy probably will be tabled for some years, although experts may continue to search for basic agreement on its outlines.

The words of Jessie Bernard provide a fitting way to conclude this Part Introduction:

> There can be little doubt that the passing of the traditional family has left a great many traumas, a great deal of suffering, a great many loose ends.... If the 1970s were a time of crisis, revolution, and moral political issues, the 1980s will be a time of putting the pieces together to develop family structures suitable for this time and place, this day and age [Bernard 1981:59].

The chapters in this book show both American families and the policies that affect them to be in transition. In the past, policies did not meet all family needs, but policy makers, family advocates, and social scientists worked to narrow the gap between needs and the programs to meet them. Now, however, when many families need more help than ever, policies and programs are moving farther away from insuring a minimum standard of living and assisting families with special needs.

Note

1. This information was provided by Karla Digirolamo of the New York State Governor's Task Force.

References

Bernard, Jessie.
1981 "Facing the Future." *Society* (Jan/Feb.):53-59.

Brody, Elaine.
1980 "Statement." Pp. 52-61 in *Families: Aging and Changing.* hearing before Select Committee on Aging, House of Representatives, 96th Congress, 2nd Session. June 4, 1980. (Comm. Pub. 96-242.) Washington, D.C.: U.S. Government Printing Office.

Cate, Rodney, et al.
1982 "Premarital Abuse: A Social Psychological Perspective." *Journal of Family Issues* 3, no. 1 (March):79-90.

Center for Women Policy Studies.
1981 "The National Coalition Against Domestic Violence." *Newsletter* (March/April):4.

Fialka, John.
1982 "Another Baby Boom Seems Near but Experts Disagree on Its Size." *Wall Street Journal* (March 4):31, 41

Harris, Louis.
1981 "Americans Believe Government Should Take Major Responsibility in Coping with the Abuse Problem." *Harris Survey* #88 (Nov. 2):1-4.

Herbers, John.
1981 "1980 Census Finds Sharp Decline in Size of American Households." *New York Times* (May 26):A1, A18.

Hochschild, Arlie R.
1976 "Communal Life-Styles for the Old." Pp. 50-57 in Beth B. Hess (ed.), *Growing Old in America.* New Brunswick, N.J.: Transaction Books.

Kamerman, Sheila B., and Alfred J. Kahn (eds.).
1978 *Family Policy: Government and Families in Fourteen Countries.* New York: Columbia University Press.

Kuhn, Maggie.
1980 "Statement." Pp. 15-21 in *Families, Aging and Changing,* hearing before Select Committee on Aging, House of Representatives, 96th Congress, 2nd Session. June 4, 1980. (Comm. Pub. 96-242.) Washington, D.C.: U.S. Government Printing Office.

Levitan, Sar A., and Richard S. Belous.
1981 *What's Happening to the American Family?* Baltimore.: Johns Hopkins Press.

Masnick, George, and Mary Jo Bane.
1980 *The Nation's Families: 1960-1990.* Cambridge, Mass.: Joint Center for Urban Studies of MIT and Harvard.

Pedersen, Inger Margrete.
1979 "Danish Law Relating to Non-Marital Relationships." *International and Comparative Law Quarterly* 28:117-27.

Steiner, Gilbert Y.
1981 *The Futility of Family Policy.* Washington, D.C.: Brookings Institution.

Suggested Additional Readings

Bernard, Jessie.
1982 *The Future of Marriage.* New Haven, Conn.: Yale University Press.

Gelles, Richard.
1979 *Family Violence.* Sage Library of Social Research, vol. 84. Beverly Hills, Cal.: Sage.

Staples, Robert.
1981 *The World of Black Singles: Changing Patterns of Male/Female Relations.* Westport, Conn.: Greenwood.

Stein, Peter J. (ed.)
1981 *Single Life: Unmarried Adults in Social Context.* New York: St Martin's.

Weiss, Robert.
1979 *Going It Alone: The Family Life and Social Situation of the Single Parent.* New York: Basic Books.

Weitzman, Lenore J.
1981 *The Marriage Contract: Spouses, Lovers, and the Law.* New York: Free Press.

25. DOMESTIC VIOLENCE: Report to the Governor and the Legislature

New York State Task Force on Domestic Violence

The Governor's Task Force on Domestic Violence was established by Executive Order #90 on May 17, 1979 to study "the traumatic effects of domestic violence and how our social and legal systems can better deal with such violence and its causes."

The police officers, attorneys, judges, shelter staff, social workers, former victims, nurses, community workers, clergy, and counselors who comprise the Task Force have voluntarily worked days and weekends during the summer and fall of 1979, identifying weaknesses in the various institutions intended to protect family members from brutalization. The Task Force's recommendations are based on the member's daily contact with victims and offenders in domestic violence situations, and represent their sense of the initial tasks that must be accomplished immediately to make the helping system responsive. The Task Force's long-term goal--the prevention of domestic violence in New York--will need to be continuously addressed by an effort among the State, localities and the Federal Government. It is hoped that the short-term recommendations contained in this report will be implemented in the 1980 Legislative Session.

I. What is Domestic Violence?

Domestic violence is not limited to wife abuse or spouse abuse. The problem encompasses child abuse, abuse of siblings, abuse of the elderly, and other intra-family violence. Although violence can occur within any intimate relationship, experience has clearly shown that the most frequent victims are women, children, and elderly family members. In fact, abuse of women and children was once sanctioned at common law. Until 100 years ago, children and wives had no legal status; they were deemed the property of their fathers and husbands and were under their exclusive control. The influence of that historical legal system has resisted explicit changes in law and ostensible changes in social values. It survives today in the form of tacit condonation of abuse of weaker family members.

Prepared by the New York State Governor's Task Force on Domestic Violence, Co-chairpersons Karen Burstein and Marjory Fields; Ilene Margolin, Executive Director, Council on Children and Families; Jeanne Kwartler, Assistant Secretary to the Governor; Karla Digirolamo, Project Director. February. 1980.

Our concern for all victims of domestic violences is integrated in this report; the focus of the recommendations is, however, on violence within couples and on the most common type of that violence: wife-beating. Future reports and recommendations will specifically address child abuse, incest, and abuse of the elderly.

In New York, acts which "would constitute disorderly conduct, harassment, menacing, reckless endangerment, an assault or an attempted assault between spouses or between members of the same family or household" (Family Court Act, sec. 812) are defined as "family offenses." ("Family offenses" do not include murder or attempted murder.) Those illegal acts defined as "family offenses" because the victim and the offender are related by blood or marriage may be prosecuted as civil wrongs in the Family Court of the State of New York. The Family Court cannot impose criminal penalties but may issue orders of protection directing the person found to have committed a family offense to cease the offensive conduct. Alternatively, if the victim chooses and the prosecutor concurs, a "family offense" may be prosecuted in an appropriate criminal court. The criminal court has the power, after conviction, to impose criminal penalties, fines and jail sentences.

Domestic violence ranges from verbal abuse to murder. A recent unpublished study of women who used the Family Court, a shelter, and a counseling program in New York City reported that in the majority of those cases, the women's injuries had been produced by beating, kicking, choking. In a significant number of cases, the incident involved a weapon: a club, a knife, or a gun. The assumptions people make about how severe individual incidents of domestic violence are determined by how significant they believe the problem is in our society. A policy maker who imagines domestic violence is limited to "a little pushing, a shoving" will not see domestic violence as a social problem at all. A policy maker who recognizes that intrafamily violence frequently involves recurrent severe attacks and prolonged beatings will identify domestic violence as a crucial social issue. The recognition is essential if decision makers are to allocate adequate resources to provide meaningful assistance to victims and their families.

How common are incidents of domestic violence? In New York, it is difficult to answer that question because the relevant data are not collected.... However, statistics that are available indicate that family violence is prevalent. Between September 1, 1978 and September 1, 1979, 17,701 family offense petitions were filed in the New York Family Court (Office of Court Administration); 278 spouse murders occurred in New York between 1976 and 1978 (Division of Criminal Justice Services). The New York City survey mentioned earlier revealed that the backgrounds of the women victims were so diverse as to defy categorization, as were the histories of their abusers. Minnesota has the best statewide profile available. Based on thousands of reports from law enforcement, medical, and social service personnel, the "typical" battered spouse in Minnesota is a white woman between the ages of 18 and 35, with children, whose husband has beaten her more than once, each episode leaving her with visible injuries such as bruises and lacerations. As in the New York City study, such assaults were recorded among women of all ages, races and socioeconomic groups.

Data from other states are equally limited. A Cleveland, Ohio survey found that physical abuse was cited as a complaint in 37 percent of divorce petitions filed by women. A New Hampshire survey found that 34 percent of a randomly selected group of families had experienced "at least one" incidence of violence in their marriages. On the national level, the recently published survey of *Violence in the American Family*, by Strauss, Gelles and Steinmetz, found that 3.8 percent of the 2,143 couples surveyed reported one or more *serious* physical attacks during the preceding year. In one-third of those cases, the wife had been assaulted five or more times during the year.

Another survey conducted by pollster Louis Harris in Kentucky concluded that "if anything, the middle class is more prone toward physical assault than the poor."

Using the frequency of spouse abuse reported by Strauss, Gelles and Steinmetz, we estimate that in New York State there are 144,000 marriages in which at least one serious assault results in visible injury each year. This is a conservative estimate because of under-reporting; the actual frequency of spouse abuse, like rape and child abuse, is always higher than the reported frequency. What we do know leads us to conclude that the cost of domestic violence to our State is clearly high--in demands on law enforcement officials, in impact on family disintegration, in psychological scarring of victims and children--and most tragically, in lost lives.

II. New York Response

The movement against wife beating started in England in 1971. A courageous woman named Erin Pizzey, feminist and maternal, opened a run-down house to which local women fled from violent husbands with their children. It was immediately filled to overflowing. Within a few years the work of that one woman led to a network of refuges throughout the United Kingdom....

> In 1972, Women's Advocates, Inc., in St. Paul, Minnesota, began a telephone information and referral service for women.... in October 1974, Women's Advocates began operating the first refuge in America for battered wives and their children.... for years [there was] only one therapist on the eastern seaboard specializing in counseling for the entire battered family.... [Terry Davidson, *Conjugal Crime*].

The movement against domestic violence reached New York in the early 70's as an outgrowth of many community-based women's groups that met in all parts of the State. Two aspects of the activities of these groups led to the decision to focus on the problems of wife beating: the informal community crisis intervention networks for women, and the more formal "rape crisis hot lines." Sensitized by the abused women seeking their help, individuals opened their homes to victims in what became known as "safe home networks." Women's groups negotiated with community centers, YWCA's, hospitals, and counseling programs to provide further services.

In 1975, Maria Roy of New York City convened the first New York State Conference on the Abused Wife, and shortly afterward, organized AWAIC (Abused Women's Aid in Crisis), which began operating a hotline. AWAIC is presently receiving 100 calls a month requesting emergency shelter. It counseled forty-five families during the first half of 1979.

In 1976, Brooklyn Legal Services attorney Marjory D. Fields contacted then State Senator Carol Bellamy with the disturbing complaint that New York's Family Courts were not enforcing existing laws against spouse abuse. Her charge resulted in the filing by Senator Bellamy and Senator Karen Burstein of a number of bills aimed at correcting Family Court deficiencies and expanding a battered spouse's legal options to include access to criminal courts. Also in 1976, a class action suit was brought against New York City Family Court and the New York City Police Department (*Bruno v. Codd*) by twelve battered wives represented by the Litigation Coalition of Battered Women. The complaint charged that neither the police nor the Family Court were enforcing existing laws against domestic violence.

The first state legislative hearings on the issue of domestic violence, sponsored by Speaker Stanley Steingut's Assembly Panel on Women's Issues and the State Minority Task Force on Women, were held in 1977 and took as their theme: "The Battered Spouse: Has the System Failed?" At these hearings, conducted in New York City, Rockland County, Albany and Buffalo, battered women, police officers, shelter staff, Family and Supreme Court judges and other persons involved in this service system testified about the problems in that system. The following excerpt from a victim's testimony is representative:

> The final break came when within a one-week period:
>
> I sat with the muzzle of a cocked 45 six inches from my face listening to a description of how my brains would look shattered against the wall.
>
> Susie was chased from the house with a bread knife because she looked like me;
>
> And, business irregularities came to light which forced him to relinquish his control and any association with the business.
>
> I know as surely as I was breathing that Tom's solution would be to kill all of us and himself... With this immediate fear superseding all past considerations, I obtained an Order of Protection. The locks were changed and metal barricades put on every door.
>
> There followed five years of repeated attempted break-ins. Always with police sirens wailing. Always ending in Police Court with a mere reprimand to him, or Family Court where I was advised to ignore him, "he's trouble." No support edicts from Family Court were honored by him and no enforcement was carried out.

As a result of these hearings, two major legal changes were enacted during the 1977 Legislative Session. First, the "concurrent jurisdiction bill" (Chapter 449, L. 1977), sponsored by Speaker Steingut and Senate Majority Leader Warren Anderson, gave battered spouses the choice of pursuing the cases in Family Court or in a criminal court. Second, the "shelter bill" (Chapter 450, L. 1977), sponsored by Speaker Steingut and then State Senator Karen Burstein, permitted the Department of Social Services to approve "special care homes" as shelters for victims of domestic violence and their children. These measures signaled a new understanding of the urgency of the problem on the part of the Legislature.

Public and legislative attention were further directed to the issue by the 1977 report, *Battered Women*, published by State Senator Manfred Ohrenstein and researched by Barbara Schwimmer. The report detailed the answers of social service, hospital, and law enforcement personnel to questions concerning the frequency of domestic violence and their services to victims. The report concluded that, because of the lack of data collection systems, "battering as a social problem or as an individual act of violence is statistically nonexistent." Reflecting this official ignorance was the absence of social and medical services, leaving "the police agency the only public agency readily accessible on a 24-hour basis in times of crisis."

The Ohrenstein/Schwimmer report made several recommendations for State action. Some of those recommendations have been implemented. For example, the report called for services to domestic violence victims to be made available through the State's Title XX program. This was done in the Department of Social Services' 1978-79 Comprehensive Annual Social Services Program Plan. Other recommendations are repeated by the Governor's Task Force in this report, since the importance of implementing them has not diminished during the past three years.

In 1978, the State Assembly Panel on Women's Issues, chaired by Assemblywoman Estella B. Diggs, conducted a series of public "workshops" for judges, attorneys, police officers, women's advocates and shelter staff to evaluate the effectiveness of the new concurrent jurisdiction law. Agreements were reached on several necessary amendments, which became law in 1978 (Chapters 628 and 629, L. 1978). These amendments clarified procedural questions concerning when a battered family member could exercise her/his legal right to choose Family Court or criminal court, thereby facilitating use of the new law.

Greater access to the legal system for victims of domestic violence was also enhanced by the settlement of the police portion of the *Bruno v. Codd* lawsuit. A consent decree, which became effective October 1, 1978, requires police to answer domestic dispute calls promptly and to make arrests when a felony has been committed or an order of protection has been violated.... The remaining part of *Bruno v. Codd*, dealing with Family Court and probation department personnel, was argued separately in the Court of Appeals. The Court ruled in 1979, stating that "the welcome efforts of plaintiff's counsel and amici in this case have no doubt alerted, even sensitized our courts to the full measure of their responsibilities," and thereby made a trial of the issue unnecessary. Most service providers, however, disagreed with the view that the courts are fulfilling their responsibilities to the victims of domestic violence.

The majority of services now available to New York's victims of domestic violence are provided by a special grants program begun by the Department of

Social Services ($1,387,550 since 1977). These grants, awarded largely to grass roots organizations, have resulted in the creation of seven special care homes, four community services coordination and safe home networks, and three research and demonstration projects exploring such issues as emergency room care, legal assistance and couples counseling. Two additional special care homes have been licensed during this period. During the 1978-79 fiscal year, the New York State Department of Social Services funded eleven domestic violence projects around the state, ranging from shelters to a legal advocacy program and counseling programs for batterers.

Simultaneously, additional community groups developed shelter/advocacy/counseling programs, some of which were supported by other state agencies such as the Office of Mental Health, the Division of Criminal Justice Services and the Division for Youth. In 1978, many groups formally organized themselves as the New York State Coalition Against Domestic Violence, a support and advocacy group representing a wide range of community-based service providers from every region of the State. The coalition functions as a political and technical assistance resource for communities wishing to expand or establish programs.

In short, the period between 1977 and 1979 was one in which government and public concern expanded throughout the state. The most recent directory of services available to victims of domestic violence shows 101 programs now operating in forty counties. As the members of the Governor's Task Force can testify from direct experience, however, much remains to be done if New York is to be effective in its efforts to prevent the continued tragic use of violence by family members against each other.

III. The Work Of The Task Force

In preparation for the issuance of this report, the Task Force established subcommittees to deal with four major areas of concern: the Justice System; Education, Training and Outreach; Data Collection and Evaluation; and Services. During the summer and fall of 1979, those subcommittees met in lengthy sessions and, with the assistance of Advisory Board members, formulated, considered and approved the twenty-one recommendations contained in this report.

The recommendations represent immediate goals. Given the correlation of domestic violence with other societal problems of unemployment, alcohol abuse, sexism, and acceptance of violence, long-term goals and objectives are described in the remainder of this report.

Recommendations

1. The Family Court Act and the Criminal Procedure Law should be amended to clarify and expand provisions for preliminary relief and enforcement of orders of protection. Family Court jurisdiction over first degree assaults should be repealed, thereby giving the criminal courts exclusive jurisdiction over the most serious assaults. These provisions are contained in an omnibus bill.

2. Legislation should be passed authorizing Family Court judges to order a batterer to participate in a "designated violence prevention and treatment program." (S5379, Pisani; A7766, Nadler, Kremer, Diggs, Engel, Farrell, Fossle, Hirsch, Jacobs, Lipschutz, Perone, Pesce, F.M. Sullivan).
3. Legislation should be passed establishing indigent petitioners' right to court-appointed counsel. Indigent respondents now have this right. (S5380, Pisani; A7771, Nadler, Siegel, Kremer, Diggs, Engel, Farrell, Hirsch, Jacobs, Lipschutz, Perone, Pesce, F.M. Sullivan).
4. Legislation should be passed requiring respondents found to have committed family offenses to pay the legal and medical fees of petitioners. (S5373-A, Pisani; A7770-A, Nadler, Kremer, Diggs, Engel, Farrell, Hirsch, Jacobs, Koppell, Perone, Pesce, Connor).
5. Legislation should be passed allowing abused former spouses and unmarried, cohabiting adults to have access to either Family Court or a criminal court.
6. The Governor should mandate each human service and criminal justice agency to produce domestic violence training designs for all staff having public contact, prior to December 31, 1980.

   An assessment should be made to determine whether statewide training programs become effective on the county level. The Governor's Task Force should provide a monitoring and review resource for these training activities.
7. The Governor should require every state agency having client contact to conduct a public information campaign to educate its constituencies about the laws and services relevant to domestic violence problems, prior to December 31, 1980.
8. The Governor should recommend to the Board of Regents that all institutions of professional education licensed by the New York State Department of Education or any other State department, including medical schools, law schools, graduate schools of social work, nursing schools, divinity schools, schools of psychology and psychoanalytic institutes, develop curriculum materials on domestic violence issues. In addition, preventive and education curriculum materials should be prepared by the State Education Department for use in New York's elementary and secondary schools.
9. A treatment protocol for emergency room staff should be developed by the State Health Department in order to insure the appropriate response of health personnel to victims of domestic violence. This protocol should be comparable to the existing procedure prescribed in cases of rape, and should include procedures for examination of child sexual assault victims similar to the protocol used in Connecticut's Sexual Trauma Treatment Program.
10. The State Health Department should institute a pilot project in several selected hospitals in which emergency room staff would submit domestic violence incident reports to the Department, using reporting forms which would *not* disclose a victim's name.
11. The Governor should direct state agencies presently collecting domestic violence data to do so in a coordinate manner, by developing a cross-agency

data collection instrument applicable to each agency's computer systems and designed to produce the most usable data base....

12. Local police agencies should be directed to collect domestic violence data in the form mandated by the Division of Criminal Justice services.
13. All agencies presently required to collect data on domestic violence should submit that data as part of their annual reports to the Governor and the Legislature.
14. The Governor and Legislature should support the creation of a statewide media campaign to inform New Yorkers about laws pertaining to domestic violence and services available to family members.
15. A *Handbook for Beaten Women*, previously published by Brooklyn Legal Services, should be updated, reprinted and disseminated statewide (S.5225-A, Pisani, A.7625-A, Nadler, Connelly, Cooke, Diggs, Grannis, Jacobs, Lipshutz, Newburger, F.M. Sullivan).
16. The state should establish a 24-hour, 7-day a week toll-free information and referral service to provide information concerning domestic violence programs and services.
17. Creative long-term methods for funding shelters, including but not limited to Emergency Assistance to Families, must be developed.... Particular attention should be aid to better utilization and coordination of Federal, foundation, State and local funding.
18. The Governor should direct the appropriate state agencies to sign memoranda of understanding coordinating appropriate programs and guaranteeing that all members of families experiencing domestic violence will be categorically eligible to receive necessary state services (alcoholism programs, child protective services, medical care, legal representation, mental health services, special care shelters, police protection, social services, public assistance, and emergency public assistance).
19. All programs dealing with domestic violence should identify and respond to the particular service needs of the abused elderly.
20. To strengthen the ability of the criminal courts to respond to domestic violence cases, the existing domestic violence program within the Westchester District Attorney's office should be evaluated so that it may be appropriately replicated.
21. The Governor's Task Force on Domestic Violence should be continued and staffed to provide the coordination and technical assistance necessary to ensure the implementation of the preceding training and outreach, legal, data collection, and service recommendations. The Task Force and its Advisory Board should also develop further recommendations concerning broader domestic violence concerns, particularly focusing on the relationship between adult and child abuse, more realistically defined as a cyclical family violence problem.

Conclusion

Violence between spouses alone accounts for hundreds of murders, thousands of divorces, and countless emotionally damaged children and adults annually. While other family crises have similar tragic effects, physical abuse of one family member by another has been shown to have uniquely shattering effects: on the batterer, the victim, and the children, who ultimately become victims as well as witnesses. The ripple effect of domestic violence forces the State to pay far too much for police services, criminal prosecutions, Family Court personnel, foster care, public assistance, and juvenile corrections.

We know there are strong connections between domestic violence and juvenile delinquency, foster care, divorce, alcoholism, and other social problems. It is, therefore, the responsibility of all New Yorkers who care about families and the State's economy to assure that preventive and treatment services are provided to families who seek them. Neither social nor economic pressures should continue to force family members to remain in situations which place them at risk of death. Such services will ultimately save Federal, State, and local governments money, because violence and its costly aftermath will be reduced.

The Task Force has no startling revelations to make about the causes of domestic violence in New York State. The survey of New York City women referred to above revealed that alcohol, money, and infidelity were the factors mentioned most often as associated with abuse. Many families, however, experience these problems without resorting to violence, while many violent families do not have these collateral problems. Clearly, the general tolerance of violence in our society, combined with the lingering effect of earlier laws making wives and children the property of their husbands and fathers, creates an atmosphere in which family violence is likely to occur. The growing lack of regard for the increasing number of older family members similarly exposes the elderly to the risk of abuse.

Any long-term preventive measures taken by government, then, must include a commitment to raise the societal status of women, children, and the elderly, as well as a commitment to reject violence as a problem-solving tool, at home and on the streets. If these commitments are not made, the need for shelters, counseling, police and other services will only increase as one generation of violent families continues to produce another.

In the short run, however, the Task Force believes that implementation of its immediate recommendations will be both a great assistance to troubled families and the first step toward demonstrating society's commitment to prevent and ultimately end the underlying causes of domestic violence.

Abuse within families is the deepest possible violation of our shared sense of what "family" means. Until we can ensure that *none* of New York's homes will be places of pain, terror, and injury, the Task Force's responsibilities will not be fulfilled.

26. NEVER-MARRIED AMERICANS AND PUBLIC POLICY POSSIBILITIES: "Single Power" in the 1980s?

Arthur B. Shostak

"The purpose of action is not to replace life with politics. The point is not to turn life into a scene of protest; life is the point."

Schell (1982:103)

Thanks largely to the risk-taking and vision of modern feminists (and their many unsung male allies) our American way of life has been compelled in recent years to provide significant, if indirect, policy aid to the nation's 31 million never-married citizens (Bureau of the Census 1979). Typical is the legal protection provided now against sexual exploitation at work, a historic hazard suffered especially by unwed young adults who, as new workforce entrants, were unfortunate enough to report to job-threatening sexists. Similarly, new legal protection against discrimination in the awarding of major credit cards has helped many young workers survive job-entry years when they were short on capital. And, seemingly divergent legal advances, such as new guarantees of job gains for handicapped job seekers, also provide never-married Americans of this type with fresh rewards and lifestyle options.

Not surprisingly, much more remains to be achieved than has yet been won. Never-married Americans,[1] still largely without a self-conscious notion of themselves as a distinct type with enormous political potential, remain essentially an inchoate statistical category, still waiting for an energizing and unifying leader to help them coalesce and apply their (latent) political clout (as did Townsend for older Americans in the 1930s; Pepper, for older Americans at present; and Friedan and Steinem, for contemporary women).[2]

In this avowedly exploratory and speculative chapter, special attention is paid to critical, steadily building policy issues that may significantly alter the quality of never-married life in this country in the foreseeable future. The issues are chosen from aspects of American life where singles are disproportionately overrepresented, such as the public policy domain of contraceptive and abortion realities, the public policy domain of job entry and job-holding realities, and the public policy domain of tenant rights and (single) consumer protection, among others. Proactive, rather than merely reactive, policy responses to these issues could help us all, single and non-single alike, make the most of a proud, unabashed, and unapologetic singlehood in this country.

The New Singlehood

To understand the policy issues at stake here is first to grasp the idea that modern singles are different from cohorts of never-married Americans that have gone before. To begin with, the nation's 31 million modern singles are a larger proportion of young adult generations than ever previously true. Given the decision of many to marry later than did their older siblings or parents, the average age at marriage has risen for both partners every year since 1958.[3] Proportionately more 18-, 19-, 20- year-olds, and so on, are unwed since that time (Feinsilber and Mead, 1980), and, as many as fifty percent of all females between 20 and 30 years of age (and 67 percent of the males) remain never-married today as compared to only about 30 percent of the females and 54 percent of the males 20 years earlier (Stein 1981:5). Although the vast majority are likely to marry at least once in their lifetime, and very few are resolute in preferring permanent singlehood all the years of their lives, the presently never-married cohort persist, *voluntarily*, as singles for several more years than did their parents or grandparents.

A second major difference concerns the educational attainment of the never-married group: both females and males have more years of schooling than any bloc of singles that has come before them (Bureau of the Census 1980). While the linkages here remain uncertain, this increase in education may help account for a third major difference--the striking status assertiveness of the entire bloc of never-married individuals.

In an unprecedented way, unwed Americans decline to apologize for their marital status. Historically many singles felt censured as immature, irresponsible sowers of wild oats, redeemable only by marriage, and that as soon as possible! To make matters even worse, many felt that their parents and married friends quietly judged them to be witless complicators in their own hapless (unmarried) fate, flawed losers somehow responsible for this sorry turn of events.

Today, however, 84 percent of the single women surveyed in a 1978 national poll thought a woman could enjoy life without ever marrying--a much higher figure than any previously secured in such surveys (Norbeck 1980:47). And as many as 44 percent of the unwed women in a 1977 poll argued that singlehood has more advantages than married life, as did 30 percent of the unmarried men in the same poll (ibid.).

This new pride in singlehood status may be profoundly altering the composition of the ranks:

> What remains the most resoundingly significant finding [in the 1980 census data] is the growth rate of the hard-core single, the "single" single, the people who live by themselves, without children, friends, lovers, or family members.... This group has increased by 64 percent, a rate more than five times that of the total population's increase (in the last 10 years) [Wolfe 1928a:35].

Only twenty-five percent of the females in this bloc are never-married, but 46 percent of the males are so designated. Even more striking, while the tally of never-married females living alone grew 89 percent from 1970 to 1980, the male tally soared beyond and rose 118 percent ("there are more men than ever queuing up for that hard-to-find studio apartment").[4]

Never-married Americans, of course, include a remarkably diverse and heterogeneous cohort--one that encompasses young factory workers and college students, "fast-track" female careerists, "living-together" couples, middle-aged confirmed bachelors and "bachelorettes," unwed childrearing teen-age mothers, and those whose physical or psychological impairments make marriage improbable (Fine & Asch 1981). These 14 million females and 17 million males differ *en masse* from their recent counterparts twenty and forty years ago in their age range (more time is being *voluntarily* spent unwed), their educational attainment (better than ever!), and their self-esteem (higher than ever!). As such, they may soon challenge American society with specific policy reform issues as meaningful and dramatic as any now associated with comparable social movements (such as Gray Power, the so-called pro-family movement, and the feminist movement).

Policy Reforms

1. Contraception gains. To begin with, a major source of discontent in the lives of sexually active singles concerns the sexual revolution that began twenty years ago with the arrival of oral contraceptives. This social change reels today from rapidly falling confidence in once-heralded contraceptors ("the current birth-control situation is defined by Age of Limitation Terminology: tradeoffs. Benefits versus risk").[5]

Singles traditionally worried about unwanted pregnancies are increasingly worried as well about the alleged risks of the Pill, and their disillusionment here may course very deep:

> Things were never easy for those who wanted sex without pregnancy. But the Pill gave us a glimpse of fantasyland. Every screw could be zipless, free of the worry of unwanted pregnancy.... Those who have rejected the Pill and its comparably risky cousin, the IUD, are worse off than their ancestors. Because no matter how many times we hear the Life is Unfair theory of contraception, it does no good. We were promised the ideal contraceptive years ago; we thought we had it. Our raised expectations were mischievously dashed.[6]

Accordingly, never-married Americans in the years immediately ahead may pressure the federal government and drug companies to launch a crash program to increase substantially the safety of the Pill. A similar "research and development" campaign could focus on minimizing or eliminating unpleasant characteristics of contraceptive barrier methods. Opposition to such pressure may be considerable, however, as politicians of the Moral Majority persuasion are bound to champion abstinence and celibacy by singles, or, parenthood-in-marriage as their strong preferences to (unwed) sex, especially if government-aided gains in contraception are thought likely to help never-marrieds enjoy less anxious sexual relations (and thereby have less of an incentive to wed).

2. *Abortion law.* Given severe limitations on modern contraception technology, the availability of legal, low-cost, and medically safe abortions would seem in the best interest of sexually active singles. Opposition to this pregnancy-termination option is considerable, however, despite the fact that a majority of the public has told pollsters for many years that it prefers to keep the law permissive on this score and leave the choice to the pregnant female (Jaffee, Lindheim, & Lee 1981).

All-too-rare research on the situation of the *male* involved in an abortion points up the need for better home and school discussion of contraceptive choices. As well, a case can be made for the imaginative use of clinic outreach efforts to draw males into the preabortion counseling process. Above all, the steady development of a cultural role for males as conscientious and active, rather than as intimidated and passive participants in the entire process, might help singles and married participants alike mature in desirable ways from an abortion experience (Shostak 1979, 1981). Females also need additional help in their own sex and contraceptive education and, in the case of indigent women without male financial aid, in locating funds to meet the costs of an abortion. Indeed, the New Federalism plan to transfer Medicaid to the states threatens to end public funding of abortions for the needy (Brozan 1982).

Unfortunately, never-married Americans are presently distracted from campaigning for these reforms by the urgent need to fight instead to preserve the very option of legal abortion itself. A new generation of abortifacients may be on the market in five years or so that will permit abortion "so early and easily in pregnancy that the line between birth control and abortion will be increasingly blurred" (Wohl 1982:88; see also Montgomery 1982). Until that time however, many single men and women will feel obliged to fight to keep pregnancy termination choices available, recognizing in anti-choice legislation a sharp threat of state interference in precious individual liberties (Fairbanks 1981).

3. *Job security.* When the Harris pollsters asked never-married and married respondents in 1978 how anxious they were about the likelihood of keeping their jobs, only 29 percent of the latter, but 43 percent of the unwed Americans, indicated considerable unease (U.S. Department of Housing and Urban Development 1978). As the present recession deepens and unemployment reaches toward post-World War II record highs, the job anxiety of young never-married Americans undoubtedly also reaches toward similar highs.

Given their relative youthfulness and their lack of seniority at work, singles are often disproportionately represented among those "last hired, first fired." To make matters even worse, many "rollback" contracts are now being negotiated by unions desperately seeking assurances of job security. Although details still remain sketchy, the suspicion grows that concessions and sacrifices are being made by Labor in the name of people not yet on the payroll, most of whom would probably be single new job entrants (Holusha 1982). Similarly, the suspicion also grows that management intends to win leeway to substitute unprecedented automation and robotics for as-yet-unhired new workers. In the words of Harley Shaiken, MIT labor relations specialist: "Now the danger is that the plant stays where it is, but the new technology goes in and decimates the work force" (cited in Holusha 1982:B6 1982).

Accordingly, the 1980s are likely to see singles become more and more interested in workplace reforms to improve their job-gaining and job-holding chances. A state law pioneered recently in California that helps reduce layoffs by letting workers collect unemployment insurance part time when their work weeks are cut is typical (Lublin 1982). Another reform enables two people to share one job, while a third reform would require both long advance notice of any impending layoff and considerable effort by the employer to retrain and retain vulnerable low-seniority employees (O'Toole 1981).

Single workers who try to improve their job-earning chances by pioneering in fields previously closed to their sex might want affirmative-action efforts substantially upgraded as well. For example, Wider Opportunities for Women, a national women's rights organization, urges that sexual harassment on the job be countered by better enforcement of antisexist regulations, increased government financing of training programs, and the strict maintaining of hiring goals and timetables (DeCourcey Hinds 1982).

4. Renters' rights. When asked in 1978 by Harris pollsters to spotlight their discontent with their urban living situation, never-married Americans gave first place to housing (47 percent), followed by shopping (32 percent), job opportunities (28 percent), and social activities (17 percent) (U.S. Department of Housing and Urban Development 1978).

Primarily renters rather than owners (though a new trend has certain contented single women now buying their own urban homes), the never-married American confronts the challenge of recognizing, clarifying, claiming, and extending policy gains as a tenant (DeVise 1979-80). Accordingly, a small but possibly growing number are joining chapters of a National Tenants Union in fifty cities across the country. United in this way, they press for a tenants' "bill of rights" that would secure for every renter, single and married alike, four major gains:

- ☐ Protection against arbitrary evictions, even with "just cause," including evictions for condominium and cooperative conversions;
- ☐ Tax credits for tenants (as the current tax regulations discriminate in favor of owners);
- ☐ Provision of federal housing grants directly for tenant-controlled low-equity cooperatives and public housing; and
- ☐ Recognition of tenants as a legitimate constituency with its own concerns [Atlas & Dreier 1980].

Focused on winning cooperation from all tenants, regardless of their marital status, the union could help its never-married members learn much about policy-reform realities of wide applicability to other areas of single life.

5. Consumer rights. As purchasers of various goods and services oriented especially to them, such as tour packages for singles only, apartment complexes for singles only, and health club memberships for singles only, never-married types can be hurt by the conspicuous absence nowadays of adequate public-policy regulations governing relevant business practices.

Problems that have been encountered by singles who have paid substantial sums for dating leads from computer dating services are typical. Introduced in 1965, these services were early marred by their use of high-powered, fast-talking, commission-hungry super-salesmen, and by the comparably deceptive use of inflated claims for match-ups. Ensuing media exposure and costly, frequently embarrassing lawsuits were often required to tone down and rehabilitate this still-promising source of contacts.

Accordingly the 1980s are likely to have never-married customers become more desirous than ever of consumer safeguards in the $40-billion-a-year singles' market (Barkas 1980: 31). Many worry about the gullibility of unwed friends who are promised new happiness by unscrupulous purveyers of this or that tonic (Lear 1980):

> Singles may not yet look or act as childish as they're drawn, but they are as vulnerable as children, and the singles hustlers appreciate this...they know their market, know that loneliness will prevail over dignity every time, and that even the most sensible people in the world will eventually crawl for company, if necessary... [Rosenblatt 1979:14].

Perhaps this assessment is correct; if so, never-married types will need to campaign soon for new legal protections, well-funded and skilled enforcement personnel, the honoring by industry of its codes of ethical conduct, the implementation of singles' industry self-policing practices, and other related improvements in public- and private-sector policies.

6. *Educational preparation.* Basic to all the preceding reforms is one that could prove more decisive than any other, and that should therefore preoccupy would-be agents of policy-based improvements in the lives of singles.

Education for the never-married life is the obvious foundation of a well-prepared life, albeit "the school of hard knocks" is a more commonly employed source of insights. Courses and workshops in singles topics could be added to the schedule of high-school students and collegians alike:

> Around the country, hundreds of discussion groups and workshops for singles are mapping out the space between the old image and the new. One such workshop, called "The Challenge of Being Single," has enjoyed a six-year run at the University of Southern California and other campuses across the country [Lowe 1977:86].

Young men could be drawn into nontraditional courses (cooking and nutrition, wardrobe selection, health care and enhancement, budgeting, etc.) even while young women are similarly helped to gain nontraditional skills (car repair, household maintenance, self-defense skills, and so on).

Particular attention might be paid in such courses, as in home-computer and videotape courses, to the bevy of love-aiding interpersonal skills relied on by never-married adults. After interviewing singles across the country for two years, for example, one researcher concluded that the search for a loving relationship was the single greatest stressor in their lives: "Almost all singles, no matter how content they are living alone, fantasize about someday having a special partner... It did not matter how long a man or woman had been single..." (Barkas 1980:172).

Unfortunately, there is much emphasis at present on cost-cutting, "back-to-basics" approaches in precollege schooling, and on a no-frills career-focused approach in the curriculum of many colleges. It will require a sustained and sensitive reform effort by highly motivated present-day singles to correct this regrettable course of events and to strengthen educational offerings in single life skills--both for those about to enter the singles life, and for others with more experience at it.

Discussion: Policy Prospects?

To understand the source of the policy needs of never-married Americans is to understand their overrepresentation in certain situationally appropriate contexts; e. g., they are disproportionately found among the users of contraceptors and abortions. They are also especially vulnerable to job denial and job loss, to custom-tailored consumer fraud, and to "garden variety" tenant abuses. Above all, however, never-married Americans are sorely under-served by educational neglect of the very curricula likely to help them get themselves off to a reasonably strong start.

To understand whether or not singles will soon act to win relevant policy reforms is to begin by confronting the *absence* here of consciousness of kind: never-married types do not identify with one another at this time, do not recognize common policy needs, and do not especially agree on political actions necessary to earn policy gains for themselves as mobilized, never-married citizens.

If America in the 1980s, however, tilts in the direction of the exceedingly controversial pro-family program of the Moral Majority (Steiner 1980), this pro-marriage shift in public policy might help galvanize unwed adults into defensive political action. Some might feel obliged to fight against efforts to end legal abortions. Others might be provoked by efforts to impede the recently expanding ability of singles to adopt difficult-to-place orphans. Many might be stirred to action by efforts to strengthen censorship campaigns and to hamper sexual freedom (including the civil rights of homosexuals). And a sizable number might rally to protest cutbacks in the already inadequate high-school and college curricula offered in sex education and interpersonal skills, to say nothing of single-life skills.

Similarly, if America in the 1980s were to tilt in the direction of the Gray Power agenda, this might help galvanize young never-married citizens into defensive political action--especially if political gains by older Americans (largely married individuals) result in ever-heavier taxes to meet the health-care bills of retired oldsters, along with even tighter laws to protect delayed retirement by job-needy seniors, almost regardless of the job-denying impact of this development on much younger job seekers.

Spurred by the possibility that gains for so-called pro-family forces and/or the senior citizen lobby might be gains at *their* particular expense, the nation's never-married Americans *may* develop an unprecedented consciousness of kind and a related political militancy.

Aid here could be secured from a commonly overlooked and undervalued source, the embryonic men's movement, an idea whose time may have arrived. After several years of incubating as an idea mulled over and argued about at various regional and seven annual national meetings of concerned men, a National Organization of Men was finally formed in the winter of 1982 (ten years to the month after the founding of the National Organization of Women). Dedicated to helping men liberate their role(s) in life and, especially, their underdeveloped potentialities as friends, lovers, spouses, and parents, the new organization will necessarily be drawn immediately into each and every policy controversy touched on in this essay, as unwed men can be expected to constitute a large segment of any pro-singles political movement (Sawyer 1974; Farrell 1975; Nichols 1975).

Such men are likely to question traditional prescriptions for never-married (and married) manhood alike:

> [M]ost of us have never quite measured up to all these ideals (super cool, a stud, a leader of men and a seducer of women). We have fallen short somewhere. Besides, we no longer believe in all these things. The world about us is changing. Our women have been changing ahead of us. And we are changing too, mostly in reaction as the shadow follows the player. We have been socialized into believing that there are only a few ways to be a man. But these old ways do not always work. New ways are needed to solve our problems. New integrations. Syntheses.[7]

Never-married personhood *might* be significantly enhanced by the self-conscious efforts of newly "liberated" males--men who "dream about another world which could be, a world of brotherhood and sisterhood...of personhood"[8]--provided that they take their pro-singles political-action role as seriously as every other personal and societal challenge ahead of them.

Summary

The 31 million never-married men and women who enter the 1980s as a statistical category, *could* leave the decade as a new political force of considerable significance. Scoffers are urged to remember that few thought Townsend could create a political force from a lot of old folks in the '30s and now, only fifty years later, the Gray Power Movement he set in motion looms as a decisive molder of current and future events. Feminists have earned similar cohesiveness and clout for another statistical category, and in far less time. Never-married Americans have fully enough needs as a group to energize the formation of their own singles' social movement, provided that they soon locate charismatic leadership, perhaps from among the readers of this chapter.

Obstacles are many, of course, and include the ability of the cohort to fragment and polarize itself. For example, singles who resent tax benefits given to child-rearing couples might form a coalition with childless married (and living-together) couples to protest this type of tax favoritism, while other singles planning to rear children themselves some day might choose to sit this one out. Similarly, never-married young adults might split off from much older singles who, in turn, might endorse Gray Power campaigns that much younger singles oppose. Competing with one another for scarce resources, the various factions of never-married Americans might downgrade the reform agenda of the cohort per se in favor of more specialized needs of this or that faction--a fate that has befallen other vulnerable social movements. This can be avoided, though the countereffort will require diplomacy, trust, and mutual caring from all the parties--a tall order that the singles' social movement will hopefully be able to fill.

Feminist Gloria Steinem (1982) reminds us that the women's movement organized only ten years ago: "Now we have words like 'displaced homemaker' and 'sexual harassment.' We didn't have those words ten years ago. It was just called 'life.'" Never-married Americans just call "'life'" today what they may soon rally instead to challenge, to revalue, and to reform--the better to help us all, single and not-single alike, profit anew from the distinct styles of life of one another.

Notes

1. Although the term "singles" is commonly used to refer to never-married, separated, divorced, and widowed individuals, the policy needs of each type are sufficiently diverse to recommend the narrowing of this chapter's focus to the largest of the four categories, and to one of most immediate concern to this reading audience. As well, never-married Americans would seem in great need of academic commentary, given a revealing and regrettable record of scholarly neglect: "[T]he never-married person has been consistently treated as a member of an insignificant and deviant group, worthy of study only for its departure from the normal married state" (Stein 1981:5). The distinct situation of the homosexual single, of course, warrants an entire essay of its own, very much like this one, preoccupied with political-reform possibilities and personhood gains for all, whatever their sexual preference.
2. Townsend created the first major movement on behalf of pension and social security rights in the 1930s. Florida Congressman Claude R. Pepper is the modern heir of this Townsend campaign, and has updated it with his surprising 1971 success in having mandatory retirement set back to 70 from age 65. On the significance of these individuals and others in helping a statistical category ("Americans over 65") become one of the nation's major political lobbies (see Clark 1980). On the significance of feminists like Betty Friedan and Gloria Steinem in helping a statistical category ("women") become one of the nation's major political lobbies, see O'Leary (1977).
3. Wolfe (1982a:35). While the decade's rise for women living alone was 51 percent, for men it was 92 percent. Nevertheless, there are more women than men living alone, 11 million to 6.5 million.
4. Ibid. Outstanding here are new research reports on the social determinants of remaining never-married and the literature on marital status as an independent variable, both available from Dr. Edward L. Kain, Cornell University, Department of Human Development and Family Studies. See also the research of Leonard Cargin and M. Melko at Wright State University, Dayton, Ohio.
5. Levy (1982:25). "We thought then that promiscuity would become the norm, the lusty peak of the bell-shaped curve. We thought that the double standard would be halved.

And we thought that no one again, ever, would have to worry about unwanted pregnancy--before, after, and especially during sex--as long as the woman took her Pill every day. We were wrong on every count."

6. Levy (1982). "Actually, you don't need a statistician to document this drop in Pill use. Ask around. If a woman is reasonable, intelligent, thoughtful, and a member of the middle or upper class, she's probably not on the Pill. If she is, she's worried about it."
7. Lewis (1981:xiv). "Men are in difficult times and they must change" (ibid. xv).
8. Lewis (1981). "Most of us will change if we are challenged to give up our sexist ways, if we are reinforced for the things we do inwardly to grow, and if we are supported for the positive efforts we make to change our environment in more egalitarian ways" (p. xv). For more information on the new organization, write to National Men's Organization, 5512 Bartlett St., Box C, Pittsburgh, Pa. 15217.

References

Atlas, John, and Peter Dreier.
1980 "Tenants' New Clout." *New York Times* (Oct. 23):A27.

Barkas, J. L.
1980 *Single in America.* New York: Atheneum.

Brozan, Nadine.
1982 "Plan Cast Doubts on Abortion Aid." *New York Times* (Feb. 8):1, 10.

Bureau of the Census.
1979 *Current Population Reports*, Series P-20, no. 349. Marital Status and Living Arrangements. March.
1980 *Current Population Reports.* February.

Clark, Robert L.
1980 *Retirement Policy in an Aging Society.* Durham, N.C.: Duke University Press.

DeCourcey Hinds, Michael.
1982 "Sexual Harassment Cited in a Report." *New York Times* (Feb. 18):C3.

DeVise, Pierre.
1979-80 "The Expanding Singles Housing Market in Chicago: Implications for Reviving City Neighborhoods." *Urban Past and Present*, 9 (Winter):30-39.

Fairbanks, James David.
1981 "Morality Legislation and Policy Analysis." *Policy Studies Journal* 10, 1 (Sept.): 249-60.

Farrell, Warren.
1975 *The Liberated Man.* New York: Bantam.

Feinsilber, Mike, and W. B. Mead.
1980 *American Averages: Amazing Facts of Everyday Life.* New York: Doubleday.

Fine, Michelle, and Adrienne Asch.
1981 "Disabled Women: Sexism without the Pedestal." *Journal of Sociology and Social Welfare*, 8 (July).

Holusha, John.
1982 "Ford's New Contract: Who May Win, Who May Lose." *New York Times* (Feb. 16):B6.

Jaffee, Frederick S., Barbara L. Lindheim, and Philip R. Lee.
1981 *Abortion Politics: Private Morality and Public Policy.* New York: McGraw-Hill.

Lear, Martha W.
1980 "Loneliness: More Common than the Common Cold." *Redbook* (Nov.):33, 202-06.

Lewis, Robert A. (ed.)
1981 *Men in Difficult Times: Masculinity Today and Tomorrow.* Englewood Cliffs, N.J.: Prentice-Hall.

Levy, Steven.
1982 "The Birth Control Blues." *Rolling Stone* (March 4):25-26, 28, 67.

Lowe, Wendy.
1977 "The Single Experience." *The Graduate*: 86

Lublin, Joann S.
1982 "Labor Letter." *Wall Street Journal* (Feb. 16):1.

Montgomery, Sy.
1982 "Abortion Suppository." *Omni* (March):40.

Nichols, Jack.
1975 *Men's Liberation.* New York: Penguin.

Norback, Craig (ed.).
1980 *The Complete Book of American Surveys.* New York: New American Library.

O'Leary, V.
1977 *Toward Understanding Women.* Monterey, Calif.: Brooks/Cole.

O'Toole, James.
1981 *Making America Work.* New York: Continuum.

Rosenblatt, Roger.
1979 "The Self as Sybarite." *Harper's* (March):14.

Sawyer, Jack.
1974 *Men and Masculinity.* Englewood Cliffs, N.J.: Prentice-Hall.

Schell, Jonathan.
1982 "Reflections. (Nuclear Arms - Part III)." *New Yorker* (Apr. 15):45-107.

Shostak, Arthur B.
1979 "Abortion as Fatherhood Lost: Problems and Reforms." *Family Coordinator* (Oct.):569-74.
1981 "Men and Abortion: Survey Data and Human Needs." Paper presented at the 1981 Annual Meeting of the Eastern Sociological Society, New York, March. (Available from the author.)

Stein, Peter J. (ed.)
1981 *Single Life: Unmarried Adults in Social Context.* New York: St. Martin's Press.

Steinem, Gloria.
1982 "Second Wave of Feminism." *Philadelphia Inquirer* (February 21):3A.

Steiner, Gilbert.
1980 *The Futility of Family Policy.* Washington, D.C.: Brookings Institution.

U.S. Department of Housing and Urban Development.
1978 *The 1978 HUD Survey on the Quality of Community Life: A Data Book.* Washington, D.C.: HUD.

Wohl, Lisa Cronin.
1982 "The New Danger: A Three-Step Abortion Plan." *Ms.* (Feb.):87-88.

Wolfe, Linda.
1982a "The Good News." *New York* (Dec. 28 - Jan. 4):35.
1982b "Taking the Worry out of Being Unattached." *Philadelphia Inquirer* (Feb. 28):H1, H8, H9.

27. UNMARRIED COHABITATION IN SWEDEN

Jan Trost

Background

During the 1960s there was mounting discussion of the nuclear family in Sweden which carried over into debate about marriage. Some felt that marriage as a religious institution was detrimental to the individual as well as to society. Others asserted that it was marriage as a legal institution that fomented problems.

It became increasingly clear that growing numbers of couples in Sweden (and in Denmark) were living together without being married, especially during the later part of the '60s. In the early '70s, this practice was also seen on the rise in such countries as the United States, the Netherlands, Belgium, and France. It seems as if initially many of these couples demonstrated against the religious and/or legal marriage. At the same time, almost all over the Western world, communes of different types started. Most of these have not endured. However, cohabitation without marriage has.

Defining Cohabitation

There is considerable confusion about what the concept "cohabitation" could or should mean. The term itself is vague; different expressions are often used as synonyms: living together, quasi-marriage, trial marriage, shacking up, semi-marriage and consensus marriage, to mention a few.

A description often used in the U.S. is "two persons of opposite sex living together without being married." Another definition is "sharing [a] bedroom during at least four nights a week for at least three consecutive months with someone of the opposite sex." These two examples build upon the cultural background in the U.S. where cohabitation is regarded as mainly occurring among college students.

Reprinted from *Social Change in Sweden*, 18 (May 1980), pp. 1-6 by permission of the Swedish Institute. The views expressed are those of the author.

For a Swede it might seem unnecessary and even superfluous to define what is meant by cohabitation without marriage; in common language the term already has a significance. But sometimes it might be necessary even in Sweden to pinpoint what you mean by the expression. In some cases it can be hard to decide when a couple cohabits under marriagelike conditions and when not. The one partner might define the relationship in one way and the other in another. Social scientists and other observers use their own criteria.

In application as well as in research we use what is sometimes called a "phenomenological" definition, meaning that we leave it to the individuals or couples themselves to indicate whether they are cohabiting or not. This requires a general consensus about the sense of the word. There is no doubt that such a consensus exists in Sweden today. In our studies we have asked the respondents what they mean by "cohabitation without marriage" and they have had no problem at all, whether they were cohabiting or not, to understand or to answer the question. The answers were very similar, describing cohabitation as "living together steadily under marriage-like conditions but without being married."

Marriage Rate and Cohabitation Rate

Historical records show that cohabitation without marriage was usual in some parts of Sweden in earlier centuries.

During the 1940s, 1950s, and the first part of the 1960s, the marriage rate in Sweden was fairly constant. From 1966 to 1973, however, it decreased by an extraordinary 40-50 percent. Since 1973 the rate has been fairly constant for all age-groups, indicating a decrease in first as well as in remarriages.

The decrease in the marriage rate has been followed by an increase in the cohabitation rate. Figure 27.1 shows the changes in the marriage and cohabitation rates among young women.

Figure 27.1

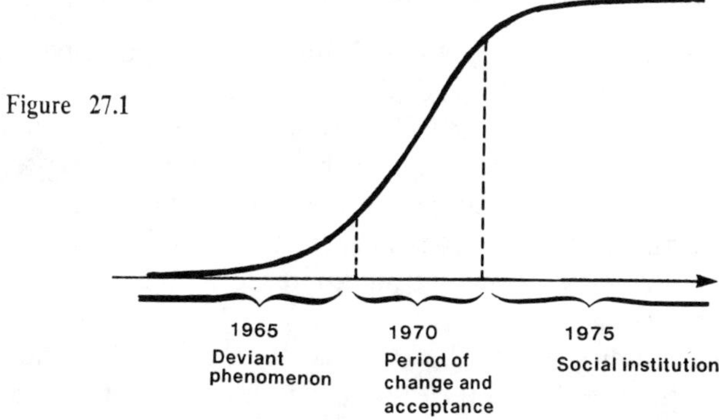

This figure indicates that the relative popularity of the dyad has increased despite the criticism of the nuclear family during the 1960s.

Table 27.1 shows the relative number of married and unmarried cohabitants in different ages in 1975. The current figures have changed slightly but more recent data for all Swedes do not exist. We can see that cohabitation is more common than marriage among younger people whereas marriage dominates in older age groups. Today the marriage rate is about half of what it should have been had no changes taken place.

Table 27.1 Married and Cohabiting Women, by Age

Age	Marrieds	Cohabitants
20-24	21.7	28.6
25-29	58.0	16.8
30-34	73.2	8.0
35-39	77.9	4.8
40-44	79.3	3.4
45-49	78.5	3.2
50-54	76.4	2.7
55-59	72.8	2.2
60-64	65.6	1.8
65-69	55.0	1.6
70-74	41.1	1.6
75-over	20.1	0.7
Total in ages above 20 years	59.5	6.9

The changes in cohabitation and marriage rates in Sweden have been dramatic with the same tendencies observed in Denmark. They also seem to be under way in Finland and Norway, delayed five to ten years. In France, the Netherlands, the U.S., and some other countries the increase has not reached the same proportion as in Sweden.

To Cohabit or to be Married--Similarities and Differences

When we asked newly married and unmarried cohabitants about the economic and legal advantages and disadvantages of cohabitation without marriage compared to being married, the majority answered that they had not noticed any advantages nor disadvantages with either form of living together. A small minority could see some advantages with cohabitation and another small minority with marriage. Studies from Sweden as well as the U.S. and France show the same trend: most people see no difference at all between married and unmarried cohabitation.

Furthermore, studies have shown that in their social and psychical commitment to each other and in their relations to friends and relatives, etc. there is no difference between married couples and those cohabiting without being married.

Do Cohabitants Dissolve their Relationship more often than Marrieds?

Swedish experience shows that the dissolution rate among cohabitants is about double the dissolution rate among marrieds.

The comparison is however misleading, since the married couples, with very few exceptions have cohabited before they married and have had a possibility to separate during this period. A substantial number of those cohabitants, who have separated, had they instead chosen to marry, would have divorced later. By this we do not mean to say that cohabitation is a kind of trial marriage but it is evident that only a part of the unmarried cohabitants can be compared with married couples. An important number of them should rather be compared with couples going steady or being engaged. Probably no one would have thought of raising the question, prior to 1965, whether engagements were dissolved more often than marriages.

Is Cohabitation a Social Institution?

There are two ways cohabitation normally starts. One is that the couple gradually moves in together. The other is that they move in together after a more or less manifest decision.

The first one occurs, for example, when one partner happens to have an apartment and the other lives in a rented room or with parents. The latter stays overnight with the former with increased frequency and after some time this situation develops into real cohabitation and a marriage-like condition. This might be a matter of weeks or months or even longer.

The second implies that the couple moves in together after a mutual decision has been made, often triggered by a concrete cause like a pregnancy, a new apartment, a new job or that one partner has to move to another community. Often this cause is perceived by the couple itself and their friends and relatives as the reason why they move in together. The real reason, however, is that they are emotionally attached to each other, that they love each other.

Many of the cohabiting couples are engaged to marry. Some of them were engaged prior to moving in together while others have done so during the cohabitation. Often the engagement seems to be some kind of *rite de passage* as indicated by the fact that the engagement is announced and celebrated, by the couple alone or together with friends and relatives. The passing seems to be from a casual going steady to a more settled going steady--both in the form of cohabitation. The engagement does not mean that the couple plans to get married.

An important question in this connection is: why do people marry? One reason seems to be that the couple wants to change their status from cohabiting without being married to cohabiting as married. The other would be that the wedding ceremony per se is the purpose: a *rite de confirmation.*

Most people find it natural that a couple living together will marry sometime in the future. Since they do not have to marry in order to move in together there is a need for a releasing factor. What factor seems to be of minor importance. The decision to get married can be triggered by an external factor like an upcoming Midsummer holiday, which is the wedding season par excellence in Sweden, or a royal wedding. This releasing factor, however, insignificant in itself, is perceived by the couple as important--since on top of a number of contributing causes it catalyzes the marriage.

In Sweden today two-thirds of the wedding ceremonies are religious and one-third civil. The majority celebrate their weddings in one way or another with friends and relatives. It is seldom that a couple will not celebrate their wedding at all. It is in fact conceived as a ritual act.

Cohabitation is not looked upon as deviant in Sweden today. It is a social institution as...[is] marriage. Thus we have two similar social institutions living side by side and to some extent collaborating. From the individual's as well as from society's viewpoint, there is no difference and much...legislation takes cohabitation into consideration.

For instance, after the death of her partner the cohabiting woman receives some basic widow's pension as a married woman if she has a child under 16. However, she is not qualified to receive the supplementary pension, which is based on previously earned, pensionable income.

At a divorce the legislation regarding the property of a married couple does not apply to cohabitants. If they separate, each partner takes what belongs to him or her. If there are children, the partner who gets the custody as a rule also gets the lease of the apartment. If there are no children the apartment remains with the partner who signed the lease unless there are very strong reasons against this.

According to the law, the mother gets custody of the children unless the couple decides to share custody or the father can prove that the mother is unfit.

A cohabitant couple with children receive the same social benefit as if they were married. If one partner dies the children--or if there are no children, the parents, sisters, and brothers of the deceased--automatically inherit unless there is a will. Finally, if one partner dies the survivor may benefit from a private life insurance policy if they have signed a special agreement.

...[C]ohabitation was considered deviant until the end of the 1960s. During the last years of the '60s and the first years of the '70s society's acceptance changed radically. From 1972-1973 [on] cohabitation without marriage was considered "normal."

In Sweden (as in Denmark) couples do not make up their minds to cohabit instead of getting married. They just move in together.

Some conclusions, which in spite of their simplifications, are valid today:

1. Sweden has for a long time had a fairly low marriage rate by international standards. It increased to some extent during the 1950s and the first half of the '60s. Then it decreased rapidly from 1966 to 1973 and has been oscillating at a very low level. It is currently about 60 percent of what it should have been had the situation not changed in the mid-'60s.
2. Sweden has the highest cohabitation rate in the world, closely followed by Denmark.
3. Practically all--more than 99 percent--of those marrying have cohabited under marriage-like conditions during some time before getting married.
4. Moving in together generally occurs in either of the following ways. One partner gradually moves in with the other; it is normally hard to define *when* the cohabitation is a fact but it is however not hard to decide it is a fact. In the other case the couple made a decision to move in together, which makes it easy to identify *when* the cohabitation started.
5. Normally people marry because it is a tradition, especially if... [they have cohabited] for a long time. The reason for not getting married is that there has been no reason to marry.
6. The time of the wedding is decided by an occurrence not significant in itself. A relevant metaphor would be drops falling into a bucket, one finally causing the bucket to flow over.
7. The wedding is normally celebrated with relatives and/or friends and can be regarded as a *rite de confirmation* rather than a *rite de passage.*
8. Cohabitation with or without marriage is looked upon by most as identical--there is no noticable difference in everyday life. The difference first becomes evident when the couple separates or one of the partners dies--in many cases not even then.
9. Separation or divorce is generally looked upon...as equal. The emotional, practical, and social consequences are, in spite of legal differences, about the same since they depend more on the integration of the couple and the duration of the relationship than on the form of the cohabitation.

Reference

Trost, Jan. *Unmarried Cohabitation* (Västerås: International Library 1979).

28. THE COOPERATIVE "FAMILY": An Alternative Lifestyle for the Elderly

Gordon F. Streib and Mary Anne Hilker

The personal and family environments of the elderly and the possibilities of alternative lifestyles have received increasing attention from gerontologists in recent years. This corresponds to the trend in American life toward openness and experimentation, and the shift away from rigid or socially prescribed modes of life. In both professional writings and in the media, there has been the tendency to extol the idea of variety--of choices--of alternatives.

The emergence of alternative lifestyles and living arrangements has been recognized in legal policy and in other public policy pronouncements concerning the life of the elderly. In the Older Americans Act of 1965, the Declaration of Objectives (U.S. Department of Health, Education and Welfare 1976:2-3) stated:

3. Suitable housing, independently selected, designed and located with reference to special needs and available at costs which older citizens can afford.
10. Freedom, independence, and the free exercise of individual initiative in planning and managing their own lives.

In 1976, the Federal Council on the Aging issued a Bicentennial Charter for Older Americans, and objective No. 10 of the Older Americans Act became No. 1 of "basic human rights for older Americans":

> The Right to Freedom, Independence and the Free Exercise of Individual Initiative. This should encompass not only opportunities and resources for personal planning and *managing one's life-style,* but support systems for maximum growth and contributions by older persons to their community [italics added].

Statements of legal objectives and public pronouncements of policies are important symbolic statements, but they are essentially rhetorical. In order to consider alternative living arrangements in sociological and gerontological perspective, we need to outline briefly the major considerations involved. Zablocki and Kanter (1976) have analyzed alternative lifestyles in relation to cultural differentiation. Although the term lifestyle has not been precisely

---

Reprinted from *Alternative Lifestyles,* 3, 2 (May 1980):167-184 by permission of the authors and the publisher, Human Sciences Press, Inc., 72 Fifth Avenue, New York.

defined in the contemporary social science writings, these authors believe it can be distinguished from other concepts such as culture and subculture. Zablocki and Kanter (1976:270) write: "A lifestyle might be defined over a given collectivity to the extent that the members are similar to one another and different from others both in the distribution of their disposable incomes and the motivations that underlie such distributions."

If one takes a historical view of alternative lifestyles, one must consider the communal movement in the United States, which was rooted in religious beliefs and utopian ideologies. In the 1960, these older trends evolved in some new forms. In addition, there was the emergence of a new counterculture type of commune in which the dominant ideology was a withdrawal from prevailing urban cultural values. Some of these forms are operating in the United States today, but many were short-lived. In addition, there has been the emergence of middle-class communes which Raimy (1979) points out are not organized in terms of a religious or political ideology. Rather, he states: "People don't join a middle-class commune to find utopian solutions for all the problems of society. Their more modest goal is, as I have said, to create a home that feels like a family or a miniature community" (1979:11).

Zablocki and Kanter point out that lifestyle is basically a set of preferences, and there may be overlap with patterns related to subcultures, social class, and status groups. However, the importance of socioeconomic considerations is paramount. In fact Zablocki and Kanter (1976:272) maintain that the best single predictor of lifestyle is [socioeconomic status or] SES. While SES and health status are obviously related, we suggest that in considering alternative lifestyles for the elderly, the factor of health--emotional and physical--exerts an independent and primary influence. The importance of physical and emotional health as major variables in the lives of older persons is obvious and has been documented repeatedly in the gerontological literature (Atchley 1977; Shanas & Maddox 1976; Shanas et al. 1968; Streib 1972).

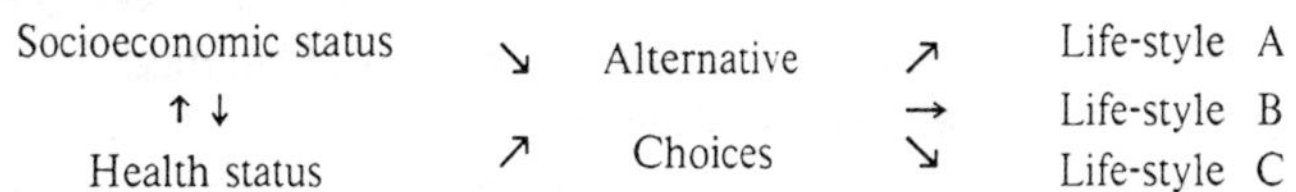

Figure 28.1

Therefore, the analytical scheme employed by Zablocki and Kanter (1976), in which socioeconomic status is the primary determinant of lifestyle, must be altered to include health status as an important independent determinant. We propose the scheme shown in Figure 28.1. Zablocki and Kanter considered primarily younger persons and their lifestyles; indeed, for those writers, persons over 30 years of age were considered "old." Thus, we suggest that a gerontological perspective on alternative lifestyles requires that health status be given primary consideration.

Field Research on Cooperative Families

This background leads us to examine one particular alternative living arrangement, Share-A-Home. We will consider the factors which lead persons to share this lifestyle, discuss how it operates, and evaluate the nature of the social interactions of the "family."

In central Florida, this alternative living arrangement has been functioning for a decade. At this writing, ten family units are in operation. The "families" are composed of ambulatory elderly persons who are not related and who share their own household and divide the expenses of running it. A paid staff performs all domestic duties. This cooperative organization is a less expensive solution than nursing homes for the isolated, slightly dependent elderly person who cannot live alone or who cannot afford to keep his or her own household. This alternative seeks to meet not only the physical needs of shelter and food, but also psychological needs of belonging to a primary group of caring people and preserving some sense of autonomy.

The materials to be presented here are part of an ongoing research project. In this limited space, it is not possible to present a detailed description of the methods employed. The study is essentially a comparative examination of naturalistic situations. The second author lived for extended periods of time in three different family units which she researched. She lived in the units twenty-four hours per day, was able to share in the everyday activities of the family units, and also was present when unusual events took place. In addition to the participant observations, formal interviews were carried out with a subsample of the family members in all the family units who were able and willing to be interviewed.

At the time of the field study, 97 persons resided in 10 homes: 76 females and 21 males, with an average age of 83.0 years. Interview data were obtained from 84 residents in either a complete or abbreviated form. Complete interviews were carried out with 51 persons; these provide the bases for the tables in this article. In the current article we will direct our attention to five main questions:

(1) How did family members make this choice of lifestyle?
(2) Do the families have primary group characteristics?
(3) What patterns of interaction are formed among the members?
(4) Does this cooperative living arrangement provide a successful and satisfying alternative lifestyle?
(5) Are alternative living arrangements for the elderly viable lifestyles that should be encouraged by social policy and perhaps supported by public funding?

Factors in the Lifestyle Decision

In answering the first question of how elderly persons chose this lifestyle, we must consider the importance of disabilities as a causative factor resulting in changes in housing and living arrangements. Newman (1976) reports survey results for a representative sample of fifteen hundred households in the United States based upon responses of persons under 55 years of age who were questioned about the disabilities of their parents, their spouses' parents, or their grandparents. Over half of the persons in the survey (that is, spouse, children, children-in-law, or grandchildren) stated that housing changes were considered as a result of the disabilities of their elderly relatives. Changes were more likely to be considered for persons who were over 75 years of age, and a much larger percentage of changes were considered for women (58%) as compared with men (42%).

Table 28.1 Perceived Capacity for Independent Living Tasks

	Meals/Housework		Shopping		Preparation		Laundry	
	N	%	N	%	N	%	N	%
Completely unable to do	21.0	11	24.0	12	27.0	14	33.0	17
Could do with some help	61.0	31	45.0	23	47.0	24	45.0	23
Could do with no help	18.0	9	31.0	16	26.0	13	22.0	11
Total	100.0	51	100.0	51	100.0	51	100.0	51

Thus, one way to index the need for alternative living arrangements is by evaluating the ability of elders to function at everyday tasks. Our respondents were asked to judge their present capacity to manage tasks of living independently. Less than one-fifth (see Table 28.1) felt they could do all of the household tasks necessary to maintain an independent living status. Only one-quarter felt they could prepare adequate meals for themselves, and only 31 percent could do the required grocery shopping unassisted. Generally, health and mobility limitations were seen as restricting the capacity for independence, and yet the survey results show that a portion felt they could perform the necessary tasks given some help.

In our study we also tried to uncover the respondents' perceptions of possible alternatives to Share-A-Home. Table 28.2 shows that about 30 percent felt they either had no alternative or were not aware of any alternative. Nearly one-quarter felt that their only alternative was an institution for the elderly such as a nursing or boarding home. Slightly more than 20 percent believed they could live with an adult child or other relative; however, nearly every individual who so responded added that they would not want to burden their families in this way.

For example:

> I could live with my son in Virginia, but I have no desire to. I want to be around people my own age who I have something in common with, who I can have an exchange with. I don't want to be taken care of [an 87-year-old female].

> My daughter says I could live with her, but I'd go to a nursing home before I'd impose on their lives [80-year-old female].

> We could live at our daughter's, but it would disrupt both families. They wouldn't really want us and we wouldn't really want to go there [a married couple in their 80s].

Another 20 percent indicated they could live in their own apartment *if* they had some help with domestic chores.

Table 28.2 Perceived Alternatives to Share-A-Home

	%	N
Child or other kin	21.0	11
Institution for aged (includes boarding homes, nursing homes)	24.0	12
Own apartment (with help)	20.0	10
Miscellaneous alternative	4.0	2
No alternative	29.0	15
No response	2.0	1
Total	100.0	51

Primary Group Characteristics

The alternative family forms being studied in central Florida are not intentional families in a true sense for, as has been pointed out, the family member chose this alternative as the more desirable of the few choices available; for some, there is no other choice. However, it must be stressed that the families are not institutions, and this can be shown by the observational and interview data.

Among the characteristics of primary groups, like families, are shared feelings and a sense of belonging together. An attempt was made to index these complex and sensitive characteristics by studying help patterns.

In the formal interview, the members were asked to describe the kinds of help, if any, they gave to each other. While 75 percent said they gave help to others, only 48 percent said they received any. Those who claimed to give help most often mentioned helping ill or handicapped members.

> I do as much as I can. I do lots of things for my roommate. She's in bad shape... I look after her, help her get ready and find things [a 75-year-old female].

> I do lots of things for the ladies. I take some of them for little walks. I get help for them if they get sick at night [an 82-year-old male].

> I help out the sick ones. One lady had cancer and I did lots of things for her [a 73-year-old female].

Those who said other residents helped them most often mentioned small tasks, such as sewing on a button or just "little things." Few mentioned receiving help during illness.

> They would do anything if I needed it, but so far I haven't [an 88-year-old female].

> They do small favors for me...like rubbing my back. One lady cared for my plants while I was away [an 82-year-old female].

It must be recalled that the sample interviewed was a select one, tending toward the healthier, more intact members. Therefore, it might be expected that these individuals would be more often on the giving than on the receiving end of help and support. However, denying that one receives help from others, expecting minor kinds of help, may also reflect a desire to retain the claim to independence. Many members commented to the researcher that one must "do" for oneself or be forced to move to a nursing home.

To whom, and in what circumstances, one member may give help or support in a very important way is affected by the domestic staff. They are expected to perform domestic tasks, but are not expected to provide personal or nursing care, although on occasion they do. Further, they are expected to adhere to the ideals of Share-A-Home by encouraging the members to maintain the highest level of independence possible so as to avoid the dreaded prospect of institutionalization.

The result is that members may be discouraged at times from providing help to certain others. The attempt to keep everyone functioning as independently as possible may conflict with the other Share-A-Home ideal, the maintenance of a sharing, supportive "family" of peers. This misunderstanding often produced confusion among the members:

> I do little things for people, but I'd do more, and so would the others, if we were allowed to. We're supposed to be a family. Well, family members help each other [an 82-year-old female].

> I help some of the old ladies, but then they ["managers"] told me not to. I guess it's against the rules [an 85-year-old male].

Such comments were not uncommon in a number of the homes. The researcher also observed several instances of the domestic staff's intervention in situations involving one member helping another. In all of these instances the staff related to the researcher that such intervention occurred only when they believed the recipient did not really *need* the help and could "do" for himself or herself.

Nevertheless, Share-A-Home seems to provide an opportunity for many older people to develop meaningful helping roles. Although it may bring them into occasional conflict with the domestic staff, the residents in most of the homes do engage in considerable support of the more disabled residents.

Variable Interaction Patterns

The Share-A-Home concept is based on the beliefs that elderly people need both personal autonomy and independence and a "family" or caring peers. One set of research questions has centered on the kinds and qualities of relationships which emerge among the residents in these cooperative settings.

Observations in the various homes revealed a wide variety of interactional patterns and styles, similar to "natural" families. In most of the homes, both large and small, the researcher observed many instances of mutual help among the residents, frequent conversation and interaction, and expressions of liking and trust for other residents. Those interviewed in these homes also tended to express high satisfaction with Share-A-Home.

A smaller number of homes, however, were less "successful," both in terms of the kinds of relationships which occurred among the residents and also in the degree of satisfaction with Share-A-Home expressed by the residents. In these homes the group members were observed to interact less, to provide less mutual aid, and to express fewer positive feelings toward other residents in both informal discussions and formal interviews. The residents in these same few homes were generally less satisfied with the home than were those in the other homes.

The most "successful" homes tended to be those with the most stable resident populations. In those homes with very unstable membership, it was difficult for residents to develop and maintain ties with each other. The reason for the higher resident turnover in some homes than in others is related in part to the natural aging process of the group. That is, the homes which had been in existence the longest tended to have proportionately more very elderly individuals. Consequently, one of the oldest and largest homes lost one-third of its membership in a four-month period because of death or permanent nursing home placements. These were individuals who had lived in the homes for several years. There was a feeling of constant and unsettling change by the residents of this home, as well as a feeling of loss of old friends.

Another factor which appears to be important in explaining differences among the homes regarding resident satisfaction and the kinds of relationships which are fostered is the mental condition of the residents. Given the advanced age of the population, it was not surprising to find a number of elderly persons exhibiting signs of mental impairment. Thus, in many of the homes there lived some members who exhibited confused and disoriented, sometimes disruptive, behaviors. In most of these homes the researcher observed instances of support and acceptance day after day for those more impaired members. One woman expressed the general feeling well:

> There are some of us who are less fortunate than others, but we love them nonetheless. Sometimes I get asked the same question a hundred times by the same person and I lose patience, but we get along [a 77-year-old female].

In general, the residents and domestic help in the homes demonstrated great tolerance and receptivity toward a member who showed signs of mental deterioration.

The crucial factor was not the presence of impaired residents but rather the number of them present in any home. In one home many of those who were interviewed felt overwhelmed by the sheer numbers of impaired residents. Some felt the need to protect themselves by withdrawing from interaction; this is the kind of response which has often been documented in studies of institutional settings. Even those who expressed strong commitment to the Share-A-Home ideals of sharing and caring sometimes felt that they did not have sufficient energy or resources to give support constantly to all who were in need.

> [The hardest thing about living here] is having to deal with people who are in need of help, and I don't quite know how to help.... They come in here to talk but I've had to close my door lately [a 69-year-old female].

> All but one or two of them needs compassion all the time.... It wouldn't be so bad if it was just one or two. I'm beginning to block it out or I might fall into their state [a 74-year-old female].

Evaluation of Share-A-Home

Our overall assessment [of Share-A-Home] is that the environments are very positive for older residents and have many familylike aspects. Different Share-A-Home families vary in the quality of their relationships--in their congeniality and sociability--just as natural families do. The families studied can be considered a social amalgam between fully independent living and institutionalization for the elderly. The organizational concept of Share-A-Home involves (1) establishing a "family" of peers who care about and support each other, and (2) freeing the individual from the burdens of housekeeping and cooking so that he or she may live an independent life outside an institution.

It was suggested that these twin ideals of sharing "family" and personal independence may cause some members to experience contradictory situational definitions, analogous to what Bateson et al. (1956) have called the "double bind." The desire on the part of the members to help certain others may meet with resistance from staff who perceive that such help would be detrimental to the others' motivations to maintain independence.

This research also suggests that mixing older people with widely different impairment levels may have negative implications for those involved. The crucial variable may not be the range of competencies but rather the proportion who are seriously impaired. Even those with strong commitment to the Share-A-Home ideal of mutual support may feel overwhelmed by the sheer numbers of those in need. Further research may uncover a critical level of heterogeneity on this factor beyond which mutual benefit stops. Simmel (Wolff 1950) points out in his discussion of the numerical aspects of social life that quantitative increases can have significant qualitative effects; in fact, changing the numbers often results in a wholly new phenomenon.

These findings on successful and unsuccessful "families" can be contrasted with the conclusions of Kanter (1973) on stable and unstable communes. Kanter notes that unsuccessful communes are characterized by failure to implement commitment mechanisms carefully or resocialize the members to provide new identities. These conclusions parallel some of ours--that the more successful homes have a spirit of group cohesiveness and group identity. However, some of the analysis of communes fails to be relevant to the situation of the elderly. First, members join the family primarily for reasons of deficit--personal decline in health or economic condition--not for ideological reasons. It is the factor of health that is paramount in the alternative living arrangements for the elderly--a factor not mentioned by Kanter in her analysis of other intentional family arrangements. Furthermore, it is declining health, particularly mental health, that poses one of the chief obstacles to integration of members in the family groups that were judged to be less successful.

A second major difference is the area of boundary maintenance. Kanter (1972) points out that stable, long-lived communes are characterized by boundary maintenance which facilitates commitment. When there are strong boundaries--physical, social and behavioral--what goes on in the commune is clearly differentiated from what happens outside. In the case of the elderly, however, it may be that rigid boundary maintenance should be avoided so as to prevent the transformation of alternative living arrangements into geriatric ghettoes. It seems that the most desirable situation for the somewhat dependent elderly is to live in a protected environment, yet be free to interact with other groups in society--family, friends, church groups, and special interest groups.

Conclusions and Policy Issues

The data we have presented indicate that the alternative living arrangement described here is a viable lifestyle and is more than a catch phrase. Moreover, in other areas of the country, a variety of other cooperative living arrangements for the elderly are now operating or are in the process of formation. These include the Shared Living housing arrangement for persons over 50 initiated in Boston by the Back Bay Aging Concerns Committee; Community Housing for the Elderly, a form of intermediate housing consisting of nine semidetached homes in a residential neighborhood in Philadelphia; a house-sharing scheme in Los Angeles; Weinfield House, a program organized by a Jewish service organization in Chicago involving apartments or a complex of town houses in which there is a strong back-up of social services provided by the sponsoring agency, linked with an array of volunteers. These alternatives are quite successful and provide family living and support. Further research is obviously needed to assess more fully the strengths and weaknesses of the various alternatives and the optimum conditions of their viability (Liebowitz 1978).

It should be pointed out that these "families" are often organized by persons other than the older residents, unlike the alternate living arrangements in earlier phases of the life cycle. People often choose this lifestyle a bit reluctantly--as the best choice available, not as the most preferred style of life. In most instances, it is entered into because of health and some dependency, not because of ideological beliefs or a commitment to the norms of communal living. Indeed, as Dressel and Avant (1978) have pointed out, there are counterideological factors present in the contemporary United States, plus some prejudice on the part of the old and young against alternative forms; in turn, these arrangements may be labeled deviant. There are also legal obstacles (such as zoning regulations) and bureaucratic blockages (such as housing inspection requirements) present in some situations.

One of the unquestioned goals currently accepted in social service systems is that keeping elderly persons in their own homes is a top-priority aim. The policy of independent living arrangements has received strong support. In his address to the 1971 White House Conference on Aging, President Nixon specifically stated: "The greatest need is to help more older Americans to go on living in their own homes" (Kamerman & Kahn 1976:315). To accomplish this, a multiplicity of services may have to be supplied: Meals on Wheels, homemaker and shopping services, transportation assistance, "Friendly Visitor" services, visiting nurses, CETA household repair services, and rent subsidies. There has been little attention given to the enormous expenditure of energy required to bring all of these separate kinds of assistance to individual homes, to say nothing of the enormous expenditures of public funds. Policy makers in the future may have to weigh whether the benefits of remaining in one's own home are worth the costs in an energy-scarce society; they perhaps should consider encouraging the wider organization of alternative family arrangements.

There is a growing awareness that American society in the future is likely to be more a society of scarcity than it has been in the past. Americans of all ages will be forced to consider adaptations to meet the stern reality of a growing scarcity of energy, a reduced rate of growth, and probably fewer dollars for human services and social benefits. Alternative lifestyles in which older persons will share living facilities such as a house and automobile and other aspects of a common lifestyle comprise one set of realistic alternatives which can be workable, economical, energy-conserving, and fulfilling in terms of the quality of life.

Note

Support for the research has been generously given by the NRTA-AARP-Andrus Foundation, Washington, D.C. A demonstration project (90-A-1656) funded by the Administration on Aging, Department of Health, Education and Welfare is supporting work on the diffusion of the Share-A-Home model. The data presented here were part of a paper, "A Variant Family Form for the Elderly: Some Preliminary Findings," by Mary Anne Hilker and Gordon F. Streib presented at the 41st Annual Meeting of the Southern Sociological Society, Atlanta, April 1979.

References

Atchley, R.C.
1977 *The Social Forces in Later Life.* Belmont, Cal.: Wadsworth.

Bateson, G., D.D. Jackson, J. Haley, and J. Weakland.
1956 "Toward a Theory of Schizophrenia," *Behavioral Science* 1:251-64.

Dressel, P.L., and W.R. Avant.
1978 "Neogamy and Older Persons." *Alternative Lifestyles* 1 (Feb.):13-36.

Federal Council on the Aging.
1976 *Bicentennial Charter for Older Americans* (no. 1976 0-207-256). Washington, D.C.: U.S. Government Printing Office.

Kamerman, S.B., and A.J. Kahn.
1976 *Social Services in the United States: Policies and Programs.* Philadelphia: Temple University Press.

Kanter, R.M.
1973 "Why They Dissolve: Problems of Short-Lived Communes." Pp. 445-449 in R. M. Kanter, *Communes: Creating and Managing and Collective Life.* New York: Harper & Row.

Kanter, R.M.
1972 *Commitment and Community.* Cambridge, Mass.: Harvard University Press.

Liebowitz, B.
1978 "Implications of Community Housing for Planning and Policy." *Gerontologist* 18 (Aug.):138-43.

Newman, S.J.
1976 "Housing Adjustments of the Disabled Elderly." *Gerontologist* 16 (Aug.):312-17.

Raimy, E.
1979 *Shared Houses, Shared Lives: The New Extended Families and How They Work.* Los Angeles: J.P. Tarcher.

Shanas, E., and G.L. Maddox.
1976 "Aging, Health, and the Organization of Health Resources." Pp. 592-618 in R.H. Binstock and E. Shanas (eds.) *Handbook of Aging and the Social Sciences.* New York: Van Nostrand Reinhold.

Shanas, E., P. Townsend, D. Wedderburn, H. Friis, P. Milhoj, and J. Stenhouwer.
1968 *Old People in Three Industrial Societies.* London: Routledge & Kegan Paul.

Streib, G.F.
1972 "Older Families and Their Troubles: Familial and Social Responses." *Family Coordinator* 21 (Jan.):5-19.

U.S. Department of Health, Education and Welfare.
1976 *Older Americans Act of 1965, as Amended* (DHEW Pub. No. OHD 76-20170). Washington D.C.: U.S. Government Printing Office.

Wolff, K.H. (ed.)
1950 *The Sociology of Georg Simmel.* New York: Free Press.

Zablocki, B.D., and R.M. Kanter
1976 "The Differentiation of Life-Styles." Pp. 269-298 in A. Inkeles, J. Coleman, and N. Smelser (eds.), *Annual Review of Sociology.* Palo Alto, Cal.: Annual Reviews.

29. THE ROLE OF SELF-HELP NETWORKS IN MEETING FAMILY NEEDS: Policy Considerations

Rosalie G. Genovese

Social networks, informal arrangements that arise out of the shared needs of participants, make important contributions to the well-being of individuals and families. They often provide participants with material goods and services, as well as mutual support. Several authors in this volume have alluded to the role played by networks in the communities they studied (see Pearce and McAdoo, Chapter 16; and Buss and Redburn, Chapter 24). During the past decade, social scientists have examined networks in a variety of settings and have begun to make distinctions on the basis of their function, membership, and location (Katz 1981; Silverman 1980; Hickman, n.d.).

However, researchers have not focused to a great extent on the policy implications of such networks or on government's role vis-à-vis them. A notable exception has been the work of Sarason and his colleagues (1977). Yet social networks may offer policy makers a way out of their current dilemma by providing necessary services to families while at the same time cutting or holding the line on government expenditures. In this chapter, some policy implications of increased reliance on networks will be considered.

Until recently government has adopted a largely hands-off stance, a policy encouraged to some extent by network members and supporters who feared that government intervention would change the character of networks, as the following statement illustrates:

> The recommendation as related to midlife women specifically excluded official financial support. To the contrary, the view was expressed that government support would deprive self-help groups of their in-dependent, informal and flexible character [*Status of Midlife Women* 1980:16].

Given changes in governmental philosophy and policy which have led to decreased funding for social programs, networks could help meet the service needs of families at a relatively low cost. Since many families must adjust to shrinking resources during this recessionary period, outside funds may be essential if existing networks are to survive:

> Family support systems are increasingly being examined as alternatives to government-funded services. However, these systems are threatened by the inflationary squeeze currently affecting American families, whose members often use discretionary money to exchange aid with one another. Inflation limits the availability of these discretionary funds, causing hardships for those members who rely on them [National Retired Teachers Association et al. 1980:108].

Yet families may have to rely even more than ever on their own resources and on informal arrangements for services, for material goods, and for support in coping with problems ranging from unemployment or catastrophic illness to adjusting to having a previously institutionalized member return home. For many low-income families, reliance on relatives and friends is not a new phenomenon. Stack (1974) and others have documented how this form of mutual help has helped generations of minority families to endure conditions of poverty and deprivation. Relatives and friends who exchange gifts become defined as kin. "In the process of exchange, people become immersed in a domestic web of a large number of kinfolk who can be called upon for help and who can bring others into the network" (Stack 1974:44).

Social researchers have pointed out several reasons for the growing importance attached to social networks. They cite, for example, the decline of the extended family and the support it can provide (Katz 1981:139). Although the prevalence of extended family arrangements in the United States has often been exaggerated while the strength of ties among family members who live at a distance today is perhaps underestimated, families cannot personally provide care for an ill relative in another city. Substitutes must be found, and networks of unrelated individuals may provide support that supplements impersonal purchased care.

Second, some families participate in informal networks because they are dissatisfied with the professional care and bureaucratic services they receive. They have found professionals unresponsive to the day-to-day problems of chronically ill or handicapped individuals and their relatives. Self-help groups have not only provided social support, but they have devised concrete solutions to members' needs, for example by designing equipment for those with colostomies (Silverman 1980). Moreover, the move toward deinstitutionalization has created many new concerns and responsibilities for families who now care at home or in a community setting for members who formerly would have spent their lives in institutions. Parents and other family members frequently look to networks composed of others in the same situation for advice and support.

Third, mental health practitioners are well aware of the important role of social support in maintaining health and in aiding recovery from illness. They often encourage former patients to become network participants and some agencies have sponsored the formation of networks by their clients (Froland et al. 1981).

Types and Functions of Self-Help Networks

Networks can be either "embedded" or "created" (Froland et al. 1981:51). Embedded networks are based on kinship, residential proximity, or organizational relationships. These are often referred to as "natural" because they have developed spontaneously (Collins & Pancoast 1976). Created networks have been fostered by a formal agency to assist people with a similar problem or need. These networks are very open, since the only requirement for belonging is an interest in participation. They tend to be oriented to short-term problem solving or to the provision of basic services (Froland et al. 1981:52-53).

In contrast, embedded networks entail long-term relationships in which participants invest considerable "time, responsibility and concern" (Froland et al. 1981:52). They tend to be flexible and to provide both material and emotional support. However, they can help only small numbers of people, and they are affected by the geographic mobility of participants, changes in family size or structure, and increased labor-force participation by women.

Networks also differ in whether or not they are based on geographic proximity. Whether in an inner-city area or a suburb, neighborhood support networks may compensate participants for services lacking in a community, as well as offer emotional support (Genovese 1981; Stack 1974). Some have the character of an extended family. On the other hand, participants in networks that assist individuals and families with special needs--for example, some form of deviant behavior--may be drawn from a much wider area: "The local area may...be inappropriate as a source of informal help when the focal problem is stigmatizing or the clients wish to remain anonymous, as in family violence or mental problems" (Froland et al. 1981:137).

Two characteristics shared by networks are exchange relationships and a fraternal structure. Exchanges may take the form of reciprocity or mutuality--"a favor given may be repaid by helping someone else with the idea that, over time, things will balance out" (Froland et al. 1981:42).

As the foregoing discussion suggests, informal networks provide a range of assistance: tangibles like food, housing and money (Stack 1974; Genovese 1981) and intangibles like emotional support, advice and influence (see Buss and Redburn, Chapter 24 and also Silverman 1980). In a study of the networks among a sample of mothers in a town near Boston, for example, Stueve and Lein (1979:5) considered the following types of exchange: "material," including lending and borrowing; "service," including child care, transportation, car repairs, pet care, and illness; "social and ritual," including holiday and vacation activities, recreation, and socializing; and "personal supports," including advice and comfort.

According to Foote and Cottrell (1965), networks that give members mutual support, both material and psychosocial, have a fraternal structure. Foote and Cottrell used the term "quasi-families" to describe them because of their resemblance to contemporary families. In contrast, the doctor-patient or professional-client relationship is more like a parent-child relationship. This distinction helps explain both the commitment of members to informal networks and the therapeutic value of such networks. In the sections that follow, networks of special significance to families are discussed.

Community-based networks. Geographic proximity often results in close-knit social networks. Women and children are especially likely to participate in neighborhood networks. Individuals and family members with limited mobility--older people, the unemployed, and the poor--also must look close to home for mutual support and ways to share limited resources.

Research on women's networks by social scientists documents how planners fail to meet the needs of women, both those who work outside the home and those who do not. Numerous recent books and special editions of journals have been devoted to planning that is responsive to the realities of women's lives (Heresies 1981; Keller 1981; Stimpson et al. 1981 Wekerle et al. 1980).

Women who live in communities almost entirely populated by women and children during the day have a special impetus to form self-help groups, as numerous observers have pointed out. Stamp (1980:189) echoes the opinion of many of her colleagues:

> In its present character, the neighborhood of the American city generally does not meet basic human needs for support and belonging.... Instead it separates its inhabitants so that problems stemming from isolation are commonplace. As women and their young children are often its only full-time occupants they are the chief victims of its isolating effects.

Rivers and her colleagues (1979:266-67) see networks as a response for women in such communities:

> Women at home have a vested interest in joining with other housewives to form networks that can offer them respites from the unrelenting demands of child care. These networks can act as pressure groups to make community organizations responsive to their needs: places to meet other adults where child care is provided.

However, networks do not necessarily consist only of women who are at home all day. Some include employed women who make informal arrangements with their at-home counterparts to provide child care during the day. Barter, not money, is the basis for many of these exchanges (Genovese 1981). In low-income communities, networks may include several generations of one family, unrelated individuals who are considered kin, and men as well as women (Stack 1974).

Community networks also differ in the nature and extent of support exchanged. In some neighborhoods major emphasis is placed on mutual support to counter isolation or to help; participants cope with changes in family status; in others, barter and informal exchanges of goods and services are the primary reasons for the network's existence.

Single parents may be particularly dependent on networks for both material and nonmaterial support. Some of these networks are geographically based. Brown (1978) has shown that a single parent's neighborhood may be a crucial factor in the family's quality of life. Informal networks can help a female household head cope with decreased economic resources after divorce and with role strain or overload. Women in communities with a substantial number of single parents are more likely to form support networks:

> We found this issue of personal ties very important. The women in our sample who did not have stable social networks were the ones most favorable to remarriage, indicating that on some level husbands and friends are interchangeable. Aside from the suburbs already mentioned, what other neighborhoods supply social networks for divorced mothers?...
>
> In general, neighborhoods that seem to provide the most interpersonal support were of three types. Some, but not all, stable working class areas enabled young divorcees to remain in contact with their high school chums who may themselves now be getting divorced. (Other such areas were hostile to her deviant status.) A second type of neighborhood was the public housing projects, where a female head of family has a lot of company. The third type, found in many areas of Boston, is the heterogeneous older neighborhood with a mixture of classes, housing types, and family organizations [Brown 1978:7].

A newer form of networking, parent networks, has been receiving attention recently. These are being formed by parents with teenaged children to bring "to sprawling, diverse economic and ethnic suburban neighborhoods a sense of mutual community values" (Teasdale 1982:LI-11). The impetus for them came from parental concern about drinking and vandalism among teenagers. Dr. Schuchard, a supporter of parent networks, calls them "an informal mutual agreement that they [parents] will stick together and stay in touch with each other and try to provide consistent guidelines for the kids, which will ease some of the pressures they feel from their friends" (ibid.). Parents whose children are members of the same circle or class get together to decide on goals and guidelines. The networks are very informal, with contact frequently made by telephone.

Networks to aid family and life-cycle transitions. Networks serve an important function in helping individuals and families adjust to changes in status and transitions--for example, to parenthood, divorce, widowhood, or the death of a child. Raikes (1981:12) found networks important to new mothers: "access to simple day-in, day-out contact that lends itself to problem-solving and help when it is needed appears to be the most important support a new mother can have." The mere presence of others seemed more important than what they actually did. Networks may be especially helpful to teen-aged mothers because they can offer both support and concrete advice about child care. Research is needed to determine whether network support exists for fathers and, if so, what form it takes. In his contribution to this volume, Shostak emphasizes that men involved in the abortion process need support. Men approaching fatherhood may too.

In addition to geographic networks, other kinds of networks provide support for single parents or for divorced men and women. Parents without Partners, an international organization, is probably the best known and most extensive, with a thousand chapters. Its members participate in meetings and receive a magazine and newsletter that provides information and advice (see Weiss 1973). Some divorced women rely primarily on informal networks of relatives and friends to help them adjust to their new status. Coughey (1981:16) found that most "tragic" cases had no support networks after divorce: "Women's social life, social contacts, household burdens and responsibilities, financial situations and their options in life are all improved when they have social networks to turn to." Her research indicated that older women were especially isolated. They saw less of relatives and friends and were less likely to have anyone with whom to discuss problems. She found that some older divorced women seemed to be excluded from their children's family activities (ibid.: 17).

Children in one-parent families also can draw support from networks composed of peers who are having similar experiences and stresses. In Cambridge, Mass., students at the Fayerweather Street School (1981) met to discuss their common problems and eventually put together the *Kids' Book of Divorce* to help others in the same situation.

Networks can be an important source of support for women alone at midlife and in later years. Widow-to-widow networks have been especially effective, since they give participants the opportunity to interact with others who have coped successfully in similar situations (Silverman 1980). Transitions to retirement, labor force reentry, or the empty nest may also be facilitated by support groups.

Older individuals derive valuable material as well as emotional support from networks:

> There is a growing interest among government agencies, social service providers, and researchers in the field of aging in the care arrangements and informal support systems of older people. There has also been a growing concern over the well-being of older women, especially very old women, who encounter particular difficulties as a result of their sex and historical location as well as their age [Stueve & Fischer 1978:1).

Exchange of material goods and services may be crucial to older low-income network participants who can manage with less income during lean economic periods (ibid.:5). In addition, networks mediate between older people and government bureaucracies, organizations, and landlords. They also enhance older people's self-image, especially their sense of usefulness and their ability to help others (ibid.:6).

Among unanswered questions about networks of older people are how those of men and women differ and how networks differ in their capacity to provide services (ibid.:17). Networks may be more effective when they include members of various ages who can help each other.

Networks for families with ill or disabled members: An unmet need. Families who care for ill, handicapped or elderly members have an obvious need for the emotional support provided by informal networks. In addition, they have a pressing need to be able to "take time off" from the pressures of caring for a homebound relative, often twenty-four hours a day. A network composed of relatives and friends helps, but a truly effective one would also provide tangible goods and services--respite care, medical transportation, home care aides, and assistance in ensuring that the rights of both the person cared for and the caregiver are protected.

Networks created by agencies can fill this growing need. Some organizations have already begun to offer a range of services, including peer support groups whose participants meet to discuss problems. The Community Service Society in New York City began a Natural Supports Program to supplement the informal services that family and friends provide for the elderly (Zimmer 1980). It would be difficult for an informal network to provide these diverse services on a voluntary basis.

Relationships among Formal Services, Professionals, and Networks

Professionals and others who provide formal services and network participants display a range of attitudes toward each other. Some informal networks developed because participants found that professionals and formal organizations failed to meet their needs (Silverman 1980:28). Some examples are the anonymous organizations like Parents Anonymous, Alcoholics Anonymous, and Al-Anon; organizations for parents of developmentally handicapped children; and those begun by individuals who are often stigmatized, for example former psychiatric-hospital patients.

Attitudes of professionals toward self-help groups are often ambivalent. If self-help groups accept professionals as the experts and define their role as an adjunct to such care, then they may be viewed favorably. Created networks have often been begun by, or with the help of, professionals or established agencies. Mental health professionals long have emphasized the therapeutic value of social support from informal groups. Recovery, Inc., for example, was formed by Dr. A. Low using methods he pioneered in treating psychiatric patients. Parents Anonymous (originally Mothers Anonymous) was started by a mother who abused her children and by the psychiatric social worker who had been treating her (Silverman 1980).

Relationships between informal networks and formal agencies may take various forms. They may coexist, or formal services may supplement network exchanges, filling gaps in services or support. On the other hand, formal services might eliminate the need for the informal or make the costs of maintaining networks seem too high, especially if they overlap (Stueve & Fischer 1978:36-37). This last possibility seems unlikely. The opposite point of view was often heard in the early 1970s, when supporters of the self-help movement were optimistic that informal groups might replace many services provided by professionals (Riessman 1982:A23). Now, however, the agreement seems to be that their impact will be minor, or that self-help groups might even be coopted by professionals (Borkman 1981:2).

If a government policy in support of networks is formulated, then the role of professionals will become an important issue for clarification. If self-help groups appear to threaten the status of professionals, especially by offering free or low-cost assistance, then action by professionals and their associations to reassert their dominance seems likely.

However, the biggest concern of network supporters today is probably not cooptation but how to find the resources to maintain and expand their activities to help those in need. Outside funding seems essential to accomplishing these aims. Until recently, government seemed to offer the best hope for providing such financial support.

Prospects for Government Policy in Support of Networks

The case for networks. Many arguments can be marshaled to support the idea that the time has come for government to provide economic support to networks. Individuals and groups with widely divergent political views have reason to favor them. Conservatives may like informal networks as an alternative to interference by government and professionals in people's lives. Moreover, informal networks are in keeping with the Reagan emphasis on voluntarism: people helping one another instead of expecting government to assume the responsibility.

At the other end of the political spectrum, counterculture groups favor self-help as an alternative to professional services, which are frequently accompanied by elitism. Self-help also gives individuals and families the opportunity to gain more control over their lives and their communities. Network participants may develop or increase skills that are transferrable to other spheres--for example, work or political action. The hope is that self-help groups ultimately will become a force for change in the professions, social services, and society as a whole (Gartner & Riessman 1977).

Whatever their political views, legislators can be expected to support networks as a relatively inexpensive way to provide services without new or enlarged bureaucracies, an important point when "big government" is criticized. Moreover, a program of aid to local networks would respect the diversity of values found across the country, instead of requiring conformity to national standards.

Numerous references to policy makers' interest in support networks for older people have already been made in this chapter. Several Congressional committee publications recommended that networks be recognized and encouraged. An important rationale underlying this position was that they required little government support. *The Status of Midlife Women* (1980:22,24) included the following findings and recommendations:

> Self-help networks have been found among the most effective programs, with virtually no cost to the taxpayer....
>
> Self-help network formation and expansion should be encouraged through the Department of Health, Education and Welfare so that private women's organizations, Y's, community centers, churches, and other groups take greater initiative.

The advantages of networks also were summarized in another report on midlife women (1979:15):

> Because they respond more quickly than formal institutions, mutual help groups are desirable carriers of change. Another advantage is that they require low or no financial backing, since volunteer efforts of members usually sustain them.... Unnecessary bureaucracy should be avoided. Governmental funding of mutual help groups, if requested at all, should be appropriate to the mode of operation of groups, lest the grant become contraproductive.

Flexibility is another advantage of networks from government's point of view. Networks that solve short-term needs may be dissolved, unlike bureaucratic organizations which tend to persist. Moreover, start-up costs are minimized if financial assistance goes to established networks.

Dangers of viewing networks as panaceas. Enthusiasm for networks may lead policy makers to expect them to accomplish much more than is realistically possible. Sarason and his colleagues (1977:187) expressed just such a reservation several years ago:

> What does concern us is that the use of the word *network* and the concept of network are becoming increasingly fashionable. They are "in the air" and that suggests they speak to something important in the lives of people. It is realistic and not pessimistic to expect that some people will view "networking" as a panacea and devise "methods" by which the new gospel will be spread. Efforts at social change never wait on proof that the values and ideas powering the efforts have validity. If "networking" takes on the characteristics of a movement, we have cause to be fearful and optimistic, fearful because we know the consequences of unbridled enthusiasm and simple answers, and optimistic that perhaps on balance there will be a desirable difference.

Riessman (1982:A23) has voiced several important cautions regarding self-help that are especially applicable to networks. First, it may serve as an excuse by government to justify reduced services, although self-help efforts cannot possibly replace those that government provides or should provide. Networks may supplement and fill gaps in services or they may meet emerging needs before programs have been established, but they are not substitutes for necessary public services.

Second, although self-help efforts make it easier for people to cope with their circumstances, especially during crises like unemployment or chronic illness, they cannot *change* those circumstances by creating jobs or by providing respite care for families with aged or chronically ill members at home. Nor do they help poor families escape from poverty; they just make survival possible (Stack 1974).

Given the dearth of alternatives, the need for self-help networks is likely to increase as more individuals and families face the consequences of depressed economic conditions and cuts in government programs. Families may be trying to devote substantial amounts of time to voluntary network activities at a time when they have to spend more hours working to make ends meet. For example, women who are the sole or prime economic support for their families have little time to devote to networks. If families are expected to assume responsibility for services formerly provided by government, without compensation, then they will be under even greater strain. (See Chapter 23, by Finch and Groves.)

It is also important to realize that networks do not reach all potential participants. The need to raise funds may result in policies that eliminate some individuals and families. For example, Parents without Partners groups have membership dues and per-meeting charges that make participation by low-income families difficult. In addition, networks reach only certain population segments. Individuals who are isolated or who are not joiners may be left out. Moreover, some individuals and families are more receptive than others to networks. In a review of research on help-seeking, Gourash (1978) found that self-help groups or networks and professional help were sought out by young, white, educated women more often than by older people, those with less than a high-school education, or lower-income individuals. (However, some networks do undertake outreach efforts.) For all these reasons, it would be a mistake to embrace networks as the one best answer to meeting individual and family needs.

Furthermore, serious limitations are placed on network activities by lack of funds. Networks under agency sponsorship or informal networks that try to provide tangible goods or services have limited effectiveness when they operate on a shoestring. They also may find it increasingly difficult to enlist volunteers as more women obtain fulltime jobs. Even largely voluntary groups need some funds. For example, Women in Transition, Inc., a self-help group that provided emotional and legal support to women coping with divorce, separation, or family violence ceased to exist because it lacked funds. Galper and Washburne (1976) concluded that such groups needed organizational and financial skills and resources to succeed. Borkman (1981:5) reached a similar conclusion in assessing self-help groups: "Most self-help groups are small, weak, often ephemeral and locally oriented. Most groups are only loosely informally organized and have few resources such as money, power, organizational skills, etc."

Conclusions

Despite the reasons why government support for networks makes sense, the prospects for funding them seems slim at present. The Reagan administration contends that government has assumed too much responsibility for meeting citizens' needs and that individuals should assume more responsibility for themselves. Consequently, it is attempting to swing the pendulum back in the direction of greater individual responsibility in its effort to rewrite "the social contract" between people and government.

Moreover, despite Reagan's emphasis on people helping one another, the administration has cut programs that provide employment at the grassroots level for low-income residents, the elderly, and others who fill community service jobs. The VISTA program has been cut, CETA jobs are being phased out, and the Department of Labor is eliminating the Senior Community Service Employment Program which provides jobs for about 55,000 older Americans who are paid the minimum wage (*New York Times* 1982:A24). Such programs as nutrition centers for seniors and Meals on Wheels must contend with budget cuts at the local as well as the federal level. The current administration is unlikely to fund new social programs when it is sharply curtailing established ones.

Thus, the need for "natural" helping networks that provide emotional support is likely to increase. Whether they can expand their activities to provide specific services and materials will depend largely on voluntary efforts. At the same time, those networks that were formed primarily to provide goods and services will find it difficult to satisfy the growing demand for services as their financial resources dwindle. Where does this leave families? They will do what they have always done--manage as best they can--until policies and programs begin to match their needs.

References

Borkman, Thomasina S.
1981 "Evolving Models of Interdependence among Mutual/Self-Help Groups and Professionals." Paper presented at the American Sociological Association Annual Meeting, Toronto, August.

Brown, Carol A.
1978 "Spatial Inequalities and Divorced Mothers." Paper presented at the American Sociological Association Annual Meeting, San Francisco, September.

Collins, Alice H., and Diane L. Pancoast.
1976 *Natural Helping Networks: A Strategy for Prevention.* Washington, D.C.: National Association of Social Workers.

Coughey, Kathleen.
1981 "Divorced But Not Alone: A Study of Divorced Women's Networks." Paper presented at the Society for the Study of Social Problems Annual Meeting, Toronto, August 1981.

"Family Support Systems and the Aging: A Policy Report."
1980 Pp. 105-13 in *Families: Aging and Changing.* Hearing before the Select Committee on Aging, House of Representatives, Ninety-Sixth Congress, Second Session, June 4.

Fayerweather Street School.
1981 *Kids' Book of Divorce.* Brattleboro, Vt.: Stephen Greene Press.

Foote, Nelson, and Leonard Cottrell.
1965 *Identity and Interpersonal Competence.* Chicago: University of Chicago Press.

Froland, Charles, Diane L. Pancoast, Nancy J. Chapman, and Priscilla J. Kimboko.
1981 *Helping Networks and Human Services.* Sage Library of Social Research, vol. 128. Beverly Hills, Cal.: Sage.

Galper, Miriam, and Carolyn Kott Washburne.
1976 "A Women's Self-Help Program in Action." *Social Policy* 6 (March/April):46-52.

Gartner, Alan, and Frank Riessman.
1977 *Self-Help in the Human Services.* San Francisco: Jossey-Bass.

Genovese, Rosalie G.
1981 "A Women's Self-Help Network as a Response to Service Needs in the Suburbs." Pp. 245-53 in Stimpson et al. (1981)

Gourash, N.
1978 "Help-Seeking: A Review of the Literature." *American Journal of Psychology* 6:413-23.

Heresies
1981 "Making Room: Women and Architecture." Issue 11, vol. 3, no. 3 (entire issue).

Hickman, Marjorie T.
n.d. "Self-Help Groups and Mutual Aid Organizations of Interest to the Social Worker in a Mental Health Setting: A Selected Annotated Bibliography, 1965-1977." New York: National Self-Help Clearing House.

Katz, Alfred H.
1981 "Self-Help and Mutual Aid: An Emerging Social Movement?" *Annual Review of Sociology* 7:29-55.

Keller, Suzanne.
1981 *Building for Women.* Lexington, Mass.: Lexington Books.

"Midlife Women: Policy Proposals on Their Problems."
1979 A summary of papers submitted to the Subcommittee on Retirement Income and Employment of the Select Committee on Aging, U.S. House of Representatives, Ninety-Sixth Congress, First Session. April 1979. (Committee Publication 96-180.) Washington, D.C.: U.S. Government Printing Office.

National Retired Teachers Association, et al.
1980 "Family Support Systems and the Aging: A Policy Report." Pp. 105-13 in *Families: Aging and Changing.* (Report prepared jointly by the National Retired Teachers Association, American Association of Retired Persons and Wakefield Washington Associates.)

Raikes, Helen H.
1981 "Social Network Supports and Perceptions of Early Motherhood." Paper presented at the American Sociological Association Annual Meeting, Toronto, August.

Riessman, Frank.
1982 "Toward Self-Help." *New York Times* (March 24):A23.

Rivers, Caryl, Rosalind Barnett, and Grace Baruch.
1979 *Beyond Sugar and Spice.* New York: G.P. Putnam's Sons.

Sarason, Seymour B., Charles Carroll, Kenneth Maton, Saul Cohen, and Elizabeth Lorentz.
1977 *Human Services and Resource Networks: Rationale, Possibilities and Public Policy.* San Francisco: Jossey-Bass.

Silverman, Phyllis R.
1980 *Mutual Help Groups: Organization and Development.* Sage Human Services Guide, vol. 16. Beverly Hills, Cal.: Sage.

Stack, Carol B.
1974 *All Our Kin. Strategies for Survival in a Black Community.* New York: Harper & Row.

Stamp, Judy.
1980 "Toward Supportive Neighborhoods: Women's Role in Changing the Segregated City." Pp. 189-198 in G. Wekerle et al. (eds.) *New Space for Women.* Boulder, Col: Westview.

Status of Midlife Women and Options for their Future.
1980 A report with additional views by the Subcommittee on Retirement Income and Employment of the Select Committee on Aging, U.S. House of Representatives, Ninety-Sixth Congress, Second Session. March. (Committee Publication No. 96-215.) Washington, D.C.: U.S. Government Printing Office.

Stimpson, Catharine R., Elsa Dixler, Martha J. Nelson, and Kathryn B. Yatrakis (eds).
1981 *Women and The American City.* Chicago and London: University of Chicago.

Stueve, Ann, and Claude S. Fischer.
1978 "Social Networks and Older Women." Berkeley, Cal: Institute of Urban and Regional Development, University of California.

Stueve, Ann, and Laura Lein.
1979 "Problems of Network Analysis: The Case of the Missing Elderly." Wellesley, Mass.: Wellesley College Center for Research on Women, Working Paper no. 50. October.

Teasdale, Patricia.
1982 "Parent Networks Catching On." *New York Times* (Feb. 7):LI-11.

Weiss, Robert S.
1973 "The Contributions of an Organization of Single Parents to the Well-Being of Its Members." *Family Coordinator* (July):321-326.

Wekerle, Gerda R., Rebecca Peterson, and David Morley (eds.).
1980 *New Space for Women.* Westview Special Studies on Women in Contemporary Society. Boulder, Col.: Westview Press.

Zimmer, Anna.
1980 "Statement." Pp. 61-65 in *Families: Aging and Changing.* Hearing before the Select Committee on Aging, House of Representatives, Ninety-Sixth Congress, Second Session, June 4.

NOTES ON CONTRIBUTORS

Terry Buss is Director, Center for Urban Studies, Youngstown State University. F. Stevens Redburn is a Social Science Analyst with the Office of Policy Development and Research, U.S. Department of Housing and Urban Development. They are the coauthors of *Shutdown: Public Policy for Mass Unemployment* and of *Mass Unemployment.*

Janet Finch is a Lecturer in Social Policy, University of Lancaster, and the 1983-84 Chairperson of the British Sociological Association. Her current research interests span sociology and social policy, especially in the fields of welfare, family and gender. Dulcie Groves is a Lecturer in Social Policy, University of Lancaster, where her major field is income maintenance. Her current interests include women and occupational pensions, the financial consequences of divorce, and income support for "carers."

Rosalie G. Genovese is a Research Associate with the Center for the Study of Women and Society, Graduate Center, City University of New York. Her current research is on dual-career families and the careers of women in the sciences. Her research and publications on advocacy planning, citizen participation, new towns, and informal suburban networks reflect a continuing interest in community and urban planning and policy issues.

Edith Grotberg is Professor of Psychology, Ahfad University, Omdurman, Sudan. She was formerly Special Assistant, Associate Commissioner, Administration for Children, Youth and Families, U.S. Department of Health and Human Services.

Beth B. Hess is Professor of Sociology at the County College of Morris. She has published several textbooks and articles in the areas of aging and women, and is coauthor of *Sociology* with Elizabeth W. Markson and Peter J. Stein.

Tom Joe, Director of the Center for the Study of Social Policy, was formerly Special Assistant to the Undersecretary of the U.S. Department of Health, Education, and Welfare. He has worked as a consultant to various federal government departments under several administrations on such human service issues as welfare, health policy, manpower, disability, urban policy, and youth services.

Susan Lehrer is Assistant Professor, Department of Sociology, State University of New York, College at New Paltz. Her major research interests center around women, work and family, especially from a historical and political perspective. She is also interested in the historical development of labor legislation from a sociological viewpoint.

Diana Pearce is Director of Research, Center for National Policy Review, Catholic University Law Center, Washington, D.C. and Harriette McAdoo is professor at Howard University, Washington D.C.. *Women and Children*: *Alone and in Poverty*, was originally written for the National Advisory Council on Economic Opportunity, September 1981. A new postscript was prepared by the authors for this book.

Arthur B. Shostak is Professor of Sociology, Drexel University, Philadelphia. He is the author or editor of twelve books, nearly one hundred articles, and consults on the uses of sociology with major labor unions, industrial corporations, and all levels of government.

AUTHOR INDEX

N

O

P

R

S

T

V

W

Y

Z

SUBJECT INDEX

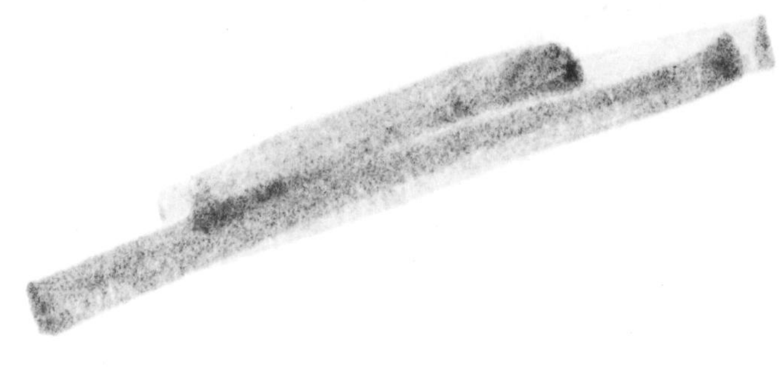

Teacher's Resource Book

6

ScottForesman

'erating English Language Learning

Authors

Anna Uhl Chamot

Jim Cummins

Carolyn Kessler

J. Michael O'Malley

Lily Wong Fillmore

Consultant

George González

ScottForesman

Editorial Offices: Glenview, Illinois

Regional Offices: Sunnyvale, California • Atlanta, Georgia

Glenview, Illinois • Oakland, New Jersey • Dallas, Texas

Visit ScottForesman's Home Page at http://www.scottforesman.com

SBN 0-673-19718-2

1.800.554.4411
http://www.scottforesman.com

2345678910 CR 0504030201009998 9796

Contents

Oral Language Scoring Rubric

To assess a student's progress, complete a copy of the scale on page 3 at the end of each unit.

	Speaking	Fluency	Structure	Vocabulary	Listening
1	Begins to name concrete objects.	Repeats words and phrases.		Uses isolated words.	Understands little or no English.
2	Expresses personal and survival needs; begins to communicate appropriately in discussions and conversations; begins to recall and retell after listening; asks and responds to simple questions.	Expresses ideas in short phrases; speaks hesitantly because of rephrasing and searching for words.	Uses many sentence fragments; has little control over tenses or other grammatical features.	Uses limited, functional vocabulary.	Understands words and phrases; listens attentively for brief periods; requires much repetition; can follow simple (1 or 2 step) oral directions.
3	Initiates and sustains conversation with descriptors and details; exhibits self confidence in social situations; begins to communicate in classroom situations; recalls, retells, and begins to question after listening.	Speaks with occasional hesitation; begins to develop audience awareness; begins to speak with clarity.	Expresses ideas in complete sentences; applies rules of grammar but lacks control of irregular forms (e.g., "writed," "feets," "not never," "more better").	Uses adequate vocabulary but with some irregular word usage.	Understands classroom discussions with repetition, rephrasing, and clarification; begins to maintain attention during a variety of activities; can follow 2–4 step oral directions.
4	Consistently contributes to classroom discussions and conversations; expresses and supports ideas; errors do not interfere with meaning.	Speaks with near native fluency. Any hesitations do not interfere with communication; demonstrates audience awareness and speaks with clarity and confidence.	Uses a variety of structures with occasional grammatical errors.	Uses varied vocabulary.	Understands most spoken language including classroom discussions; follows complex oral directions.

Oral Language Scoring Scale

Name ______________________________

Date ______________________________

Speaking	1	2	3	4
Fluency	1	2	3	4
Structure	1	2	3	4
Vocabulary	1	2	3	4
Listening	1	2	3	4

Reading Skills/Strategies Checklist

Name ______________________________

Date ______________________________

Skill/Strategy	1st 6 weeks	2nd 6 weeks	3rd 6 weeks	4th 6 weeks	5th 6 weeks	6th 6 weeks
Emergent Reader						
Tracks left/right, up/down.						
Uses pictures to retell storyline.						
Uses predictable patterns to tell/recall story.						
Can locate words in a text.						
Can recognize a few words.						
Developing Reader						
Reads short, predictable texts.						
Begins using reading strategies.						
Begins to self-correct.						
Has small, stable sight vocabulary.						
Displays awareness of sounds/symbols.						
Reader						
Reads familiar material on own.						
Uses several reading strategies.						
Figures out words and self-corrects.						
Has large stable sight vocabulary.						
Understands conventions of writing.						
Independent Reader						
Reads appropriate material independently.						
Uses multiple strategies flexibly.						
Makes inferences; draws conclusions.						
Monitors and self-corrects for meaning.						
Chooses to read.						

Comments

Process Writing Checklist

Name ________________________ Date ________________________

Writing Process	1st 6 weeks	2nd 6 weeks	3rd 6 weeks	4th 6 weeks	5th 6 weeks	6th 6 weeks
1. Prewriting Strategies						
Chooses topic before writing.						
Decides purpose for writing.						
Outlines or makes graphic organizer.						
Locates details about topic.						
2. Writing Strategies						
Organizes work and workplace.						
Sets goal for writing.						
Refers to notes and graphic organizer.						
Adapts techniques as necessary (e.g., writes without stopping to correct mistakes).						
3. Postwriting Strategies						
Rereads and reviews.						
Gets feedback from others.						
Rewrites and revises.						
Edits and proofreads.						
4. Applications and Interests						
Communicates in writing (letters, etc.).						
Seeks guidance in writing.						
Writes in all curriculum areas.						
Discusses his/her writing.						
Shares writing with others.						
Edits writing of others.						

Comments

Written Language Scoring Rubric

To assess a student's progress, complete a copy of the scale on page 7 at the end of each unit.

	Composing	Style	Sentence Formation	Usage	Mechanics
1	No clear central idea or ideas are apparent to an observer; may be able to read or explain own writing.	Uses known vocabulary in very simple sentences.	Uses frequent non-standard word order; writing contains many run on sentences and sentence fragments.	Shifts from one tense to another; errors in basic conventions.	Rereads to check meaning only; misspells even simple words; makes basic errors in punctuation and capitalization.
2	Shows evidence of central ideas but they are not well focused; can read own writing back to an audience.	Uses basic vocabulary that is not purposefully selected; uses mostly simple declarative sentences.	Uses some non-standard word order; writing contains some run on sentences and sentence fragments.	Makes some errors with inflections, agreement, and word meaning.	Begins to make corrections while writing; makes errors in spelling and punctuation that detract from meaning.
3	Focuses on central ideas but they are not evenly elaborated; includes digressions; utilizes some kind of organization plan.	Uses more varied vocabulary and structures; writes in a variety of forms; beginning to develop a sense of authorship.	Uses mostly standard word order; writing contains some run on sentences or sentence fragments.	Uses mostly standard inflections, agreement, and word meaning.	Recognizes the need to revise and edit and uses revision strategies and the editing process; makes some errors in mechanics that do not detract from meaning.
4	Develops central ideas clearly within an organized and elaborated text; shows confidence as a writer by taking risks.	Purposefully chooses vocabulary and sentence variety; employs a distinctive voice to affect reader; initiates independent writing.	Uses standard word order with no run on sentences or sentence fragments; uses standard modifiers and coordinators and effective transitions.	Uses standard inflections, subject/verb agreement, and standard word meaning.	Uses such conventions as capitalization, punctuation, spelling, and formatting effectively.

Written Language Scoring Scale

Name____

Date____

Composing	1	2	3	4
Style	1	2	3	4
Sentence Formation	1	2	3	4
Usage	1	2	3	4
Mechanics	1	2	3	4

Self-Assessment of Oral Language

Name ______________________________

Date ______________________________

Read each statement. Check (✔) the box that is most true for you.

When I use English...	**Always**	**Often**	**Some-times**	**Never**
Listening				
I can understand many words I hear.				
I can understand the teacher's directions.				
I can understand others when we work in a group.				
I can understand friends outside of class.				
I can understand when the teacher explains something.				
Speaking				
I can name pictures and objects.				
I can ask questions in class.				
I can talk to friends outside of class.				
I can retell a story.				
I can make a presentation in class.				

Self-Assessment of Reading Activities

Name ______________________________

Date ______________________________

Read each statement. Check (✔) the box that is most true for you.

Statement	At Least Once Each Week	At Least Once Each Month	Never or Hardly Ever
I tell a friend about a good book.			
I read about something because I am interested.			
I read on my own outside of school.			
I write about books I have read.			

Statement	Very True of Me	Kind of True of Me	Not at All True of Me
Being able to read is important to me.			
I can understand what I read in school.			
I learn important things from school.			
I am a good reader.			

Other comments about your reading:

____

____

____

Self-Assessment of Writing Activities

Name ____

Date ____

Read each statement. Check (✔) the box that is most true for you.

Statement	At Least Once Each Week	At Least Once Each Month	Never or Hardly Ever
I write letters at home to friends or relatives.			
I take notes when the teacher talks at school.			
I take notes when I read.			
I write a personal response to reading.			
I write a summary of what I read.			
I write stories or poems.			

Statement	Very True of Me	Kind of True of Me	Not at All True of Me
Being able to write is important to me.			
Writing helps me think more clearly.			
Writing helps me tell others what I have learned.			
I am a good writer.			

Other comments about your writing:

____

____

____

My Reading Log

Date	What is the title?	Who is the author?	What did you think of it?

My Writing Log

Date	Working Title	I especially liked:	My readers liked:	What's next?

Anecdotal Record of Reading Skills and Strategies

Name ____

Date ____

Reading Selection

Title ______________________________ Pages ________

Type (circle as many as apply)

fiction	nonfiction	poetry
biography	content text	other:

Context (circle one)

individual	small group	large group

Fluency in reading aloud (pauses, miscues, etc.)

Comprehension (recalls main ideas and details)

Strategies (e.g.: uses prior knowledge, predicts, infers meaning, etc.)

Personal response (relates to personal experience)

Recommendations for instruction

Portfolio Conference Questions on Reading

Name ______________________________

Date ______________________________

Reading Selection

Title ______________________________

Type (circle as many as apply)

fiction	nonfiction	poetry
biography	content text	other:

What did you like best in the reading?

What strategies helped you read it?

What do you do to help you remember what you read?

What will you do to become a better reader?

Portfolio Conference Questions on Writing

Name______________________________

Date______________________________

Title of writing sample

____

What do you like best about this piece of writing?

What strategies helped you write it?

How did you choose a topic for writing?

What will you do to become a better writer?

Portfolio Peer Assessment

Name ______________________________

Your partner's name ______________________________

Title of writing sample ______________________________

1. Read your partner's writing sample.

2. What do you like best about your partner's writing?

3. What did your partner do well?

4. What do you think your partner could make better?

5. What advice would you give your partner?

Portfolio Self Assessment

Name ____ Date __________

Title of writing sample ____

1. Look at your writing sample.

2. What do you like best about your writing?

3. What did you do well?

4. How could you make your sample better?

5. What are your writing goals? Write one thing you need to do better.

About My Portfolio

1. What I Chose

2. Why I Chose It

3. What I Like and Don't Like

4. How My Work Has Changed

Introduction to the Graphic Organizers

1. **Idea Web:** This can be used for brainstorming activities in which students name the words they know about a topic. It can also be used to organize ideas into groups if circles with subtopics are added around the central circle.

2. **K-W-L Chart:** This can be used to introduce a theme, a lesson, or a reading. It can help generate students' interest in a topic and help students use their prior knowledge as they read. Students can complete the chart at the end of a unit or lesson.

3. **T-Chart:** This chart can be used to help students see relationships between information. It can be used to list cause (left column) and effect (right column) or to list words (right column) associated with a topic or story character (left column).

4. **Venn Diagram:** This can be used to help students understand comparisons and contrasts in a text. It can be used when the question asks, "How are the two things alike? How are they different?"

5. **Story Sequence Chart:** In this chart, students can list the beginning, middle, and end of a story and gain a sense of story structure.

6. **Story Elements Chart:** In this chart, students list the main elements of stories, including setting, characters, problems, and important events.

7. **Main Idea Chart:** This chart can be used to help students see and chart main ideas and supporting details.

8. **Character Trait Web:** In this chart, students can list the important qualities of characters in stories and how the characters' actions reveal those qualities.

9. **Step Chart:** This chart can be used to list events in sequence, such as events in a story or steps in a process.

10. **Problem-Solution Chart:** This chart is used to list problems and solutions in a story.

11. **Word Log:** Students can use this log to list important words in what they are reading or to list words that they want to learn.

Idea Web

K-W-L Chart

Topic: ______________________________

What We Know	What We Want to Know	What We Learned

T-Chart

Venn Diagram

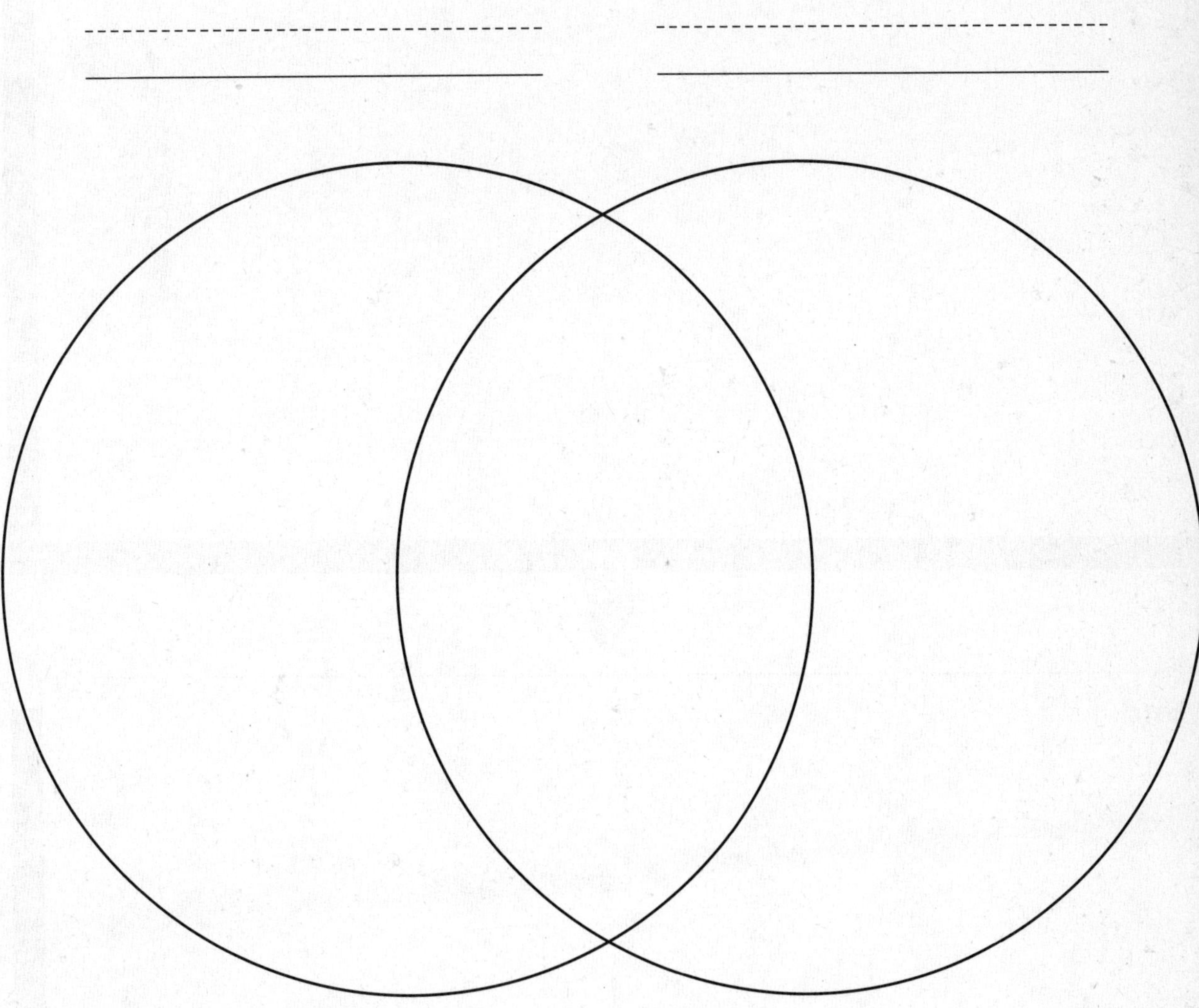

Story Sequence Chart

Beginning

Middle

End

Story Elements Chart

Title:

Setting:

Characters:

Problem:

Events:

Solution:

Main Idea Chart

Main Idea

Details

Character Trait Web

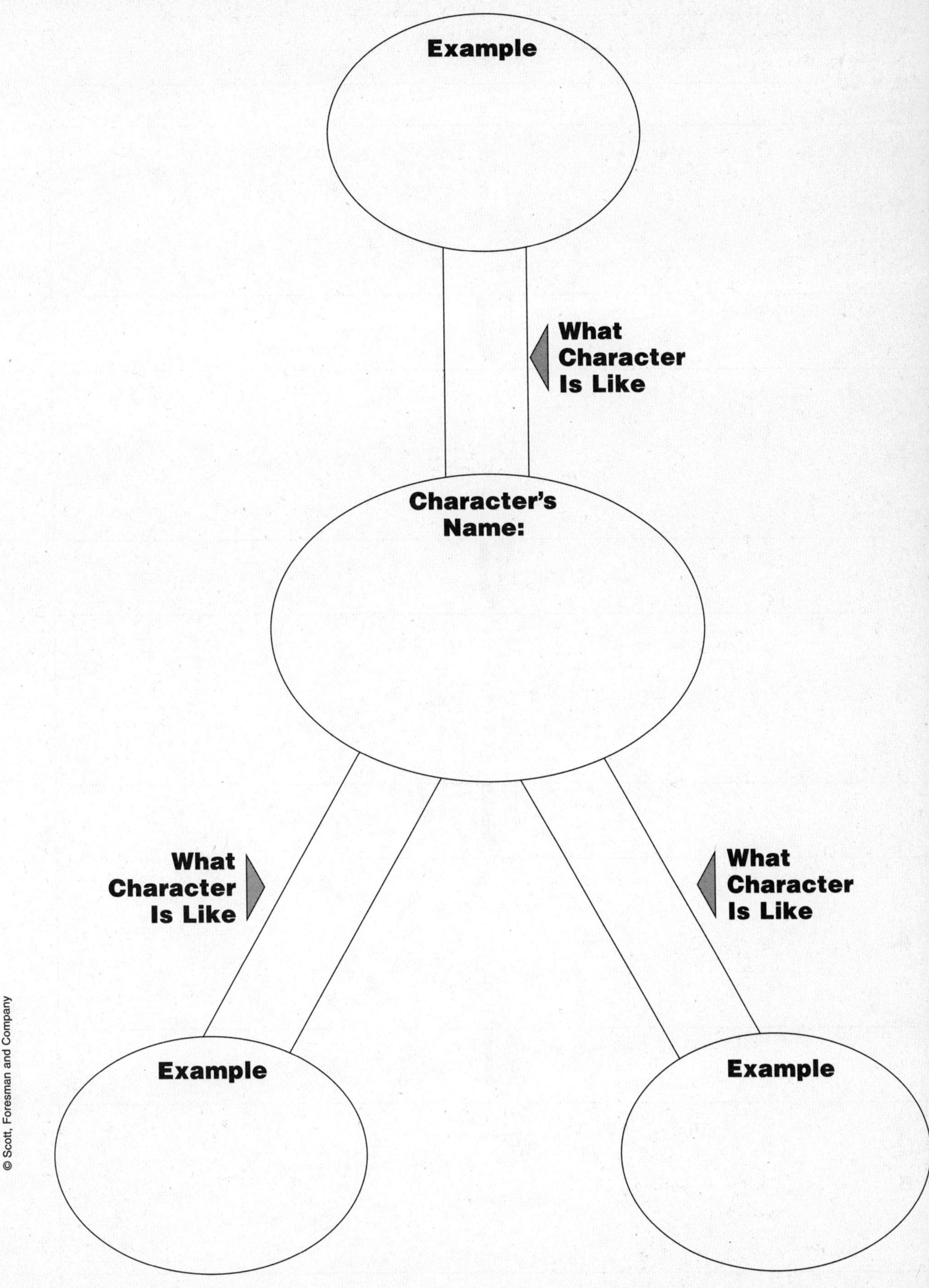

Step Chart

How to ______________________

1.

2.

3.

4.

5.

Name ______________________________

Problem-Solution Chart

Problem 1:

Solution

Problem 2:

Solution

Problem 3:

Solution

Word Log

Date	New Words I Learned

Chapter Self Assessment

Name ______________________________

Date ______________________________

Chapter number ______________________________

This chapter was about ______________________________

Read each statement. Check (✔) the box that is most true for you.

Statement	Not very well	OK	Well	Very well
I understand the main ideas in the chapter.				
I can ask and answer questions about the main ideas.				
I can tell someone about the main ideas.				
I can write about the main ideas.				

Write something you learned in the chapter.

____

____

____

____

____

____

____

An Invitation

Dear Family,

Please come to

____

____

on____

at___________ a.m./p.m. to see and hear about our latest project. Taking a few minutes to visit with us can be an important part of showing your child how important school is .

Please come.

Sincerely,

Teacher

An Invitation

Dear Family,

You are invited to see the latest class project your child has been working on. Please come to

____

____

on____

at______________a.m./p.m.

You will be able to see what the class is learning and share in the learning process.

Thank you.

Sincerely,

Teacher

Letter to the Family

Dear Family,

For the next few weeks, our class will be studying how scientists learn about the past. Students will find out how scientists learn about dinosaurs (the study of paleontology) and how scientists learn about ancient cultures (the study of archaeology).

Students will make museum displays about dinosaurs and ancient Egypt. They will make models of various dinosaurs and prepare a display about ancient Egypt.

You may have things at home that the students can use to help prepare their displays. These things include

- markers
- cardboard

The class will use these things to prepare their museum displays.

Thank you for helping with our unit called "Digging Up the Past."

Sincerely,

Teacher

Letter to the Family

Apreciada familia:

Durante las próximas semanas, estudiaremos cómo investigan el pasado los científicos. Averiguaremos cómo recogen datos acerca de los dinosaurios (lo que se conoce como paleontología) y acerca de culturas antiguas (lo que se conoce como arqueología).

Los estudiantes prepararán exhibiciones de esculturas de dinosaurios y de escenas del antiguo Egipto. Harán varios modelos de dinosaurios y una exhibición del antiguo Egipto. Éstas son algunas de las cosas que se necesitan para este proyecto y que ustedes podrían aportar:

- marcadores
- cartones

Nos servirán para las exhibiciones. Gracias por colaborar al estudio de esta unidad titulada "*Digging Up the Past*" ("Desenterremos el pasado").

Atentamente,

Maestro/a

Letter to the Family

មកដល់គ្រួសាររបស់សិស្ស

ក្នុងរយៈពេលពីរបីសប្ដាហ៍ខាងមុខនេះ កូនរបស់លោកអ្នកនឹងសិក្សាអំពីរបៀបដែលអ្នកវិទ្យាសាស្ត្រស្រាវជ្រាវរឿងអំពីអតីតកាល ។ គឺ សិស្សទាំងអស់នឹងស្វែងរកឲ្យដឹងនូវរបៀបដែលអ្នកវិទ្យាសាស្ត្រស្រាវជ្រាវអំពីសត្វដីណូស័រ (ការសិក្សាបាសិណភូតវិទ្យា) និងរបៀបអ្នកវិទ្យាសាស្ត្រស្រាវជ្រាវវប្បធម៌ជំនាន់ដើម (បុរេវិទ្យា) ។

ដោយវាជាផ្នែកមួយនៃការសិក្សាវិជ្ជានេះ សិស្សានុសិស្សទាំងឡាយនឹងបង្កើតសារៈមន្ទីរមួយដែលមានតាំងរូបសត្វដីណូស័រ និងវត្ថុ បូរាណនៃសញ្ជាតិអេហ្ស៊ីប ។ លោកអ្នកប្រហែលជាមានវត្ថុដូចរៀបរាប់ខាងក្រោមនេះដើម្បីជួយដល់កូន ឲ្យយកមករៀបចំការដាក់តាំងនៅសាលា ។ របស់ទាំងនេះមានដូចជា :

- បិចសំរាប់គូសចំណាំធំៗ
- ក្រដាសកាតុងសំរាប់គូរគំនូរ

សិស្សនឹងប្រើរបស់ទាំងនេះ ដើម្បីរៀបចំសារៈមន្ទីរនៅក្នុងសាលា ។ យើងសូមអរគុណលោកអ្នកដែលបានជួយដល់ការសិក្សារបស់ យើងដែលមានចំណងជើងថា "ការជីកស្រាវជ្រាវរឿងអតីតកាល" ៕

ហត្ថលេខា

គ្រូបង្រៀន

Letter to the Family

親愛的家長：

我們班上在下幾個星期中要學習科學家研究過去歷史的問題。學生要學習科學家怎樣研究恐龍(古生物學)及科學家怎樣研究古代文化(考古學)。

同學們要作有關恐龍和古代埃及的博物館展覽。他們要作各種恐龍的模型，及準備古代埃及的展覽。

你家中可能會有他們準備這次展覽的東西。這些物件包括：

- 記號筆
- 紙板

班上同學要用這些東西準備他們的博物館展覽。謝謝你對我們「發掘過去」這一單元的幫忙。

忠誠地

老師

Cantonese

Letter to the Family

Nyob Zoo Txog Tsev Neeg,

Ob peb vas thiv tom ntej no, peb yuav kawm txog yog ua cas cov neeg kawm paub txog toj raub hauv pes nroj tsuag xyoob ntoo (scientists) ho yuav kawm txog yav tag los. Peb tsev kawm ntawv yuav kawm txog ua cas scientists ho paub txog cov tsiaj dai naus xaum (dinosaurs) (ntawm qhov kev kawm txog toj raub hauv pes, nroj tsaug, xyoob ntoo "paleontology") thiab ua cas scientists ho kawm txog cov neeg txheej thaum ub lub neej (kev kaw txog kev tshuam xyuas tib neeg lub neej puag thaum ub).

Cov me nyuam yuav ua ib qho chaw tso cov khoom qub no tau saib txog dais naus xaum dinosaurs thiab cov neeg Egypt puag thaum ub. Lawv yuav npaj ua ib lub yeeb yam txog ntau yam dinosaurs thiab npaj ib co khoom saib txog cov qub neeg Egypt puag thaum ub. Tej zau koj yuav muaj tej yam khoom nyob tom tsev ua cov me nyuam yuav siv tau rau tom qhov chaw tso saib ntawd. Cov no xws lis

- cwj mem sim (markers)
- thawv ntawv

Cov me nyuam kawm ntawv yuav siv tej yam no coj los npaj rau qhov museum chaw txo saib ntawd.

Ua tsaug rau koj kev pab rau peb kev kawv txog fab hu ua "Dig Txog Yav Tag Los."

Sau Npe,

Xib Hwb

Hmong

Letter to the Family

Kính thưa quí vị phụ huynh

Trong vài tuần tới đây, các cháu sẽ học về cách thức các nhà khoa học nghiên cứu về quá khứ. Các cháu sẽ được biết cách thức các khoa học gia sưu tầm về các loại khủng long (khoa di tích học) và cách thức các khoa học gia sưu tầm về các nền văn hóa cổ (khoa khảo cổ học).

Các cháu sẽ thực hiện cuộc trưng bày di tích xưa về các con khủng long và về nước Ai Cập thời cổ. Các cháu sẽ lập nên các mô hình của vài loại khủng long và chuẩn bị cho cuộc trưng bày nước Ai Cập vào thời cổ. Có lẽ ở nhà quí vị có thể giúp cháu chuẩn bị cho các vật để trưng bày này. Chúng gao gồm:

- vài bút long màu
- thùng giấy

Các cháu sẽ dùng những món này để chuẩn bị cho buổi trưng bày di tích.

Xin cám ơn quí vị đã giúp cho bài học "Đào sâu Quá khứ" này.

Thành thật,

Giáo-viên

Vietnamese

ame ____

Chapter 1 Language Assessment

. Complete the sentences. Use the words in the box.

era	meat-eaters	skeletons
fossils	plant-eaters	

1. A large number of years is called an ________________.
2. Scientists can tell which dinosaurs were ________________ from their flat teeth.
3. Dinosaurs with sharp teeth were ________________.
4. After millions of years, dinosaurs' teeth and bones turn into stone ________________.
5. Scientists fit bones together to make ________________.

. Write **dinosaurs** after the facts about dinosaurs. Write **scientists** after the facts about scientists.

1. They divide history into eras and periods. ________________
2. We know from their footprints that some of them were quick and nimble.
   ____
3. They get information by studying fossils. ________________
4. Their name means "terrible lizards." ________________

dinosaur	egg	tooth	foot	fossil

. Fill in the blanks. Use words for more than one.

1. Some dinosaurs walked on four ________________.
2. Meat-eaters have sharp ________________.
3. Dinosaurs laid ________________ just as birds do.
4. ________________ lived before humans.
5. Dinosaur bones turned into ________________.

Name ______________________________

Chapter 1 Listening Assessment

Listen carefully. Dr. Paleo has just found some fossils for a new dinosaur. Circle the pictures that show what Dr. Paleo has discovered.

1\.

2\.

3\.

4\.

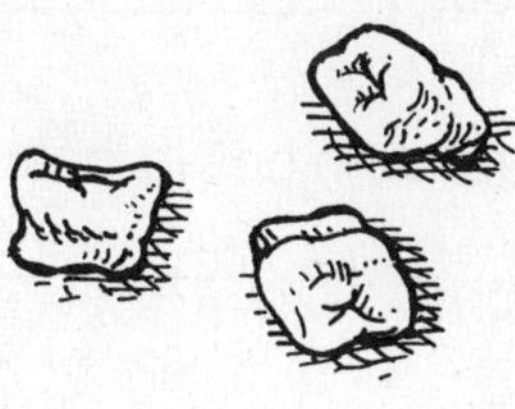

5\.

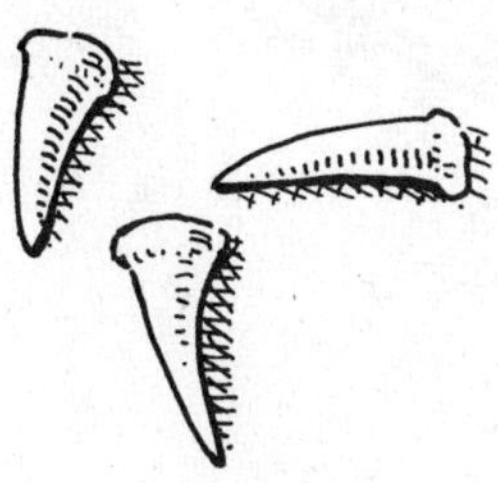

6\.

lame ______________________________

Chapter 2 Language Assessment

. Complete the sentences. Use the words in the box.

ancient	archaeologists	pyramids
mummies	hieroglyphics	pharaohs

1. The ____________________ Egyptians lived more than 3,000 years ago.
2. The ____________________ were Egyptian kings.
3. ____________________ are scientists who study about people who lived long, long ago.
4. Scientists discovered ____________________, which are preserved dead bodies wrapped in special cloth.
5. Tombs of some Egyptian kings were hidden in huge ____________________.
6. Scientists found ____________________ written on the walls of tombs.

. Use the words in the box to label the artifacts.

furniture	game	jewelry	weapon

1. ____________________

2. ____________________

3. ____________________

4. ____________________

Name ___

Chapter 2 Listening Assessment

Listen carefully. You will be told to draw items in the pyramid.
Draw the things you hear on the tape.

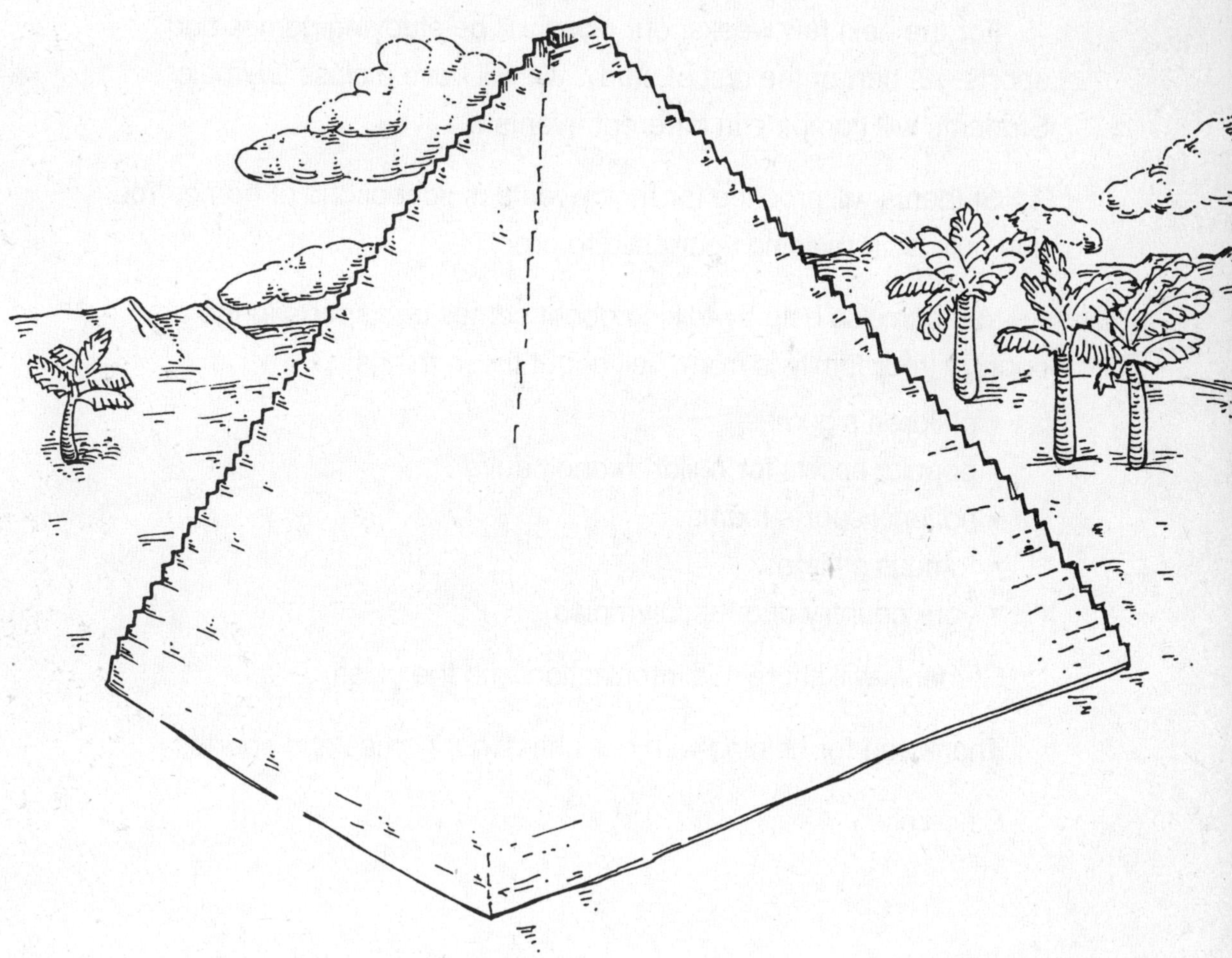

Letter to the Family

Dear Family,

For the next few weeks, our class will be studying games and sports. As part of the unit of study, we will have a class Olympics. Students will compete in different events.

Students will practice for their events at school and at home. You can help by reminding your child to practice.

You can also help by talking about games and sports in the country your family is from. Tell about these things:

- children's games
- popular sports for children and adults
- national sports teams
- famous athletes
- your country and the Olympics

Students will share this information with the class.

Thank you for helping with our unit about games and sports.

Sincerely,

Teacher

Letter to the Family

Apreciada familia:

Durante las próximas semanas, trataremos el tema de los juegos y los deportes. Como parte de esta unidad, realizaremos una olimpiada escolar con diversas competencias.

Los estudiantes entrenarán para las competencias tanto en la escuela como en la casa. Por favor, recuérdenle a su hijo/a que practique.

También podrían colaborar hablándole de los juegos y deportes propios de su país de origen, como por ejemplo:

- juegos infantiles
- deportes populares para niños y adultos
- equipos deportivos nacionales
- deportistas famosos
- participación del país en las olimpiadas

Los estudiantes transmitirán esta información al resto de la clase.

Gracias por ayudarnos con la unidad acerca de juegos y deportes.

Atentamente,

Maestro/a

Letter to the Family

មកដល់គ្រួសាររបស់សិស្ស

ក្នុងរយៈពេលពីរបីសប្តាហ៍ខាងមុខនេះ កូនរបស់លោកអ្នក នឹងសិក្សាអំពីល្បែងនិងកីឡា ។ ដោយវាជាផ្នែកមួយក្នុងការសិក្សាមេ រៀន នេះ យើងនឹងមានបើកការប្រកួតនៅក្នុងសាលារៀន ហើយកូនសិស្សទាំងឡាយនឹងធ្វើការប្រកួតប្រជែងល្បែង និងកីឡាផ្សេងៗ ។ ដូច្នេះ កូនរបស់លោកអ្នកនឹងហាត់សំរាប់ការប្រកួតនោះនៅផ្ទះ និងនៅសាលា ។ លោកអ្នកអាចជួយកូនរបស់ខ្លួនដោយជួយរំ ឭកឲ្យកូនខំប្រឹងហាត់ ។

លើសពីនេះទៀត លោកអ្នកអាចជួយនិយាយប្រាប់កូនរបស់ខ្លួនអំពីល្បែង និងកីឡាផ្សេងៗដែលមាននៅក្នុងស្រុកកំណើតរបស់ក្រុម គ្រួសារអ្នក ។ ចូរនិយាយប្រាប់កូនទូវរឿងដូចតទៅនេះ

- ល្បែងកូនក្មេង
- កីឡាទាំងឡាយដែលក្មេងៗ និងមនុស្សចាស់ចូលចិត្ត
- ក្រុមកីឡាប្រចាំជាតិ
- ឈ្មោះកីឡាករល្បីៗ
- កីឡាអូឡាំពិចនិងប្រទេសរបស់លោកអ្នក

កូនសិស្សនឹងយកពិតមាននេះ មកនិយាយប្រាប់មិត្តរួមថ្នាក់របស់គេ ដូច្នេះយើងសូមអរគុណដល់លោកអ្នកដែលបានជួយក្នុងកម្មវត្ថុ សិក្សា អំពីល្បែង និងកីឡារបស់យើង ៕

ហត្ថលេខា

គ្រូបង្រៀន

Letter to the Family

親愛的家長：

在下幾個星期中，我們班上要學習有關遊戲和運動的問題。我們要舉辦一個班級奧運會。同學們將從事各項競賽。

同學們要在學校和家裡練習他們的項目。請提醒他們經常練習。

你也可以跟小孩談論你們家鄉的遊戲及運動。請跟孩子談論下列事項：

- 兒童遊戲
- 兒童及成人流行的運動
- 代表國家的運動代表隊
- 你國家和奧運的關係

同學們會把他們在家所學的帶到班上與其他同學分享。

謝謝你對我們「遊戲與運動」這一單元的幫忙。

忠誠地

老師

Letter to the Family

Nyob Zoo Txog Tsev Neeg,

Ob peb vas thiv tom ntej no, peb tsev kawm ntawv yuav kawm txog kev ua si kis-las sports. Ua yog ib fab ntawm peb kev kawm, peb yuav muaj ib hoob Sib Tw Olympics. Cov me nyuam tub kawm ntawv yuav sib tw rau ntau yam kev kis-las.

Me nyuam kawm ntawv yuav xyaum rau cov kev sib tw ntawd rau tom tsev kawm ntawv thiab hauv vaj hauv tsev. Koj yuav pab tau xws lis yuav tau hais kom koj tus me nyuam nco qab ntsoov xyaum.

Koj kuj pab tau koj tus me nyuam xws lis nrog nws tham txog kev ncaws pob sports nyob rau lub teb chaws us koj tsev neeg tuaj ntawd. Qhia txog tej yam raws lis nram no:

- me nyuam kev ua sis games
- yam kev ua sis me nyuam yaus thiab cov laus nyiam
- tej pab tub ncaws pob hauv teb chaws
- tus neeg ncaws los yog ntaus pob muaj npe nrov
- koj lub teb chaws thiab ntawm kev sib tw Olympics

Cov me nyuam yuav pauv tswv yim txog tej yam no rau hauv tsev kawm ntawv.

Ua tsaug rau koj kev pab ntawm fab kawm txog kev us kis-las sports.

Sau Npe,

Xib Hwb

Letter to the Family

Kính thưa quí vị phụ huynh

Trong vài tuần tới đây, các cháu sẽ học về các môn chơi thể thao. Trong phần của bài học này chúng tôi sẽ thực hiện một Thế Vận Hội cho lớp học. Các cháu sẽ tranh tài với nhau trong nhiều trận đấu khác nhau.

Để đấu trong các trận, các cháu sẽ phải tập dợt ở nhà và tập dợt ở trường. Quí vị có thể giúp cháu học bằng cách nhắc nhở cháu tập dợt.

Quí vị cũng có thể giúp bằng cách kể lại các môn thể thao ở quê hương xứ sở của quí vị. Hãy kể đến:

- các môn thể thao cho trẻ con
- các môn thể thao bình dân cho người lớn và cho trẻ con
- những đội banh quốc gia
- những cầu thủ nổi tiếng
- nước của quí vị và các nước trong Thế Vận Hội

Các cháu sẽ trao đổi chuyện này với lớp học.

Xin cám ơn quí vị đã giúp cho bài học các môn thể thao này.

Thành thật,

Giáo-viên

Vietnamese

Name ____

Chapter 3 Language Assessment

A. Label the parts of the body. Use the words in the box.

elbow	heart	lung	muscle	shoulder

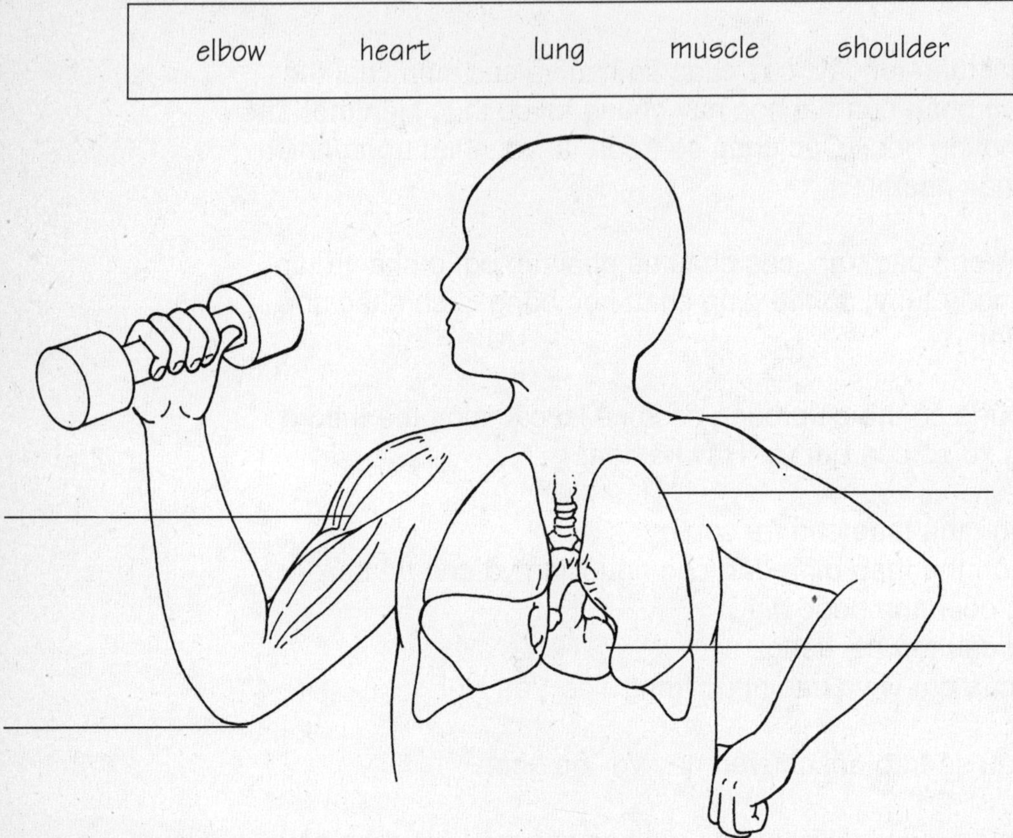

B. Draw lines from the kinds of fitness to their meanings.

Kinds of Fitness	**Meanings**
1. cardiovascular fitness	a. how easily you can move your joints
2. muscular endurance	b. how strong your heart and lungs are
3. flexibility	c. how much force your muscles can produce
4. strength	d. the amount of fat in your body
5. body fatness	e. how long you can use your muscles without getting tired

Name ______________________________

Chapter 3 Listening Assessment

Write the sentences you hear. They are steps in an exercise.

1. ______________________________

____

2. ______________________________

____

3. ______________________________

____

4. ______________________________

____

5. ______________________________

____

6. ______________________________

____

lame ______________________________

Chapter 4 Language Assessment

. Complete the sentences with the past tense of the verbs in parentheses.

The Olympic games __________ (begin) in ancient Greece. Athletes __________ (go) to lympia. There they __________ (compete) in such events as foot races and chariot races. he ancient games also __________ (include) speaking contests. The prize for winning __________ (is) a crown of leaves.

. Complete the sentences. Use information from the chart. It shows the order runners finished in the race.

Runner	Time
Sonya	2 hours 45 minutes
Peter	2 hours 47 minutes
Carlos	2 hours 55 minutes
Miyoko	2 hours 56 minutes
Ana	2 hours 57 minutes

Example: Sonya finished ___first___ in the race.

1. Carlos finished __________ in the race.
2. Peter finished __________ in the race.
3. Ana finished __________ in the race.
4. Miyoko finished __________ in the race.

. Write the sport next to its description.

baseball	diving	track and field	gymnastics

1. This is a team sport. __________
2. This sport is done in the water. __________
3. Races are part of this area of athletics. __________
4. This sport requires a high degree of balance and agility. __________

Name ______________________________

Chapter 4 Listening Assessment

Listen carefully. Circle the sports you hear talked about.

Letter to the Family

Dear Family,

For the next few weeks, our class will be studying oceans. We will build an ocean model in the classroom.

You can help your child learn about oceans. You may have things at home that students can use to build their models. These things include

- wax paper
- plastic wrap
- plastic shopping bags

Students will also learn about pollution. They will study ways to help protect the environment. You can help by talking about these topics:

- what things your family recycles
- how you prepare things to be recycled
- where you take things to be recycled
- what recycled products your family uses

Students will use these facts in class discussions of how to protect the environment.

Thank you for helping with our unit about oceans.

Sincerely,

Teacher

Letter to the Family

Apreciada familia:

Durante las próximas semanas, estudiaremos el tema de los mares y construiremos un modelo de un océano.

Para ayudar a su hijo/a en el aprendizaje de este tema, podrían aportar algunas cosas que necesitamos para este proyecto, como:

- papel encerado
- plástico de envolver
- bolsas grandes de plástico

También investigaremos acerca de la contaminación y de cómo proteger el medio ambiente. Les sugerimos que conversen con su hijo/a acerca de los siguientes temas:

- cosas que reciclan en su casa
- cómo las preparan para reciclarlas
- a dónde llevan los objetos de reciclaje
- qué productos reciclados usa la familia

Estos datos le servirán a su hijo/a para participar en las charlas acerca de la protección del medio ambiente.

Les agradecemos por ayudarnos con la unidad acerca de los mares.

Atentamente,

Maestro/a

Letter to the Family

មកដល់គ្រួសាររបស់សិស្ស

ក្នុងរយៈពេលពីរបីសប្តាហ៍ខាងមុខនេះ ថ្នាក់រៀនរបស់យើង នឹងសិក្សាអំពីសមុទ្រ ។ ដូច្នេះ យើងនឹងបង្កើតសមុទ្រគំរូមួយនៅក្នុង ថ្នាក់រៀន ។

លោកអ្នកអាចជួយបង្រៀនកូនខ្លួនអំពីសមុទ្រផងដែរ ដោយរកវត្ថុដូចតទៅនេះ (ប្រសិនបើមាន) ដើម្បីឲ្យកូនយកមកសង់រូបសមុទ្រគំរូ នៅនឹងសាលា ។ របស់ទាំងនោះ មានដូចជា :

- ក្រដាសមានជាតិក្រមួន
- ផ្លាស្ទិកសម្រាប់រុំ ឬខ្ចប់
- ថង់ផ្លាស្ទិកដាក់ឥវ៉ាន់

សិស្សានុសិស្សនឹងសិក្សាអំពីភាពក្រខ្វក់របស់ទឹក និងរបស់បរិអាកាសផងដែរ ។ គេនឹងរៀនទូវរបៀបការពារបរិយាកាស ដែលមាននៅជុំវិញខ្លួនយើងនេះ ។ លោកអ្នកអាចជួយ ដោយនិយាយប្រាប់កូនទូវរឿងទាំងឡាយដែលប្រធានដូចតទៅនេះ

- របស់អ្វីដែលគ្រួសារលោកអ្នកតែងតែដាក់ក្នុងធុងសំរាម ដើម្បីឲ្យគេយកទៅរំលាយធ្វើជាអ្វីសំរាប់ប្រើឡើងវិញ
- របៀបដែលលោកអ្នករៀបចំរបស់ ទុកឲ្យគេយកទៅរំលាយធ្វើជាអ្វីមួយសំរាប់ប្រើសាជាថ្មី
- ទីកន្លែងដែលលោកអ្នកដាក់របស់ ទុកឲ្យគេយកទៅរំលាយធ្វើជាអ្វីមួយសំរាប់ប្រើសាជាថ្មី
- ប្រដាប់ប្រដាដែលគេអាចយកទៅរំលាយធ្វើជាអ្វីមួយសំរាប់ប្រើសាជាថ្មីដែល ក្រុមគ្រួសាររបស់លោកអ្នក ទិញប្រើ ។

សិស្សានុសិស្សទាំងឡាយនឹងយករឿងនេះមកពិភាក្សាគ្នានៅក្នុងសាលា ហើយរកមធ្យោបាយការពារបរិយាកាសរបស់យើង ។ យើងសូមអរគុណលោកអ្នកដែលបានជួយដល់កម្មវិធីសិក្សាអំពីសមុទ្ររបស់យើង ៕

ហត្ថលេខា

គ្រូបង្រៀន

Letter to the Family

親愛的家長：

我們班上在下幾個星期中要學習海洋問題。我們要在班上建造一個海洋模型。

你可以在家幫孩子學習海洋。他們要學習保護環境的方法。跟孩子談論下列的題目會幫助他們了解這一單元的內容：

- 你家拿來循環使用的東西
- 你們怎樣準備要用來循環使用的東西
- 你們把東西拿到那裡去讓它們能重新被再次使用
- 你家用那些由循環使用材料製造的產品

同學們將用這些資料在班上討論保護環境的方法。

謝謝你們對我們「海洋」這一單元的幫忙。

忠誠地

老師

Letter to the Family

Nyob Zoo Txog Tsev Neeg,

Ob peb vas thiv tom ntej no, peb tsev kawm ntawv yuav kawm txog hiav txwv. Peb yuav tsim ib lub qauv hais txog hiav txwv rau hau tsev kawm ntawv.

Koj kuj yuav pab tau koj tus me nyuam kawm txog hiav txwv. Tej zaum koj yuav muaj tej yam khoom nyob hauv tsev ua cov me nyuam kawm ntawv yuav siv tau coj los ua lub qauv hiav txwv ntawd. Cov no xws lis yog

- ntawv lo ciab (wax)
- ntawv roj hmab qhwv
- hnab ntawv ntim khoom

Cov me nyuam kuj yuav tau kawm txog pa roj pa av. Lawv yuav kawm txog txoj kev yuav ceev kom tsis txhob muaj khoom phem nyob puag ncig yus. Koj kuj yuav pab tau nws yog koj nrog nws tham txog tej yam lis nrag no:

- yam khoom nej tsev neeg xa rov qab coj mus siv duav yog yam dab tsis
- cov khoom nej xa rov qab coj mus siv duav ntawd nej npaj lis cas
- nej coj cov khoom xa rov qab mus siv duav ntawd mus rau qhov twg
- yam khoom siv nej tsev neeg coj mus siv duas ntawd yog dab tsis

Cov me nyuam tub kawm ntawv ntawd yuav muab tej yam tseeb no coj mus tham txog kev ceev kom txhob muaj tej yam khoom phem nyob puag ncig yus.

Ua tsaug rau koj kev pab txog ntawm peb kev kawm fab hiav txwv.

Sau Npe,

Xib Hwb

Letter to the Family

Kính thưa quí vị phụ huynh

Trong vài tuần tới đây, các cháu sẽ học về các biển cả. Chúng tôi sẽ tạo ra một mô hình biển cả trong lớp học.

Quí vị có thể giúp cháu học về biển cả. Có thể quí vị có vài món đồ mà các cháu sẽ dùng vào việc tạo ra mô hình biển cả. Những món đó bao gồm có:

- giấy sáp
- miếng ny lông mỏng
- bao ny lông

Các cháu sẽ học về sự ô nhiễm nữa. Các cháu sẽ nghiên cứu về những cách thức bảo vệ môi trường. Quí vị có thể giúp bàn về những đề tài sau đây:

- gia đình quí vị tái chu kỳ (dùng đi dùng lại) những món gì
- quí vị sắp xếp như thế nào trước khi cho món đồ đi vào tái chu kỳ
- quí vị mang các món đồ đến đâu để cho tái chu kỳ
- gia đình quí vị dùng những món đồ gì đã được tái chu kỳ

Các cháu sẽ sử dụng những sự kiện này để thảo luận trong lớp hầu để biết cách bảo vệ môi trường.

Xin cám ơn quí vị đã giúp đỡ trong bài học về biển cả này.

Thành thật,

Giáo-viên

Name ____

Chapter 5 Language Assessment

A. Draw lines to match each ocean word with the sentence that tells about it.

Ocean Words	**Sentences**
1. shore	a. This fills the ocean. You don't want to drink it!
2. salt water	b. Some of these are the tops of volcanoes.
3. sea animals	c. These can be very, very deep.
4. light zone	d. These include fish, whales, and dolphins.
5. islands	e. You will find shells here.
6. trenches	f. Many fish and plants live in this level of water.
7. coral reef	g. These are found near the shore and have colorful fish.

B. Complete the sentences. Use the words in the box.

darker	less food	more light	warmer

1. Trenches are ____________________ than coral reefs.
2. Fewer fish live in the dark zone. There is ____________________ there.
3. Many plants live near the top of the ocean because there is ____________________ there.
4. The light zone is ____________________ than the dark zone.

Name ____________________

Chapter 5 Listening Assessment

Listen carefully. Circle the areas of the ocean you hear talked about.
Circle the numbers you hear.

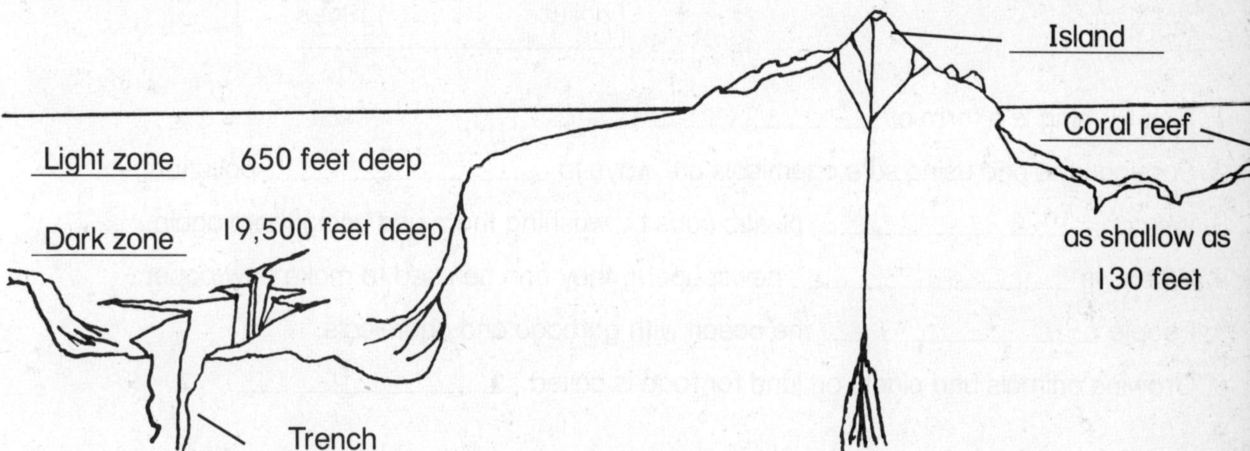

Name ______________________________

Chapter 6 Language Assessment

A. Complete the sentences. Use the words in the box.

agriculture	recycle
aquaculture	reduce
pollute	reuse

1. Fish farming is a form of ________________.
2. Passing laws and using safe chemicals are ways to ________________ pollution.
3. We can ________________ plastic cups by washing them and using them again.
4. When we ________________ newspapers, they can be used to make new paper.
5. People ________________ the ocean with garbage and chemicals.
6. Growing animals and plants on land for food is called ________________.

B. Write **cause** under the causes of pollution. Write **effect** under the effects of pollution.

1. Oil tankers spill oil into the oceans.

____

2. People throw garbage on the beach and into the water.

____

3. Animals are harmed and killed.

____

4. Farmers use chemical fertilizers. These chemicals run into the ocean.

____

5. Plants are harmed and killed.

____

C. Complete the question with the correct word.

Who	What	Where	When	Why

__________ started the recycling project? Sixth-graders in Smith School.
__________ did they start the project? Last September.
__________ do they do? They collect cans of paper and take them to recycling centers.
__________ do they collect cans? They collect from areas around the school.
__________ did they start the project? They wanted to protect the environment.

Name ______________________________

Chapter 6 Listening Assessment

Listen carefully. Circle the projects that the school is doing.

1.

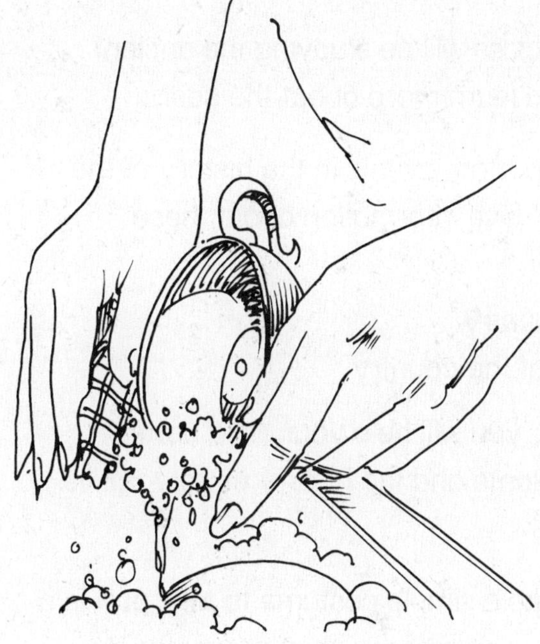

2.

3.

4.

Letter to the Family

Dear Family,

For the next few weeks, our class will be studying the ancient Romans. You can help your child learn more about the past.

Talk with your child about important events in the history of the country you are from. You might give information about these topics:

- the early history of your country
- main events in the history of the country

By providing this information, you will help your child better understand both the history of Rome and the history of your native country.

Students will be asked to make a simple costume to take part in a Roman Day. You can help gather some of the costume materials. These include

- old bed sheets
- string or cord

Thank you for helping us with our study of Rome and with our Roman Day.

Sincerely,

Teacher

Letter to the Family

Apreciada familia:

Durante las próximas semanas, estudiaremos el tema de los antiguos romanos.

Para ayudar a su hijo/a a entender el pasado, háblenle acerca de su país de origen. Pueden contemplar los siguientes temas:

- orígenes e historia patria
- principales sucesos históricos del país

Esta información le ayudará a su hijo/a a entender mejor tanto la historia de Roma como la de su país de procedencia.

Los estudiantes elaborarán un sencillo disfraz para participar en "El día de Roma". Quizá ustedes puedan aportar algunos de los siguientes materiales:

- sábanas viejas
- cuerdas o cordeles

Gracias por colaborar al estudio de los romanos y a la celebración del día dedicado a Roma.

Atentamente,

Maestro/a

Letter to the Family

មកដល់គ្រួសាររបស់សិស្ស

ក្នុងរយៈពេលពីរបីសប្តាហ៍ខាងមុខនេះ ថ្នាក់រៀនរបស់យើងនឹងសិក្សាអំពីបុរាណកាលនៃជនជាតិរ៉ូម៉ាំង ។ លោកអ្នកអាចជួយកូនលោក អ្នក ដោយបង្រៀនកូនអំពីរឿងអតីតកាល ។

ចូរនិយាយប្រាប់ក្មេងអំពីព្រឹត្តិការណ៍សំខាន់ៗ ដែលមាននៅក្នុងប្រវត្តិសាស្ត្រនៃមាតុភូមិរបស់លោកអ្នក ។ លោកអ្នកអាចនិយាយប្រាប់ នូវរឿងដែលមានប្រធានដូចតទៅនេះ

- ប្រវត្តិដំបូងនៃមាតុភូមិរបស់លោកអ្នក
- ព្រឹត្តិការណ៍ធំៗដែលមាននៅក្នុងប្រវត្តិសាស្ត្រនៃមាតុភូមិរបស់លោកអ្នក

ដោយការនិយាយប្រាប់នូវរឿងរ៉ាវដូចខាងលើនេះ លោកអ្នកនឹងជួយឲ្យក្មេង បានយល់កាន់តែច្បាស់អំពីប្រវត្តិសាស្ត្រទាំងពីរ គឺប្រវត្តិ សាស្ត្ររបស់ជនជាតិរ៉ូម៉ាំង និងប្រវត្តិសាស្ត្រនៃមាតុភូមិរបស់លោកអ្នក។

យើងនឹងសុំឲ្យសិស្សទាំងអស់ធ្វើវត្ថុអ្វីមួយជាគំរូ ដែលបង្ហាញអំពីទំនៀមទម្លាប់ក្នុងសម័យដើមរបស់ជនជាតិរ៉ូម៉ាំង ។ ដូច្នេះ លោកអ្នក អាចជួយរកសម្ភារៈដែលបង្ហាញពីទំនៀមទម្លាប់ឲ្យកូនរបស់លោកអ្នកបានស្គាល់ ។ របស់ទាំងនោះមានដូចជា :

- កំរាលពូកជំនាន់ដើម
- អំបោះ ឬខ្សែ

យើងសូមអរគុណដល់លោកអ្នក ដែលបានជួយដល់កម្មវិធីសិក្សា អំពីបុរាណកាលនៃជនជាតិរ៉ូម៉ាំងរបស់យើង ៕

ហត្ថលេខា

គ្រូបង្រៀន

Letter to the Family

親愛的家長：

我們班上在下幾個星期中要學習有關古代羅馬的事蹟，你可以幫孩子多學習些有閱過去的事情。

跟你小孩談論你國家歷史上重要的事件。你可以談論下列的題目：

・你國家的早期歷史

・你國家歷史上的大事

跟孩子談論這些題目，可以令他們對羅馬歷史及你家鄉歷史有更深的了解。

我們要同學們準備一件簡單的服裝來參加學校的「羅馬日」。你可以幫孩子準備一些製造服裝的材料。這些材料可以是：

・舊床單

・細繩子或燈芯絨線

謝謝你對我們學習「羅馬」這一單元及我們「羅馬日」的幫忙。

忠誠地

老師

Letter to the Family

Nyob Zoo Txog Tsev Neeg,

Ob peb vas thiv tom ntej no, peb tsev kawm ntawv yuav kawm txog cov neeg txheej puag thaum ub hus ua Romans. Koj yuav pab tau koj tus me nyuam kawm txog yav tag los.

Nrog koj tus me nyuam tham txog tej yam tseem ceeb us muaj yav tag los nyob rau lub teb chaws koj tuaj. Tej zaum koj kuj muaj txog tej yam pab vav txog lis nram no:

- pab vav hais txog puag thaum ub hauv koj lub teb chaws
- tej yam muaj nuj nqis muaj pab vav haus lub teb chaws

Pab tau tej yam no, koj yuav pab tau koj tus me nyuam to taub zoo dua txog ntawm pab vav hais txog Rome thiab pab vav ntawm nej lub teb chaws.

Cov me nyuam kawm ntawv yuav npaj tej yam tsoos tsho ua yooj yim hais txog Roman Lub Neej Thaum Ub. Koj yuav pab tau tej yam khoom tsoos tsho. Xws lis tej yam no

- ntaub pua txaj qub
- hlua los yog cov

Ua koj tsaug rau kev pab ntawm peb kev kawm txog Rome thiab neeg Roman thaum ub.

Sau Npe,

Xib Hwb

Letter to the Family

Kính thưa quí vị phụ huynh

Trong vài tuần tới đây, cháu sẽ học về các người La Mã vào thời cổ. Quí vị có thể giúp cháu học thêm về quá khứ.

Quí vị cùng bàn với cháu về những sự kiện quan trọng trong lịch sử của quê hương xứ sở của quí vị. Thiết tưởng quí vị có thể cho biết các đề tài sau đây:

- lịch sử lúc ban đầu mới dựng nước
- những sự kiện chính xảy ra trong lịch sử sủa quê hương xứ sở quí vị

Khi cho biết các dữ kiện như vậy, quí vị giúp cháu hiểu rỏ cả vừa lịch sử của La Mã vừa lịch sử của chính quê hương xứ sở của quí vị.

Các cháu sẽ được yêu cầu làm ra một bộ y phục đơn giản để tham dự vào Ngày La Mã.

Quí vị có thể giúp cháu thâu nhặt vải để làm y phục này. Các món ấy gồm có :

- các miếng vải trải giường cũ
- dây thừng hoặc dây gai

Xin cám ơn quí vị đã giúp trong bài học La Mã và ngày La Mã.

Thành thật,

Giáo-viên

ame ______________________________

Chapter 7 Language Assessment

. Complete the sentences. Use the words in the box.

aqueducts	arenas	forum	law	shops
arches	army	Latin	roads	temples

1. Roman ____________ let rich men and poor men vote.
2. The Romans were the first to use ____________ in their buildings.
3. The ____________ was the center of the city and of government.
4. The Romans built ____________ to honor their gods.
5. The Romans built ____________ to connect Rome to other parts of the empire.
6. The Romans enjoyed sports events at ____________.
7. People could get things they needed at ____________ in the city.
8. The ____________ language spread through the empire.
9. A strong Roman ____________ helped the empire to grow.
0. The Romans built ____________ to carry water to cities.

. Complete the chart. Write the meaning of each prefix and the meaning of each word.

Prefix	Words	Meaning of Prefix	Meaning of Word
1. pre	pregame		
2. re	rewrite		
3. uni	unicycle		

. Add the containers for the items used in the recipes. Use the words in the box. Use each phrase one time.

a bag of	a jar of	a bottle of	a carton of	a can of

____________ tuna

____________ honey

____________ dates

____________ eggs

____________ salad dressing

Name ______________________________

Chapter 7 Listening Assessment

Listen carefully. A student is talking about what she learned about the ancient Romans. Circle the places that she mentions.

Name ____

Chapter 8 Language Assessment

A. The things listed in the box were found in the ashes of Pompeii. Some things were in houses. Some things were in other parts of the city. Write the five things that were in houses.

atrium	forum	shops
bakery	kitchen	snack bar
dining room	pots	temple
dishes	roads	

Things Found in Pompeii Houses

1. ____________________
2. ____________________
3. ____________________
4. ____________________
5. ____________________

B. Complete the sentences. Use the past tense of the words in the box.

come	run	sink
make	ring	watch

1. The farmer's plow __________ into the ground.
2. Smoke __________ out of the hole, and there were rumbling noises.
3. The farmer and his son __________ for the village.
4. The farmer __________ the bell to warn people.
5. All night, the people __________ the mountain grow.
6. The soldiers __________ people move away.

C. Write the words that relate to volcanoes on the lines. Then match each one to its definition.

erupt	flood	lava	storm	cinder	shield	hurricane

1. ______________ a. burst out

2. ______________ b. hot rock

3. ______________ c. type of volcano

4. ______________ d. pieces of burned rock

Name ______________________________

Chapter 8 Listening Assessment

Listen carefully. Write the sentences.

Letter to the Family

Dear Family,

For the next few weeks, our class will be studying the physics of movement. Students will do experiments to learn basic science facts.

Your child will be participating in a project in which students describe and record examples of various types of motion that children engage in on playgrounds.

You can help your child learn. Ask him or her about the project on a regular basis.

You may have things at home that the class can use for its experiments and observations. These things include sport equipments such as

- soccer balls
- hockey sticks
- skates

Students will use these sports equipment to study friction, gravity, and other rules of physics.

Thank you for helping with our unit about physics.

Sincerely,

Teacher

Letter to the Family

Apreciada familia:

Durante las próximas semanas, estudiaremos la física del movimiento. Los estudiantes harán experimentos que les permitirán aprender conceptos científicos básicos.

Su hijo/a participará en un proyecto que consiste en describir y anotar ejemplos de los movimientos que hacen los niños en los patios de juego.

Para ayudar a su hijo/a en el aprendizaje del tema, pregúntenle con frecuencia cómo va el proyecto.

Para los experimentos y observaciones necesitamos algunos objetos que quizá ustedes puedan aportar:

- balones de fútbol soccer
- palos de hockey
- patines

Con ese equipo deportivo los estudiantes investigarán los conceptos de fricción, gravedad y otras reglas de la física.

Gracias por su colaboración en el estudio de esta unidad.

Atentamente,

Maestro/a

Letter to the Family

មកដល់គ្រួសាររបស់សិស្ស

ក្នុងរយៈពេលពីរបីសប្ដាហ៍ខាងមុខនេះ ថ្នាក់រៀនរបស់យើង នឹងសិក្សាអំពីរូបវិទ្យានៃចលនា ។ សិស្សទាំងឡាយ នឹងធ្វើការពិសោធន៍ ដើម្បីរៀនភាពពិតដែលជាគោលនៃវិទ្យាសាស្ត្រ ។

កូនរបស់លោកអ្នក នឹងចូលរួមក្នុងសកម្មភាពមួយ ដែលសិស្សទាំងអស់នឹងកត់ទុកជាឯកសារ និងអធិប្បាយជាឧទាហរណ៍នូវសកម្មភាព អ្វីមួយរបស់ក្មេងដែលកំពុងលេងនៅក្នុងសួន ។ ដូច្នេះ លោកអ្នកអាចជួយកូនរបស់ខ្លួន ដោយសួរអំពីការងារដែលគ្រូដាក់ឲ្យនេះ ឲ្យ បានញឹកញាប់ និងទៀងទាត់ ។ នៅផ្ទះ លោកអ្នកប្រហែលជាមានរបស់ដូចរៀបរាប់ខាងក្រោមនេះ សំរាប់ឲ្យសិស្សប្រើក្នុងការធ្វើ កិច្ចពិសោធន៍ស្រាវជ្រាវនេះហើយ ។ របស់ទាំងនោះមានដូចជា :

- បាល់ទាត់
- ឈើលេងហក់គី (Hockey)
- ស្បែកជើងដែលមានបាតធ្វើពីដែកស្រួចៗសំរាប់ពាក់ដើរលើទឹកកក

សិស្សនឹងយកសម្ភារៈកីឡាទាំងនេះទៅប្រើ ដើម្បីសិក្សាអំពីភាពត្រដុសឬកកិតគ្នា អំពីទំនាញផែនដី និងអំពីក្បួនផ្សេងៗរបស់រូបវិទ្យា ។ យើងសូមអរគុណដល់លោកអ្នក ដែលបានជួយដល់កម្មវិធីសិក្សារបស់យើង ៕

ហត្ថលេខា

គ្រូបង្រៀន

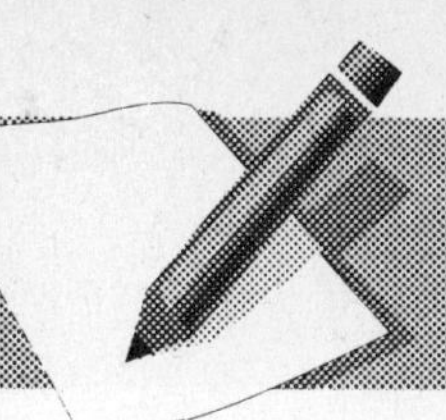

Letter to the Family

親愛的家長：

在下幾個星期中，我們班上要學習移動的物理作用。學生要做有關基本科學事實的實驗。

你的小孩要作一個研讀項目作業。在這個作業中學生們要描述和記錄小孩在操場上做的各種和動有關的活動。你可以在家幫他們學習這個題目，請經常查詢他們作業的進度。你家裡可能有班上能借用來作實驗和觀察的物件。這些物件多是運動器材，如：

- 足球
- 曲棍球球棍
- 溜冰鞋

同學們要用這些運動器材來學習磨擦力，地心引力，和其物理規則。

謝謝你對我們「物理作用」這一學習單元的幫忙。

忠誠地
老師

Letter to the Family

Nyob Zoo Txog Tsev Neeg,

Ob peb vas thiv tom ntej no, peb tsev kawm ntawv yuav kawm txog physics us yog yam txawj txav. Cov me nyuam tub kawm ntawv yuav xyaum kawm txog hauv paus ntawm science qhov tseeb.

Koj tus me nyuam yuav tau koom tes rau qhov kev kawm ua lawv yuav hais txog thiab muab sau piv txwv txog ntau yam me nyuam yaus tau siv ua sis nyob rau hauv chaw ua sis. Koj yuav pab tau koj tus me nyuam kawm. Nug nws txog yam nws kawm txog ntawd rau txhua lub sij hawm. Tej zaum koj kuj yuav muaj tej yam nyob tom vaj tom tsev us peb yuav sis tau rau peb kev xyaum thiab saib no. Tej yam no kuj xws lis khoom kis-las.

- lub npas ncaws
- pas ntaus hockey
- khauv caij dej khov (skates)

Me nyuam kawm ntawv yuav siv cov yam khoom no coj los kawm txog, yam khoom nyob tsis tau ua ke, tej yam sib thiab hyav, thiab lwm yam ntawm physics.

Ua koj tsaug rau kev pab ntawm peb kev kawm fab physics no.

Sau Npe,

Xib Hwb

Letter to the Family

Kính thưa quí vị phụ huynh

Trong vài tuần tới đây, cháu sẽ học về các qui luật vật lý của động tác. Các cháu sẽ làm các thí nghiệm để học những sự việc khoa học căn bản.

Cháu sẽ tham gia vào một dự án trong đó các học sinh mô tả và ghi chép xuống những loại chuyển động mà trẻ con đang chơi trong sân trường.

Quí vị có thể giúp cháu học bằng cách thường xuyên hỏi về cái dự án ấy. Quí vị có thể có những món đồ ở nhà mà các cháu dùng được trong lớp để làm các bài thí nghiệm và quan sát. Những món đó bao gồm các dụng cụ thể thao như:

- trái banh
- que chơi hockey
- giầy trợt trên băng đá

Các cháu sẽ dùng những dụng cụ thể thao này để học về sự cọ sát, về trọng lượng, và về các qui luật vật lý khác.

Xin cám ơn quí vị đã giúp cho bài học vật lý này.

Thành thật,

Giáo-viên

Name ____

Chapter 9 Language Assessment

A. Under each picture, write the word that tells about the action. Use the words in the box.

blow	kick	pull
jump	push	throw

1. ________________ 2. ________________ 3. ________________

4. ________________ 5. ________________ 6. ________________

B. Draw a line from each word to its definition.

Words

1. motion
2. force
3. friction
4. gravity

Meanings

a. the force that draws objects toward the center of the earth

b. the force that slows down the motion of surfaces that touch

c. the movement of an object from one place to another

d. the power to cause motion, or to stop or change motion

Name ____________________

Chapter 9 Listening Assessment

Listen carefully. For each item, circle the pictures you are told to circle.

1.

2.

3.

Name ___________________________________

Chapter 9 Language Assessment

A. Complete the sentences. Use the words in the box.

curves	motor	down
stops	motion	work

1. Energy is the ability to do ____________.
2. A roller coaster builds up energy from ____________.
3. A roller coaster needs a ____________ to climb the first hill because it hasn't built up any energy yet.
4. A roller coaster uses energy from going ____________ the first hill to go up the second hill.
5. When a roller coaster goes on twists and ____________, it uses energy.
6. When a roller coaster uses up all its energy, it ____________.

B. The words in the box all tell ways to move. Write each word under the heading that tells whether it means to move slowly or to move quickly.

crawl	inch	rush	zoom
dash	lumber	stroll	

To move slowly	**To move quickly**
____________	____________
____________	____________
____________	____________
____________	____________

C. Complete the conditional sentences. Use the verb in parentheses.

1. If I rode a roller coaster for two days, I ________________ (be) tired.
2. If I could ride any roller coaster, I ________________ (want) to ride the Cyclone.
3. If I could build a roller coaster, it ________________ (have) a lot of curves.
4. If I could go on a tall roller coaster, I ________________ (be) very excited.

Name ____________________

Chapter 10 Listening Assessment

Listen carefully. Follow the directions. Number the pictures of the roller coaster.

☐

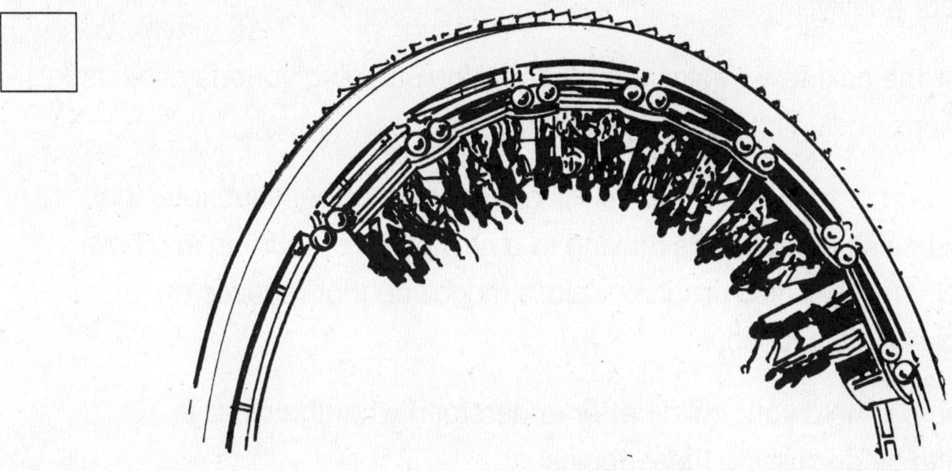

☐

☐

Letter to the Family

Dear Family,

For the next few weeks, our class will be studying various aspects of change, including handling stress.

As part of the unit, students will act out skits about situations that can cause stress, such as moving to a new place or starting in a new school. They will also prepare a class magazine that focuses on changes in life situations.

You can help your child better understand what the class is studying by discussing these topics:

- changes that your family has faced since you moved to the United States
- ways your family handles changes as they come along

Thank you for helping us make the project a successful one.

Sincerely,

Teacher

Letter to the Family

Apreciada familia:

Durante las próximas semanas, estudiaremos varios aspectos del cambio. Uno de ellos es cómo manejar la tensión nerviosa.

Como parte de la unidad, los estudiantes representarán escenas teatrales sobre situaciones que pueden causar estrés, tales como el traslado a un nuevo lugar o el ingreso a una nueva escuela. Además, harán una revista colectiva dedicada a diversos cambios en la vida.

Para ayudar a su hijo/a a entender mejor el tema, conversen acerca de lo siguiente:

- Cómo ha cambiado su vida desde que llegaron a los Estados Unidos.
- Cómo ha enfrentado la familia esos cambios.

Gracias por ayudarnos con la realización de este proyecto.

Atentamente,

Maestro/a

Letter to the Family

មកដល់គ្រួសាររបស់សិស្ស

ក្នុងរយៈពេលពីរបីសប្តាហ៍ខាងមុខនេះ ថ្នាក់រៀនរបស់យើង នឹងសិក្សាអំពីទស្សនៈទាំងឡាយនៃការផ្លាស់ប្តូរ ហើយនិងវិធីដោះ ស្រាយវិបត្តិ ។

ដោយវាជាផ្នែកមួយនៃការសិក្សា កូនសិស្សជាច្រើននឹងសម្តែងជារឿងមួយ ដោយស្តីអំពីស្ថានការណ៍ដែលបណ្តាលឲ្យកើតមានវិបត្តិ ដូចជា ការរើផ្ទះទៅនៅក្នុងកន្លែងថ្មីមួយ ឬការចូលទៅរៀននៅក្នុងសាលាថ្មីមួយជាដើម ។ លើសពីនេះ សិស្សទាំងឡាយនឹងរៀប ជាទស្សនាវដ្តីសំរាប់សិក្សាមួយ ដែលនិយាយអំពីការផ្លាស់ប្តូ រស្ថានភាពក្នុងការរស់នៅ ។

លោកអ្នកអាចជួយក្មេងឲ្យយល់បន្ថែមនូវអ្វីដែលយើងកំពុងសិក្សានេះ ដោយពិភាក្សានូវរឿងទាំងឡាយដែលមានប្រធានដូចតទៅនេះ

- ការផ្លាស់ប្តូរដែលក្រុមគ្រួសាររបស់លោកអ្នកបានជួបប្រទះ នៅពេលដែលបានរើមកនៅក្នុងសហរដ្ឋអាមេរិកនេះ
- របៀបដែលក្រុមគ្រួសាររបស់លោកអ្នក ដោះស្រាយបញ្ហាពីការផ្លាស់ប្តូរនេះ នៅពេលដែលខ្លួនបានជួបប្រទះ

យើងសូមអរគុណលោកអ្នក ដែលបានជួយធ្វើឲ្យកម្មវិធីសិក្សារបស់យើងនេះ បានសម្រេច ៕

ហត្ថលេខា

គ្រូបង្រៀន

Letter to the Family

親愛的家長：

我們班上在下幾個星期中要學習有關變遷的各種情況，包括對生活壓力的處理方法。

班上同學將演出各種能製造生活壓力情況的短劇，例如搬到新地區或到新學校上課的情況等。他們還要編寫一份和生活改變有關的雜誌。

如果你能和孩子討論下列的題目，這能幫助他們對班上所學的有更深的認識：

・你們搬來美國所遭遇的變遷

・你們家裡處理生活壓力的方法

謝謝你幫我們使這一研讀項目成功。

忠誠地

老師

Cantonese

Letter to the Family

Nyob Zoo Txog Tsev Neeg,

Ob peb vas thiv tom ntej no, peb tsev kawm ntawv yuav kawm txog ntau yam txog kev pauv thiab txawv txav, nrog rau kev tuav xam ntawm kev ntxhov siab.

Fab kev kawm no, cov tub kawm ntawv yuav ua yeeb yam txog tej qhov yuav ua rau tib neej muaj kev ntxhov siab, xws lis tsiv mus rau qhov chaw tshiab los yog pib kawm ntawv rau ib lub tsev kawm ntawv tshiab. Lawv yuav npaj sau ib phau ntawv magazine hais txog kev pauv neej.

Koj yuav pab tau koj tus me nyuam kom nws to taub zoo txog kev kawm yam no hau tsev kawm ntawv yog koj tham raws lis cov ntsiab lus lis no:

- Kev pauv ua tau muaj nyob rau hauv nej tsev neeg txij thaum nej tuaj poob rau teb chaws Asmislikas no
- txoj kev ntawm nej tsev neeg tswj kev ntxhov siab zoo lis cas yog thaum muaj

Ua koj tsaug rau nej kev pab ntawm peb kev kawm ua yog ib qho mus tau zoo.

Sau Npe,

Xib Hwb

Letter to the Family

Kính thưa quí vị phụ huynh

Trong vài tuần tới đây, các cháu sẽ học về nhiều trạng thái của sự thay đổi, kể cả cách xử sự trước tình trạng căng thẳng tinh thần.

Trong phần của bài học này các cháu sẽ giả đóng tuồng về các hoàn cảnh có thể gây ra sự căng thẳng tinh thần, như dọn nhà đi nơi khác và khởi đầu đi học trường mới. Các cháu cũng soạn thảo ra một cuốn báo ảnh cho lớp, đặt trọng tâm vào những sự thay đổi trong các hoàn cảnh của cuộc đời.

Quí vị có thể giúp cháu hiểu rõ hơn về các bài học ở trong lớp bằng cách thảo luận những đề tài sau đây:

- những sự thay đổi mà gia đình phải chịu từ khi dọn đến ở Hoa Kỳ
- các phương cách mà gia đình dùng để xoay sở khi gặp tình trạng thay đổi

Xin cám ơn quí vị đã giúp đỡ chúng tôi hoàn thành dự án này được mỹ mãn.

Thành thật,

Giáo-viên

Name ____________________

Chapter 11 Language Assessment

A. Write each word from the box under the picture where it belongs.

angry	happy	sad	worried
excited	nervous	scared	

Pleasant Feelings

____

____

____

____

____

Unpleasant Feelings

____

____

____

____

____

B. Draw lines from the words to their definitions.

Words	**Definitions**
1. stress	a. the act of sweating
2. emotion	b. quick in thought or action
3. alert	c. any strong feeling
4. perspiration	d. a hormone that speeds up the heartbeat
5. adrenaline	e. strain or pressure

Name ______________________________

Chapter 11 Listening Assessment

Listen carefully. Draw lines from the words to the pictures you hear described.

1. Student 1

2. Student 2

Name ____

Chapter 12 Language Assessment

A. Complete the sentences. Use the words in the box.

computer	encyclopedia	magazine	newspaper	textbook

1. A ________________ is what you bring to class almost every day.
2. An ________________ is a set of books that has information about almost any subject.
3. A ________________ is often published every day. You use it to find out what is happening in the world or in your community.
4. A ________________ is an electronic device that stores information.
5. A ________________ is a publication that usually comes out every week or every month. It contains articles and pictures.

B. Read the article. Then answer the five W questions below.

On Saturday, October 15, sixth-graders from Fulton Middle School will collect plastic and newspaper to recycle. They want to help the environment. Students will collect one box of newspaper and two bags of plastic from around their neighborhoods.

1. Who? ____
2. What? ____
3. When? ____
4. Where? ____
5. Why? ____